AUTOGENESISM

AUTOGENESISM

A
RATIONAL
THEORY
OF
EVERYTHING

Kevin Brian Carroll

Luin InterRealm Ltd.
Cincinnati, Ohio USA

First Edition 2015

ISBN: 978-0-578-16911-8

Cover Design and Layout: Rick Carroll

Light in the Darkness" image: coolbaba19, http://OldtimeWallpapers.com

Interior Layout: Rick Carroll

Interior Illustrations: Rick Carroll, unless otherwise attributed

Luin InterRealm Ltd.
1724 Hopkins Avenue
Cincinnati, OH 45212
http://LuinInterRealm.com

This book is dedicated to two wonderful people, without whom its successful completion could never have been accomplished. First, to my wife, Karen, whose quiet and agreeable acceptance of the fact that I am who I am and see things as I see them, without feeling the threat that so many others would find a need to indulge, allowed me the personal and intellectual space I required as it increasingly became the case that my revelations clashed openly with her own most cherished and deeply held traditional views. And then to Lucy, my constant partner in this effort, whose priceless curiosity drew my examinations forward as her relentless refusal to accept any determination as brute fact forced me to discover the means of supporting every intuitive leap that her curiosity inspired in me.

"How does it happen that a properly endowed natural scientist comes to concern himself with epistemology? Is there no more valuable work in his specialty? I hear many of my colleagues saying, and I sense it from many more, that they feel this way. I cannot share this sentiment . . .

Concepts that have proven useful in ordering things easily achieve such an authority over us that we forget their earthly origins and accept them as unalterable givens. Thus they come to be stamped as "necessities of thought," "a priori givens," etc. The path of scientific advance is often made impassable for a long time through such errors. For that reason, it is by no means an idle game if we become practiced in analyzing the long commonplace concepts and exhibiting those circumstances upon which their justification and usefulness depend, how they have grown up, individually, out of the givens of experience. By this means, their all-too-great authority will be broken."

~ *Albert Einstein*

Contents

Preface   **1**

- Concerning Empiricism, Prediction, and the Scientific Method
- A Brand New View of the Same Old Data

Introduction   **15**

- What's Happening to Reality?
- There's No Place Like Home
- So, What Is Real?
- A Functional ToE: Basic Requirements
  1. The Genesis of Physical Reality
  2. Coherence
  3. The Existential Foundation of Order
  4. A Sufficient Explanation For . . .
  5. The Arrow of Time
  6. The Emergence of Spatial Environment
  7. The Existence of Natural Laws
  8. Quale: The Experience of Experience
  9. The Why of Esotericism
  10. The Fundamental Requirement
- . . . And In This Corner . . .
- . . . And So

Section I   **49**

- The Basis of Everything
- There's Real and Then There's *Real*
- The Quantum: A Quick Overview
- Bits, Pieces, and the Material Realm
- It's a Small World After All
- You Are What You Do
- Some Philosophy Concerning Existence

- To Be . . . Period
- Now, Before We Get Ahead of Ourselves
- Everything You Know is Wrong
- The Perfectly Coordinated Change
- Extra Dimensions and Stuff
- The Metaphysics of Identity Survival
- The Precedence of Precedent
- It's all About Context
- Building the Real
  - Managing Context Via the Informational Continuum
- Reality: The Contextual Environment
- The Emergent System
- The Real You That You Are
- The Isolated You
- And Then, There's the Lizard Brain
- Concerning Ghosts, Demons, and Other Monsters
- Let's Summarize What's Been Covered
  - The Quantum of Everything
  - Time's Arrow
  - The Existential It
  - Humanity: The Epitome Fundamental

Section II   **147**

- A Theory of Everything
- In The Beginning . . .
- And, Concerning Those Damn Atheists . . .
- Do You Think They Know This About Each Other?
- AutoGenesism: A Rose By Any Other Name

Track#1: From Nothing to Everything   **161**

- Existential Genesis
- Determining the Instant of Genesis
- The Emergence of the Relative Being State
- . . . And Away We Go!
- Wash, Rinse, Repeat
  - The Initial Confluence Suite

- The Quantum of Now
- The Push for Reliable Survival
- Serving the Whole
- It's Alive!!!
- It Thinks, Therefore, It Is
- The Change/Event Achieves Permanent ID Survival
- The Sentient Brain and Its Sapient Mind
- "I Am Not An Animal!"
- The Soul of Man
- The Personality Development Trajectory
    - Stumbling Into Maturity
    - Building the Ultimate You
- The Eternal Human Being
- I Breed, Therefore, I Am

Track#2: Detailing a Divine Gestation   **243**

- Why the Ethereal Must Be Examined
- Labels and Quick References
- Impetus and Obstacles
    - The Biology of Creation
    - Coming Upon the Notion
    - The Power to Connect
    - Defining the Goal
    - Building on the Need to Succeed

- The Process
    - The Sub-Environment as a Placenta
        - Sheep to the Right — Goats to the Left
        - Where to Go? The Hierarchy of Kind in Action
        - Butching Up the SDI
    - Behold . . .
    - A God is Born
- And So . . .

Section III — Digressions and Speculations   **307**

- Concerning My Specific Methodology

  - Item#1: Reality — The Ultimate Frame of Reference
  - Item#2: System Coherence — "As Above, So Below"
  - Item#3: The Meta-Law
  - Item#4: Time — In Proper Perspective
  - Item#5: Information — It's Physical Nature and Role
  - Item#6: The Inapplicability of Math to Any ToE
  - And So . . .

- Contextual Precedent and the Mechanics of Progressive Development

  - Time as a Dimensional Isolate
  - Getting Specific Through System Definition
  - And So . . .

- Our Emergent Universe: How the Change/Event Became Spatial

  - Fields, Energies, and Mass
  - Kinetic Energy: The Basis of Matter
  - Emergent System Confluence Suite
  - The Initial Confluence Suite
  - Change/Spatial Emergence: An ID Survival Pursuit
  - And So . . .

- Human Consciousness and the Personality Development Trajectory

  - The Emergent Mind
  - Managing the Initiation of Perception
  - The Executive Brain
  - What It Means to be Human
  - The Personality Development Trajectory
  - Free Will?
  - PFS versus RFS
  - Summary

- From Here to There: The Crossing Over Event

  - But, First . . .
  - Corporeal Conscious Awareness
  - The Corporeal Perspective
  - The Eternal Mind
  - The Actual Crossing-Over Event
  - The Traditional Narrative
  - "You? You Ain't Goin' Nowhere, Pal"

- Entanglement: The Laws and Dynamic of Contextual Association

  - A Rising Tide Lifts All Boats
  - The Hierarchy of Kind
  - The Environmentally Imposed Entanglement

Speculations   **413**

- Time Dilation and Gravity: General Relativity or Identity Survival Enforcement

  - The Atomic Clock

    - History
  - Mechanism
  - Gravitational Field Strength is an Environmental Factor
  - And This Has 'What?' to do With Identity Survival?
  - "You Can't Hold Us Here Forever!"

- Determining the Unit Rate of Change

  - The Duration of Now
    - Velocity Time Dilation Tests
    - Gravitational Time Dilation Tests
    - Velocity and Gravitational Time Dilation Combined-Effect Tests
    - Muon Lifetime
  - Working With the Data

- Dark Matter: How the Change/Spatial Trajectory Serves the URC-Defined Macro-System

  - The Big Bang: A Traditional Speculation

- Displacement Fact Sets and Macro-System Identity
- The Displacement Fact Set Continuum Matrix

So, What Have We Learned?   **447**

- The Introduction
- Section I
- Section II
  - Track#1
  - Track#2
- Section III
  - Digressions
  - Speculations
- And In the End . . .

About the Author   **457**

Preface

"Tell them what you are going to tell them, tell them, then tell them what you told them." It was either Dale Carnegie or Paul White (the first director of CBS News) that first proposed that axiom in one of the various forms that it's been preserved over the years. As a quick truth concerning the art of effectively communicating specific information, it's pretty tough to improve upon.

"It is not once, nor twice, but times without number, that the same ideas make their appearance in the world." This bit of rock-solid truth can be directly linked to Aristotle, and while it examines the communication of specific information from an entirely different perspective, its accuracy has earned it its own level of axiomatic permanence.

Since I'm going to attempt to teach you what I've learned about the true nature of Reality, the first of these two quotes will be my own guide concerning how best to present what I know will be — for some — a serious intellectual challenge. In fact, I've watched the whole of this presentation fail to gel in the minds of absolutely brilliant thinkers even after each structural constituent has been thoroughly examined and agreed upon, and the coalescence itself logically vetted. Yet, this is not to suggest that what I've got for you is exceptionally difficult or hopelessly obscure.

Tell them what you are going to tell them, tell them, then tell them what you told them. And, yes, this is what I'll do at every stage as we move forward together. However, it's the enduring truth of the second of these two quotes that will probably prevent most folks from ever experiencing this presentation as being anything more than yet another interesting abstraction.

As Aristotle stated, the wisdom of our world is based on very few notions. This is true, in spite of the myriad of unique ways the human mind has invented to rebrand each of them as new and novel. These same ideas continue to make their appearance in the world in ways that are both negative and positive; meaning that they frame the basic argument concerning the nature of Reality regardless of whether they've been embraced or flatly rejected. And this is the nature of their resilience as fundamental tenets.

Embraced or rejected, these truths have become self-evident as a result of simply showing up whenever the big questions arise. I'm going to admit here that this has caused me a lot of frustration, and not just because these implausible truths prevent us from looking deeper into so much of what we really need to reexamine. I get incensed because so much misery and hopelessness is so directly attributable to the impact that this sacrosanct muddle has had on our past, has on our present, and will have on what we create as the future of our own little version of humanity.

Still, I realize that we love this crippled hulk and we cling to it because it's our security and our emotional-intellectual-psychological foundation. To us, this writhing confusion of flippant claims and irresponsible definitions is what's real about Reality, and we need to believe that we can know what is real. For us, the anxious embrace of even the most impossible *real* is far better than the raw terror of having no *real* available to embrace.

But, what if we could somehow free ourselves from the anxiety associated with embracing this incoherent mess as universal and fundamental? What if we could discover that we don't owe our emergence, or anything else, to this collection of baseless secular dogmas; that we're children of an entirely different world that features a much more recognizable and sympathetic fundamental structure?

I don't know. By now, would it even matter?

Y'know, it's said that unless it can make your readers rich, thin, or get them laid, then there's no use in writing about it. That may be true, and maybe nobody really cares about what's real and what isn't real, but imagine if you could become absolutely freed from the oldest and most universal terrors to ever stalk the human race as a result of simply reading a book and taking the time to fully understand the implications of what that book contains. Imagine if the key to unlocking every prison cell that's ever held anyone in eternal bondage could be as easily possessed as a general knowledge of the basics of a high school science class.

Wouldn't you want that key for yourself and for those you love? It wouldn't make you rich, or thin, and it wouldn't get you laid, but at some point, all that stuff isn't going to matter to you anymore. At some point, all that's going to

AutoGenesism: A Theory of Everything

matter to you is whatever it might be that sits just beyond your ability to perceive and to verify as being real. That, and — if there is anything out there at all — whether you're prepared to deal with it.

AutoGenesism is a full Theory of Everything. It's the only full Theory of Everything that exists. This is what makes it singular among the many theories that have begun to pile up within the worlds of cosmology, physics and metaphysics in recent years.

It's not a unification theory addressing the profound schism between the way that macro and micro systems operate. It's not a theory focused on reducing the mathematics of material reality to an elegant (if necessarily cryptic) equation that balances one side of the "=" against the other with miraculous precision and without leaning on any infinite values or convenient absences (like gravity or time progression). It's certainly not yet another bland attempt to reveal the science behind any of the handful of traditional religions that have dominated human culture over the course of recent millennia.

AutoGenesism is unlike any Theory of Everything that's ever been proposed, and yes, I fully realize how many times this claim has been published in connection with Natural Philosophy; the centuries-old and on-going effort to define the macro-system that contains everything that is real. This AutoGenesism will prove to be a very different revelation, regardless of how it is measured, compared, or contrasted, and whether it is the world's modern scientific dogmas or its traditional wisdoms that are used as contextual reference.

AutoGenesism fully addresses all questions concerning the true nature of Reality.

- It reveals how Reality came into existence.
- It reveals why Reality came into existence.
- It reveals how spatial dimensions emerged.
- It reveals why spatial dimensions emerged.
- It reveals how Time began.
- It reveals why Time began.
- It reveals the true structure of material existence.
- It reveals the truth concerning precedent and its relationship with the laws of nature.
- It reveals the actual parameters of our universe.

3

AutoGenesism fully addresses all questions concerning the true nature of the human being.

- It reveals how humanity is unique within the material realm.
- It reveals why humanity knows it is unique within the material realm.
- It reveals the eternal nature of the human being.
- It reveals that the full human being is not a material manifestation, and why.
- It reveals how easily a fully developed human being can become imprisoned and explains why it can end up being literally impossible to free such a prisoner.
- It offers the most plausible explanation for our species' belief in gods, demons, heavens, and hells.
- It reveals the false connection between deism/theism and human *after-life*.
- It reveals the physics behind all that humanity has known to be true about itself.

AutoGenesism addresses these basics, and how they each relate intimately with one another, as it completely fleshes out Reality's structural foundation without the introduction of anything that hasn't already made its own case for being fundamental within the last century of scientific research. In fact, what might be most astonishing will be the complete lack of anything new to reveal. That said, all that's become common knowledge will be properly placed and accurately attributed, with the net result being a fully functional matrix that is both familiar and completely counterintuitive — well, until the utter simplicity of it as a thoroughly natural response to raw physical existence itself becomes obvious, and its conceptual elegance forever invalidates all other explanations.

Yes, when AutoGenesism — as a thorough explanation of what is real and why Reality is what it is — suddenly gels within your mind, it really is an amazing perspective transformation. Of course, at first it can be startling, but then it becomes increasingly reassuring; especially as its capacity to explain begins to expand ever further before you. And, this is what's so wonderful and valuable about finally and forever knowing what's real about Reality. Okay, so it won't make you rich or thin (although it won't prevent you from becoming rich and/or thin) and it won't get you laid (although it's been proven that people are physically attracted to potential mates who can display evidence of possessing above average intelligence) but there really is a stability and an emotional/intellectual

AutoGenesism: A Theory of Everything

comfort that comes with knowing what's real, and especially about knowing what simply cannot be real.

As a sapient being, believing that you know what is real is as critical for your peace and stability as a strong sense of self. In fact, if you can't believe that you can ever know what's real, then imagine the impact on your ability to even have a full sense of self; let alone one that's strong. What I'm going to teach you is the fundamental structure of Reality and how you actually fit in as both appropriate and necessary to all that physically exists.

As research and technology drag us farther and farther from what once was a blissful ignorance, the endlessly repeated and reinvented traditional wisdoms [unknowable mysteries, unfathomable purposes, omniscient consciousnesses, and infinite presences] and their secular alternates [empiricism, chaotic randomness, anthropocentricism, and rigid reductionism] have crippled our ability to even recognize useful questions concerning Reality and our place within it. In fact, our devotion to restricting all serious thought to proving the legitimacy of pursuing either one or the other of these two general avenues persists in spite of so much clear evidence that both are dead ends. It's no wonder that our modern world is so fractured and frantically unstable.

The truth is that both of our world's secular and nonsecular pathways are based on faith in the agreed-upon dogmas, imposed by brilliant, powerful personalities who were (let's face it) men of their times. This is easy enough to declare when describing the tenets of those mystical and religious pathways toward truth, since these are based on wisdoms that are centuries, if not millennia, old. But what of those theoretical pursuits that are based on the scientific breakthroughs of the 20th century? How can this general trajectory also be based on faith? Surely, if this avenue is also a dead end, then why have so many predictions that are based on its most widely embraced determinations been successfully validated via repeated experimentation? That is a good question. Perhaps we need to examine the nature of experimentation, prediction, and the scientific method.

Concerning Empiricism, Prediction, and the Scientific Method

A primary requirement of any scientific theory is that it be predictive. Now, in physics, a theory must successfully predict system behavior and/or response to direct stimuli and/or interaction. In biology, a theory must successfully predict genetic development that results from system manipulations [breeding and/or environment] imposed on a much broader scale and over a greater period of time. The larger the system under scientific scrutiny, (our solar system is a good example), the less predictive a theory can be, and the more a theory will depend on observation and inference. Macro-systems (our universe is a good example) are too large for any theory to be predictive, and much too expansive for even indirect observation to be of much use, so induction is generally how scientists reach their theoretical conclusions.

> Induction — a process of reasoning, used especially in science, by which a general conclusion is drawn from a set of premises, based mainly on experience or experimental evidence. The conclusion goes beyond the information contained in the premises, and does not follow necessarily from them. Thus an inductive argument may be highly probable, yet lead from true premises to a false conclusion.
>
> **http://dictionary.reference.com/browse/induction?s=t**

Obviously, the larger the system under scrutiny, the less successful should be the theories, but this is not how the Scientific Method has worked over the years. In cosmology, the capacity to isolate and manipulate the systems under examination is nonexistent, so scaled experimental representations, math equations, and computer simulations serve as induction stand-ins with theoretical conclusions that have since been built upon (becoming the scientific foundations for — in most cases — additional layers of foundation-providing theoretical conclusions) in spite of the obvious dielectric that exists between the models being used and the actual systems under examination. For quite a while, this seemed to be a successful strategy, but as our measuring and observing technologies have become increasingly sophisticated, clashes between *settled science* and newly emerging empirical indications have developed; some extreme enough to directly challenge some of our most *settled* of scientific foundations, even taking acknowledged levels of applied predictability into account in these cases.

Clearly, the Scientific Method has been shown to have inherent limitations, even if that's not yet a universally held view. Concerning my own view of the role that empiricism [observation, experimentation, and prediction] and induction play in the theoretical determination of Reality, the following apocryphal tale has always been valuable as an analogy. I've tried to run down the original source for this story, but it's been too many years since I discovered it, and all attempts to Google it using phrases and such have only revealed my own uses of it at various times over the years. In fact, I'm not even convinced that I've remained true to this tale's original moral. I do know, however, that it makes my point concerning the Scientific Method as being only one tool in the process of validating a successful theory.

An island native stumbles upon what is for him an odd item. It is a digital wristwatch. The watch — its band having broken — fell off the wrist of a research team member, and remains as the only indication that a modern era human being was on this specific island at some point in the recent past. No other indication persist, and this includes any memories of such a person having been witnessed by any island native inhabitant.

In fact, this island hasn't changed in culture or outer-world awareness at all for many centuries. This lone digital watch, lying in the open on this one path on a remote side of this island, is the very first failure of modern researchers to remain completely unobserved by the stone-age inhabitants of this remote island. Other than the broken watch band, this piece is in perfect working condition, and is properly set to the time zone of this island as it relates to these months of spring and summer.

We'll name this artifact's discoverer XXZXX, and suggest that while he is an intelligent and curious man, he is no more or less than a man of his time and of his culture. XXZXX is certainly not a holy man or a community authority. That said, he's more interested in larger thoughts than the average member of his community, and very sober and analytical in his personal approach to whatever it is that might present itself as a novel indication. As a result, he keeps the discovery of this unusual item to himself, and in his spare time, he devotes himself to studying it.

What he learns immediately is that he's never felt such a smooth surface before, and he has nothing whatsoever to compare its round, flatness to. Perhaps a skipping stone, but even so, this item's shape and texture is much too precise and as far as XXZXX is concerned, it has the feel of intelligent craftwork. This is obviously not a naturally shaped object. It clearly belonged to someone or something that visited the island. But who?

When XXZXX gets the object to a secluded place for deeper analysis, he realizes that on one of the smooth, flat surfaces, there's a lot of activity happening, and it's happening all by itself. He can't reach the activity with his fingers, but he can watch it happen. To his own mind, it seems alive, even if he can't relate the bizarre shape-shifting behavior to anything he's ever witnessed before.

7

After some study, he begins to realize that the activity is not at all random; that it is based on a repeating set of patterns. He sees this as a true breakthrough, and commits himself to unlocking the mystery of what this artifact is, and what it means to the larger whole that he understands Reality to be. After all, it exists, as does everything else that shares the world with it. This means that whatever this thing is, it has a role that it serves relative to the rest of Reality. It fits in somewhere, and since it does, he knows that if he can find where it fits in, he'll also discover something equally important about the true nature of what is real. XXZXX is rapidly becoming a scientist.

Over weeks, XXZXX becomes deeply focused on translating the relentless activity that continues just beneath the smooth, hard surface of the artifact he's discovered. What at first seemed chaotic and spastic in its tight, jerky reconfigurations, has become much more organized and evenly measured to XXZXX's observational perspective. The design reconfigurations, while initially appearing to be complete and novel, have, over time, revealed themselves to be progressive and highly predictable. In fact, XXZXX has begun to recognize a series of design patterns that repeat and follow other design patterns. His sketches have begun to form a distinctive body of research concerning the behavior of this artifact, even if he has yet to formulate a larger purpose behind this behavior.

Being a human being, XXZXX hasn't neglected his own need to make larger sense of what his research has revealed to him. His pattern determinations, his careful documentation of each angular design that fills the mysteriously isolated field of activity, his painstaking attention to each empirical indication aside; XXZXX is not immune to the larger speculations concerning this item's true role within the world that he's known to exist as real and dependably so.

One day, XXZXX is, yet again, comparing his notes with the endless design reconfigurations of his artifact, and it suddenly strikes him that each defined pattern is repeated within a larger defined pattern, with each repetition of the lesser pattern triggering a small acknowledgement within the design of the larger pattern. This indicates that there are multiple layers, a structure of patterns, being represented by design configurations. This artifact's cycles are much larger than he suspected. He's definitely breaking new ground in his research of this thing's behavior.

He names the smaller pattern cycles OOAAOO and the larger pattern cycles AAOOAA, and begins charting anew. Over the next few weeks, he's determined that over the course of a full day, the artifact winds through two full AAOOAA cycles. One during the day and one during the night. This is something that he sees as being extremely important, since each AAOOAA cycle can now be tied directly to the span of a day. XXZXX now knows that his artifact's role in Reality has something to do with the occurrence and re-occurrence of each day. It's here, where XXZXX realizes that he might be in over his head, and he brings his artifact and his research to the wisest men in his community; the council of elders.

XXZXX's presentation of the artifact and his months of research stuns the council. These men have centuries of traditional wisdom between them and at their disposal. With their much larger command of what's become reliable interpretations of common and not-so-common empirical evidence, these men are much more capable of determining what XXZXX has discovered. The otherworldly nature of this auto-animate device clearly suggests that it was constructed by beings that are much more powerful and important than any they've ever encountered.

When XXZXX experimentally demonstrates the artifact's tracking of the sun's movements via design reconfiguration, they inductively determine that this device is not simply tracking the movement of the sun, but that the beings who created this device used it to control the movements of the sun. They also know that its existence must be kept secret from the community at large, and especially from all enemies of the community.

They ask XXZXX if he's shown anyone else what he's discovered, and when they're assured that he's kept his find completely to himself all along, they have him immediately executed. The watch is then taken to a location, deep within a series of caves, where it is buried and each member of the team that completed this mission is also executed.

To their own interpretation of XXZXX's research, the verdict is obvious. This device controls the cycles of days, seasons, ages, and who knows what else. It's too much power to be allowed to exist among fallible human beings, and for the sake of the entire world, it must be hidden away forever.

Like I said, the original story of the digital watch and the islander belongs to someone else, and I remember it being much less dramatic than this, but the moral of the story is the same; the Scientific Method can take you only so far, and system observation/prediction certainly won't prove to be any more valuable than your own data interpretation will allow it to be. XXZXX was certainly able to responsibly observe, successfully record, and accurately predict a relationship between the alignment of design patterns and the sun's movements, but his proper adherence to these staples of the modern Scientific Method did nothing to help him accurately determine the functionality of the watch, its larger role in nature, or the true nature of its relationship with the sun. For that, XXZXX would have needed to learn an entirely new perspective concerning time, the Earth as a physical system within the larger solar system, the existence of other cultures with written language and numeral representations, the concept of time measurement, and a long list of other things that I'm in no mood to include here.

Yes, XXZXX was able to predict, and yes, the theoretical conclusion that the elders inductively arrived at, as a result of XXZXX's successful predictions, did offer what they viewed to be a perfectly reasonable explanation for the predicted results, but let's face it, that watch was just a digital watch that had fallen from the wrist of a research team member that had come and gone from that island, unseen by the inhabitants, regardless of what the research and the successful predictions insisted.

Does this mean that the Scientific Method is of no value whatsoever? Of course not. It does mean, however, that its use should be considered as part of a larger context that includes system coherence, the cohesion of functionality within each larger system that contains and therefore is affected by the system under examination, and the nature of a system's experimentation preparations that are required for a specific prediction's results to be successful. The more profound the impact of any of these contextual considerations, the less likely it is that the Scientific Method, alone, can be conclusive as a theoretical proofing determinant.

This is especially true when working to determine the actual nature of Reality as a macro-system. In the case of a Theory of Everything, there's no reasonable means that exists by which the Scientific Method can be used to prove such a theory's validity, regardless of what's been considered acceptable science to date. Certainly, its use (in the case of XXZXX and his artifact) brought no one closer to the truth concerning that digital watch and its power over the earth's daily cycles.

Was Einstein's curved starlight the result of a warped spacetime fabric, dimpled by the sun's mass as successfully predicted, or did some other, unrelated fact of open space cause that one gathering of photons to appear to bend around the Sun as that photo was taken? Perhaps, as some insist, no more than a plasma thermal refraction, in sort of the same way that a mirage causes images

AutoGenesism: A Theory of Everything

that exist over the horizon to appear above the horizon when the thermal conditions are just so. Yes, these predicted result have been repeated, but when the implications are enormous, how sacrosanct is the theorist's own specific interpretation of the prediction's cause if that interpretation causes the larger definition of Reality itself to become internally contradictory? Can one prediction's success obliterate the requirement that system coherence and macro-system cohesion persist and remain instructive concerning the true nature of what is real?

And what of the ± nature of most experiment predictions? How broad can the slop range be before it gets to the point that a prediction is dismissed? How many misses are allowed? How many hits per misses constitute a successful prediction? Yes, nothing is exact, but what does this mean, or is it always a subjective call that each research team gets to make? Considering the elaborate system preparations of many such experiments, at some point shouldn't they be seen in the same light as those equally elaborate system preparations that professional illusionists employ to an even greater degree of success? When does system artificiality become an issue? Or does it ever?

AutoGenesism is an explanation of the way that Reality works, and if there's any prediction that can be made as a result of AutoGenesism, it's that whatever it is that has achieved existence will strive to remain existent until it can no longer succeed in that effort. What can also be predicted is that the definition of existential survival will involve the contextual Identity of the existent something, and will not necessarily conform to our own interpretation of physical existence as being restricted to material structure.

AutoGenesism also predicts a wide arrangement of holon structural responses to the imperative demand of Identity Survival: from the emergence of change/event trajectories; the emergence of spatial trajectories; the achievement of orbital spatial trajectories; the structural matrixing of spatial trajectories as entangled change/event trajectories and our perception of these structures as particles and matter; the emergence of information-centric holon structuring that involves the external migration of Identity to otherwise isolated holon structures that combine in common cause to create even larger, and more resilient identified wholes (otherwise known as life) as a successful Identity Survival strategy; the ultimate material system survival breakthrough (the central nervous system) and its revolutionary processing structure that converts DNA dictates into action items [the brain]; and the ultimate emergence of the dynamic information hybrid that upended Reality and redefined what it means to exist.

These are not predictions that can be experimentally verified in a lab under controlled conditions, but Darwin's Natural Selection, and the entire field of Cosmology is also resistant to that sort of falsifiability. As I stated, the larger the system under examination, the less amenable it is to the Scientific Method as a theoretical proving tool. Also, the employment of induction should never take the place of the responsible examination of the direct and indirect ramifications of embracing a theoretical structure that clearly violates what has been reasonably determined to be a broadly reliable and rational system that supports multiple layers of holon structure. Science should never be pursued in abject isolation. Each system under examination should be viewed as integral to the larger system that is Reality itself.

In the end — the contributions of the Scientific Method acknowledged — Reality is what it is, in spite of what predictions we make, and especially in spite of what lengths we go to in order to ensure that we get those predictions to succeed.

A Brand New View of the Same Old Data

AutoGenesism launches a new debate concerning the true nature of Reality, and not by asking questions, but by offering new answers and new interpretations of what's already been revealed to be true about our world and our place within it. The research has been done. The experiments have been conducted. It's time now for the available data to be properly analyzed, and for the indications to be accurately aligned with the basic logic structure that has proven to be existent and in charge. There's no need for a newer, larger, super anything. The truth is that we've already got all the data we'll ever need to make sense of everything. All that's needed now is a bit of clear, critical thinking.

The following presentation is broken into very specific sections, and each section serves a very specific function. These sections combine to explain what AutoGenesism is, and why it is unique as a Theory of Everything.

- **Introduction** — This section details what a full Theory of Everything must address. Forget the math formulas, this is where you'll learn the requirements of a theory that seeks to explain everything.
- **Section I** — This section lays out the fundamentals of Reality. Precedent, context, the event, information, the emergent system, identity

and what is being pursued by that which exists; this is where the table is set and the water poured in preparation for the feast to come.

- **Section II** — This section is the main event. It's divided into two independent tracks due to the fact that (yes, it's possible) there might exist (along with the original and naturally occurring *universe*) intentionally initiated *universes* (no, this is not an acknowledgement of the existence of a multiverse, but something entirely different). As a full Theory of Everything, this possibility does exist as part of that everything, and therefore must be explained in full.

  - **Track#1** — This narrative fleshes out the instant of existential genesis, the progressive development of material complexity and sophistication, the impetus and opportunity for life, sentient life, and finally, the emergence of the human being.

  - **Track#2** — This overview sketches out the impetus, the opportunity, and the logic structure that may exist beneath the relentlessly incompatible concept of gods, demons, heavens and hells, and what (if anything) may be behind this uniquely human construct. At best, it answers all the questions about why we believe in what most of us believe in. At worst, it's a really good masters class in applying the logical infrastructure of AutoGenesism to a perfectly reasonable (and highly plausible) conundrum that could easily exist within the realm occupied by fully viable human beings.

- **Section III** — This section features extended examinations of a variety of notions and their implications that are relevant to what's been revealed and discovered by scientists over the years. Stuff about Dark Matter, Dark Energy, time dilation, the nature of human consciousness, and other mysteries that lose their mysteriousness when you start looking at them from this very unique perspective.

The fact that nothing new is dropped out onto the table here should not be seen as an admission that any of this information has ever been presented in a published form of any kind, because the truth is that even the basis of this theory has never been offered by anyone other than myself, and even then, only in relatively cryptic chunks to a select few — mainly to get a feel for exactly how counterintuitive the bits of this entire premise might actually be for the traditional thinker. This is absolutely revolutionary thought, and I need you to go into this with that in mind.

You've never been presented with this way of seeing Reality before. I can assure you of that. I can also assure you that while each brick in this structure will be extremely familiar, there will be that moment when the structure itself, as an emerging whole, will suddenly seem as though it can't possibly exist as it's being presented. It's then, that I'll have something in place to help you make traditional sense of what's being suggested, and I can only hope that you'll stick with me, and allow me that moment to help you move forward.

One last thing that I can assure you is that if you do finish this presentation, and if you are able to fully conceptualize and internalize this view that I've discovered to be accurate and authentically real, then there will never, ever, be another instant — as you make your way through the whole of your own physical existence — when you'll feel threatened or incapable of completely managing all aspects of what's become of that instant.

Desiderius Erasmus once said, *"In the kingdom of the blind, the one-eyed man is king."* When, as a result of learning what I've learned, you can see what I can see, you'll be that king. It will only be the one eye, but with the whole of our own world blindly deadlocked between mysticism and what's become of the Scientific Method, that one open eye will certainly be a source of endless advantage.

What's Happening to Reality?

. . . or, can a paradigm shift within freefall?

One hundred years ago, the Western World was struggling through a cataclysmic paradigm shift that most people could never have seen coming. A relative handful of scientific leaders were quietly defining a wave of revolutionary ideas concerning the fundamentals of Reality that would ultimately lead the new century through social and technological transformations that no one could've ever anticipated; eventually reinventing the human experience forever. Yet, for most folks, each day began as usual, offering little more than what had already become commonplace as the whole of the modern world confidently planned a version of the future that would never unfold.

As we warm up this second decade of a new century, the Western World is again experiencing a cataclysmic shift in how the fundamentals of Reality are to be viewed. However, this time no one is leading the way, and for all too many regular folks, the future is anything but confidently planned.

Radical ideas are flying wildly from one end of the earth to the other, and rapidly losing definition with each translation, each iteration, as yet another visionary plants his or her brand on whatever patchwork of convoluted notions and assertions it is that they've presented as their ticket to Internet notoriety. Nothing's being quietly defined and none of these ideas are revolutionary. They're frustrated. They're rebellious. They're certainly tilting firmly against the status quo, but they're not revolutionary, so much as reactionary.

Unlike the early years of the 20th century, when the revolution arrived before anyone had even realized that it was needed, the 21st century's revolution is long past due, with only the gathering anxiety over how late it is in coming giving out any indication that we're in yet another significant moment of transition. What's also different about this century's paradigm shift is that it will suffer through its wrenching labors in public. The world will finally get to see how truly terrible the process of radically redefining Reality has always been for those so tasked.

A recent list of books, penned by significant — if not eminent — scientists and science professionals is evidence of just how clearly the need for this transition is being felt within the two scientific disciplines that deal most directly with the question of Reality fundamentals; Cosmology and Physics. The most influential of these offerings; Prof. Lee Smolins' *"The Trouble With Physics: The Rise of String Theory, The Fall of Science, and What Comes Next"* and his *"Time Reborn: From the Crisis in Physics to the Future of the Universe"*; Sheila Jones's English translation of Alexander Unzicker's *"Vom Urknall zum Durchknall"*, *"Bankrupting Physics: How Today's Top Scientists Are Gambling Away Their Credibility"*; and Jim Baggott's *"Farewell To Reality: How Modern Physics Has Betrayed the Search for Scientific Truth"*, are must-reads for anyone with even the most casual interest in just how blatantly preposterous big-money theoretical science has become. There is also no shortage of lesser works and articles — news and opinion — feeding on what can only be described as a growing frustration over what seems to be a loss of intellectual discipline within the elite echelons of the professional academic community.

This gnawing unrest is much more palpable when you descend into the Internet's popular science fandom community. Here, the distress of the professional community is magnified exponentially, although with much less focus and definitional specificity. Here, the nature of Reality itself is literally disintegrating before those who are the most feverishly engaged; their world becoming increasingly and more profoundly fragmented as the planet's thought leadership begins to stumble and reach for those long-established reality anchors that — if the most recent indications are true — have never actually been there to provide support.

Then, there's the wild-eyed tribe of *Theory of Everything* visionaries, sweeping in with its own contribution to the carnage. And the arrival has done nothing but deepen the confusion and further calcify the resolve of those devoted to the opposition of any theorist that claims to know exactly what it is that sits at the substructure of physical Reality.

The resulting battle lines [super-symmetries, superstrings, and whatever it is that M Theory might be, representing the mess that defines the state of physics on one side, versus a literal smorgasbord of completely indefinable existential

AutoGenesism: A Theory of Everything

jumpstarts from those who believe that the cosmos is where we'll find the clues concerning our true genesis narrative, on the other] have begun to really solidify, and yet we're still no closer to actually understanding who or what we are, what's real, or why it is that some modern scientific theories have begun to sound just as cartoonish as the most preposterous of ancient myths. Even with blackboards full of math formulas and billions of dollars' worth of single-application technologies that spit out impossibly undecipherable data backing up these newest faith-based Reality narratives, it's as if we're completely lost while making great time as we career ever further into the depths of nowhere whatsoever.

There's No Place Like Home

Wandering through the world of theoretical science is like following Oz's Yellow Brick Road. It's fascinating, but each magical fantasy melts away quickly, leaving only the smallest residual impact on the mind as the very next astonishing absurdity leaps into the frame with its own demand to suspend all belief in what's already established itself as real and reliably palpable. So much to be entertained by, and yet, nothing at all to hold onto that's actually connected to what continues to sit simply and patiently at the ready once the tour has ended for the day. Scientific fiction presented as science, and an entire generation of thinkers being taught to ignore the fact that none of it can be aligned even slightly with the world that they see, touch, smell, taste, hear and experience as inescapably real.

Young minds are being persuaded that the factual nature of Reality does not, and cannot, actually make sense with what can be perceived as normal and mundane. But, what happens when these brilliant, yet recklessly prepared, minds eventually take the reins? Imagine yourself in such a position.

How do you plan for the future if you believe that Time itself has been scientifically proven to be nothing but an illusion? If you believe that science has determined that you live in just another of an infinite number of replications of the very same universe [each featuring the exact same molecules, features, fundamental laws and people, with the only defining difference one small shift in direction taken by you or any of that universe's other trillions of possible decision makers] how do you take any decision seriously? What's the point if each decision (made by each of the trillions of inevitable deciders that exist within each of any already infinite number of insignificant universe manifestations) will bring an infinite number of replicate universes erupting into immediate existence that are the result of each possible decision that was, and wasn't, made.

As a thought exercise, it's tough enough to quantify the ramifications, but try to imagine if, for you — as the direct result of your deepest, most fundamental understanding of the true nature of Reality — this is not just a thought exercise. Try to imagine that this is what your modern secular culture has fully embraced as the most rational and scientific explanation for why things are as they are. How do you actually function with such a Reality view, or does it transform the business of life itself into an exercise in senseless futility?

So, what are the long term ramifications of embracing a Reality view that can never, ever, be reconciled with what can be proven, or even reasonably associated with perceptible experience? If the Dark Ages that held the whole of Europe in frozen bondage for centuries after the fall of Rome are any indication, a scientifically approved faith-based Reality view has its minuses. Combine the current failures of all traditional theological narratives with popular science's most recent promotion of its own reckless schism between what's declared and what's known to be real, and it's no wonder that the reflective, intellectual mind is caught within a building crisis.

For the truly self-aware, life itself is constantly stripped of the positive momentum that it might have otherwise achieved if what's experienced cannot be rationally aligned with that which has been declared to host each moment and frame it with reference. And in the end, this is the true damage that is done when the intellectual sophistication of a society is not respected by those tasked with responsibly presenting its most sober and rational secular explanations. Yes, wandering through the world of theoretical science is a lot like following Oz's Yellow Brick Road, and yes, it can be wonderfully fascinating. But, there's a reason why Dorothy was so desperate to get back home to the dreary sepia tones of dust-bowl Kansas. Kansas made sense to her, and nothing — not even the rich, Technicolor of Oz, or her newly-won celebrity within that magical kingdom — could ever compete with the need she felt deep inside for the real of Reality to make sense to her.

So, What is Real?

If you type *Theory of Everything* [we can shorten this to ToE here and there] into your search engine, you'll get 621,000 results from *Bing* and a whopping

AutoGenesism: A Theory of Everything

13,300,000 results from *Google*. Granted, there are plenty of duplicates, and I think I saw a movie or a TV show of some sort clogging up both front pages with that title, but the point is that there's no shortage of published materials concerning some sort of description of what it is that Reality itself is based on.

Most entries are likely unrelated to the topic in the broader sense of what they are. Probably a number of jokes and/or casual references. Internet forum posts and whatnot. Still, with millions of links referencing *Theory of Everything* in one sense or another, it's clear that there is activity out there that's being pursued on behalf of figuring out the true nature of Reality. Considering the enormity of the endeavor, it's worth noting that the lay community has jumped into the arena with its own unique contribution (adding a distinct freshness to what's long been assigned to academia and theology) for perhaps the best and most obvious reason; a clear and empirically defensible description of Reality is now needed by more of these folks than has ever been the case.

Still, as you'd expect, the Theories of Everything that are most widely considered to be legitimate are those being professionally pursued within either physics or cosmology, with Physics' *Superstring Theory* clearly leading all others with (according to John W. Moffat — in his book, *"Reinventing Gravity"*) anywhere between 1000 and 1500 theoretical physicists, each professionally engaged in mathematically proving at least one of $10^{5^{\,\infty}}$ versions of String Theory. Of course, this includes those theorists working on M-Theory (whatever that actually is). In fact, as the ToE game goes, strings seem to be where one focuses if one is really bent on breaking through with a theory that will garner serious consideration, and it's been that way for 40 years or so.

That said, there's no actual string-based theory that's emerged as falsifiable, or verifiable, or even quantifiable for that matter, but String Theory research, in general, has one thing going for it that keeps the lion's share of activity and money pouring into it; it claims to offer the promise of explaining where particles come from, and that's pretty powerful stuff in the ToE game. After all, as a hangover from the 19th Century's fixation on materialistic reductionism, particles have thoroughly failed to provide anything more than a point of theoretical failure, and a non-dimensional, non-locatable point at that.

No, String Theory hasn't delivered on that promise of breaking through the particle barrier . . . yet. There are still a few issues with getting String Theory to *work*. These are pretty big issues, though. They might even qualify as intractable issues. Let's take a look.

- The most viable string theories require 10 dimensions [9 spatial and 1 Time] to function — some string theories require up to 26 such dimensions. Meanwhile only three dimensions can be proven to actually exist; four if you define Time as being a dimension in its own right.
- There are no viable string theories that allow for the mathematical inclusion of Time.
- There are no viable string theories that are *"background independent"* — meaning that these strings require the pre-existence of the Universe itself as a physical environment within which to then emerge and function. Neither the genesis nor the physical geometry of the Universe itself is addressed by any string theory.
- There is no explanation for how these one-dimensional strings came into existence, or how it is that a one-dimensional object can actually vibrate, open and close [a feat requiring such an object to be at least two dimensional and to physically traverse an additional dimension of Time] while remaining one-dimensional.
- There is no explanation for what the primordial imperative is that compels these one-dimensional strings to vibrate, or open and close, or to even emerge into physical existence at all.

There are other significant problems with String Theory — as a whole and with each of the estimated $10^{5\ \infty}$ (yes, that's 10 followed by 500 zeros) unique versions of String Theory — but then, there are entire books solely devoted to these problems; complete with math formulas and historical references [names, dates, symposiums and the like]. The point being made here is that the Physics community, while it does seem to own the ToE effort relative to popular legitimacy, is no closer to solving this single greatest question (what is the factual basis of everything?) than any other entity — professional or amateur, solo or collective — that is likewise engaged.

Then again, the Cosmology Dept. isn't faring much better. Like Physics (with their *squarks, sprotons, gravitinos,* and *photinos*) they've got their own conceptual placeholders [Dark Matter, Dark Energy, Spacetime Singularities, and perhaps the most persistent conceptual placeholder of all time, the Big Bang], but while each of these assertions parades across the popular media as settled science, each flounders (as any conceptual placeholder will) when placed onto the table and examined under a bright light.

AutoGenesism: A Theory of Everything

The more adventurous cosmological theorists offer infinite quantities of universes. Each, existing as either a bubble, a slice or a rinse-repeat reincarnation, joins an infinite litter within an eternal multiverse in some well-regarded cosmological genesis narratives, with Time itself as a permanent environmental block that contains all versions of each of us as concurrently existent slices (like bread, I suppose) that render the past, present and future as illusory states of existence that we each make our way through, one slice following the last slice.

Of course, the more staid hold tightly onto Einstein's own view of Time as incidental and inherently malleable even as the days, months and years of their own lives slip into the rearview mirror with irony and quiet relentlessness. Again, as with Theoretical Physics, what Cosmology proposes as the basis of Reality leaves no actual fingerprints upon what's obvious, dependable, and immediately available to the average person, offering nothing whatsoever to those simply looking for an anchor of some sort (something real to orient themselves to) as they make their way through an increasingly counterintuitive world.

The distance between what either of these ToE component suites offers, and what a human being deals with from day to day, is just too vast for either, or both (in what's become an increasingly unlikely tandem) to ever really address what a functional Theory of Everything must address. The problem is that explaining the dynamics of open space, or explaining the counterintuitive nature of Quantum Mechanics for that matter, isn't the same as explaining the functional nature of everything. There's an entire range of Reality that exists between these two scale extremes, and neither scientific discipline seems at all interested in finding a way to connect its unique Reality narrative to what's definitively real about the swath of Reality that is most familiar, and most immediately available, to the human being.

This brings up an obvious question concerning the actual purpose of a functional Theory of Everything. If a ToE is an actual theory of everything, then shouldn't it explain the functional basis of everything?

Everything includes time, space, proximity, contextual juxtaposition, existence, being state, precedent, now versus then, here versus there, us versus them, mine versus yours, yes versus no, similar versus different, integral versus ancillary, and why anything at all does what it does regardless of the level of developmental sophistication it possesses.

Everything includes the existential structure, as well as the emergence of the concept of structure, as well as the primordial requirement that structure serves, as well as the universal means by which structure is initiated and progressively developed.

Everything includes the impetus behind existence, all that's come into existence by default, and all that's been actively and purposely brought into existence, as well as what it is that drives that which exists to do and/or be what it is; including why that which is capable of actively and purposely bringing anything at all into existence is driven to bring what it brings into existence.

Reality functions as a unified whole; not only at the quantum level and from one end of the Universe to the other, but right there at the end of our finger tips. We experience the things that we experience, and that experience itself is integral to the whole that is Reality. We fit into the whole of Reality, and the whole of Reality makes sense with the way that we are. Reality exists as a physical system, and it cannot be compartmentalized as contradictory pockets of experiment indication translations.

I realize that the universality of this *everything* may be more traditionally suited to the Philosophy Department due to its inherent incompatibility with falsification via blackboard equations, but it's a definitional focus that a true and functional ToE must be fully capable of addressing. After all, if a ToE doesn't also explain the everything that directly affects the lives and minds of those it's meant to serve, then what is it really a theory of? Something . . . yes. But, everything . . . ? No, not everything.

A Functional ToE: Basic Requirements

Until the physical substructure of Reality is determined, and that substructure is successfully connected to everything that is perceptible, inferable, or in any way definable — from the farthest reaches of the universe to the darkest corner of the most troubled imagination — what's real will continue to be shapeless, valueless, and functionally inaccessible to the human mind. It is only through a true, and clearly functional, Theory of Everything that the physical substructure of Reality can ever be determined, and this makes the rational and responsible pursuit of a true ToE much more important than the current crop of theories might suggest. In fact, when all prominent theories and hypotheses are gathered together, compared and contrasted, and then highlighted against what's become a reliable and inarguably coherent backdrop comprised of proven and immediately applicable scientific and technological staples, an impression emerges that regardless of the math, the funding, or the media attention, this ToE effort is treated as more of a parlor game than as serious science.

AutoGenesism: A Theory of Everything

There doesn't even seem to be a broadly agreed upon definition of what constitutes a Theory of Everything, and this is after many billions of dollars and entire professional careers invested over decades of effort. In fact, what's been produced is an absolute chaos of contradictory claims concerning what does and does not exist, can and cannot exist, versus what will and will never be actually proven to exist; each being offered as the mathematically determined fundamental basis of Reality. Okay, none that have actually been mathematically determined as such, but there are those breakthroughs that have definitely been declared — as a result of increasingly ingenious mathematical convolutions — to be determined fundamental to something that may lead science to a viable approach of the fundamental basis of Reality. Then again, it's not as if anything that can be defined as a fundamental basis has ever been agreed upon by those working to determine the true nature of everything.

This lack of a definitional foundation within the ToE pursuit itself has allowed all kinds of existential structures [pure esoteric mathematics, sacred geometry, point particles, one dimensional strings, quantum vacuums, and infinitely present multiverse expanses] to be offered as primordial launching pads, when obviously, not one of these most seriously considered constructs has any intrinsic capacity to plausibly define, let alone address, the primordial requirement that must necessarily rest at the foundation of an enterprise as focused and relentlessly dynamic as the progressive development of Reality. It's this reckless management of what should've been an orderly process of disciplined investigation that is at the heart of the failure of modern science to even establish a general center within which to then refine an increasingly accurate approach.

A true Theory of Everything must be an actual theory about the factual nature of everything that exists. It must explain what allows and what requires Reality to be the way that it is, and it must explain why we are required to perceive Reality as we perceive it. A true ToE can lose its specificity as it approaches those levels of progressive development that are inherently subject to those whims of circumstance-driven expression that exist solely within the highest strata of evolutionary sophistication, but it cannot break down at the most primordial levels, where all that's yet to become is finding its footing. A true ToE also must maintain its own progressive nature as it makes its way from detailing the most primitive to the most sophisticated. It must start out simple, and build in complexity in the same manner as everything it seeks to explain. A true Theory of Everything must resemble the *everything* that it explains.

The obvious existence of a material universe that contains clearly defined non-material, yet consequential, forms of physical manifestation (such as ideas, fears, devotions, and misunderstandings) also presents a very specific suite of demands on a true Theory of Everything, and unless every demand can be fully addressed, you may have a theory of something, but it's not a theory of everything.

In fact, you could create a thoroughly elegant math formula that wraps up every loose end pestering the worlds of cosmology, physics and biology — a brilliant theory that has everything zeroing out precisely in ways that have the Swedes eating out of your hand — but unless you can detail why mathematics exists to explain anything at all, or why you've got a mind that's even capable of caring about why anything exists as it does, you're still wandering out there in the dark.

The truth is that the application of esoteric mathematics as a theoretical tool has become more abuse than use in recent decades, with completely impossible assumptions being built one upon the other due to nothing more than the fact that the newest fantasy allows the previous fantasy to balance out on the blackboard. This would be fine if what was being built with these formulas was understood to be confined to the musings of those brilliant minds communally engaged in whatever thought experiment these chalkboard scrawling actually represent. But, that's not what's been happening with all this unrestrained creativity.

So, what's the problem with basing a ToE entirely on math? Well, for one thing, mathematics works only within a stable, context-controlled environment, and the wilds of physical Reality are anything but free of contextual contamination. Reality is a progressively developing set structure that evolves rapidly, featuring contextual mayhem of every conceivable nature, with depth-defying ramification structures that are relentlessly emerging at a pace that's just as inherently inscrutable. It's not true chaos, but it's certainly not a relationship matrix that can be boiled down to a simple math formula.

And why is it a required article of faith that pure, simple, elegant math is the structural basis of Reality? Perhaps Reality is no more than a set structure, but what can any math equation tell us about why color exists? What can it tell us about the functional net difference between the human brain and all other material brains? What can a math equation tell us about what it was that actually caused physical Reality to spring into existence? Nothing. Not a damn thing, and the reason is that the set structure of pure, esoteric math is only an idealized,

AutoGenesism: A Theory of Everything

extremely simplified interpretation of Reality. Reality is the physical basis of the human mind, which is the actual physical basis of the idealized set structure that even the most brilliant calculations are based on. Yes, this may come across as blasphemy within most scientific communities, but mathematics is a tool. It's never been anything more than a tool, and an inherently limited tool at that.

As for proving math-based theoretical formulations by confirming predictions via laboratory testing, I'll go ahead and make everyone cringe yet again. Physically isolating a severely defined experimental system with intricate preparations will give you an anticipated indication in exactly the same way that isolating and precisely preparing a stage will give a Las Vegas illusionist the same results night after night to the degree that he can bet his own life on those results being exactly as anticipated. Of course the results aren't natural or indicative of the larger reality that the illusionist exists within, but no one expects that to be the case.

Those sensational and famously counterintuitive scientific study results we've all heard about aren't natural or indicative of the larger reality that those studies existed within either. And, those results were just as heavily dependent on a carefully prepared and precisely controlled system as the results achieved night after night by any one of the many professional illusionists working the Vegas strip. Yet, the entire scientific community has taken those results and, over many years, has built additional layers of study conclusions that are (in most cases) even more confounding, basing them on increasingly unassailable assertions that are — themselves — based on the irresponsible definition of each contextually antiseptic system as being fully representative of true Reality; a thoroughly organic and hopelessly contaminated contextual environment.

And contextual contamination is just that; contextual contamination. It doesn't matter whether it's an unexpected change in stage rigging or ineffective precision within an entanglement procedure involving two or more photons. Any dirt in the system will still threaten the predicted results, and that's the point, since Reality is a system founded upon dirt.

And what is *dirt* anyway? If you're working to mathematically define Reality, then how can Reality's contaminates be anything other than necessary sets within your logic structure? Yes, the established methodology insists on a carefully controlled and soberly developed set structure, but let's be honest here, the mathematical set structure that's evolved over the last 100 years has been one that is simply not representative of Reality. You can calculate and calculate all you like, but your calculations will only ever be as useful as the sets you're working with.

In fact, what one actually learns by factoring in the relentless turmoil of change that defines what exists, is that the whole of physical Reality is the direct result of constant contextual contamination. Carefully scripted experimentation results are no more indicative of Reality than anything else that is achieved as a result of carefully scripted preparations. Maybe achieving a predicted outcome within the lab does teach us something about a tiny slice of Reality and how it would work under a very carefully engineered condition, but such system conditions fail to accurately reflect the conditions that exist *'in the wild'*, making any such research extremely limited in its capacity to actually explain Reality to any degree whatsoever.

It might be instructive here (in specific reference to this issue of basing scientific research solely on a failed mathematical set structure propped up by precise system preparation, control and manipulation) to make note of the famously mysterious nature of Quantum Mechanics, and let loose a small secret concerning the bizarre notion of *quantum superposition*; namely, why on Earth such an assertion was ever granted the legitimacy that it's enjoyed for such a long time. The resolution that was actually achieved by quantum superposition suggests it to be an entirely different proposition when the actual theoretical dilemma itself is viewed within this shaft of sunlight provide by Ervin Laszlo in this book *"Science and the Akashic Field: An Integral Theory of Everything"*.

> "Even more weird is the finding that — until it is measured or interacted with in some way — a quantum exists in a state in which all of its possible real states are superposed. Schrödinger's wave function relates the quantum's superposed wave state to its real state. (A "real" state is a classic state, with unique location and normal measurability) However, there are no laws of physics that can predict which of its possible real states the particle will select. While in the aggregate the shift from virtual into the real state conforms to statistical rules of probability, there is no way to tell just how it will occur in a given instance. Unless each shift takes place in a separate universe (as Everett suggested in his "parallel universes" hypothesis), individual quantum jumps are indeterminate, not subject to any laws of physics.

Granted, Dr. Laszlo's statement is not intended to suggest anything more than what it explicitly states, but in my own view of what this statement suggests, I see the concept of superposition (and parallel universes, for that matter) as being a belligerent refusal to accept the fact that even within the relatively

AutoGenesism: A Theory of Everything

context-free world of Quantum Mechanics, there's been no real means of mathematically predicting Reality's dynamic nature and how it will affect even the purest of entities. Again, defining and redefining Reality itself in deference to what was a recklessly stated assumption, with no thought paid to the inescapable conclusion — even after 100 years of famously bewildered fits and starts — that the set structure in use must be wrong.

I give Heisenberg and his contemporaries credit for coming up with a creative solution to what must've been a maddening effort to achieve a predicted outcome within the quantum realm. That said, inventing a jargon-riddled excuse for bailing out on a failure that infers the existence of a factual (even if technically virtual) physical state that doesn't, and can't logically, exist, didn't do a damn thing for the larger effort of figuring out what's true about Reality. A long afternoon with Google is all one needs to get a good feel for just how convoluted even the most learned assumptions about the nature of Reality have become since (and as a result of) just that one instance of bloviated obfuscation. No wonder a functional ToE has become so hard to manage in spite of the existence of so much available information concerning such enormous swaths of physical Reality.

So, how can anyone begin to figure out what's true about Reality? If mathematics can't provide a realistic basis from which to then proceed, how can a basis be established? In his book *"Science and the Sociopath"*, author Joseph D'Agnese describes an interesting means of taking a second look at what's become of *settled science* when it's gotten bogged down without resolution or forward progress. Devised by Dr. Gordon Rugg (an unlikely Scottish educator who made news in 2004 when he presented a plausible means of creating the legendary Voynich Manuscript as an elaborate, yet thoroughly achievable, hoax) the Verifier Method has the feel of simple common sense as it could pertain to the reexamination of highly technical theoretical fundamentals. Here, I've taken the exact description of the method as presented within Joseph D'Agnese's *"Science and the Sociopath"*, and simply bulleted the steps for easier reading.

Dr. Gordon Rugg's Verifier Method involves seven steps:

1. Amass knowledge of a discipline through interviews and reading
2. Determine whether critical expertise has yet to be applied in the field
3. Look for biases and mistakenly held assumptions in the research
4. Analyze jargon to uncover differing definitions of key terms
5. Check for classic mistakes using human-error tools

6. Follow the errors as they ripple through underlying assumptions
7. Suggest new avenues for research that emerge from steps one through six

As you can see, most of it is common sense, and what isn't, is the intellectual independence to allow yourself to seriously challenge what has become *'settled science'* without psychological or cultural restrictions.

> Did you know that Schrödinger's Cat was actually presented to Einstein (within a personal letter from Erwin Schrödinger concerning the Copenhagen Interpretation) as a ludicrous example of how inane the idea of superposition is? The thought experiment itself, as described by Herr Schrödinger starts off with *"One can even set up quite ridiculous cases."* And yet, Schrödinger's Cat is invariably offered as a serious explanation of Quantum Mechanics and just how weird Reality has been "proven by Quantum Physics" to be.

Clearly, there is room for, and plenty of reason for, the application of Gordon Rugg's Verifier Method within the *settled science* that bases the search for a true and functional Theory of Everything.

Before we proceed any further, maybe it'd be good to specify exactly what a true and functional ToE should explain. This could be important to definitively determine, especially since the traditional route of scientific inquiry is to become extremely specialized in focus and scope when establishing a factual basis, and then to inductively expand what's been determined as a result of that extremely specialized investigation to explain a lot more than should be reasonably allowed. The fact that most scientists actually think that getting the math of String Theory to finally work out will somehow explain anything at all says a lot about just how far afield the traditional route of scientific inquiry has wandered when it comes to theory and the larger questions concerning Reality in general.

In pursuit of a theory of the initiation and development of everything, as in the pursuit of any theory concerning anything that has occurred, impetus — Aristotle's *final cause* — is where the investigation begins. Nothing just happens, and establishing the *why* of an occurrence will always eliminate those theories concerning *how* that ultimately have no business clogging up the process of getting to the truth. So, let's see if we can determine a few things that a proper ToE must be capable of addressing. Some *why* questions that should be answered, or at least answerable to a reasonable extent.

Obviously, a math equation isn't going to explain much of anything that's real and organically existent, and a successful Theory of Everything is going to have to handle a lot more inquiry than what four established fundamental forces of nature have in common with one another. In fact, let's make a list, of what a successful ToE should be able to explain, and really let our list be driven by what we already know to exist as real and fundamental to everything else that's incidental or circumstantial (and therefore, less specifically determinable).

And let's allow our requirements to emerge free of any restraints concerning what has been determined to be achievable regardless of the scientific discipline that has imposed such a restraint. After all, this is a theory of everything, and not just a theory of gravity or space or time or emergence. Why not let this list even include questions that have long been considered unanswerable, just as long as they're relevant and inherently foundational? Why not? It's just a list after all.

In light of what we all know to exist as everything, a true Theory of Everything should explain:

1 — The Genesis of Physical Reality

In the beginning has to mean something. Conceptual placeholders — let's look at two such placeholders; the *quantum vacuum* and the *spacetime singularity* — might be allowable as philosophical constructs, but if what's being presented is being declared to be the actual initiation of physical Reality, then these kinds of constructs are obvious points of theoretical failure. Not only are they pure abstractions, they're not even physically compatible with what would have had to emerge from them in order for what has been proven to exist to have ever had any shot at existence. And that's not conjecture. That's the factual nature of the wall that stands between any one of these established theoretical launching pads and the rest of what actually exists. Here, let me see if I can sketch out the fundamental problems that exist concerning just the two highlighted above, since they are by far the most popular ToE existential points of origin.

When looking at the term *quantum vacuum*, the first thing that catches the discerning eye is the term *quantum*. Yes, this has become a very popular word, and if you simply look at what it gets attached to these days, you might think it means *magic* or *miracle*, but it's actually not a get-out-of-dealing-with-Reality-free designation. It's a term that was introduced into the modern physics lexicon by Max Planck to describe the smallest, and therefore inherently indivisible, unit of something that exists as physical and ultimately quantifiable. It was originally assigned to uniform, block units of length, time, activity, and energy transfer before being hijacked by popular culture and used to describe everything from marketing strategies to the least amount of solace one might expect to receive as a result of a given situation. In this case it's been added to *vacuum* to describe a vacuum that isn't even an actual vacuum if the term vacuum suggests a space that has had everything that was within it extracted, leaving it negatively pressurized relative to the larger environment that physically contains it.

In fact, this quantum vacuum isn't empty at all; certainly not a void. It's allegedly teeming with activators; an actual, physically existent Metaverse of creative potential as described by Ervin Laszlo, in his book *"Science and the Akashic Field: An Integral Theory of Everything"*;

> Cosmologies of the Metaverse are in a better position than the Big Bang theory (which is limited to our universe) to speak of conditions that reigned before, and will reign after, the life-cycle of our universe. The quantum vacuum, the subtle energy and in-formation (sic) sea that underlies all "matter" in the universe, did not originate with the Bang that produced our universe, and will not vanish when the particles it created by that explosion fall back into it. The subtle energies and the active information that underlie this universe were there before its particles appeared and will be there after they disappear. The deeper Reality is the quantum vacuum, the enduring in-formation and energy sea that pulsates, producing periodic explosions that give rise to local universes.

And that's what a quantum vacuum is and does, with minor description variations here and there depending on the specifics of the proposed theory that leverages the quantum vacuum as its emergence platform (of course, despite terminology differences, this includes all theories that feature parallel universes and any form of multiverse arrangement). As to where this quantum vacuum came from, and how and why it came into being, nothing is ever suggested. This is why I consider this Metaverse to be no more than another conceptual placeholder. The term vacuum doesn't really fit with the clear and definitive description of this roiling primordial soup, and as for the term quantum (defined as a uniform, indivisible unit of any of a very clearly defined variety of physical things) I don't see it working here either.

But terminology aside, the infinite nature of this quantum vacuum Metaverse is enough to sideline it as a qualified point of initial genesis. The whole premise comes across as just another secular description of the creator god; complete with endless quantities of pulsating energy, and proactive in-formation (a primordial form of information that is donated by each prior local universe upon its inevitable demise) that instructs new local universes on how

AutoGenesism: A Theory of Everything

to progress in the best, most efficient manner possible; this Metaverse learning from each previous local universe as it births universes for whatever reason it is that it does what it does. Again, too much being assumed and asserted, and without any acknowledgement of the *"turtles all the way down"* issue that this theoretical basis suffers with when it is examined in light of the next obvious question; how did Reality itself emerged to then host this Metaverse.

Now, trying to fit the conceptual spacetime singularity into the same Reality that we actually exist within is even more difficult, regardless of how it is that you maneuver it. Maybe on a chalkboard this notion comes across with a measure of viability, but when you take a few steps back and allow some daylight in to freshen the room a little, the spacetime singularity, or any singularity for that matter, loses its connection with Reality and does so rapidly.

Yes, the notion is the mathematical result of theoretical cosmology's running of our expanding universe back toward what they believe sent it outward in the first place; the Big Bang, and whatever it was that made it bang as it did. And yes, Einstein did suggest that if spacetime were to become gravitationally crushed into an infinitely dense mass that all laws of physics would be off the table. But, with all that acknowledged, there are still some really important issues that need to be addressed before anything can bang after being gravitationally crushed into a superheated singularity. Here are just a few that I can think of without actually giving it much thought.

- If gravity is the net impact on material structures of warpages in spacetime, then where did the gravity that initially crushed spacetime into a superheated singularity come from?
- Where did the stuff (that spacetime stuff) that was crushed into a superheated singularity come from? What is spacetime anyway?
- Why did that crushed stuff become crushed into a superheated singularity? What purpose was being served?
- What made the Big Bang bang when it banged?
- What did the Big Bang explode within when it banged? In other words, what was present that wasn't the Big Bang when the Big Bang banged, allowing it to explode relative to that which wasn't exploding?
- Where did that Big Bang hosting environment come from, and how did it form?
- What is the Big Bang's hosting environment made of?

31

I won't bother addressing the logical problems that exist for anything labeled a singularity that does or has ever existed relative to whatever it is that it's exploding into or has ever exploded into, since the term's being used in this case to describe

> "a location where the quantities that are used to measure the gravitational field become infinite in a way that does not depend on the coordinate system."

> http://en.wikipedia.org/wiki/Gravitational_singularity

I have no idea how such a location can ever be determined, even if I could actually connect what we do know about Reality (in any sense whatsoever) with the notion itself, but as I noted above, a full enough set of conceptual difficulties already exists with this specific spacetime Big Bang singularity concept without digressing over the logical issues inherent with any physical *"something"* described as having the inherent capacity to literally straddle two completely incompatible being states. I realize that it's just a term, but at some point terminology has to mean something definitive and terms have to related to what they (as actual words that are in active use elsewhere) structurally imply.

A true Theory of Everything cannot be a play on words or be based on an irreducible *quantum* composite of any kind. A quantum vacuum that contains quantities of *"subtle energies and in-formation"* is obviously such a composite that is being presented as irreducible, as is any gravitational singularity capable of Big Banging into the entire universal composition that we call home — with the entirety of it all merely spreading out at the speed of light or coalescing into matter, as the case may be. The genesis of Reality may as well be a voice ordering the whole of everything into existence for all the clarity such theories bring to the discussion.

A responsible Theory of Everything will answer the question of existential genesis. It will explain how and why physical existence came into existence, and it will do so without relying on infinite reduction, primordial unknowns, or just-so stories. Even if such a feat is based on the application of established fundamentals in a manner that some find counterintuitive, it will be based, and must be based, on the clear and responsible application of those established fundamentals that are pervasive throughout the physical whole of Reality. If not, then it's not a true Theory of Everything.

AutoGenesism: A Theory of Everything

2 — Coherence

Coherence is what a system possesses if it is *"logically or aesthetically consistent so that all the separate parts fit together and add up to a harmonious or credible whole."*

That definition is italicized because I took it directly from my Word 2007 dictionary. I realize that the physics definition refers to . . .

"an ideal property of waves that enables stationary (i.e. temporally and spatially constant) interference."

http://en.wikipedia.org/wiki/Coherence_%28physics%29

. . . but, I'm not going to confine the definition of *Coherence* to the tiny slice of everything that sits under the scrutiny of physics. We're looking at a Theory of Everything here, and physics — while definitely something — is certainly not everything. This being true, a bona fide ToE must transcend physics, as well as cosmology, biology, metaphysics, psychology and whatever else exists as contributing to the whole that is everything. And it must explain why all of it comes together as a harmonious and credible whole. If it can't, then it's a theory of something, and maybe even a unification theory of some sort, but it's not a Theory of Everything.

Back in Newton's day, they called the search for a Theory of Everything *Natural Philosophy*, and macro-system coherence was a leading requirement, even if there was universal acknowledgement that such coherence was elusive unless a god of some sort was tossed into the theoretical mix to provide the functional interdependence between clearly disparate systems. But, that was a long time ago. We've gathered a lot more to work with since those days. In fact, I honestly believe we've got all the secular perspective required to sew this all together without even the smallest god jammed in there to make it all squish in tightly with cohesive precision. So, in light of this requirement, let's take a look at some of what a true ToE must be able to reconcile with one flat statement of commonality:

- What it is that causes Einstein's *"spooky action at a distance"*.
- Why it is that an electron (or any other particle, atom, molecule, or specific system) will always exhibit the precise characteristics that are typical of what it is.
- Why it is that our own universe is so precisely *"fine-tuned"* to allow for all that exists within it to successfully exist.

- What it is that is common to all that exists — from the quantum to the cosmological to the ineffable — connecting all of it together as one holistic and definable system.

To date, there has been no such Theory of Everything with the power to accomplish this, with the net effect of universal system coherence losing its status as a primary requirement to achieving much less associable mathematical symmetries and the elimination of bothersome infinities within the calculating minds of those in hot pursuit of the ultimate ToE. Still, it remains obvious that since everything that exists does so as part of an structurally coherent whole, and since the survival of any such whole specifically depends entirely on its functional cohesion, that a universal coherence must exist between everything, making the specific nature and identity of what it is that provides that coherence, and how this is accomplished, a critical requirement that a true Theory of Everything must satisfy.

3 — The Existential Foundation of Order

In Lee Smolin's *"Time Reborn: From the Crisis in Physics to the Future of the Universe"* he ponders the existence of a law that sets the stage for all other laws [physics, cosmology, nature, etc.,] to be what they are.

> The idea that laws evolve has the promise of making fundamental physics more predictive. But it brings with it one final dilemma. It is natural to ask whether there is a law that governs how the laws evolve. We can call such a law, which acts on laws rather than directly on elementary particles, a meta-law. It might be hard to observe the action of this meta-law, as it may act only during violent episodes such as the Big Bang. However, if we want a complete explanation for our universe, one that fully realizes the ambition of the principle of sufficient reason, shouldn't there be such a meta-law?

I have to admit that I really appreciate this specific observation, especially as I consider the requirement of coherence within any functional system; regardless of how complex such a system might be. Of course, if such a meta-law exists, it would have to make sense with the full nature of our own universe — from the most primitively material of default ramifications to the most intellectually sophisticated of inaccessible esotericisms — for it to be useful (and for it to thereby qualify as a plausible meta-law candidate within a reasonable, responsible ToE).

AutoGenesism: A Theory of Everything

To date, there are a few physically authoritative substructures that have been offered within the confines of declared Theories of Everything (oscillating superstrings with the power and wisdom to break quantum symmetries on behalf of initiating the miracle of physical existence; quantum vacuum seas of percolating energies and in-formation exploding reincarnated universes that instinctively know to pick up where the last universe left off; and informed bosons that scurry about like bellhops issued from ubiquitous fields of force potential to act in kind upon whatever it is, to spur on whatever it is that initiates, for whatever reason it might serve) but none that actually present a fundamental impetus that directs how all existent things deal with the very finite issues that each faces from instant to instant. For a Theory of Everything to be a theory of everything, shouldn't its meta-law explanation explain the single overarching reason why everything does what it does, even if that explanation necessarily serves that function from an extremely high overhead point of perspective?

And contrary to Prof Smolin's suggestion that a meta-law's sphere of influence should be indiscernible and restricted to instances of natural law emergence, a true existential meta-law shouldn't stop being the direct basis of order and process once everything has gotten up off the floor and started ambulating. Yes, eventually contextual precedent does stabilize a system's foundational development structure, but context is inherently malleable within any dynamic confine. That's what keeps a living, progressive system alive and progressing.

Within such a system, the meta-law must always be present, densely laced throughout the whole of that system, and it should be immediately recognizable for what it is. If not, then how can it be considered the fundamental law that governs the evolution of all emergent laws; the anchor that holds the whole of the system together? The entire system itself should immediately reflect the intrinsic essence of its meta-law; from its most defined and exclusive processes, to the very least of what each and every thing does from instant to instant within that system's embrace.

We all know that evolution is an ongoing process. If our universe's natural laws did evolve (which really does seem to be the only explanation that doesn't ultimately encounter a theoretical brick wall) then their structure and application are, and will always be, subject to an ongoing developmental process. This being true, the meta-law that governs our universe — if there is such a law — will always be an ongoing requirement.

A quality, plausible meta-law should be capable of equally addressing the following issues:

- Why it is that all forms of life replicate or procreate?
- Why is gravity so relentlessly omnipresent and unusually applied within large systems?
- Why it is that Time's arrow points in only one direction?
- Why it is that Newton's 2nd Law of Thermodynamics [increasing entropy] fails to explain progressive development and increasing structural complexity over Time.
- What is the point of creativity and intellectual curiosity?
- What is the reason for *it is* and *'I am'*.

The existence of a meta-law does make sense. That said, it's not an easy call. Lee Smolin is the first major voice to suggest a need for it, even if others have offered their own versions of what must sit at the bottom of all that exists as real. Professor Smolin is right. What sits at the base of everything that physically exists must be a requirement. It cannot itself be physical, whether particle, energy, or field of potential. It must transcend all of what has emerged within this system, and it must be pervasive even now throughout the whole of it. Only a requirement — a meta-law — can be what it is that set the stage for all that's come into existence. The right Theory of Everything will offer such a requirement, and it will be immediately recognizable for what it is.

4 — A Sufficient Explanation for . . .

"The Principle of Sufficient Reason" states that nothing exists without a reason for its existence. Generally, attributed to Leibniz, it seems like an extreme requirement, bordering on determinism, but let's take a quick look at how this principle can be expressed.

> The principle has a variety of expressions, all of which are perhaps best summarized by the following:
>
> - For every entity X, if X exists, then there is a sufficient explanation for why X exists.
> - For every event E, if E occurs, then there is a sufficient explanation for why E occurs.
> - For every proposition P, if P is true, then there is a sufficient explanation for why P is true.

AutoGenesism: A Theory of Everything

A sufficient explanation may be understood either in terms of reasons or causes, for like many philosophers of the period, Leibniz did not carefully distinguish between the two. The resulting principle is very different, however, depending on which interpretation is given.

http://en.wikipedia.org/wiki/Principle_of_sufficient_reason#Formulation

My own interpretation of sufficient explanation is perhaps a bit more precise than the interpretation that Leibniz, and likely most of his contemporaries, would have embraced. My interpretation requires that there be no point within a Theory of Everything where an entity, event or proposition is allowed to exist without a full explanation concerning why it exists, how it came into existence, and how its physical existence satisfies Reality's most primordial and pervasive existential meta-law requirement. Yes, this does require that this meta-law be established as the primary impetus, but all of these ToE requirements necessarily lean against one another. This is as it should be, since all of physical Reality intersects and interconnects as one multilayered hierarchical matrix of shared dependency and support.

If a one dimensional vibrating superstring exists, then a true ToE will detail why it exists, how it came into existence, and how its vibrating serves the meta-law requirement that bases the whole of physical Reality. If this cannot be accomplished, then the superstring can't be physically existent, let alone the unitary quantum basis of material existence. If the presence of a seething, percolating quantum vacuum sea of energy and in-formation can't be fully explained (regardless of what sort of metaverse it is alleged to exist within) then that sea of energy and in-formation must be relegated to the lengthy collection of myths, legends, and metaphysical speculations as a pretty cool idea, but certainly nothing more than that. In essence, if it is described as possessing physical presence anywhere in any manner, but its initial physical genesis can't be described in the terms listed above, it simply cannot physically exist.

This does not mean that a true ToE must be reductionistic in nature. Physical emergence has been well established, and Reductionism didn't survive the 20th century as a viable scientific theory. It does mean, however, that something cannot simply be. That said, emergence has taught us that raw requirement can bring something unique and novel from that which has a true and literal absence of anything directly associable (in functionality and relative to existing property set) with what's been brought into existence, as long as that requirement can be fully associated with what has been established to be primordial as well as pervasive to the degree of ubiquity within the whole of Reality. With that stated, if

37

a ToE cannot account for the existence of any one thing that does exist, or if it requires the existence of any one thing that is inherently inexplicable, then it might be a theory of something, but it's not a Theory of Everything.

5 — The Arrow of Time

When a cup falls and shatters, for it, there's no going back to when it existed as whole and unshattered. If something breaks, it can't be unbroken. Newton's 2nd Law of Thermodynamics (entropy) observes that this is true, and while it does detail an observable direction for time's arrow, it doesn't explain why this is true. Entropy also doesn't explain why growth and increasing complexity in living structures also moves forward along the very same entropy-driven arrow of time, yet with completely different net results over a significant percentage of its existential trajectory. While a string of natural laws can be fitted together to describe the observable processes, we all know that there must be a much more fundamental structure that keeps each of these laws moving those processes in one direction, and lining them up in a way that allows them to work so seamlessly together as they do.

Some Theories of Everything dismiss Time as either irrelevant or illusory, but a true ToE has to deal with the fact that (specious theoretical claims and reckless experiment results interpretations aside) Time moves in one and only one direction, and always has. A successful ToE will be able to detail why Time exists, what Time is, and how the meta-law is served as a result of Time's arrow pointed in that one direction.

6 — The Emergence of Spatial Environment

There's a very real difference between being here and being there. It's called relative proximity, and while our own perception of it may be individual, flexible, and clearly subject to the specifics of Relativity, it's more than just an illusion. In fact, you can prove this is true by driving a car into a pole, forcing two discrete objects to occupy the same proximity point simultaneously. To allow for proximity, and the difference between being here and being there, spatial environment must exist as a real quantity. That seems pretty obvious, but what isn't so obvious is how the very first instance of spatial dimension came into physical existence, and how its emergence served the existential requirement basis when it emerged.

AutoGenesism: A Theory of Everything

A true Theory of Everything must be able to fully explain how space came into being, and when I use the term space, I'm referring to the basic open space between here and there that obviously exists and obviously persists.

And speaking of space, a full Theory of Everything must be capable of detailing the physical structure of space (as in outer space) and precisely why it is what it is, and what is being served by its existence. This explanation must make sense [have system coherence] with every other explanation offered by that same Theory of Everything, and if this cannot be achieved, then it's no Theory of Everything.

Why is open space expanding? Why are the furthest galaxies accelerating outward? What is Dark Matter? What is Dark Energy? Is open space a 3 dimensional vacuum, or is it a 2 dimensional membrane stretched across something or other as a result of some sort of inflation of some sort?

If a ToE can't make responsible heads or tails of these enormous questions without violating its own carefully designed existential structure — tasked with also explaining why the smallest of everything else is what it is and does what it does — then it's no Theory of Everything. After all, *Everything* is everything, and a Theory of Everything is a theory of everything that exists.

7 — The Existence of Natural Laws

Where did they come from? Why do they exist? Did our universe come into existence as a result of them or did they evolve as a result of the progressive development of our universe? While we may have decided for or against an actual *"law of laws"* (a meta-law, as it were) such a meta-law would not let us off the hook regarding how natural laws come to be. Are they the net response to intrinsic requirement, or of emerging functionality? Can they be tied to Time? Are they proof of the possibility of information as a physical quantity? Exactly what can we know about Reality as a direct result of the existence of natural laws?

Of course, we can declare them to be *brute fact* — that natural laws simply are what they are — but then we can declare a lot that isn't particularly useful or accurate. We've been doing that for centuries. The point of a true ToE is to NOT declare anything to simply be whatever it is, but to connect whatever it is to a larger, more fundamental order that is integral to how the whole of Reality itself is successfully served and stabilized as the persistent whole that it obviously is.

The progressive stability of natural laws is clearly necessary to the success-ful stabilization of structure within our own universe. That much isn't hard to accept as true and undeniable, and most professional theorists wouldn't see that as a particularly controversial statement. However, what this actually means is that to suggest that one area of the universe is ruled by a completely different set of natural laws is to insist that there is a way of establishing and enforcing arbitrarily determined regional demarcation zones that feature differing funda-mental physics. And, this would insist that these proximity zones factually exist in what would have to be primordial isolation, based entirely on criteria that (if these criteria exist as, at all, definable) only exist within the imaginations of theorists. Yet, that hasn't stopped entire hypotheses from evolving from theories that are based on the adventurous musings of theorists who've traversed the depth of space with their imaginations, and returned with math-approved cer-tainties that bear no resemblance to anything that's ever been observed, or even remotely indicated by anything that's ever been observed.

But, then, intellectual discipline (or lack thereof) is what sets a true and functional Theory of Everything apart from the run-of-the-mill popular science-based fiction that has become plausible reality for so many within modern soci-ety (professional and laymen alike). A true and functional ToE can't simply toss conjecture out as fact, any more than it can draw a line between what's indicated and what's simply assumed. Natural laws exist, and a true Theory of Everything will connect the emergence of each such law with every other fundamental as-pect of Reality as a whole. Even if it ends up being a case of radically differing expressions of the exact same impetus across the board, nothing will be allowed to *simply be* whatever it is. It will make sense and the specific dots will be con-nected, or it won't be a Theory of Everything.

8 — Quale: The Experience of Experience

> "The sensation of color cannot be accounted for by the physicist's objec-tive picture of light-waves. Could the physiologist account for it, if he had fuller knowledge than he has of the processes in the retina and the nerv-ous processes set up by them in the optical nerve bundles and in the brain? I do not think so."
>
> — **Erwin Schrödinger**

The human mind exists, and its experience of existence also exists. This might be an area of examination most suited to the fields of psychology and philosophy, but when addressing the true and full nature of everything, the experience of experiencing does exist as part of everything, even if only for a very small percentage of that which also exists as part of everything. What is most important about qualia is their connection to the very question of the nature of Reality, and the fact that there'd be no such question if qualia did not exist. Yes, Reality would exist and persist without the existence of qualia, but qualia do exist, and their existence has profoundly affected the whole of Reality in ways that will definitely continue to manifest as the future unfolds.

The experience of conscious experience is inherently subjective, and while there are no math formulas that can objectively define subjectivity, it exists and a true, functional ToE should be able to fully explain what subjectivity is relative to the phenomena of qualia; the human experience of conscious experience. It should be able to explain how the brain produces it, and the physical nature of what conscious subjective experience is based on once it has emerged from the brain.

Most importantly, that explanation must achieve coherence with the impetus and requirement structure that permeates Reality from the instant of existential emergence to the fully realized whole that is the entire universe itself. It cannot exist in conceptual isolation from the rest of what exists as real and definable. If this can't be achieved, then it may be a theory of something, but, again, it's not a Theory of Everything.

9 — The Why of Esotericism

The human mind is unique within the whole of physical reality in that it can both conceptualize and literally embrace that which it has never perceived, will never perceive, and cannot ever perceive as real and definable. The concept of mysticism isn't something that swept down from the heavens to impose itself upon the mind of humanity, it grew out of the depths of the human mind, and *why* is a profound and important question that must be addressed within any Theory of Everything. Esotericism has been a defining attribute of human civilization since well before recorded history revealed just how integral it's always been to the intellectual development of humankind. You can dismiss it all out of hand, but you've severely crippled the success and functionality of your ToE by doing so.

The truth is that unless a Theory of Everything can explain how such a bizarre manifestation of certainty and relentless devotion could have initiated within the survival focus of only one species of Earth's vast array of life, it's not a true, functional ToE. Especially when you consider that a full 86% of the Earth's human population believes in the existence of populated worlds that are inherently imperceptible and based entirely on centuries-old mysticism. The initial emergence of this unshakable belief in what can't ever be perceived (and to the point of dedicated self-sacrifice on its behalf) actually makes no sense if examined from a strictly causal approach, even when one allows for its noumenal nature, and yet nothing is more pervasive, more powerfully instructive, or more central to what it means to be human, regardless of the culture or corner of the world. If a ToE can't explain why, then it's no Theory of Everything.

10 — The Fundamental Requirement

When the mysterious phenomenon of Emergence occurs, there's a point that is reached within the specific confluence where the introduction of a relative intangible is introduced, and that introduction transforms that otherwise mundane collective into a spontaneous manifestation that is whole, irreducible, and unique in form and physical properties. It could be the direct introduction of a precise temperature [causing flammable materials to suddenly ignite] bringing actual fire into existence, or perhaps the tipping point infestation [a sudden balance shift within an emotional-psychological configuration] that turns a crowd into a violent mob. It's not material or structural in nature, but whatever it ends up being, it clearly presents what's necessary for that specific transformation to occur. What's also clear is that it exists in a manner that is unique when compared to the rest of what's gathered in material confluence, as if awaiting its call to transformation.

When examining the structural nature of everything that exists, reductionism brings you to a similar point where pattern and unitary existence gives way to a relative intangible in this very same manner, and why wouldn't it? The Emergent System — among physical manifestations that are actually available to be examined — most replicates the result of existential genesis; albeit in the most tangential manner. In fact, true to its repeat and replicate nature, Emergence is woven throughout the fabric of Reality as the existential basis of every fundamental from kinetic energy to life to the conscious appreciation that there's anything at all worth taking the time to wonder about.

Over the years, there have been existential requirements theoretically presented as the bases of Reality [symmetry, simplicity, mathematical elegance] with some of these requirements more focused on subjective aesthetics than on

AutoGenesism: A Theory of Everything

an actual need that pulls everything forward at all levels of progressive development. A need that everything that exists has as fundamental to what each and every thing shares with everything else that also exists. Certainly it can't be symmetry, since true symmetry is perfect balance; another way of describing system death. Simplicity and/or mathematical elegance is a subjective description, and not something that exists and is capable of actually pulling progressive development forward.

Yes, a functional Theory of Everything should only feature what's absolutely necessary, and it should have an inherent elegance, but that's not a fundamental requirement. A fundamental requirement must describe WHY everything — including a meta-law (if such a law does exist) — must do what it does. If a Theory of Everything does not feature such a fundamental requirement — one that exists at all levels of progressive development, pulling literally all existence and all laws forward in the same manner — then it's yet another incomplete and unfunctional ToE.

... And, In This Corner ...

What's also important to establish is the legitimacy of the basic approach being taken by any specific ToE theorist. For centuries, Theories of Everything were theologically based, and no one in their right mind would've suggested that Reality wasn't the handiwork of God in one sense or another. The notion simply wouldn't have been taken seriously by anyone in a position to grant it legitimacy, and there are still enormous centers of societal authority that definitively lay claim to more than the requisite number of answers to all questions concerning who, what, where, why, how, and even how many can dance on the head of a pin. Contrast that group with the equally heralded secular alternates whose ToE dilemma can be summed up with: *why doesn't gravity make sense with the other three forces of nature?* and you realize that the definition of everything can change dramatically depending on who it is that's using the term. That said, it does seem as if there is bedrock consensus concerning what it takes to achieve a reasonable, responsible ToE point of perspective, and who's allowed to legitimately offer such a perspective.

I read a statement recently that — while it didn't exactly distress me — set me back a little into my chair.

> A theory that could successfully predict or explain the value of any constant of Nature would attract the attention of every living physicist. The

43

truth of this statement is readily appreciated by those scientists who receive a large amount of mail from misguided members of the public announcing the discovery of their new 'Theory of the Universe' (the author
has received two during the last week alone).

John D. Barrow — "New Theories of Everything"

The author goes on to have at a little fun with the basic psychological profile of such theorists (basically motivated by a desire to dethrone Einstein, which
may be true for some, if not most), but then he makes a significant point that —
for me, anyway — rescues the entire paragraph's seeming descent into crass
elitism. He describes the focus of these *"eccentrics"* as being totally committed
to the numerical values of the constants of Nature (and from a variety of unique
approaches), but then pivots that observation, regarding it as indicative of a
much larger point; that an explanation of the constants of Nature is widely regarded as the ultimate ToE goal of modern physics. In other words, for the modern physicist, everything is limited to the properties of particles, the four fundamental forces, and the geometry that contains it all.

Then again, Physics is the science of physical interactions between material
wholes, involving fundamental forces and the background geometry that gives
it all an environment within which to do what it does. So, should the ToE of a
theoretical physicist be taken seriously if Physics itself is so limited in scope?
As we noted in the last subsection, there's a lot more to everything than particles,
forces and background geometry.

But, isn't it true that each scientific discipline is inherently siloed in a similar manner? Even Cosmology, as grand a science as it is, is helpless when tasked
with simply connecting what it declares to be true about Reality directly to the
kind of litter that defines the average person's daily life. Curved spacetime,
black holes, and dark energy make for great symposium topics, but if that extremely broad level of examination is the primary scope of your work, then what
percentage of everything are you actually qualified to describe? Isn't your training in such a field of study as much an impediment as any other extremely specific regimen if the effort itself requires the capacity to bridge many such isolated disciplines?

But, then, who is to be considered legitimately qualified on the subject of
everything if the whole of humanity's ToE subculture can be readily divided
between the learned [the professional whose highly trained intellectual focus has
been purposely narrowed to a point of irrelevancy] and the rest of the herd [those

AutoGenesism: A Theory of Everything

whose presence is generally defined by the loudest of those carnies who've successfully propagated the most controversial, and therefore marketable, notions]?

When it comes to breaking through the present miasma, Prof. Lee Smolin, in his book *"The Trouble With Physics: The Rise of String Theory, The Fall of Science, and What Happens Next"*, offers a description of the kind of person that he feels is needed.

> "It goes without saying that people who are good at asking genuinely novel but relevant questions are rare, and that the ability to look at the state of a technical field and see a hidden assumption or a new avenue of research is a skill quite distinct from the workaday skills that are a prerequisite for joining the physics community. It is one thing to be a craftsperson, highly skilled in the practice of one's craft. It is quite another thing to be a seer."

Prof. Smolin goes on to further illustrate the nature of this seer, using a familiar example within the same chapter.

> "History demonstrates that the kind of person who becomes a seer is sometimes mediocre when compared with the mathematically clever scientists who excel at problem solving. The prime example is Einstein, who apparently couldn't get a decent job as a scientist when he was young. He was slow in argument, easily confused; others were much better at mathematics."

And yet, how does such a person — a seer — break through with a novel yet relevant question, let alone an answer, if (as author John D. Barrow admits) professionals who have been tasked with determining the nature of everything *"receive a large amount of mail from misguided members of the public announcing the discovery of their new 'Theory of the Universe'"* on a regular basis? Or is it a case where such a seer must emerge from one of the various siloed scientific disciplines that have been officially designated as suitable cloisters for those so qualified to determine the true nature of Reality? If so, then we'd best hope that such a person does exist, and finds his (or her) transcendently novel perspective before this modern world's collective capacity to *hold two or more conflicting notions* concerning the fundamental nature of Reality itself crashes, creating a paradigm shift in its own right.

So, what about the legions of metaphysicists and *quantum* spiritualists who have seized on the opportunities that widespread confusion has always offered such folks? If Prof. Smolin's seer doesn't emerge from professional academia, then how will he (or she) ever clear a way through that shrieking fog of insanity and establish a market presence with any legitimacy whatsoever? With the towering ivied walls of traditional science pressed so firmly against the brightly festooned barbed-wire barricades of popular *scientific* infotainment, where does such a person find that revolutionary, yet responsible, pathway forward anymore? Or has such a pathway ever actually existed?

Probably the best way to deal with the fact that no Theory of Everything will ever have the inherent power to fully emerge as a true game-changer, is to accept that information, once released, will always have its own unique impact upon the macro-system as a whole, and to embrace that process of change in whichever manner it ultimately manifests. An authentic paradigm shift may no longer be possible, given the specific nature of modern society and how hyper-transactional information has become as a result. Still, even the smallest impact can initiate a change trajectory. And who knows, perhaps in time . . .

Nevertheless, it's best to simply focus on the task at hand; a plausible, reasonably responsible explanation of Reality. Something that can actually be accomplished.

. . . And, So . . .

As we look at everything and how it's possible that it all came to be, we'll be gauging our success or failure against our very concise and clearly detailed list of ToE requirements. I will admit that I'm not persuaded by the arguments that the Scientific Method is the only means of falsifying what can be inferred by what exists as clearly verifiable. That may be true about any one of so many tiny slices of Reality, and may be useful when establishing ways of applying bits of that tiny slice to the ongoing business of improving the survivability of humankind within the Material Realm, but we're not *"doing physics"* here. We're not restricting our view to any box, with plans to then project our tiny findings across enormous stretches of Reality via the miracle of Inductivism.

We're not going to follow any method that allows us to speculate (although I will feature very specific, and properly highlighted, digressions called ***Speculation Alerts***, meant to take a moment to play with an idea). We'll be letting what's clearly evident, overwhelmingly commonplace, and inarguably relevant as evidence, be our reality anchors, and with our process firmly stabilized, we'll be applying a suite of deductive devices as we rigidly define what can be logically inferred directly from what's been firmly established.

AutoGenesism: A Theory of Everything

The following deductive logic structures will be our methodological basis going forward;

Modus tollens

If the watch-dog detects an intruder, the dog will bark.
The dog did not bark
Therefore, no intruder was detected by the watch-dog.

Modus ponens

If it's raining, I'll meet you at the movie theater.
It's raining.
Therefore, I'll meet you at the movie theater.

Hypothetical syllogism

If I do not wake up, then I cannot go to work.
If I cannot go to work, then I will not get paid.
Therefore, if I do not wake up, then I will not get paid.

examples courtesy of Wikipedia.com

While most tangential or minute developmental specifics can't be fully ascertained with these deductive devices (the complexities of a hyper-dynamic system being what they are), the fundamentals that bring those (and all other) specifics into existence certainly can be defined and structurally established deductively. And by combining this deductive methodology with our target list of very specific requirements for a functional ToE, this is what we'll do.

Kevin Brian Carroll

Section I

The Basis
of
Everything

Since I am one who never reads the Preface or the Introduction of any book (and since I know that there are many others like myself in that sense) before we get into this Section I, I'm going to repeat a statement that is aggressively detailed and defended in those two sections that (let's face it) many folks just don't bother with. Now, I know that what I'm about to state may come across as pretty bold. In fact, most academic professionals might even consider it to be a very irresponsible statement, considering the years of hard work they've already put into objectively examining the physical nature of Reality. Especially if such a statement comes from someone who's never even sat through an algebra class, and who has no idea what some of those precious little chalk squiggles mean or why they have the power to bring the fullness of existence into razor sharp focus for those who've made it their life to draw them across blackboards. Still, as we begin here, it's important that we're all on the same page, so I'm going to say it as clearly and succinctly as I can; what I'm about to share with you is the only full Theory of Everything that actually exists in a finished, published form.

Now, anyone can make this claim, and these days, plenty of people are. As we've already covered in the previous two sections, there are all kinds of theories, and they range from vibrating strings to formless infinite *"potentials"* to primordial sources of pure consciousness that sit beneath all that emerges into material and/or nonmaterial physical existence. Of course, these visionaries can't all be right. The substructure of Reality can't be based solely on both vibrating strings and a pure, all knowing consciousness. That seems fairly obvious on the face of it. And formless unlimited *"potentials"* has the feel of a theoretical placeholder as opposed to an actual determination of anything.

If this specific Theory of Everything — AutoGenesism — was as unfinished and unsubstantiated as (let's say) Superstring Theory, or M Theory (whatever that actually is), or what the Metaphysics world is labeling their infinite, formless, all-knowing consciousness energy field theory these days, then it wouldn't be the subject of this or any other book. And, it's critical that this very specific point is clearly established up front. This theory is not a reductionistic dead end or a philosophical semantics quagmire. In fact, this is the first and only ToE that promises to take you all the way back to just before the emergence of physical existence, and to walk you slowly through that unprecedented instant, with plenty of detail concerning how that instant launched the fundamental Reality from which all that is real has ultimately emerged. And, this is a promise that no one has ever been able to honestly and successfully make, be they scientist, shaman, or sequestered cenobite soliciting sectarian sanctification.

In fact, you can search all you want through the most authoritative statements or determinations — peer reviewed or otherwise — for a definitively objective description of anything truly primordial, but you won't find one. Not if, by primordial, you mean that the described *anything* is the basis of the ultimate emergence — or manifestation — of a larger material or conceptual whole, while possessing no contributive components or any physical characteristics that possess a component nature. And really, it's all about a complete absence of divisibility when what you're searching for is an existential foundation, regardless of what sort of foundation it is. This has got to be accepted as fundamental to what constitutes a primordial point of physical existence. Definitely, if what is being pursued is the true and objective basis of Reality itself.

In this first section, that's what we'll be pursuing. After all, as I stated, until the true basis of physical Reality itself has been accurately determined, nothing can be theorized about anything, let alone everything. And in this section, I will eventually do just that, but only after clearing up a few crippling misconceptions so that an accurate foundation will exist upon which to build.

There's Real and Then There's *Real*

When taking on the true nature of Reality, what we have to do is determine what's real and what is the product of our own interpretation of what's real. Now, this can get pretty tricky because all we know about Reality is what we've interpreted as being real. And not only what we've interpreted as being real, but

AutoGenesism: A Theory of Everything

what we — as members of any one of a myriad of defined societal collectives — have agreed amongst ourselves to accept as constituting an accurate interpretation of what is real. That wide range of possible Reality interpretations acknowledged, we've also got to deal with the fact that (as anyone who has ever worked within a committee knows) a lot can happen to an accurate interpretation of anything as it makes its way along the road to consensus.

What also stands as a buzz saw in that doorway out of any room where ignorance reigns is the subjective nature of human perception, as well as the fact that we — as Earth's only species that is involved in any effort to actively determine the nature of Reality — have only interpretations of our own subjective perceptions upon which to build new perception interpretations. Of course, the struggle is made that much more difficult when one takes into account the fact that each progressive addition to our knowledge base is predicated on information that was determined and approved by thought leaders who have, time and time again, proven themselves to have been *men of their times* concerning their capacity to validate the accuracy of that information.

In fact, as one reaches deeper into the past and examines the foundations that were laid for us so many centuries ago, it becomes increasingly clear that our collective perception of who we are, what we are, and how it is that we exist, is built on layers of patchwork efforts that still exist to prop up one obvious error after another, with each produced in dedication to the preservation of the oldest and most foundational failures. It was inevitable that we'd finally arrive at a moment when some of our most brilliant minds would be insisting that material Reality itself can only exist as an illusory projection of the human mind. After all, our research technology was eventually going to present us with indications that could not be reconciled with a wisdom structure that had been built, and rebuilt, in deference to men whose capacity for accurate information was clearly commensurate with the times within which they lived.

With our entire knowledge base exposed as patently suspect (at the very least), and with the vulnerability of subjective perception affecting our only means of finding our way toward any semblance of objective Reality (even if only one step closer than where we now languish in bewildered inertia), how can we ever hope to determine where we stand, let alone what it'll take to move forward toward clarity. One strategy that's used in efforts that are similar in focus, if much smaller in scope, is an elimination strategy. But is there any means of even accomplishing this, relative to such enormous questions?

Fortunately, we have a tool called deductive inference to help us eliminate the impossible, the implausible, and the highly unlikely. And, if we diligently apply this brilliantly dependable device in tandem with the requirement of maintaining system coherence between what's suggested and what has already been fully established as reliable, we can make some real headway in our effort to cleanse the debate of what simply makes no sense at all. Then, once we can see what's left standing after all that, perhaps we can then determine what's to be done with it.

As for how to approach an elimination strategy, I feel that the very first target must be whatever it is that — while being absolutely wrong — grants any level of plausibility to other equally inaccurate assertions. Preferably, it should be the one inaccuracy that grants this plausibility to the most powerfully and broadly effective assertions. While acknowledging that this is a subjective call, I can think of only one such target; the entire concept of infinity as being anything that can actually exist beyond the imagination of the human mind. The claim that infinity is anything other than a human invention.

Yes, that's right. I want to take on infinity before moving on to anything else. Why? Because if we can eliminate the entire notion of physical infinity, we can completely eliminate a majority of other impossible notions about what is real without doing any other work. As I see it, you hit the root when killing a tree. You go first for the core. The fact that so much depends on the factual existence of physical infinity makes it the most egregious myth . . . that is if it's true that infinity is nothing but a myth. But is there any way to determine the truth concerning infinity?

Depending on a person's Reality view, taking the time to debunk the concept of actual physical infinity is either a ridiculous waste of time, or a ridiculously difficult challenge to begin this overall effort with. And this is the point. Even in the most disciplined fields of science, it's obvious that there exists deep division concerning the validity of infinity as more than a mathematical placeholder. Out here in the world of laymen and the casual observer, infinity is much more available for use when thought moves to those topics that concern issues that are larger than what's on TV or how to make the most of what's just landed on the plate. Out here, infinity (as a quality that something that is physically existent and materially present can possess; e.g., infinite size, presence, distance, degree of any other property) is real for most folks.

However, the truth is that infinity isn't real, and regardless of whether you already know this or not, in this second decade of the 21st century, the fictional nature of infinity is not common knowledge among the billions of people who collectively define what it means to be human on Planet Earth.

Now, for those who believe that infinity simply cannot be debunked, the heavy lifting for this specific task has already been accomplished, and was started over 100 years ago by a physicist name Max Planck. Not only that, but what Max established — as a direct result of eliminating the erroneous notion of infinity — has been the basis of 20th century physics. Not that you'd ever suspect such a thing if you didn't take the time and effort to apply simple deductive inference to what Max Planck determined to be true about the nature of activity and its impact on the least of material existence. Well, we are going to take that time and effort, and when we do, we'll ultimately be able to apply what we've established to an entire spectrum of fundamental inaccuracies; eliminating them, again, with simple deductive inference. This alone will transform the entire Material Realm. At least, for us it will.

So, what did Max Planck discover that can be used to debunk the entire concept of infinity — infinite distance, infinite presence, infinite knowledge, infinite power, and infinite anything — as being nothing more than the human mind's refusal to accept its own temporary inability to know all that it feels entitled to know? What Max discovered was the Quantum.

Okay, so he didn't actually discover it. He suggested that it must exist, but that suggestion did lead to the mathematical — and then empirical — proof that it does, indeed, exist. In fact, the lowly Quantum has been the brightest star in physics ever since, becoming the basis for an entire field within the discipline itself; Quantum Physics. And as we all know, this new approach to what is and how it all works together at the tiniest, most primordial levels of material existence has revolutionized our world in ways that are too numerous and too disparate for me to go into here.

The truth is that Quantum Physics is still reaching into the darkest corners of the Material Realm and pulling out things that bother the more traditional among us, so it's not as if we can fully qualify the impact of Planck's Constant on our view of Reality even now. And yet, what does Max Planck's notion of the Quantum have to do with the validity of the concept of infinity? Let's take a look and see.

Kevin Brian Carroll

The Quantum — A Quick Overview

First, let's define the Quantum itself. Even if I look at Wikipedia.com, the definition seems to be pretty unambiguous, and it's hard to suggest that, as a definition, the opening statement is lacking in either scope or specificity.

> In physics, a quantum *(plural: quanta)* is the minimum amount of any physical entity involved in an interaction. Behind this, one finds the fundamental notion that a physical property may be "quantized," referred to as "the hypothesis of quantization". This means that the magnitude can take on only certain discrete values. There is a related term of quantum number. An example of an entity that is quantized is the energy transfer of elementary particles of matter *(called fermions)* and of photons and other bosons.
>
> **http://en.wikipedia.org/wiki/Quantum**

Any physicist, physics student, or lay person with an interest in physics will readily agree with this definition, but what are the implications of what's been declared here? Let's take a moment to examine what the quantization of physical Reality actually implies.

The definition above states *"This means that the magnitude can take on only certain discrete values"*. This is a key property of quantization, and is actually the primary quality that quantization brings to the existential table; physics-wise. The problem that the quantization of physical action solved (this problem was the primary impetus for the establishment of this entire concept), was the mathematical impossibility of a dependable, stable orbit of electrons around the nucleus of an atom if true linear magnitude of action was possible. It's complicated, and we're going to take a closer look at what Max was dealing with, but let's first look at what linear magnitude is. The following is a simple equation question that illustrates the issue of true linear magnitude using discrete units represented by numbers.

$$1 < X < 2$$

Seems pretty simple, until you're tasked with presenting the complete range of possible answers for X. Those who embrace the concept of true linear magnitude will claim that X can represent an infinite quantity of possible answers, and perhaps they are correct; concerning that specific equation as a purely esoteric conundrum that is not limited to whole numbers or to the numerical representation of real physical units. However, Quantum Physics has proven that an infinite number of possible unitary delineations between 1 and 2 is not true

AutoGenesism: A Theory of Everything

if 1 represents the end of one actual discrete event and 2 represents what imme-diately follows the end of the very next actual discrete event within an actual event trajectory (or chain of events, if you prefer). And this is due to what was realized when the mathematical structure of the orbit (specifically, the orbit of an electron around the nucleus of an atom) was examined.

In Figure 1-A, what must become of that electron's orbit structure under classic Newtonian Physics is illustrated.

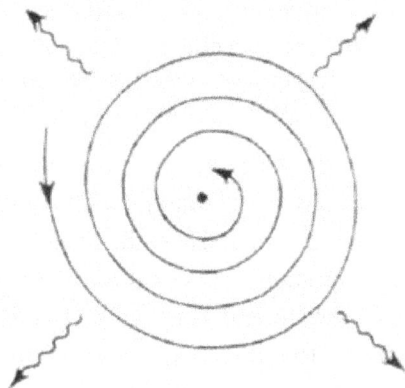

Figure 1-A

The squiggly arrows represent photons being emitted (which happens all the time within this relationship) as the electron drops into a closer relative orbit within the atomic structure. The spiraling arrow represents the electron orbit de-scending and ultimately crashing into the nucleus of the atom, since each photon emission causes the electron to lose energy, which causes it to change relative orbit, which causes it to emit yet another photon, which causes it to lose more energy, and on and on until it crashes.

The following is an excerpt from a very simplified overview I found on the following web page:

http://abyss.uoregon.edu/~js/21st_century_science/lectures/lec12.html

It's the same page that provided us that spiraling electron crash illustration (above), and it does a much better job of clearly explaining the electron orbit problem than I just did.

Kevin Brian Carroll

[1]The UV Catastrophe and the dilemma of spectral lines were already serious problems for attempts to understand how light and matter interact. Planck also noticed another fatal flaw in our physics by demonstrat-
ing that the electron in orbit around the nucleus accelerates. Acceleration means a changing electric field *(the electron has charge)*, which
means photons should be emitted. But, then the electron would lose energy and fall into the nucleus. Therefore, atoms shouldn't exist!

To resolve this problem, Planck made a wild assumption that energy, at the sub-atomic level, can only be transferred in small units,
called quanta. Due to his insight, we call this unit Planck's Constant (*h*).
The word quantum derives from quantity and refers to a small packet of
action or process, the smallest unit of either that can be associated with
a single event in the microscopic world.

So, it's clear that there are practical issues concerning the viability of infinite linearity (such as the existence of atoms), and that this has been well established within the field of physics. In essence, the equation $1 < X < 2$ (at least as
it relates to the movement of an electron as it orbits around the nucleus of an
atom, and the photons that are emitted as a result) would not feature an infinite
number of possibilities for X. But, does this mean that this *quantum* delineation
exists beyond the simple orbital revolutions of an electron? Let's see what else
we can learn about how this quantization of activity affected the other stuff that
Max Planck and his contemporaries were working on. Again, we'll refer to that
efficient physics overview that's featured above, if only for the clarity that it
provides what could otherwise become an exhausting exercise in withering digression.

All phenomena in submicroscopic systems *(the realm of quantum mechanics)* exhibit quantization: observable quantities are restricted to a
natural set of discrete values. When the values are multiples of a constant least amount, that amount is referred to as a quantum of the observable. Thus Planck's constant *h* is the quantum of action, and *h*/ (i.e.,
h/2) is the quantum of angular momentum, or spin.

Changes of energy, such as the transition of an electron from one
orbit to another around the nucleus of an atom, is done in discrete
quanta. Quanta are not divisible. The term quantum leap refers to the
abrupt movement from one discrete energy level to another, with no
smooth transition. There is no "in between".

The quantization, or "jumpiness" of action as depicted in quantum
physics differs sharply from classical physics which represented motion
as smooth, continuous change. Quantization limits the energy to be
transferred to photons and resolves the UV Catastrophe problem.

AutoGenesism: A Theory of Everything

So, that sums up the story of what Max Planck's idea did for the field of physics, but can anyone point to an unrelated breakthrough that occurred as a result of this unlikely idea that motion and energy [which is just motion too, when you get right down to it] are not infinitely linear within the material realm? There's the birth of the term *photon*. Let's read on from that same featured overview we've been examining.

> An unusual phenomenon was discovered in the early 1900's. If a beam of light is pointed at the negative end of a pair of charged plates, a current flow is measured. A current is simply a flow of electrons in a metal, such as a wire. Thus, the beam of light must be liberating electrons from one metal plate, which are attracted to the other plate by electrostatic forces. This results in a current flow.
>
> In classical physics, one would expect the current flow to be proportional to the strength of the beam of light *(more light = more electrons liberated = more current)*. However, the observed phenomenon was that the current flow was basically constant with light strength, yet varied strongly with the wavelength of light such that there was a sharp cutoff and no current flow for long wavelengths.
>
> Einstein successfully explained the photoelectric effect within the context of the new physics of the time, quantum physics. In his scientific paper, he showed that light was made of packets of energy quantum called photons. Each photon carries a specific energy related to its wavelength, such that photons of short wavelength *(blue light)* carry more energy than long wavelength *(red light)* photons. To release an electron from a metal plate required a minimal energy which could only be transferred by a photon of energy equal or greater than that minimal threshold energy *(i.e. the wavelength of the light had to be a sufficiently short)*. Each photon of blue light released an electron. But all red photons were too weak. The result is no matter how much red light was shown on the metal plate, there was no current.
>
> The photoelectric earned Einstein the Nobel Prize, and introduced the term "photon" of light into our terminology.

So, this does suggest that Max's theory was immediately applicable to explaining real and observable physical activity. In fact, the 20th century became the century it became, primarily because of the realization, by physicists, that the Material Realm is not infinitely linear when one seeks to determine the possible answers to the identity of **X** in the equation $1 < X < 2$. Yes, we're still sitting on that original question.

Kevin Brian Carroll

It seems (if one starts stacking up physics formulas as evidence) that h [Max Planck's h] has roundly debunked the infinite nature of linearity between **1** and **2** if that linearity refers to what physically exists within the Material Realm and not to what solely exists within the theoretical confines of the human mind. But, what are the larger implications of having eliminated infinite linearity between two established points (be they quantities of energy, movement, distance, or time) as a valid Reality staple? Well, that would depend on your definition of *infinity*.

The dictionary on my desk defines *infinite* as:

Infinite

- Having no limits or boundaries in time, space, extent, or magnitude
- Extremely or immeasurably great or numerous: infinite wealth
- All-embracing, absolute, or total: God's infinite wisdom

I'm going to suggest that we focus on definition **#1** for our purposes, since it's the one that most relates to physical/material structure, where this definition of *infinite* either does or does not exist to affect us directly. Now, we have just learned that it has been proven that infinite linearity does not exist between quanta. In fact, there's no argument that successfully defends the notion that if these designations represent actual physical units of anything whatsoever, that the **X** that sits between the **1** and the **2** (in our equation above) can factually represent an infinite quantity of possibilities. This means that infinity does not exist when dealing with what can physically exist between two discrete physical units; be they movement, energy, distance, magnitude, or time. In fact, because this has been so soundly proven, we can declare that this full one half of infinity within the Material Realm (the half that Zeno's *"Infinite Divisibility of Space"* paradox seeks to address) has been literally debunked. But, what does this actually mean for the existence of infinity (in any form whatsoever) within the Material Realm? Let's look again at the definition **#1** of infinite.

1. Having no limits or boundaries in time, space, extent, or magnitude

Again, we have to impose the requirement of system coherence as we examine the actual, physical ramifications of allowing the existence of infinity as described above. If there are no intrinsic limits whatsoever within the Material Realm, then how can the quantum of anything exist? No limits means exactly that; no limits. No limits on expansion nor contraction. On neither big nor small. Infinity isn't just about enormous expanses that go on forever. Infinity is also about minute divisions that never end. An infinite gradient is infinite in both directions or it doesn't exist at all.

So, what does all of this mean when we bring it back to the original question of infinity? I'm going to suggest that it means that infinity (as an actual property or capacity that can be attributed to anything that either exists as physical or that exists as fully capable of interacting with that which exists as physical) doesn't actually exist itself, beyond the musings of the philosophical or mathematical mind. And the implications of this are enormous when you take this clearly defensible determination and examine the ramifications it imposes on pretty much everything that the average 21st century human being believes to be true; from an infinite God to that primordial microdot of infinite energy that big banged our universe into material existence.

Let's take a look at one persistent axiom that cannot survive this determination; the reigning adage among those who strive to prove the principle assertion of their theologies through science — *"energy cannot be created or destroyed"*.

Yes, this phrase does exist within the whole of the Law of Conservation of Energy, but if you step back a little and let the entire description stand, this statement suggests a very different axiom than the one that equates energy with a godlike presence:

The Law of Conservation of Energy

In physics, the law of conservation of energy states that the total energy of an *isolated system* cannot change—it is said to be conserved over time. Energy can be neither created nor destroyed, but can change form; for instance, chemical energy can be converted to kinetic energy.

http://en.wikipedia.org/wiki/Conservation_of_energy

I call your attention to where that difficult phrase is couched in terms of how energy exists within an isolated system. Yes, the application of this specific axiom was originally based on the [perhaps accurate] definition of our universe as an isolated system, but if you go ahead and scour the legitimate sources that exist concerning energy conservation, you'll discover that an infinite energy source — one that simply is; having no beginning and no end — is not what this law suggests at all. It describes a closed system that has already had a sourced energy presence included as integral to what it is as an isolated whole. The initial genesis of that energy presence is not addressed within the parameters of the law itself.

And let's not forget the issue of infinity's own failure to survive deductive scrutiny. Certainly energy can't be infinitely existent — as relentlessly asserted by those who've been careless with their reading of the Law of Conservation of Energy. Beginning-less infinite physical existence is not possible. We've just proven infinity itself to be a logical nonstarter regardless of what end of a physics formula you wish to begin from. Max Planck's *h* simply denies that any such property can be integral to what is, what was, or what can ever be part of our physical realm.

And that's just the beginning of what Max Planck and his quantum established to be true about our Reality. In fact, let's take a look at the quantum again, and see what else we can infer from it.

Bits, Pieces, and the Material World

What's really important to understand about the quantum is that it is a concretely defined unit, and that no one has limited it in terms of what it represents as a physical manifestation. In other words, it can represent a transfer of energy, a movement from one physical point in space to another physical point in space, a change from one relative state to another relative state, and the list goes on to include every possible way that physical existence can be determined to manifest. It describes the smallest, and therefore indivisible, unit of physical existence, and it's this very specific fact concerning the physical nature of Reality (that it is quantized and not infinitely divisible) that is going to be of particular significance as this examination continues.

As I stated, we're going to employ strict deductive inference in tandem with what we can know to be true about physical Reality. With this strategy we're going to drill down to the very sub-structure of physical existence to see if we can better define what can and cannot be real. Of course, the first issue to examine is the larger nature of physical existence itself; specifically, what actually constitutes physical existence, if there are more than one primary physical form, and if there are, then where are we to draw the lines between these various forms that exist.

It's only been recently, within the last century or so, that this very important examination has been possible, and it was the discovery of action quantization that broke the seal on what had always been considered unknowable. Knowing that the smallest unit of all physical (and not just material) existence can potentially be uniformly determined provides us a Reality anchor with astounding implications if we're careful with how we build our deductive structure.

AutoGenesism: A Theory of Everything

Of course, it will require that we let go of some traditional ways of thinking, but only within the confines of what can reasonably and responsibly be asserted; given the very strict inferences and direct implications that emerge along our journey. In fact, I suggest that we refrain from overt speculation within this very critical part of our overall effort. Later, perhaps, we can enjoy a few wild notions, as long as each serves a larger point or helps illustrate a difficult description, and is properly tagged as a ***Speculation Alert*** to ensure that no one is led astray as a result of a little fun.

So, what is the revelatory breakthrough that the quantization of physical existence suggests? For that, we need to take a tiny bit of material existence apart, and see if we can figure out — by way of deductive inference and the conceptual quantum itself — just how small physical Reality can be as we do.

It's a Small World After All

For years they have been smashing billions and billions of particles together in those supercolliders scattered about the planet, and they've been doing so in hopes of finding clues concerning how the universe might have behaved when it was just starting out. They've been smashing particles together for other reasons as well. Like finding out just how small things get until they don't get any smaller. In both pursuits, however, what they're looking for is the material quantum; the indivisible unit of matter. And as of the writing of this presentation, the search continues, as tinier and tinier particles produce even smaller bits, with even the very least of these bits creating pieces that suggest there is no end to how small material Reality can be.

Since 2001, the European Organization for Nuclear Research [CERN] has performed a trillion such collisions, and still the pieces show up by the thousands. So, after all this mayhem, what has been found to be the smallest particle? Well, it's more like a class of particles. They're called quarks, and they're not uniform in size or behavior, as they'd be if they were the indivisible quantum units of material existence. In fact, no one really knows what they are, or if they're divisible. The following description seems fairly conservative, so let's assume it to be widely supported:

> Quarks are believed to be one of the basic building blocks of matter. Quarks were first discovered in experiments done at the Stanford Linear Accelerator Center in the late 1960's and early 1970's.

61

Three families of quarks are known to exist. Each family contains two quarks. The first family consists of Up and Down quarks, the quarks that join together to form protons and neutrons. The second family consists of Strange and Charm quarks and only exist at high energies. The third family consists of Top and Bottom quarks and only exist at very high energies. The Top quark was finally discovered in 1995 at the Fermi National Accelerator Laboratory.

http://education.jlab.org/glossary/quark.html

So, the quark [one of two classes of Fermions] is the smallest *"building block"* particle, meaning that most everything that is materially structured is composed of combinations of quarks. Not that protons and neutrons are much larger. In fact, each is comprised of only three quarks, with the Up-Down quark charge configuration being the difference between one and the other. That said, electrons [a Lepton, the other class of Fermion] aren't made up of quarks, so that eliminates the quark as the quantum unitary basis of material Reality. After all, electrons are material, meaning that they are detectable, measurable, and that they physically interact with the rest of the Material Realm.

So, if *quantum* is the term used to refer to the indivisible unitary basis of any and all forms of physical existence, then what is its material equivalent? It's right here where we may want to start employing some deductive inference, since it's obvious that the hands-on empirical aspects of the Scientific Method [observation, experiment, measurement] are not going to help us break through the quark and go smaller. But, can we actually break into the quark and determine what, if anything, comes together to make the quark? No, we can't. Not actually. At least not with the technology we possess. That said, there's nothing preventing us from determining whether such a breach is possible.

Now, we know from the very simplified description of the quark (above) that there are three *families* of quarks. We also know that (at the very least) the electron is a lepton, and not composed of an assembly of quarks. And with just this much information, we can actually determine quite a bit about the place that the quark does NOT occupy within the progression from the smallest to the largest within the Material Realm.

Now, there no such thing as a *family* of quanta, with each *family* member possessing distinct and disparate properties. There's only one quantum of action, one quantum of energy transfer, and one quantum of event progression. In fact, the quantum of anything itself is identical to all other quanta of the same thing regardless of what it is that's been quantized. This suggests that at the very sub-

Autogenesism: A Theory of Everything

structure of Reality, it gets extremely simple and extremely uniform. But can we assume that all of material existence (albeit, a manifestation of larger Reality in its own right) adheres to that same simple, uniform basic structure? Let's look at the one common bit of material existence that we've already determined is not based on the quark — the electron — and see if we can detect even a hint of uniformity.

Now, the electron isn't a building block particle, but then, what is a particle? It can get pretty vague if you take the time to really look into particles, especially if you're trying to connect what is officially known to what we've all assumed to be the physical nature of particles. In fact, the term *point particle* (and this is no theoretical outlier by any means) actually refers to a quasi-conceptual idealization of particles that lacks any spatial properties whatsoever. It's nothing more than . . .

> "an appropriate representation of any object whose size, shape, and structure is irrelevant in a given context. For example, from far enough away, an object of any shape will look and behave as a point-like object."
>
> http://en.wikipedia.org/wiki/Point_particle

And the particle doesn't really get much more concrete as you get closer to what has been declared to be resoundingly material either. The functional success of the Standard Model acknowledged, theoretical speculation seems to be the basis of a larger share of what's considered settled science than one would've assumed before diving deep into the White Papers that actually define what's been achieved over decades of particle physics research. That said, what we're examining is whether there is quantum uniformity at the primary unit level of material existence, and since we're not really sure of the quark building block particle as a primary unit, we're fully justified in bringing the electron in, since it is widely considered to also be a primary unit of material existence.

So, are all electrons similar in size? As laypeople with no formal training, we'll be depending on the hyper-competitive fact-police who relentlessly work to maintain Wikipedia.com's ongoing relevance for ensuring the factual nature of each of the following statements about the physical properties of the electron:

> The invariant mass of an electron is approximately 9.109×10−31 kilograms, or 5.489×10−4 atomic mass units. On the basis of Einstein's principle of mass–energy equivalence, this mass corresponds to a rest energy of 0.511 MeV. The ratio between the mass of a proton and that of an electron is about 1836. Astronomical measurements show that the

proton-to-electron mass ratio has held the same value for at least half the age of the universe, as is predicted by the Standard Model.

http://en.wikipedia.org/wiki/Electron#Fundamental_properties

The last sentence in that statement seems to suggest that all electrons are identical in mass, and that this uniformity is very stable. Okay, but what about charge? Are all electrons identical in charge?

Electrons have an electric charge of −1.602×10−19 coulomb, which is used as a standard unit of charge for subatomic particles. Within the limits of experimental accuracy, the electron charge is identical to the charge of a proton, but with the opposite sign. As the symbol e is used for the elementary charge, the electron is commonly symbolized by e−, where the minus sign indicates the negative charge. The positron is symbolized by e+ because it has the same properties as the electron but with a positive rather than negative charge.

Looks like existing electrons all have the exact same charge as well. So, what about the way that these elementary particles behave? Can you identify one electron from another by observing them at play?

The electron has an intrinsic angular momentum or spin of 1/2. This property is usually stated by referring to the electron as a spin-1/2 particle. For such particles the spin magnitude is $\sqrt{3}/2$ ħ. while the result of the measurement of a projection of the spin on any axis can only be ±ħ/2. In addition to spin, the electron has an intrinsic magnetic moment along its spin axis. It is approximately equal to one Bohr magneton, which is a physical constant equal to 9.27400915(23)×10−24 joules per tesla. The orientation of the spin with respect to the momentum of the electron defines the property of elementary particles known as helicity.

Okay, so it looks as if there's no actual way to identify one electron from another, and this suggests uniformity among electrons. Just as you'd expect if you were to embrace the idea that (like the quantum of action, exchange, and emission) the whole of Reality is uniformly uniform at the indivisible level of physical existence.

Now, to be fair, we are only applying deductive inference here, and it may be decades before traditional physics proves that the quark (with its multiple ways of being and behaving) is not the unitary building block of material existence, but we have arrived at a point where it can be responsibly suggested that the quark is yet another stage of organized development, with components yet to be discovered; as was the atom until late in the 19th century. After all, the uniformity of the electron (similar to the uniformity of the quantum) does suggest that this overwhelmingly particular distinction is common to all elementary material units, despite the otherwise unique characteristics that delineate them.

So, where is all of this taking us? Actually, it's taking us back to the quantum and to the electron, whose atomic orbit revealed the requirement that physical activity consist of identical, indivisible units of action.

You Are What You Do

An atom is literally defined by what is happening within the confines of its composite structure. The identification is based, in large part, on the atom's atomic radius. Now, the atomic radius actually describes the orbital reaches of however many electrons it possesses as they loop in stable repetitive trajectories. Each orbit consists of action quanta, which, as we've learned, are identical, indivisible units of action that — in this case — are obviously aligned in a highly organized manner. And, as we've learned, this quantized, and highly organized activity allows each electron's orbit to remain stable and repeatable enough to be integral to the physical structure and ultimate identity of the atom itself. And while that observation may come across as fairly obvious, the direct implications, if we (again) apply a little deductive inference, are pretty impressive.

What seems clear is that this activity itself (specifically the orbit tracks that exist as each electron has settled into a very specific and very defined relationship with the nucleus of the atom) is not only a full component of the atom's atomic structure, it is also integral to its identity relative to other atoms with similar or dissimilar orbit structures. In fact, it is the electron activity itself that identifies an atom under observation.

Clearly, activity (all by itself) is central to what it means to exist as a material whole within physical Reality. But is it possible that activity, in the form of the quantum of action, could actually be the primordial unitary basis of the material realm; the material quantum being sought by particle physicists? That's an enormous question, and one that's not all that easy to fully define, let alone answer. If ever there was a moment to focus on the nature of a notion via digression, this is that moment.

Note — I'm isolating this specific point because it is central to the theory that this book is based on. It's not this theory's sole departure from traditional philosophical and scientific thought, but it is central to most

of the departures that AutoGenesism suggests to be appropriately conceived and accurately determined. As this presentation continues, it'll
become increasingly obvious where Auto-G breaks from established and
traditional descriptions, but it's here where it all begins, so I feel that it's
important to make this first break obvious.

Digression Alert — The question is not whether matter is truly solid.
No one actually believes that matter is solid. Sure, it feels solid, and to the
unaided observer, it looks solid, but ever since the discovery of the atom
and its proton-neutron-electron atomic structure, the concept of material
solidity has been . . . well . . . conceptual in nature. What's being questioned
here is something much more central to the nature of physical existence;
specifically the true physical nature of particles and the structure of matter
in general.

The truth is that I'd be really surprised if anyone in the theoretical
physics game seriously believes that the quantum of material structure is
an undiscovered fermion, boson, or some other sort of infinitesimal particle
that has avoided detection (and therefore classification), as the Standard
Model suggests in its default manner by avoiding the notion entirely. After
all, unless one believes that undefinable stuff (stuff with no actual component nature or means of existential emergence) just started collecting into
particles as the *"molasses"* of the Higgs Field gummed it all together, then
at some point the whole question of what it is that's been collecting into
matter from the moment that matter sprang into existence must become an
actual question; one that is approached as possessing a legitimate answer.

So, I want to quickly abstract an overview of what I'll be detailing
later in this presentation concerning this very critical question, and what
I'll be working to define as a reasonably inescapable answer to this question. It's not easy to conceptualize, but it's much harder to successfully
explain, so I hope that you'll bear with me as I make this as clear and concise as I can. Please keep in mind, however, that this entire presentation (all
175,000+ words of it) works relentlessly to explain in depth how it all
works with several other primary aspects (that are equally revolutionary)
to fully and successfully describe the true nature of physical Reality.

I'm going to start with the statement that matter is nothing more than
inescapably obvious densities of precisely defined, deeply entangled (structured) activity that we — this planet's only scientific observers — long ago

collectively defined as material solidity (a concept that we invented to represent the difference between these centers of dense, structurally entangled activity and those spatial regions that exist in close proximity that are devoid of such activity). As this planet's only scientists, we noticed these stable, intricately intertwined, event confluences, and we were the ones who defined them as solid matter. We defined them long before we were capable of imagining their true physical nature; defining them in direct comparison to how we perceived ourselves as fellow solid delineations of material structure.

This is a very important point, and an extremely valid notion, since it certainly wouldn't be (it certainly has never been) abnormal for the human brain/mind perception-translation system to interpret an observation in a way that is directly affected by how it believes itself to physically exist. After all, perception is subjective, and the brain/mind system is not capable of more than perception and its own intellectual translation of that perception.

Yes, this notion (that material existence is actually layers upon layers of contextually entangled activity trajectories) is a revolutionary idea, but once you've carefully laid out exactly how such a dense matrix of highly structured activity would naturally be perceived by the human brain as solid matter (since it too exists as a dense matrix of highly structured activity) it becomes startlingly plausible. Especially when you consider the fact that [and this is really, really important to note] identical action quanta must share a common rate of change (one quantum giving way to the next quantum). That fairly obvious notion [the quantization of activity and all the other basics that emerge as a result of activity, as determined and proven by those giants of physics from the turn of the last century] actually requires that all change be literally locked into a rigid synchronicity at the sub-structural level. So, what does this have to do with whether matter is comprised of things or not?

This quantization of physical Reality is a really big deal. It doesn't just affect activity at the quantum level. Since everything that exists is literally structured from the quantum level, this rigid synchronization locks everything into this permanent lockstep of change that nothing can break free of. So, what do we call each of these shared quantum units of existence that stretch from one quantized change event to the next? We call these spans *Now*.

There's no possible means of truly experiencing the shared exchange of one span of *Now* for the next span of *Now*, and this is the point that I wanted to make here concerning the factual nature of material structure. This quantization of *Now* (this rate of quantum unit change that we share with all that exists as physical within our entire Reality) actually requires that all sub-structural change be perceived as relative stasis by the observing brain/mind system since its own material structure is similarly locked in. The net impact on us and our capacity to accurately assess the true nature of the Material Realm, and of Reality in general, through traditional scientific means should be obvious, and we'll get into a lot more about all of this as we progress through this presentation.

This isn't all that we're going to examine in this Section I, but as I stated, this assertion is the first major departure I'll be presenting. There's a lot more to come, and while it's going to take quite a bit of work (including the reintroduction of an entire suite of primordial staples and imperative expressions that have been relegated to the Philosophy Department for far too long) when we're done, I'm confident that you'll have a solid foundation concerning what's real and possible, and even more important, what can't possibly be true about physical existence. Enough to build upon as we move into Section II, and start really putting this existential structure together.

Some Philosophy Concerning Existence

If you really want to get a firm grip on what's real, then you've got to be open to challenging the traditional basics. Not with haphazardly cobbled fits of nonsense (as has become a popular option in recent years) but with hard, reliable determinations that can be proven to be true when set side by side with what's already been proven to be true and reliably so. And it's not as if this sort of work kills off the thrill of breaking new ground. In fact, once the factual basis of Reality is completely exposed and firmly established, its true majesty really starts blossoming, and it doesn't stop until there's a lot more to heaven and earth than you could've possibly dreamt of in your philosophy.

It is exciting stuff, but you've got to start at the very beginning — allowing what's real to be counter-intuitively simple; primitive. And as your examination slowly builds its theoretical structure, keeping the process pointed properly forward takes serious discipline. It also takes more Reality clarification than you might assume, but the good news is that most of what you need to know is already common knowledge; sort of. What I mean by this is that the simplest, most common sense staples [those intangibles that you've probably referenced all your life — like true and false and logic and the difference between this and that] actually represent real and powerful determining factors that shape the physical nature of everything that exists.

Now, while it's true that terms like *truth* and *logic* are man-made and have been traditionally defined as philosophical in essence, the forces and structures they represent are as real as anything that can be reproduced in a laboratory setting. That said, they are much more primitive in nature than anything that can be materially reproduced, and as such, they are resistant to the examination protocols that have been largely based upon what they provide to the fundamental real as a whole. As a result (at least in my own efforts to teach this premise) I've noticed that people have a lot of difficulty accepting these profoundly pervasive staples as having any actual physically influential presence. This has generally been most difficult for those folks with the highest level of formal education. I suspect that this is due to cultural bias and the conservative nature of higher education.

Traditional wisdom will never allow the common, mundane aspects of physical existence to be integral to the esoteric nature of what it has always declared to be transcendent. And secular scientific knowledge doggedly refuses to lift its eyes from whichever trough it has set before itself for rigid and detailed examination. It's as if these two cultural authorities have staked out very specific and widely separated territories, and neither is willing to violate the terms of whatever truce it was that forged the uneasy peace that's held since the Renaissance lifted the Western world out of the Dark Ages.

And this willful isolation persists even as so many brilliant discoveries continue to aggressively avoid any push toward true revelation as if such a destination is a no-man's land, littered with the horrific evidence of humanity's violent hatred of itself. Then again, when one considers the long, terrible history of this difficult relationship, it's not hard to understand why this might be the case.

Well, it's now the third millennium since the religionists seized the larger questions concerning Reality for their own, so we're going to step right out there and violate all of those established protocols. I see no reason to respect the treaties of those who've failed so spectacularly to find their way toward any semblance of truth. Especially considering the fact that we've finally reached the point where keeping the eternal and the incidental artificially separated has become a toxic requirement. Yes, this Section I is about taking on the controversies that arise when challenging the sort of ideas that have always drastically affected the way people see themselves, and giving these big ideas the kind of dispassionate scrutiny that they've been spared for far too long.

To begin with, let's see if we can establish a working definition of the term *existence*. And when I say *existence*, what I mean is *physical existence*. I'm going to see what my favorite quick reference source says about the term.

> The word **existence** comes from the Latin word *existere* meaning "to appear", "to arise", "to become", or "to be", but literally, it means *"to stand out"* (**ex** — being the Latin prefix for "out" added to the Latin verb **stare**, meaning "to stand").
>
> http://en.wikipedia.org/wiki/Existence#Etymology

So, if something physically exists, then it physically *"stands out"* from whatever it is that isn't it. But, what does this actually mean? Apparently, it's not all that clear when applied to the actual effort to define what is real. In fact, there are many conflicting views, even though the requirement itself — to stand out — seems fairly straightforward.

At one end of the philosophical divide concerning the nature of physical existence are claims that nothing exists unless it's being actively observed; that the conscious mind itself creates existence. In its most extreme manifestation, this belief in the primacy of self is called Metaphysical Solipsism.

> **Metaphysical Solipsism** is the "strongest" variety of solipsism. Based on a philosophy of subjective idealism, Metaphysical Solipsists maintain that the self is the only existing Reality and that all other Reality, including the external world and other persons, are representations of that self, and have no independent existence
>
> http://en.wikipedia.org/wiki/Solipsism

Solipsism does seem to suggest that a robust sense of self is possessed by its adherents, but does this notion square with the requirement that the physically existent *something* physically stand out relative to whatever it is that isn't it? Can the act of observing something cause it to actually stand apart from all that is not it if there is nothing else that is intrinsically unique about it? No, of course not. To be observed as being unique and separated requires (at the very least) that the separation already be in place and available for observation. After all,

AutoGenesism: A Theory of Everything

while it may be argued that observation affects the relationship between what is being observed and the broader contextual setting that hosts it, it can only affect that relationship if that relationship is already in existence.

It's pretty rare to run into a true Solipsist. Most who embrace this mind-projecting-Reality notion [primarily those who embrace a westernized version of Buddhism] simply declare that unless something is observed, it cannot be said to exist. This watered-down version of Solipsism is actually more troublesome than the version noted and referenced above, since the observer concedes to the existence of the observed something, while insisting that it must not exist while not being observed.

The sheer effort involved in compelling everything (from that which sits directly before such an observer, to whatever it is being potentially observed in the farthest reaches of the remote corners of the universe itself by who knows what sort of observing mind it is that exists to observe it) to relentlessly come into and go out of physical existence in direct and immediate response to the notice (or lack of notice) of any one of countless observing observers, seems to be exactly the sort of absurd entanglement that Occam's Razor was devised to slap down as an example of completely irresponsible intellectualism. Hell, at least the hardcore Solipsist is cutting Reality a break by demanding that it only respond to his (or her) instants of observation.

The direct opposite view of what can and cannot exist is held by the Materialist, where physical existence is limited to material and energy (which they correctly view as a type of material). A more progressive version of Materialism is Physicalism, which allows for material relationships and specific forces that result from these relationships to possess existence that can be defined and determined, although this progressed version runs into issues involving mind-states and the existence of Quale [basically the experience of interpreting subjective perception by the human mind].

As you can see, *existence* itself is a brutal quagmire for the best and brightest minds that the world has to offer, but only if you strive to qualify and quantify the whole of *existence*. We won't be attempting any such thing in this section. All we want to establish in Section I is what sets the existential table, providing the basis for whatever it is that then proceeds to spring into existence.

If anything, I suppose that this could be considered a Realist approach, but even then, there are bits of Physicalism here and there, in the form of acknowledging the role of Emergence within the progressive development ramification structure, so I'm not comfortable suggesting that we'll be leaning on any one established philosophy of Physical Existence. The truth of what is, and of what lays the foundation for what is, actually sits somewhere just off to the side of what's been declared to be true, regardless of what it is that's being pointed to as the established truth. It's not completely counter to what has been embraced by the best and the brightest. It's just located off to the side of it.

What is true, however, is that Reality is not something that we each have the authority to agree on, or agree to disagree about. Not if we're serious about determining what is actually and universally true. Real is a definitive quantity, and this must be stated right up front. If your mind is completely incapable of allowing for a definitive existential real, then we will have to agree that this be the buzz saw that prevents you from proceeding any further with this examination. That might seem like a cop-out, but it's not. Let me explain.

The refusal to accept the existence of a real and objective primordial substructure cannot be fully addressed within a quick overview of existential fundamentals, and I won't insult your intelligence by claiming that such a refusal can be overcome by even the most brilliantly presented deductive inference and ramification structure. Logic and ramification depend on the existence of an objective primordial substructure, and a refusal to allow for the existence of such a definitive basis renders even the most persuasive presentation, if based on deduction, inference or implication, completely inconsequential. I guess it's akin to using bible scripture to argue the authority of biblical scripture. The effort fails due to the inherent nature of what it is.

Concepts like Truth and Logic and Reality are difficult to master, and for most laypeople, a lot of the trouble stems from the many definitions that are in use for each of these terms. When discussing these existential staples, it often occurs that semantics overwhelms the exchange, and nothing more is achieved concerning whether anything is true, logical or real, than fighting over the definitions of these terms. The net result is a general agreement that language itself is central to this shifting, seething controversy over stuff that may never even be popularly established as existing beyond human imagination. In other words, battling over whether Truth, Logic and Reality exist is a complete waste of time. Well, it's a waste of my time.

In this presentation, I will introduce some primordial existential staples, and when I do, I will explain my reason for depending on each as a basis of my own determination of what constitutes Reality, and how and why that Reality emerged. That said, I won't do battle with those who've made it their careers to dismiss what obviously sits beneath all that stretches out before us and comes together to allow each of us to make up our own mind concerning what is, what might be, and what can't possibly be more than our own human arrogance imposing itself upon an indifferent real. I honestly see no value in that effort.

To Be . . . Period

And finally, as I did in the last subsection, I want to introduce yet another fundamental theoretical departure, this one pertaining to the specific issue of physical existence at all levels. It's much simpler and easily explained than the last one, so I see no need to digress it (although I did provide it with its own subtitle).

As we make our way through this Section I and through every bit of the rest of this book, what we are examining (and taking into account as we examine what we examine) is the initial, emerging, and net impact of raw survival on literally everything that exists, and everything that occurs between all that exists. The structured emergence of Reality is nothing more or less than that. Be it a simple oscillation, or the search for significance in a raised eyebrow, what drives everything that exists to do whatever it does, or to be whatever it is, is nothing more or less than the extension of its own existence and for as long as possible.

As you'll soon discover, this sole existential imperative is expressed in many ways, and due to the nature of direct, indirect, and emerging ramification, it can be very difficult to immediately recognize the connection between a given response and the survival requirement it ultimately addresses. And this is why I'm alerting you to the fundamental fact of survival as central to what constitutes Reality before we get into the nuts and bolt of how it all works.

It's all about survival, and that's the whole of what it's all about. There's no spiritual battle between good and evil. No primordial struggle between right and wrong. There isn't and has never been such thing as justice beyond the invention of the human mind as it struggles to recognize (or impose) a pattern that it can find comfort within. There is only the fact that when something becomes physically existent, it does what it does to remain existent until that existence is lost forever. Survival is the one existential imperative that drives everything that exists, everything that has ever existed, and everything that will ever achieve existence.

What you'll learn is that this lone imperative ultimately shapes the Reality that we all share as a result of what happens when some things succeed and other things fail. In fact, it's safe to say that it is this endless fundamental scramble for survival — by all that exists at all levels of progressive development — that ultimately affects who you are and what you are as a human being. As promised in the last subsection, this will all be relentlessly fleshed out as this presentation moves forward.

Now, Before We Get Ahead of Ourselves . . .

> "Einstein's discontent comes down to a simple insight. A scientific theory, to be successful, must explain to us the observations we make of nature. Yet, the most elemental observation we make is that nature is organized by time. If science must tell a story that encompasses and explains everything we observe in nature, shouldn't that include our experience of the world as a flow of moments? Isn't the most basic fact about how experience is structured a part of nature that a fundamental theory of physics should incorporate?"
>
> "Everything we experience, every thought, impression, action, intention, is part of a moment. The world is presented to us as a series of moments. We have no choice about this. No choice about which moment we inhabit now, no choice about whether to go forward or back in time. No choice to jump ahead. No choice about the rate of flow of the moments. In this way, time is completely unlike space. One might object by saying that all events also take place in a particular location. But we have a choice about where we move in space. This is not a small distinction; it shapes the whole of our experience."
>
> **Lee Smolin — Time Reborn: From the Crisis in Physics to the Future of the Universe**

We are getting ready to wander around within some very complicated areas of thought, and I want to make sure that you're prepared for some of what lies ahead. In fact, this might be the most critical sub-topic that we spend any time on, so I want you to really devote your attention to what I'm going to discuss here. You see, the truth is that if I fail to present this part of the entire premise effectively, or if you fail to take the time to successfully internalize it, then the rest of this book may as well not exist at all. That said, I'll do my best to hold up my end of the exchange.

If you've spent any time watching the dramatic Youtube videos or reading those breathless paperbacks that have been put out in recent years by New Age and Popular Science experts concerning humanity's miraculous past, present and future, then the subject of dimensions is old hat for you. The 5th Dimension of Human Ascension, the 10 (or 11 or even 26) Dimensions of String Theory,

Autogenesism: A Theory of Everything

infinite dimensions that contain infinite universes that continue to collect with every choice that you (and the rest of us) do and don't make; it seems as if dimensions are the answer to every mystery, every unknown that we know of, and plenty of unknowns that we can't even imagine to exist. Well, for the purposes of this examination, I want you to focus on the four dimensions that we all deal with every day.

Four dimensions? Yes, there are four, and they break out as follows:

- Length
- Width
- Depth
- Time

Now, the first three are easy enough to understand, and while the fourth (Time) seems fairly straightforward, when mentally placing a three dimensional item (like you, perhaps) within the movement of Time, the dimension of Time becomes much less intuitively manageable for most people.

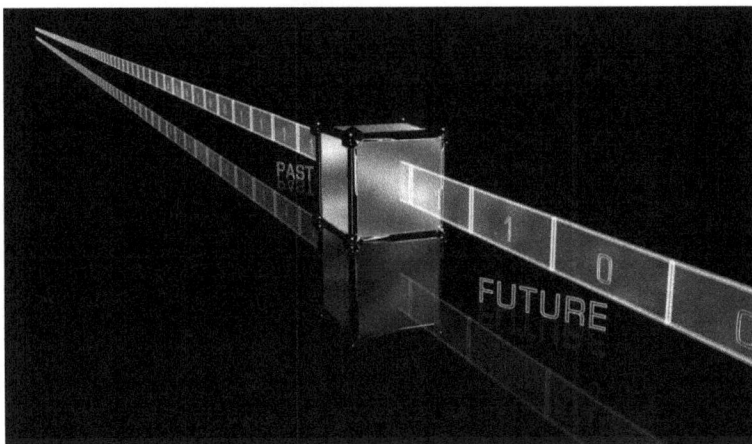

Figure 1-B
A good illustration depicting the progression of time as quantum units replacing one another — http://cdn.physorg.com

This is due to the fact that we are all used to seeing spatial movement, and while these changes in spatial position are also movements through Time, we're simply not capable of immediately perceiving the movement through Time in the same way that we can immediately perceive spatial movement. And this is because (as I introduced a couple subsection ago) we — as observers — are also

75

sharing the exact same movement within Time as the item that we are observing, and change is perceived as the difference between what was and what is. If no change is being perceived then we perceive no movement at all.

In the next few subsections, we'll be examining how it is that everything that sits around you can be in relentless, hyper-active reconfiguration, while you sit there and see nothing but the stable, solid consistency of *Now*. And yeah, it's going to take some effort to line up what's real with what seems real to you as you look around the room. I'm going to be using a term — *trajectory* — to describe how these things move through Time, even if some of it never budges an inch from where it's been anchored since the instant it came into existence. I'll refer to these trajectories as **Change/Event Trajectories**, and I'll need you to remember that I'm not referring to spatial trajectories (such as a ball literally rolling across the floor) even though if an item is engaged in a spatial trajectory it's also (and always) existing somewhere along the line within its own Change/Event Trajectory. This is because everything that exists as material, in any way, is placed at some point along the arc of a Change/Event Trajectory while it exists, and for as long as it exists. For that item [for any material item] the end of that trajectory's arc is the end of its existence.

When we start getting into contextually entangled Change/Event Trajectories, it's going to get even more complicated, but this topic [how Change/Event Trajectories become intrinsically associated, or entangled] is really important to get settled in your mind if you want to fully comprehend how it is that Reality exists as it does while appearing to exist as it's been erroneously described by everyone from bible-beating tent revivalists to Nobel Prize winning quantum physicists. And when we start digging into the survival imperative, and how it forces Change/Event Trajectories to become literally entangled in deference to its existential edict, if you haven't already internalized the difference between a spatial trajectory and a Change/Event Trajectory, then there's no way that you'll ever be able to keep up with the rest of the class. Your Change/Event Trajectories will all be orbits and shots careening from here to there, and none of what I have to teach you will ever make sense to you.

I guess we'll see just how well this notion survives as we proceed, but I do promise that I'll be working constantly to reinforce this critical fact of how physical Reality works. All I'd ask of you is to assume that when I use the word *trajectory* without *spatial* or *change/spatial* preceding it, that you visualize something [your parents, perhaps or whatever you wish] aging gracefully and with dignity. This is the kind of trajectory that we'll be dealing with. The linear trajectory of each *Now* being replaced by the next *Now*, as they all appear before us, only to tumble out behind as the history concerning who we've become.

And with that settled, let's continue.

Everything You Know Is Wrong

I wasn't sure how blunt I wanted to be in this segment, and to be honest, I pulled back a lot in the end. I could have been a lot less diplomatic, and I was for a while. In the end, I decided to relax and simply state my case. I will only go so far as to state here, and for the record, that everything that you probably assume to be true (everything that they taught you about you and the world around you) is wrong.

"How wrong?" you may ask. To which I would have to honestly reply, *"Absolutely wrong, but only wrong about the fundamental core of what they taught you."* Everything else, the tinsel and the ornaments that adorn that core, and present it as the festive celebration of life that it is, they seem to be fairly good at detailing.

> ***Note*** — I'm going to acknowledge that there may be instances where those amongst you that are exceedingly bright may suspect that I'm engaging in excessive reiteration, but I need you folks to understand that while the broader points are repeated, there are subtleties and nuances that are slowly emerging within each iteration. These small expansions are ultimately critical to the larger explanations (yet to be revealed) that are predicated on the broader points that are being reiterated, so resist the urge to blow through these subsections. I can assure you that nothing is being unnecessarily repeated anywhere in this book.

Okay, so with that out of the way, let's get about the business of explaining how the whole of humankind could have gotten it all so wrong, and for such a long period of time. It can be blamed primarily on perception and how in-sync perspective can cause even an obviously erroneous perception to seem like Reality. Proposed by Galileo and ultimately codified by Newton within his 1st Law of Motion [*An object at rest remains at rest unless acted upon by a force. An object in motion remains in motion, and at a constant velocity, unless acted upon by a force*] it has been established that uniform velocity remains uniform unless affected by conflict of one form or another. This specifically pertains to spatial velocity, of course, but I want to introduce the impact on human perception that this law can have before I move on to suggest how this kind of in-sync uniformity can exist in other forms, and how human perception can be similarly affected by all versions of uniformity.

Now, this can be pretty hard to illustrate, but I'm going to try something here. I have an analogy that might work, but this whole perception issue is extremely complicated, so don't assume that you won't have to help with the heavy lifting here. This analogy is pretty good, but it won't save you from having to do some thinking for yourself.

The first thing I want you to do is imagine that you're orbiting the earth as a member of a team assigned to the international space station. We've all seen the footage, as one of the crew steps off into space and works on a solar panel or a robotic arm or some other issue to be addressed, so I don't feel the need to describe what you'd experience as you push off and begin your first spacewalk. In fact, I would imagine that it'd feel like nothing much whatsoever. Very still. Very little in the way of actual physical sensation. It'd be almost tranquil in its sheer absence of anything at all, as the earth slides silently beneath your feet and the stars lay out to the end of the universe itself.

Okay, I want you to shelve that thought for a moment, and now imagine yourself identically tethered to a similar projectile that is screaming across the sky only 30,000 feet above the surface of the earth, at a speed of nearly 18,000 miles per hour. Tranquil isn't a word that you'd use to describe the very brief experience of being completely shredded by the violence of that ride. And yet, as you float effortlessly along, leashed to the space station, you're traveling along at that very same speed. What is different is your relationship to the environment that contains you and your moment of sailing along at 18,000 miles per hour. For you, that environmental relationship is the difference between quietly appreciating the beauty of the Earth, and salting a long stretch of Earth with your flaming remains.

In this analogy, as you hang silently in your 18,000 mph orbit, the space station is sailing right along with you, and with no atmosphere (a literal sea of gas molecules in their own relative harmony of movement) to provide a direct and violent opposition to the contextual agreement that you and your space station have established concerning motion, the experience of careening through the void at 18,000 mph is surprisingly serene. All of the pieces involved are in a contextual harmony, and this is experienced by the space walker as motionlessness.

AutoGenesism: A Theory of Everything

The truth is that you can only perceive changes in velocity; acceleration or deceleration. If you're integral to a spatial trajectory that encounters no change to its established velocity, your experience of its ongoing momentum is nonexistent. Einstein observed this phenomenon with his statement that:

> "If a system of coordinates K is chosen so that, in relation to it, physical laws hold good in their simplest form, the same laws hold good in relation to any other system of coordinates K' moving in uniform translation relatively to K."
>
> **Albert Einstein: The Foundation of the General Theory of Relativity**

Of course, only in a material vacuum is this possible, and this is why I presented this space walker example of the perceived motionlessness of uniform velocity.

The same can be said about how we, as corporeal human beings, experience our lives in relative context with what we are and what embraces us as a universal environment. Our corporeal bodies are a collection of bits and pieces that come together to complete us as auto-animate wholes. We all know that. We know about atoms, and cells, and quarks, and some have theorized that there are strings at the bottom of it all, and those strings vibrate and set everything into motion.

We've already got that figured out, but what we don't seem to fully appreciate is that we're not only bits and pieces of this and that, we're also immutably finite instances of physical existence that are locked together within a common unit rate of change as a relentless forward trajectory of cause, effect and emergence. This causes every combination and sub-assembly to constantly reconfigure in precise coordination within this very consistent and universal event trajectory. So, as *Now* replaces *Now*, we cease to exist as we are, but then we reemerge as something that is completely reconfigured — a whole new structural arrangement — at the most elemental level.

The most obvious net result is that we, as material wholes, don't actually maintain consistent structural existence from moment to moment. Then again, neither does anything else that surrounds us — with atoms and molecules in the same sort of constant change and assembly reconfiguration at all times.

But, even more important to our capacity to perceive all of this as real is the fact that the entirety of all sub-atomic activity is moving through linear time with the same precise and immutable unit rate of change, with change itself (pieced out in those indivisible quantum units we know as *Now)* occurring in universal time sync to create a universal sub-structure of contextual commonality. I'll often refer to this universal sub-structure of contextual commonality as a **Contextual Environment** if I am working to describe its structural nature, but most of the time I'll just call it Reality.

This structural progression of change is experienced by us as relative stasis, since what we each are and what we each perceive is in sync with this universal change rate. And, this is where my analogy of whipping around the earth at 18,000 mph in the calm of unified context fits in as somewhat appropriate, even if not all that effective.

The Perfectly Coordinated Change

Now, this issue of the **Unit Rate of Change** [we can call it the **URC** to save print space] is extremely important, and we need to devote some additional attention to it. This uniform exchange of one quantum of action for the next is not a new concept, but when taking this thoroughly proven notion to where we need to take it, some people can get pretty turned around without specific guidance. Besides, the real world ramification of universal quantization of action that we've been addressing [the specific impact it has on human perception and perspective] is not one that's received much scrutiny, and there's precious little that's been published. Especially relative to the largest question; what is real versus what could very likely be the inevitable result of this overwhelming factor's impact on the human mind's interpretation of empirical evidence.

In referring to the philosopher Heraclitus, Plato declared that *". . . you could not step into the same river twice"*, and while there is some controversy whether Heraclitus actually meant what Plato meant, when he said whatever it was that he actually said to inspire Plato to paraphrase him, there is a point here that is worthy of examination in its own right. Whether a river is a concrete physical thing that can be dealt with as if it were a structurally constant whole is a fundamental question, even though Plato had already moved beyond the simple question of the river's relative capacity for true physical identity.

In a very real sense, a river is an event that contains an amazing collection of smaller events that begin, happen, and then complete, as the main event of the river itself allows all those lesser events an overarching identity relative to the rest of the world around it. And while each event is occurring, they're happening in flow with the larger river event as a whole, and multiplying with one another to actually become that overarching river event from moment to moment as a collection of concurrent and consecutive events that are in unified association (or contextual entanglement). And what we see is a river that never changes; flowing steady to the sea, like it always has since anyone can remember.

Now, it's pretty easy to conceptualize a river as being an event, but when we lean against a table, it's harder to imagine that table as being like that river; an event that is a collective of lesser events, with all of these lesser events combining from instant to instant to create the overarching event that is the table itself.

Then again, our physical relationship with that table is actually a lot more like the relationship between that astronaut and the space station in my analogy featuring the both of them spinning around the planet in a serene vacuum environment. It's difficult, but if you can imagine everything around you, and everything within you [everything that combines to create the material human being that you are] hurtling through open space at the exact same rate of speed, and with no atmosphere to offer any resistance at all [like that space station in orbit above the earth] then you can begin to picture what is actually in constant play as you sit there and experience a stable and reliable here and now.

Now, I need you to change that mental picture by replacing that movement through open space [surrendering your whole material existence within one precise location for your new whole material existence within the next precise location as you move along] with that same kind of movement through time [surrendering your whole material existence in the same way for your next interval of whole material existence], even as you experience no progressive change whatsoever. This idea [it's not easy to hold for very long once you've captured it] will allow you to accurately appreciate what the Material Realm really is as a physical structure; an immeasurably broad configuration of deeply entangled trajectories of Change/Event Units that all share a leading and tailing edge of actual existence that is spanned only by the extremely brief, razor-thin duration of the quantum of *Now*. Each one of uncountable Change/Event Trajectories existing only from one quantum of *Now* to the next, even though we (as observers that are fully entangled within it all) experience the richness of material existence in full color 3-D sensurround.

Yes, that's a hell of a thing to conceptualize, but if you can't accomplish this one abstraction, then the rest of this is going to be extremely difficult for you to grasp. This one extremely counterintuitive fact of material structure is going to be yet another foundation that the whole of this premise will rest upon, and due to that, I will expound a bit on it, hopefully illustrating it a bit better as I do.

By now, even school kids know that matter is anything but solid. Each bit that interacts, attracts, repels, gravitates, magnetizes, spins around, and engages in dynamic interplay within ourselves as an organized end result has its own cacophony of tightly coordinated mayhem that is responsible for its own moment of existence. I invite you to visualize for yourself all that is occurring within your own body. Sure, it looks solid and feels solid, but there is more space between bits of activity than there is substance that makes up those bits, and within those bits, the story is exactly the same.

In *"How to Know God: The Soul's Journey into The Mystery of Mysteries"*, Deepak Chopra states on page 29 that . . .

> "At the quantum level, nothing of the material world is left intact. It is strange enough to hold up your hand and realize that it is actually, at a deeper level, invisible vibrations taking place in a void. Even at the atomic level, all objects are revealed as 99.9999 percent empty space. On its own scale, the distance between a whirling electron and the nucleus it revolves around is wider than the distance between the earth and the sun."

And none of it is capable of maintaining a consistent state of relative association with anything that's near it. In fact, movement is the literal basis of all that is material, which ensures that nothing we see, touch, hear, smell, or taste persists in a true and lasting concrete sense.

Deepak Chopra goes on to state in the above quoted paragraph that . . .

> "But you could never capture that electron anyway, since it too breaks down into energy vibrations that wink in and out of existence millions of times per second."

Now, I have my own ideas about things *"winking in and out of existence . . ."*, since I have to surrender to the fact that once something ceases to exist it doesn't reemerge as existent, but the larger point he makes is one that I agree with. Matter isn't solid in any sense of the word.

The truth is that nothing that we have declared to be real is in any way real at all. Not in the way that we have decided to define real; referring to that which is solid, material, and physically consistent. What we call *real* is as fluid and circumstantial as downtown traffic. Our perception of solidity is nothing more than our incapacity to isolate our observation from the quantum unit change synchronization that we, as fellow material structures, share with what we are observing.

That means that you, my friend, don't actually exist at all. At least, not in any sense of being a real, solid and concrete chunk of anything. Your material body is an event that is comprised of uncountable lesser events that keep on happening, and will continue to happen until the whole of it stops happening. Then, it will never happen again, and that is the bottom line of you as a corporeal human being with a life that is the apical holon event stretching out like an umbrella over every event that occurs as units within that trajectory connecting your birth and death events.

Then again, it's not like the rest of the universe around us is solid either, so I try not to get too frustrated when I encounter humanity's universal refusal to accept (or even imagine) this most foundational of Reality fundamentals. After all, we each can only perceive the quantum instant of Now, causing the leading edge of our life's Change/Event Trajectory (an uncountable entanglement of structural Change/Event Trajectories that are in a perfect lockstep exchange of one unit of *Now* for the next) to serve as our only window on Reality. So, unlike the spatial trajectories we observe and intersect with from minute to minute, hour to hour, day to day and year to year, we can abstract, but we can't ever perceive, the arc of a Change/Event Trajectory.

We can examine time-lapse footage. We can note the passing of time by the changes it imposes upon all that exists around us. We can intellectualize the concepts of past, present and future, but there's no way to lift our own selves out of the Change/Event Trajectories that populate our own lives to then examine the full nature of those trajectories. We're contextually locked into the quantum rate of unitary event exchange — one Change/Event Unit replacing the last — of our entire Contextual Environment and everything that exists as real within it. As each instant of Now happens, this entire environment shares that *Now*, making that progression of quantized transitions completely imperceptible; just a perpetual *Now* ruling everything, perceived by the human mind as relative stasis and physical consistency.

So, does this mean that there is nothing of a solid, immutable, concrete nature in physical existence? No. In fact, there is plenty of a solid and concrete nature that provides a very real anchor for what spins, shifts, adjusts and mutates. And we'll get to that shortly.

Kevin Brian Carroll

Extra Dimensions and Stuff

The Material Realm is real, but it's real in the sense that it occurs, even though it ceases to exist as soon as it occurs. In fact, change/activity is a full half of what constitutes the whole of physical existence. And when I say that, I'm not being esoteric or engaging in analogy. Change, literally, is one of two basic forms of physical existence.

Change can be reduced to the indivisible Change/Event Unit, even if we have no means to actually measure that unit. Now, I should probably go ahead and explain where I'm getting all this from, since for most folks, this quantized change/event business is pretty counterintuitive. Truth is that Quantum Physics established all of this over the last 100 years or so, and we've transformed our entire world as a result of leveraging that very dependable Reality anchor. So, I'm not pulling any of this out of my hat. As for how long it takes for the change/event quantum of *Now* to fully play out, there's some established thought on that too.

The Physics Department has declared that the quantum of *Now* [1 unit of Planck time] is the time it takes one light photon to travel a distance of 1 Planck length within a vacuum. One Planck length is equal to 1.616199(97)×10−35 meters. This measurement (about 10−20 times the diameter of a proton) was determined by working with three fundamental physical constants: the speed of light in a vacuum, Planck's constant, and the gravitational constant. For what it's worth, the math looks like this:

$$\ell_P = \sqrt{\frac{\hbar G}{c^3}} \approx 1.616\ 199(97) \times 10^{-35}\ \text{m}$$

Planck length
Figure 1-C

The speed of light within a vacuum is exactly 299,792,458 meters per second. We know this because they based the meter itself on the speed of light in a vacuum. So, given that the accepted standard insists that Planck time is the duration of the photon's journey across an entire Planck length (within a vacuum, of course) each quantum of Now lasts a full 5.4x10^−4 4 sec before, as a Change/Event Unit, it ceases to physically exist and is replaced by the next change/event quantum unit of Now of identical duration. Again, here's the math:

AutoGenesism: A Theory of Everything

$$t_P \equiv \sqrt{\frac{\hbar G}{c^5}}$$

Planck time
Figure 1-D

So, what was the point of this quick physics lesson? I wanted to prove that this indivisible quantum of *Now* stuff isn't anything new to those professional types whose business it is to accurately determine what is and what isn't crazy talk. As to whether these formulas actually represent the Unit Rate of Change within our Reality confine, there's no way to ever know. The measurements themselves have a ± accuracy range, so there's that. The rest is the result of working with fairly arbitrary numbers that, while based on quantified results, are more accurately defined as agreed-upon estimations than as hard numbers with any actual precision. Still, what's important to note here is that the quantization of Time (as yet another real physical dimensional aspect that comes in indivisible units) is very well accepted as an established concept within the most responsible academic circles.

So now, let's take a look at how physical existence is gathered into what I prefer to call Contextual Environments as opposed to dimensions, or planes of existence, or whatever buzzword exists to describe the physical embodiment of a universally shared, and therefore encompassing, contextual commonality between otherwise independent material wholes.

If you've been poking around the field of physics, or even metaphysics, in recent years, you've run into plenty of talk concerning vibrational dimensions and higher spatial planes and whatnot, and it all sounds pretty technical until you really dig into what some of this talk is based on. In Lee Smolin's book *"The Trouble With Physics: The Rise of String Theory, The Fall of Science, and What Happens Next"* there's a wonderful overview of how one String Theorist devised an imperceptible spatial dimension in order to make his theory work out mathematically.

> " . . . Alexander Polyakov had suggested that in certain cases the emergent strings associated with a gauge theory might behave like fundamental strings. Yet, the gauge-theory strings would not exist in our world; instead, in one of the most remarkable feats of imagination in the history of the subject, Polyakov conjectured they move in a space that had one additional dimension.

"How did Polyakov succeed in conjuring up an extra dimension for his strings to move in? He found that when tested quantum-mechanically, the strings that arise from gauge theory have an emergent property, which, it turns out, can be described by a number attached to each point on the string. A number can also be interpreted as a distance. In this case, Polyakov proposed that the number attached to each point of the string be interpreted as giving the position of that point in an additional dimension."

Personally, I love how Polyakov did that, but let's face it, you can't create actual spatial dimensions by reinterpreting numbers that someone else designated to a diagram of a string to mean that the string itself (not just the diagram) now has one end passing through to the dimension that you just invented as a result of your brilliant argument. Reality doesn't have lawyers because it doesn't need lawyers. Reality simply is what it is and does what it does in spite of us and our brilliant imaginations.

For now, I will only be screwing around with one dimension (Time) and mainly because, as you'll see, it's the only dimension that actually has the power to permanently isolate. In fact, Time is the primordial determinant concerning inclusion within a defined Contextual Environment.

The first thing I want to do is explain that last statement: *"Time is the primordial determinant concerning inclusion within a defined Contextual Environment."* I think that a diagram will work best to start us off here. What we have here are two Change/Event Trajectories that are not in sync with one another.

Out-of-Sync Unit Rate of Change (URC) Progression

Figure 1-E

As you can see, the transition points between Event 1 and Event 2 and Event 3 are not happening at the same instances for this pair of event trajectories. Yes, it could happen that there could conceivably be exchange points that align every now and then, but the incompatible duration of these units of *Now* will always keep these two event trajectories from ever existing within the same Contextual Environment [Reality]. They'll simply never sync up, and this is the long and short of what determines what is included as part of one Contextual Environment or another.

As to perception (which is where we human beings come in on this issue of extra dimensional relationships), there's literally no means of perceiving the contents of an alternate Contextual Environment [again, Reality]. Here, let's try a couple more diagrams to see just how the in-sync versus out-of-sync thing works when all you're trying to do is notice what's there in front of you. Of course, perception (a product of your material brain that we'll soon examine as existing in *Burst Units*), while in sync with the URC, is considerably slower, hence the longer span of perceived *Now*.

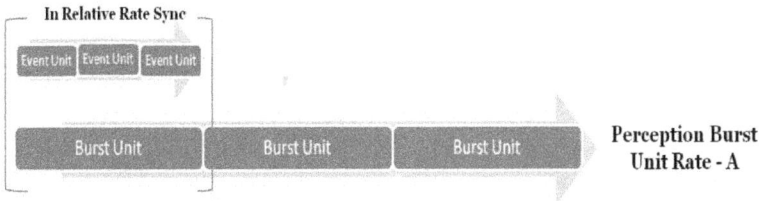

In Relative Rate Sync

Event Unit | Event Unit | Event Unit

Burst Unit | Burst Unit | Burst Unit

Perception Burst
Unit Rate - A

URC and Change Progression Perception Synchronization
Define a Permanent Physical Environment

Figure 1-F

It becomes obvious that when two URCs are not compatible, time-locked perception can't overcome the difference. This makes extra-environmental perception physically impossible.

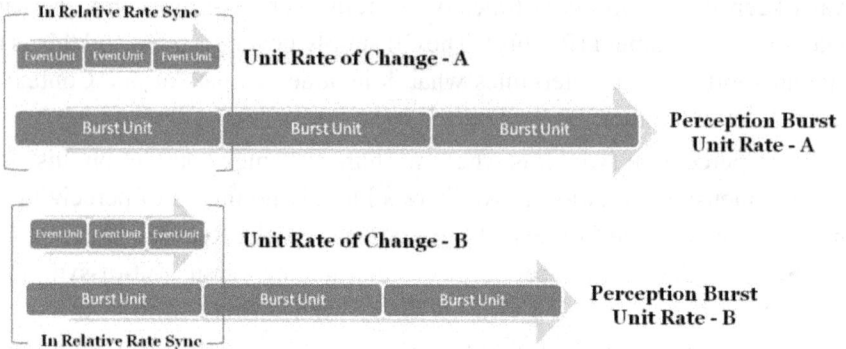

URC and Change Progression Perception Differences
Create a Profound and Permanent Physical Isolation Dielectric

Figure 1-G

But, what (if anything) does this mean to claims of extra-dimensional travel and/or physical ascension? I guess it all depends on whether you believe these dimensions to be spatial, and if so, how you make the math work out to prove that they do actually exist.

The truth is that theoretical physicists have been *"rolling up"* tiny dimensions that fit between the frequency bands of the light spectrum for decades just to make their String Theory math calculations add up. If these guys can't make extra dimensions that are inhabitable (or even descriptively realistic), then I have my doubts about anyone's capacity to wink in and out of those dimensions that they've imagined to populate their own version of Reality.

That said, as you'll learn (once we get out of this no-imagination science section here) there are plenty of reasons to believe that some people do experience those extra dimensions. But experiencing something isn't the same as actually doing or being whatever it is that you're experiencing. In fact, human experience isn't representative of Reality at all, and we'll get deep into that soon enough.

The Metaphysics of Identity Survival

At this point, I am going to introduce one of the more controversial assertions of AutoGenesism. It's the literal bottom line relative to existence and what it means to exist, and this theory lives and/or dies on the factual nature of this staple. This being the case, I'm going to do my best to fully explain what it is and why I've determined that it must be universally true and necessary to the nature of Reality. I guess we'll just have to see how it goes.

As we learned, for something to exist, **it** must stand out apart from whatever it is that isn't **it**. **It** doesn't have to be observed as standing out, but it must be truly separated at some level from that which is not **it**. This is the essential requirement.

Now, in spite of my respect for, and acknowledgement of, the centuries of brilliant minds that have slaved over a proper definition of the word, I want you to use the word *Identity* to refer to what it is that permits the existent something to exist as whatever it is that it is, relative to all that is NOT it. I want us to agree that if something has Identity, then it stands out from all else that exists, as well as from non-existence (which we'll have to agree involves a lack of Identity, since Identity provides physical existence by allowing whatever it is to *'stand out'* as existent).

This also means that if Identity is what establishes physical existence (and this is regardless of whether observation is present or not) then Survival [the lone existential imperative] is actually (and only) about the survival of Identity for the existent something. Grasping this basic premise is going to be more than critical to your being able to fully understand the true structure of physical Reality, so I'll be coming back to Identity Survival again and again as we move forward. For now, I'm going to give you a very basic feel for Identity Survival and how it manifests at a variety of levels that should be familiar to you.

Digression Alert — Identity Survival is the fundamental pursuit of all that physically exists; Aristotle's *"final cause"*. Now, I realize that as a person with places to go, things to do, and people to see, you don't see the preservation of existential Identity as being on your radar, let alone at the top of your to-do list from day to day, but the truth is that it drives you (and everything else) to do and not do, to be and not be, whatever it is that you (and everything else) end up doing and being.

Think about it. You buy, you create, you accomplish, you express your opinion, you bring your progeny into this world, and all of it is yours. It all belongs to you. Like a male cat spraying your territory, you mark the world around you, and you make it identifiably associated with you and you alone. Your body, your wife, your husband, your car, your house, your career/job/business/art, your children, your parents, your family, your life, your sickness, and finally, your death. You tag it all, you defend your ownership of it, you care for it, and you push it forward to positively express your ongoing identity through having made it yours.

What you can't own, you've established direct association with. Your school, your community, your church, your company, your friends, your city, your ethnicity, your race, your heritage, your country; all of it establishing and preserving your Identity through your direct membership. Assuring and preserving your existential presence within the environment; the survival of your Identity.

And regardless of your level of selflessness [*"spiritual enlightenment"*] you don't exist in a way that transcends the primordial pursuit of Identity Survival. No one does. You simply pursue that survival in whatever way it is that you feel is suitably transcendent as you establish and preserve of your unique Identity with the same resilient devotion as the most viscerally carnal among us.

It's this way for everything else that exists. Sketch out the ongoing development of anything you wish, and you'll discover this same basic existential formula. What's most fascinating is that if you examine the composite parts of any unified collective, you'll find that each part is also in ongoing pursuit of Identity Survival. That said, how such structural units pursue it is a bit more counterintuitive at first glance.

I'll be using the term *"holon"* (coined by author Arthur Koestler to describe something that is both whole and part) to refer to whole and unique items that gather in common pursuit of prolonged Identity presence via direct association with the next greater (and therefore, more survivable) holon; forming a definable structure as they do. I like that word *holon*. The reason I like it is that it illustrates the nature of the most fundamental of Identity Survival strategies in an immediately relatable manner whenever it's used.

> ***Note*** — One of the best examples of a common holon hierarchical structure is Major League Baseball. Each baseball player is a holon who joins in common cause with coach holons and manager holons (each are unique kinds of holons in their own right) to create the greater holon that is the team, and each team is a holon that combines with other team holons to create the league conference (American or National) holon. From there, the two conference holons (as well as the specific legal and management holons that serve to fill out the precise organizational requirements involved) enter into dedicated common cause to create Major League Baseball as the apical holon that gives all holons within that

specific structure the long and storied Identity that each holon gains as part of the whole that is Major League Baseball.

Holon structure is not as obvious in lesser examples, but the fact that your cells and your atoms persist in serving the apical holon that is your material body, is evidence that they (as holons in their own right) are driven by the very same Identity preserving and promoting Survival imperative that holds all such holon structures together. From the least to the greatest, it is only Identity Survival that exists as a true existential imperative, driving all that exists to be what it is.

Speculation Alert — While this is officially a speculation, I'm not all that convinced that it qualifies as pure speculation. Still, I did promise to only declare that which I could responsibly assert to be true or reasonably self-evident. As you'll see, however, as a working hypothesis, this little notion has pretty good legs upon which to stand.

The most overwhelming and pervasive example of the relentless nature of Identity Survival is the mysterious relationship that is evident between physical systems at all levels of existence. Depending on the significance of the systems involved, this relationship is perceived as manifesting in a variety of manners that have been labeled the four primary forces of nature; Electromagnetism, Strong Interaction, Weak Interaction, and Gravity. In essence, these four unique manifestations are the result of the one existential imperative — Identity Survival — as each physical system either competes or combines with greater and lesser physical systems for raw preservation of its own contextual identity.

Through the specific force (and/or combination of forces) most effective in maintaining its own critical holon structure, each system fights to remain whole and/or to increase via holon structural inclusion wherever possible. The Strong Interaction and Electromagnetism are indicative of each atom's battle for holon structural integrity (proton/neutron nucleus cohesion, and electron orbit stability respectively), and Gravity's far reaching assurance that macro-systems will remain intact even as its *"weak"* influence allows for widespread intra-system holon structural survival; after all, each surviving holon structure is as integral to the contextual Identity of such a macro-system as the environmental background that presents that holon structure's delineation with its own unique Identity.

Of course, Gravity and Electromagnetism also offer holon structure

ID Survival through inclusion within dynamic spatial trajectories; (a primordial evangelism of sorts) inviting material wholes to link their own lesser systems together in common cause to a far greater and more resilient activity. Again, Identity Survival through holon structural Increase, as we observe, measure, and work to relate it all to what makes the most sense when compared to what we (as neither macro nor micro systems) can readily relate to.

Now, it's important to make the point here that serving a primordial existential imperative is not something that is chosen. There's no choice involved. In the case of the most unitary, pre-matter examples of this drive, there are obviously no choices being considered. We'll be examining indivisible units of activity [quanta] and their devotion to Identity Survival imperative expressions (such as Isolation and Increase) as they form entire Change/Event Trajectories that are clearly organized and predictable, but I certainly don't expect to feel required to suggest that these quantum units of activity are consciously choosing to organize and produce follow-on quantum units of activity in service of this primordial existential imperative.

We don't have to anthropomorphize quanta in order to understand what drives activity, or why activity organizes into event trajectories as it does. We can extrapolate from what we can observe in higher forms of physical existence, and make the required intellectual adjustments as we do. Again, it is well established that holons gather in common cause, even at the most primitive and unitary levels of physical existence, to preserve and promote their own individual Identities by way of contextual inclusion within the next larger holon collective's Identity.

What's also important to point out is that Time itself [the progressing exchange of one unit of Now for the very next unit of Now within a quantized universal system] cannot be affected by the gravitational force of any macrosystem that is integral to [therefore a lesser part of] that quantized universal system. A time-keeping system's precise process of structural entropy can be affected, but it will still remain a quantized process of relative entropy, with Time itself remaining based on the Unit Rate of Change that locks the entire universal system together as the apical holon that it is and that rigidly ensures its Identity Survival regardless of what does or doesn't happen.

As we'll see in the next sub-section, shared relative contextual association (or you can use the term *entanglement*) is what places each contributing holon

AutoGenesism: A Theory of Everything

within the internal contextual structure (or you can use the term *historical composition*) of a greater, more resilient holon. As long as that greater holon survives (or survives as historically integral to an even greater holon), the Identity of each contributive holon also survives, since the Identity of the greater holon is contextually defined by the Identities of all such contributive holons. This is extremely significant to keep in mind when you're dealing with the survival pursuit of extremely primitive change/event quanta. After all, the quantum of *Now* is nearly over before it begins, but a Change/Event Trajectory can last a lot longer. When you consider the kind of orbital spatial trajectory that the Earth is engaged in as it circles the Sun, the difference in longevity (since every spatial trajectory is also a Change/Event Trajectory) becomes obvious.

As we get into Section II's examination of a typical progressive development structure, I'll be sure to amplify this critical aspect of how physical Reality works, especially relative to the initial stages of physical development's climb out of that literal void. It's there where the Identity Survival imperative is most clearly seen for what it is, since there's literally nothing else to point to in connection to each quantum unit of existence showing up on the heels of the last until the whole thing starts to catch. It's there that the very same primordial impetus that forces an artist to commit his entire life to the incredibly unlikely off-chance that he will someday create a masterpiece, is laid open for full inspection. Because, like I said, from the least to the greatest, it is only Identity Survival that exists as a true existential imperative, driving all that exists to be what it is.

Note — In July of 2012, CERN physicists announced the indication of what they believe to be a possible candidate for the Higgs boson. This was big news due to the nature of the prevailing theory concerning how physical matter forms from what is otherwise random elementary particles and energy waves. Actually, the presence of the Higgs Field (suggested as the physical means by which particles are "slowed down" enough to begin coalescing into larger, more complex material wholes) isn't a true theory, but it could be one if the Higgs boson were to be proven to exist. As of this summer of 2013, the jury is (essentially) still out on whether the class of particles discovered is a close enough match to the proposed Higgs boson without possessing properties that clash with those anticipated to the extent of disqualifying this boson from consideration.

And yet, to date, no one has bothered to explain exactly where the Higgs Field itself came from, why it exists, how it came into existence, and what its own properties are. Apparently, all that's required for the

Higgs Field Theory of particle coalescence to be deemed a successful explanation of how physical matter gathers within our Universe is for a predicted particle (or one reasonably similar in mass, spin, and rate of decay) to turn up.

In Section II: Track #1 we'll take a fresh look at the whole topic of matter, energy, and how (and why) stuff coalesces into material structure, and I'll detail a point of emergence that physically links the Change/Event Trajectory to the spatial trajectory as that Change/Event Trajectory pursues its own Identity Survival. And, with that, we'll establish Identity Survival as the literal link between Time and everything else that exists as a result of Time.

As has been well established, it's only through the entanglement of kinetic energy (the spatial trajectory) that hierarchical material holon structure is ultimately established. There's no other means of creating it. There's certainly no such thing as an orbital Change/Event Trajectory. There are only event trajectories that exist as *Now* followed by the next *Now* followed by *Now* yet again, regardless of how entangled they become.

In a Reality that is solely driven by holon Identity Survival, repetitive momentum [the existence of kinetic force propelling an orbital trajectory of action quanta that are looping endlessly as a defined holon structure] definitely brings something valuable to the table. After all, as each orbital spatial trajectory returns to zero and starts anew, it also persists as a Change/Event Trajectory. In fact, that orbital spatial trajectory [the ultimate basis of matter, and then of the entire Material Realm by direct progressive extension] can be most accurately viewed as the most successful means by which the much more primitive Change/Event Trajectory (which is itself the primordial Identity Survival strategy of the quantum of *Now*) physically pursues Identity Survival as an identified holon structure in its own right.

Yes. As endlessly intricate as Reality gets, the basic concept remains surprisingly simple. Everything that exists — everything that it is and everything that it does — is all about the primordial pursuit of Identity Survival. Every bit of it.

AutoGenesism: A Theory of Everything

The Precedence of Precedent

Precedence

noun

- Law. A legal decision or form of proceeding serving as an authoritative rule or pattern in future similar or analogous cases.
- any act, decision, or case that serves as a guide or justification for subsequent situations.
- the right to precede others in ceremonies or social formalities
- the order to be observed in ceremonies by persons of different ranks, as by diplomatic protocols

Precedent

noun

- act or fact of preceding
- the right to precede in order, rank, or importance; priority
- the fact of preceding in time; antedating

I have included the dictionary definitions of the terms *precedence* and *precedent* (above) as my own way of acknowledging that these terms were coined to describe exactly and only what the above stated definitions specifically suggest. That said, what I am going to do is make the case that all natural laws [as is the case with most of what the human mind has invented for its own application] are structurally based on what exists as naturally and progressively preferred [precedence] as a result of established wins and losses [precedent] within the physical realms that the human mind straddles. As I do so, I'll be freely using the terms *precedence* and *precedent* to refer to this naturally emergent tag-team cause/effect basis of all that has evolved to become concretely established within the whole of Reality.

Just as the esotericism of mathematics is based on the simplicity of Set Logic (the precedence structure that affects potential relationship dynamics that can exist between things that are composites of lesser things), our laws (and the precedents that defined those laws with interpretation preferences) are based on the ramification structure that evolves (and has evolved) as a result of actual physical relationships between existent things and the impact of those relationships on how Reality, and the lesser systems that populate it, work in a default manner [promoting precedences]. The Laws of Physics, Natural Laws, the yes/no

95

basis of all demonstrable logic (including Set Logic); all real and definable, and all the clearest of evidence that precedence is the natural result
of precedent within a system based on successful survival, and not something that the human mind created out of whole cloth.

Recently, I discovered something (a fact concerning the general nature of
physical Reality as viewed by the mainstream of theoretical physics) that I'm
still struggling to come to terms with. Apparently, while the notion of an infinitely populated multiverse (featuring an endless amount of universes packed
with no less than 9 spatial dimensions and 1 dimension of Time) is accepted as
plausible (perhaps absolutely required), the concept that precedence exists at all
is viewed by the most adventurous to be suspect, and is more widely viewed to
be *"laughable"* as an actual existing dynamic that affects progressive development.

In this subsection I want to initially address this issue as aggressively as I
can. In the end (while I will hold off on fully detailing exactly how and why
precedent brings system precedence into existence as it does until a more appropriate segment within this overall presentation) I hope to detail why it is that I
am incapable of agreeing with this very specific mainstream view, and prove
that I haven't come upon my own (apparently) unique view of Reality by way
of irresponsible inference or undisciplined thinking.

Over the years that I've been working to develop and strictly define my
Reality view as a quantifiable ToE, I've always assumed that system preferences
simply exist, and have always existed. In fact, I've assumed that without the
definition provided by some form of emergent structural precedence, progressive organizational development could never be possible. Of course, I knew that
there were those belief systems that fully embrace the hands-on Supreme Being
(with such a being eliminating the need for any sort of progressively developing
natural order whatsoever) but I also knew that this notion presents an infinite
regression conundrum that can't be reconciled with what's been proven and
firmly established as real.

Concerning settled science, I just assumed that the existence of factual
precedent's hand in a naturally emerging order at all levels of physical existence
(as a default ramification of simple wins and losses occurring within each competitive theater of physical survival) had been established long ago. How could
anyone explain away the impact of preferred outcome on the evolutionary de-

AutoGenesism: A Theory of Everything

velopment of physical Reality when confronted with the obvious evidence contained within every system that exists, from atoms to human behavioral predilections?

I recently discovered that I was wrong to assume that simple precedence within systems is a universal assumption. In final rewrites, I decided to include a variety of quotes and book passages from noted authors and theoretical physicists. Of course, this meant that I would take some months to read and fully comprehend the books that contain the passages I'd chosen. One author/physicist that I found to be the most compelling and eminently quotable is Prof. Lee Smolin; not only due to his clarity of expression, but also due to his clarity of thought concerning recent controversies over the direction of Theoretical Physics as a scientific discipline. It was while reading his latest book — *"Time Reborn: From the Crisis in Physics to the Future of the Universe"* — that I happened upon a *'breakthrough'* notion of his that he calls the *'principle of precedence'*.

This discovery led me to several hours of intense investigation into what it could be that makes Prof. Smolin believe that *precedence* is conceptually unprecedented relative to what is known and/or suspected concerning how physical Reality made its way from a very primitive state to the extremely robust and ultra-sophisticated state it clearly enjoys at this moment. I found the following paper:

Lee Smolin: Precedence and freedom in quantum physics,

arXiv:1205.3707v1, 17 May 2012

Abstract:

A new interpretation of quantum mechanics is proposed according to which precedence, freedom and novelty play central roles. This is based on a modification of the postulates for quantum theory given by Masanes and Muller[4]. We argue that quantum mechanics is uniquely characterized as the probabilistic theory in which individual systems have maximal freedom in their responses to experiment, given reasonable axioms for the behavior of probabilities in a physical theory. Thus, to the extent that quantum systems are free, in the sense of Conway and Kochen[1], there is a sense in which they are maximally free.

We also propose that laws of quantum evolution arise from a *principle of precedence* according to which the outcome of a measurement on a quantum system is selected randomly from the ensemble of outcomes of previous instances of the same measurement on the same quantum system. This implies that dynamical laws for quantum systems can evolve as the universe evolves, because new precedents are generated by the formation of new entangled states.

I want to take a look at the very last sentence in the abstract, since it seems to sum up what I found to be incredible about this entire notion.

This implies that dynamical laws for quantum systems can evolve as the universe evolves, because new precedents are generated by the formation of new entangled states.

First, I want to acknowledge that Quantum Mechanics is a unique field of science, and that those who labor within it are presented with many unexpected and often counterintuitive indications. It is also true that there is much controversy surrounding the validity of what has emerged as the primary focus of Theoretical Physics — Superstring Theory — and I am impressed with Prof. Smolin's courage and clarity in leading the way on this very difficult issue. That said, I struggle to understand how it could be that anyone trained in science (let alone an individual as clearly impressive as Prof. Smolin) could suddenly suspect, after so many years as a world class theorist, that the assumption — that progressive development of this Material Realm has so successfully evolved (and from such elemental, primitive origins) without the existence of emerging states of system precedence aiding in that evolution — has been an incorrect assumption all along. After all, isn't Darwinian and Neo-Darwinian Evolution based entirely on the principle of precedence?

If the principle of precedence is not predicated on Nature's repetition of what has proven to be a successful precedent, then perhaps I'm not fully understanding what is being suggested. However, if it is, then the field of Quantum Physics hasn't merely gone off the rails (as it were) but, more troubling perhaps, it's never been on the rails to begin with. To be succinct, I probably should bullet point my questions concerning the implications as I see them:

- How could Darwinian and Neo-Darwinian Evolution possibly exist as successful science without the principle of precedence?
- How could it be that biological evolution is not seen as the study of physical interaction between physical systems that exist within a larger shared system; meaning that this discipline is also physics at its basis.
- How can anyone, regardless of their specific scientific discipline, assume to know where to draw the line between the physics of biological

Autogenesism: A Theory of Everything

systems and the physics of any other system, relative to what can and cannot exist as determining factors within each?

I applaud Prof. Smolin's realization of the obvious existence of an impact on quantum systems by the precedence-establishing precedents that have, themselves, been established within those systems and similar systems, but I have to wonder — if this notion has never been considered by those who work as experimental physicists, then what's been the point of carefully and precisely isolating those systems used in experiments from all manners of contextual contamination? I understand the need to eliminate physical contaminants, but when creating quantum entangled pairs, it seems obvious that the entire technical point of preparation is to create two photons that are as precedent-free (contextually speaking) as possible. This suggests that contextual precedent (which is what gathers to determine precedence within any system) is and has been a known concern for quite a while.

It's here, after having established that at least three specific disciplines within the field of science have been working with the net impact of the principle of precedence all along, that I will cut to the principal focus of this subsection; the intricate and logically precise nature of contextual precedent and how it contributes to the definition of each and every physical system that exists or has ever existed.

It's All About Context

In a new study published in the journal *Nature*, researchers have shown that a weird aspect of quantum theory called contextuality is a necessary resource to achieve the so-called magic required for universal quantum computation.

One major hurdle in harnessing the power of a universal quantum computer is finding practical ways to control fragile quantum states. Working towards this goal, IQC researchers Joseph Emerson, Mark Howard and Joel Wallman have confirmed theoretically that contextuality is a necessary resource required for achieving the advantages of quantum computation.

"Before these results, we didn't necessarily know what resources were needed for a physical device to achieve the advantage of quantum information. Now we know one," said Mark Howard, a postdoctoral fellow at IQC and the lead author of the paper. "As researchers work to

build a universal quantum computer, understanding the minimum physical resources required is an important step to finding ways to harness
the power of the quantum world."

Weird 'magic' ingredient for quantum computing: Contextuality: Science-Daily.com

Ref; Mark Howard, Joel Wallman, Victor Veitch, Joseph Emerson. Contextuality supplies the 'magic' for quantum computation. Nature, 2014; DOI:

If Identity Survival is what drives everything to do what it does and be what it becomes, then I would imagine that the next step in our establishment of the true nature of Reality should be to lay out exactly how Identity is achieved and/or determined. As indicated by this subtitle, to accomplish this, we're going to take a moment and look at the nature of internal and relative context. This is due to the fact that context — the specific balance between internal and relative context (or *"contextuality"*, as labeled in the above quoted article) — is what establishes and preserves existential Identity, regardless of what it is that has become existent as a direct result of that contextual confluence. And this is due to the fact that if something physically exists, it does so relative to everything else that also physically exists, and that very specific relationship that the phys-ically existent thing has with every other physically existent thing is what Iden-tity is all about.

I will try to make this as accessible as possible, and lay off the dry technical stuff when I can. In fact, I'm going to go ahead and attempt a narrative analogy to illustrate how internal context [historical provenance] makes even the least of things unique and special. I may even try and relate it to you as a person here and there, to suggest how you can begin to view your own emergence process.

Soaring high above a full orchestra's rendition of a symphonic master-piece, a solo violinist offers a packed house a stunning performance. Some in the crowd swoon under the spell of each note's strength and nuance, while others focus on the entire presentation as a whole. There are those who find themselves enjoying the performance in spite of a preference for other forms of entertainment, and then, there are those who can never be satisfied with what this or any other violinist can produce.

In fact, the music that each mind in that hall *hears* is unique, even though the notes that soar from the stage to the farthest reaches of the hall are simply what they are and nothing more or less. With this in mind, as the violinist pulls passage after passage from his instrument, and fills the evening with the art that drives him to such intense devotion and disciplined dedication, a question becomes, at what point does the man, himself, end, and the man's art begin?

When the violinist draws his bow across the strings of his violin, where does the violinist — the human being wrapped in skin — end, and the music that transcends that corporeal confine, begin? Is it at the end of his fingertips, where the strings are set to vibrate? Is it as the sound waves leap from the violin's soundboard to touch the air in the hall? Is it where those sound waves press against the inner ear of the listener? Or is it within the mind of the listener as the whole of it is translated into what that specific mind has determined to be music?

And what of the mind that is — due to any of a host of reasons — incapable of perceiving that sound as music? How do we factor in the unique perspective of the listener, and how that perspective was built until that instant when the violinist's sound waves struck that listener's mind to be either accepted or rejected as that which can be defined as music? Or does the music always remained trapped within the mind of the violinist, with the effort to release it, a repeating failure that can never be rectified?

That's a really good question. In the same sense, where does the human brain become the human mind? Does it ever become the mind? Where does the person emerge from the material human being, or does the person ever truly emerge? This is basic philosophy, and you can debate it forever, as evident in any freshman college classroom in the early weeks of the fall semester. And yes, we will get to it.

But first, we need to focus on the issue of context, and to look at how internal context creates intrinsic identity. After all, *it* does not exist if *it* cannot be fully delineated from all that surrounds *it*. Again, let's look at this violinist and note all that his performance delivered to his audience. This time, let's shift the focus to the question of context and what it is that establishes the isolation of intrinsic identity. Maybe we can find a transition point between the effort and the art if we dig in deep enough?

When we look at just a short list of unique physical components that came together as the music that was created (the brain-nerve-muscle coordination of the violinist, his hands and his fingers acting upon the strings, the bow drawn across those strings, the strings vibrating and resonating against the bridge of the violin itself which caused the wood to resonate, the sound waves pushing through the open air of the hall, the reverberation of the walls and ceiling that smoothed out the harsh tone of the raw sound of the strings and made it sing as it did, the ears of the listeners, and finally, the minds of each listener at that instant that the sound became music as interpreted by each mind) we have to accept that if we took away any single entry from just this list of contributing aspects alone, the result would cause the music in question to either be radically altered, or destroyed entirely.

Then there are the preparatory components. When the violinist struck his first note of the evening, that note was a C#, but to simply state that it was a C# is to lose sight of all that this single note presented to the unique identity of this particular moment. This C# note did not, does not, exist in a vacuum. It didn't simply appear from nowhere to launch this specific performance.

As the first note of a composed symphony, it was selected and placed by that symphony's composer. That choice imbued this C# with all that came about (as historical context) to create that choice. What historical context is that? Let's see.

This composer lives (or once lived) a life full of instances that contributed to the notion of choosing and placing that note in that specific part of the composition. In fact, it stands to reason that the composer spent some time and thought about which note to place in that specific part of the piece. He likely spent considerable time deciding how long the note should last, how loud it should be played, and whether it should be physically manipulated by the musician in such a way as to provide it a specific expressiveness at any point within its existence as a performed musical note. As the definite result of such a causal chain of events (inspiration, experience, consideration) this C#'s historical context becomes a primary identifier when selecting it out from any such expression suite for precise examination.

In this case, circumstance is not the only progressive chain that brought this C# to lead off this orchestral arrangement. There is also the direct contribution from the author's own progressive intellectual continuum to consider. This composer provided mundane (non-compositional) intellectual context to that note, and that context grants a broad distinction to that specific note that is actually shared with all other notes in that musical piece. The entire composition came as a result of study and experience, as well as the direct impact of those specific events on the inimitable human expression that separates any composer from any other composer — or any other human being, for that matter. Of course, this adds further density to the inimitable nature of that note, and made that note unique before it was even performed.

AutoGenesism: A Theory of Everything

Now, on this particular night, that note was performed, and this isolated it even further as its singular identity was more precisely defined with the additional impact of the performer's involvement. After all, this was an audible note, and not just a conceived note, within this particular composition.

When the violinist struck that note, he added his own contextual contribution to that specific note on that specific evening. This piece was not composed by him, but the creation of that C# note as sound (the physical interpretation of that note by way of the violin as a sound generation tool) was accomplished solely by the violinist. What flowed through the hands and fingers of that violinist as he struck that C# note, represented all that had been his life to that point in time, and the whole of it caused that C# to suddenly belong to him as an artist who had taken the composer's suggestion and had had his way with it — for good or ill, as the case may be.

The years of study, practice, and personal sacrifice; the career that he'd already had, or still envisioned; the surging elements within his own body and brain; all came together as this artist hit that first C# and gave its execution his own unique signature. Combining with the historical and intellectual context that the composer had already provided, this is the historical and intellectual context that the violinist provided to further distinguish this first C# note as a contextually isolated unique whole that expressed the unique identities of both artists in a manner that is both actual and logical.

But there are other contextual layers to consider. There is the instrument itself.

The musician's violin is a rare and valuable model that was produced by a celebrated craftsman who died hundreds of years ago, and since its creation, it has been played by a line of brilliant musicians who've carefully preserved its beauty, its tone and its overall utility. The very fact of its unique excellence, and the history behind that excellence, contributed its own level of context to the sound of this first note, as well as the causal impact on the violinist's psyche (again, flush with critical context) as he skillfully honored this rare treasure with his committed effort to produce that sound.

This blend of circumstantial and intellectual context (somewhat different in nature than the blending of purely intellectual context that two artists in tangential collaboration would contribute to the identity of the piece, but just as powerfully isolating in its impact) was yet another contribution to what had already come together to distinguish this first C# of this particular musical piece.

Then, we must include the actual event and physical environment into the contextual whole, since the note did reach into a real environment during a real moment in time. For this, we must include the environmental aspects of the concert venue itself; the relative humidity of the atmosphere and its impact on the violin's tone and the *"carry"* of the note within the structure of the hall, the impact of competing and sympathetic frequencies from the other notes filling the hall, and whether people were buzzing among themselves as this note was struck, or even if the hall was full or whether people were still finding their seats. From there we can continue to add contextual qualifications until we run out of atoms and quarks and strings to pick over.

So, where does the artist end and the art begin? I don't know. There may not be a point where one ends and the other begins, and that may be exactly the point. Context identifies and isolates, but it can also unify and relate one unique item with another. Our violinist — as he struck that C# — became forever associated with that composer through the contextual confines of what both men contributed to that one note, even as that C# broke free and isolated itself from the whole of Reality with its full load of inimitable context, never to be duplicated again as the fact of its existence lives on into eternity.

The artist adds to the whole, while establishing his or her art as both contribution and identification. Of course, as humans we each experience Reality in relation to ourselves and to our own need to establish unique identity, so we focus on the identifying-isolating aspects within the artistic expression, and we look for that point where the art itself becomes released from the artist. After all, that release must exist if we are to take from the artist what we see as beautiful and claim it as part of our own identity.

So, what was the point of that analogy? Besides enjoying a bit of philosophy and realizing that the separation between the art and the artists may not even exist, we established how context separates and isolates things (even information) into unique and definable wholes. And when you examine the provenance of anything that exists as physical, those same layers of indelible history are revealed like rings within the trunk of a tree. Nothing exists devoid of internal context, and that history is a major part of what combines to create intrinsic identity. And intrinsic, inimitable identity is the sole requirement when determining if something exists.

So, now it's time to look at another major contributor to the establishment of inimitable identity. And again, we'll be examining context, since isolation is not the only thing that context inflicts upon the Identity of each bit of physical existence. In fact, context is also what causes completely dissimilar things to suddenly become relatively similar. Yes, that sounds like I'm giving context a lot of credit, but relative context is the only thing that can cause such a transition to occur. Again, let's try an analogy and see how it works to illustrate how relative context brings isolated things together in tangential association.

Let's imagine that you work in a large customer service center, and you are one of fifty employees who have been isolated into five product support groups of ten employees for as long as you've worked for this company. This is due to the established organizational data routing structure and to the actual physical cubicle layout, with the result being that it is rare that any of you engages with anyone that works outside of your assignment group. Even the group work schedules are staggered over five 1/2 hour periods, to ensure a constant and somewhat extended coverage of customer service activity throughout the day. In essence, your associations — professional, and as a result, personal as well — within that specific society are constant, having been rigidly determined by the structure established for that society.

Now, let's imagine that you take a vacation, and you travel to Europe. While you're in Europe, you happen upon another employee of your firm, and although that person works in the same customer care center as you do, they do not belong to your specific product group. You recognize them, having seen them before, but within the strict environmental context of your job, this person does not share contextual association with you as a member of your ten person team.

But the two of you have just discovered each other in a bar in Hamburg, Germany, and regardless of what you do about it, this fact has immediately caused a major change in your relationship. The company's structure that prevented contextual association between you as employees, has now (by default ramification) established a new level of direct contextual association between you as employees of that same company in the US. In fact, this environmental shift has established a definitive in-kind contextual relationship that you did not share before this change. What you now share is relative context as two people with a similar contextual history, relative to the local environment. After all, this is a bar in Germany; not your work center in America.

This contextual bond will now survive while you continue to associate in this or any subsequent environment that pits you both as a relatively similar pair against this over-arching attribute (the fact that where you are is an equally foreign environment for both of you) that will be a dominant factor within each of these environments, relative to your established identities.

If any other contextual similar becomes part of the equation, (let's say, the cashier from your company cafeteria bumps into you both as you're walking together to another Hamburg bar) you will both adopt that similar, (whether conceptually or in fact) and this new association will exist for the duration that each of you shares the same level of relative contextual isolation within the environment you're presented with.

Of course, if that level of relative context changes (say, the cafeteria cashier hooks up with a local and becomes less of a *"relative foreigner"* as a result) then the relative association between the three of you will adjust accordingly. In fact, it's likely that the initial two of you will establish an even closer relative contextual bond, since now you both are also without local romance in Germany, unlike the lunch lady.

So, as you see, context works both ways; isolating and associating this and that. And in doing so, it creates the internal and relative attributes that combine to give whatever it is that exists its own unique Identity, ensuring that nothing can ever be completely replicated (and thereby replaced) by anything else. This is the basic essence of what constitutes physical existence, and it's accomplished through passive default ramification. But how is all of this internal and relative context [precedent that exists as a result of each instance of circumstance within the progressive development, and ongoing existence, of every single relationship that contributes to the Identity of a specific existential whole] precisely established and then managed in a stable and predictable manner? Especially if, as I just stated, it's all done passively and through default ramification? Well, the short answer is — information.

Building the Real

What I want to do, over the next few pages or so, is to introduce you to an amazing matrix of hierarchical control and stability that exists literally everywhere. It's a physical structure that, without the aid of a single conscious notion or directive, is directly responsible for all that has ever come into physical existence, all that's ever lost its tenuous hold on existence, and everything that's ever happened as a result of anything that's ever existed. This miraculous achievement is airtight, perfectly indifferent, and everything from natural law to the mathematics of Set Logic is based solely on its profound predictability. It's also dynamic and evolutionary, but only within the rigid confines provided by default ramification and historical precedent.

AutoGenesism: A Theory of Everything

This matrix is so rock-solid that even the most brilliantly effective legal systems and the most amazingly efficient production processes (while firmly based on its wondrous framework) are only dim shadows when presented in comparison. And yet, the average person fails to even notice its existence, and if pressed on the subject, most prefer to give credit for so much of its stunning success to any of a number of ringers (from an overworked deity to their own genius capacity for hyper-real delusional projection) with some folks becoming absolutely incensed at the idea that such brilliance could be the result of rote response to immediate incident.

So, what am I talking about? I'm talking about how context and Identity Survival come together within the theater of dynamic confluence, and Reality itself emerges as a result. This next bit of explanation may require some dedicated effort on your part, but I want you to trust that while I'm going to introduce the basics of this infrastructure here, we'll be working with it a lot going forward, and this means that you will become completely familiar with it as long as you don't get frustrated and give up on me at the first sign of complexity. This will be our first test of your patience with my capacity for complex elucidation, and I hope we get through it intact and pushing forward. I guess that all we can do is jump in and see what happens.

Managing Context via the Informational Continuum

In the two previous analogies, the one structure that featured unshakable consistency was the gathered arrangement of historical context. This history [the collection of specifics that isolated the violinist's C#, and the hierarchy of circumstances that ultimately brought you, your coworker, and the lunch lady together as contextual cohorts in Hamburg] exists as information; information that gathered over the course of days, months and years within what is known as an Informational Continuum.

The Informational Continuum [I'll refer to it here and there as the Residual IC] is all the residual information that's comes into existence as a direct result of things that have happened within a URC-Determined Environmental Confine, and it's just as simple as that. Whenever a quantum unit of change or activity happens, the fact that it happened is information [a residual Fact Set, actually] that instantly exists as a result of it happening. When the next quantum of change/event happens, the fact of it happening is added to the existing residual Fact Sets that represent what previously happened as yet another fact, with all of them gathered as an entangled mass of residual Fact Sets. Of course, the addition of each new residual Fact Set (to the collection of existing residual Fact Sets) changes the nature of the Information Continuum itself, even if only changing the amount of residual Fact Sets that comprise the Residual IC and nothing more. More often than not, however, emerging residual Fact Sets (each permanently entangled within any one of an uncountable number of residual Fact Set continuums) present significant changes to this informational relationship matrix that physically defines Reality as the macro-system that it is.

So let's make sure that you know what I'm asserting here. The Residual IC is not just an esoteric listing of what's factually happened. Residual information is not conceptual. It's one of two fundamental forms of physical existence (the other form being the Change/Event Unit). The residual Fact Sets and residual Fact Set continuums that make up the Informational Continuum do fully and physically exist. In fact, each residual Fact Set can only come into existence as a result of a Change/Event Unit that brought it into existence. This means that each Change/Event Unit that occurs (and has ever occurred) is fully and permanently represented by its very own residual Fact Set as if it (the Change/Event Unit itself) were still physically present.

Now, the same holds true for each and every Change/Event Trajectory that plays out, with each leaving behind a representative residual Fact Set continuum that fully and permanently maintains the impact ramification that the Change/Event Trajectory's occurrence inflicted upon Reality. Of course, that actual Change/Event Trajectory ceased to physically exist as soon as its string of entangled quanta came to an end, but the enduring impact of that Change/Event Trajectory's occurrence does persist due to the residual Fact Sets that make up the residual Fact Set continuum that will always exist as a direct/default ramification of that once existent trajectory.

And if that residual Fact Set continuum represents a specific contextual relationship development that emerged within Reality (as well as within any affected lesser system that contributes to the identified whole that is Reality) as a direct or indirect result of that Change/Event Trajectory's occurrence (including any change it may have inflicted on either another concurrent Change/Event Trajectory or on the overall contextual Identity of any defined system) then that residual Fact Set continuum must enforce that exact contextual relationship development. Then, when another Change/Event Trajectory's occurrence inflicts a change that directly or indirectly affects that very specific contextual relationship development (one way or another), yet another relationship adjustment (as

AutoGenesism: A Theory of Everything

dictated by the new residual Fact Set continuum brought into existence by that new Change/Event Trajectory's occurrence) will emerge to permanently exist, adding yet another strand to the intricate web of contextual relationships that we refer to as physical Reality.

This all may seem horribly rigid, but it's this very simple action-reaction protocol that creates the logical and actual structure that is historical precedent. Reality could not exist if not for residual information and its default response to the instance of change and/or activity.

As far as how precedent does what it does on behalf of Reality, this system of residual Fact Set representative ramification works as it does because (as far as Reality is concerned) there is no difference between the Change/Event Trajectory's impact and that of the residual Fact Set continuum that represents that trajectory's impact. And, because information is the only permanent form of physical existence, all ongoing contextual relationships that define any physical system actually exist only between the residual Fact Sets and residual Fact Set continuums that were left behind to represent those Change/Event Trajectories, regardless of the truth that these information sets only exist to represent those ramifications and influences that came into existence as a result of those actual changes that were inflicted upon those systems.

Of course, how all of these residual Fact Sets blend to create a precedent-based system of contextual influence (and those emerging suites of lesser system precedence) gets a lot more complicated than this, since such system development is the result of Reality's own pursuit of Identity Survival as it leverages the fact that information has no half-life rate of physical decay. Yes, as I've been relentlessly hinting here, all information is physically eternal; once it has emerged, of course.

Note — Concerning the word *Eternal* — The dictionary on my desk (The New International Webster's Family Dictionary of the English Language — 1999 Trident Press International) offers a range of definitions for the term eternal. For this specific examination, and throughout this entire book, I will only be using #4 from Webster's list of acceptable definitions, which reads exactly as follows:

Independent of time or its conditions; unchangeable; immutable.

No other definition of eternal is operative in connection with this premise, nor will any other definition of the word eternal be allowed in connection with this premise.

So, with all this eternal information representing so much emerging Reality-defining contextual ramification, you might think that after a while the webbing created by this permanent linkage between the things that are maintaining physical existence would begin to get pretty dense and complicated. And if you thought so, you'd be right. It does get dense, and it affects everything that happens after a while, with change and activity becoming more and more organized, and much of it becoming repetitive; especially if it's become obvious that something's working out pretty well. Activities that don't work out so well tend to decrease in frequency, and evolutionary biologists refer to this general phenomena as natural selection.

For now, we'll simply acknowledge this proven aspect of progressive development, and (since this is only Section I) attribute it to the ongoing influence of internal and relative context (with a matrix of information sets, factually and permanently representing contextual relationship adjustments between the actual macro-system changes that occurred and affected the existence of unique and identifiable things) and how this system promotes successful ID Survival efforts (manifesting as increasingly complex — and thereby increasingly survivable — holon material structures) in default service of Reality's need to increase its own complexity as an inimitable relationship matrix (which is how it pursues its own Identity Survival). After all, as I will continue to clarify, once any change/event has occurred, all that is left is the information set that represents that occurrence, and this is added to what's physically real; that which is left behind to persist and become increasingly detailed, as this constantly developing contextual balance also persists.

By the way, did you notice how I established that the residual information of the Informational Continuum impacts and manages Reality by permanently representing the full ramifications of internal and relative context on its own pursuit of Identity Survival? Just in case you missed it, that's what I did over the last flurry of paragraphs, after making a big deal about how context works in general. And it does this by just being what residual information is — existential packing peanuts that keep things from shifting around. This is going to become extremely important later, so keep this in mind, even if all you remember is that information manages everything by never allowing Reality (as a progressively developing relationship matrix) to *forget* what's happened as a result of contextual ramification and the new contextual relationships that have emerged and developed as a result. If you remember just that, you'll be all set.

AutoGenesism: A Theory of Everything

Note — For a more extensive examination of how this works, Section III includes a digression concerning this very issue, titled *Contextual Precedent and the Mechanics of Progressive Development*. I figured it best to isolate the larger digressions and speculations and prevent the reader from becoming bogged down from overview to overview.

Reality — The Contextual Environment

Note — To make things easier, from here on, I'm going to refer to the information sets that represent contextual specifics and/or contextual relationships as being — in fact — those contextual specifics and/or contextual relationships. I'm also going to state that the specific term *Informational Continuum* (as opposed to any other term that also contains the word *continuum*) refers only to the universal factual representation of all change and activity that's taken place within one URC-Determined Environmental Confine. Let's just see how well this works as a means of preventing this entire effort from collapsing under the weight of its own capacity for digressional complexity.

So, we've covered the fact that information sets come into existence as a result of events and changes that have occurred, and that this causes contextual relationships (between information sets that represent the ramifications of those events and changes having occurred) to emerge and develop over time (what with representative information sets persisting indefinitely), creating a phenomenon that physicists commonly refer to as *entanglement* when they encounter it within their research efforts. We're now at the point where it needs to be established how all of this emergence and contextual entanglement comes together to form a unified physical whole.

Of course, it's the most primitive and pervasive common attribute that unifies that which is at all associable into the most permanent contextual entanglements. For information sets, the most enduring bond is common or contextually associated authorship; i.e., shared historical context [provenance]. But, when dealing with the intricate blend of information sets and the wide range of ongoing material structural developments [countless Change/Event Trajectories] that populate a universal Reality confine, the unifying sub-structural commonality ends up being a lot more primitive. Actually, we've already examined what establishes that relationship for even the most complex arrangement of disparate collectives. Still, this is a good place to reiterate what it is that unites the largest relationship matrices that can possibly exist, even if only to place what we've already determined within a fresh context.

111

The term I will use for these most comprehensive relationships is *environment*, and environments exist as a result of the most primal and inclusive level of similarity that is, in the end, shared between even the most seemingly dissimilar forms of physical existence. Another term *sub-environment* will refer to any otherwise sub-structurally defined environment that has been brought into existence within the contextual confines of a preexisting environment, even if that preexisting environment is also, itself, a sub-environment.

The term that is commonly used to describe the relationship matrix that is established by the most primal and inclusive sub-structural contextual commonality is *Reality*, but as I work to detail the nature of contextual relationship matrices we won't be using that term because it's got a lot of cultural baggage associated with it. And, that baggage could cause some people difficulty if I haven't taken care to properly qualify that term every time I use it. So, I'll stay away from it for now unless specifically applied and fully qualified. Such as the term *Reality Confine*, which seems to qualify its application sufficiently; suggesting established parameters that have been imposed within an otherwise more comprehensive relationship matrix, short of creating a true sub-environment.

Besides, *environment* is a term more descriptively suited to those contextually determined relationship holons that can be relative to one another, even existing as wholly identifiable within a larger relationship confine (as sub-environments, of course). These confines can also be temporary, so we'll stay with *environment* as our primary term for contextually entangled relationship matrices. No sense in making any of this harder than it has to be.

I guess a good way to illustrate this concept of a sub-structural contextual commonality and how it unites things to establish an environment, is to consider a group of sealed containers within a room. Within each container there is a specific arrangement of parameters that are unique to that container, and this makes each container different from any other container in the room. You could claim that each container is its own environment, and in a sense, you'd be right.

However, you'd only be right in the sense that those specific properties do give each individual container a relatively unique Identity when compared to the others. You'd still have to acknowledge that all of these containers share at least one sub-structural physical and/or contextual commonality, and all it takes to place everything within one environment is for one such commonality to unite the entire arrangement at its most pervasive level. One property that comes to mind is that it's likely the same instant of *Now* within each container as it is in the room that contains them all; placing all the containers in the room within the same contextual environment, regardless of how unique one container's interior is relative to any other container's interior.

The differences between the interiors of the containers [shape, size, relative humidity, air pressure, or whatever it is that could be adjusted to make one interior unique from all others] would never be enough to override the fact that it's (for ease of reference) 2:05 PM no matter which container you're within, or if you're outside all of the containers.

> ***Note*** — Yes, some of these examples, illustrations, and analogies might seem unnecessarily obvious, but you'll find that we'll be establishing a lot of obvious things as this theory is built. And there's a serious reason for that. Many people have made strident claims about the true nature of Reality and humanity, and some have even declared that there's a god (and what that god looks like and what it demands from us), and yet very few have bothered to establish the validity of their claims beyond referencing one ancient papyrus or another, or tossing out a bewildering arrangements of numbers and symbols. When detailing Reality, the small things matter, since all that exists rests solidly upon those small things. This being the case, I will also be building upon those small things as we move forward and they'll each need to be solidly presented. That sort of attention to detail takes time and effort.

Concerning this effort to detail the nature of the contextual environment, it is important to make the case that since it is the same instant of *Now* within each container as it is outside all containers — as well as in all locations within the room, regardless of how well you isolate each unit — this time-determined and time-sealed contextual environment will always embrace all the containers, as well as whatever is physically isolated within each sealed unit. The contextual entanglement that is imposed by this shared instant of *Now* (because it is so pervasive) establishes the physical union of everything in that room, and locks it all within the same environment.

This union also requires that all representative Fact Sets and Fact Set continuums that emerge as a result of whatever occurs to alter or define the contents of the containers, the containers themselves, or the room itself as a whole, will become a thread within the Informational Continuum that represents and defines what we've already termed the **URC-Determined Environmental Confine** that contains everything that's the result of the quantized Unit Rate of Change — including the whole of that room.

Yes, we have just reiterated that the quantized unit progression of change (that quantum of *Now*) is the sub-structural contextual commonality that establishes and enforces the nature and Identity of the Contextual Environment (or Reality, if you prefer).

Note — Two really important takeaways here:

- You're going to be reminded again and again that in-sync change progression is the primordial establisher of Contextual Environments, and in a bit you're going to discover why this is the case. That said, I need you to always keep in mind what take-away #2 here has to offer as a qualifying caveat concerning this most pervasive environmental determinant.
- All things (be they incidental or permanent) that share environmental origin, also share permanent informational representation within the same Informational Continuum. This means that regardless of all other factors, no residual Fact Set continuum can ever become separated from the originating continuum "trunk" that established the historical precedent responsible for its eventual existence. Keep this very specific fact in the front of your mind as we progress with this examination, because eventually we'll be looking at developments where the environmental origin of an Informational Continuum will rigidly determine how it reacts to those developments. It'll be good if you begin preparing your understanding of how historical context affects permanent existence.

As to the physical parameters of our own universe [*universe* being yet another synonym for *URC-Determined Environmental Confine*], laying out Einstein's measuring rods isn't going to give us our answer, regardless of how many such rods we use. You see, unlike the common wisdom concerning our expanding (or not expanding) universe, the truth is that the difference between our universe and what either does or doesn't lie beyond it isn't dimensional or spacetime specific or even materially quantifiable. The difference between here (universally speaking) and not here is simple change progression quantization, or Unit Rate of Change. If a Change/Event Trajectory or Fact Set continuum is based on our universal URC, then it physically exists relative to everything else that exists within our universe. If not, then it just doesn't.

This means that there isn't a membrane or location or physical proximity that isolates one environment (like our own universe) from another such environment. It is only the Unit Rate of Change [the duration of the quantum of *Now*], Reality's most primordial contextual attribute, that creates this kind of

AutoGenesism: A Theory of Everything

universal environmental confine. This is why I invented the term *URC-Determined Environmental Confine* for use when being technically descriptive. Our universe isn't expanding into anything, even if it is expanding. As the totality of all Change/Event Trajectories and Change/Event Trajectory matrices, and all the Fact Set continuums that comprise the Informational Continuum, its expansion is inevitable and ongoing.

The truth is that as each Change/Event Trajectory brings a new Fact Set continuum into permanent physical existence, some of these emerging Fact Set continuums represent three dimensional spatial displacement events that did, in fact, occur. And it's also true that some of these three dimensional spatial displacement events featured enormous material systems (think planets, stars and entire galaxies) that inflicted enormous relative spatial displacements. What's important to fully appreciate is that the Identity of the URC-Determined Environmental Confine (and by extension, what it takes for it to pursue its own Identity Survival) is necessarily defined by all relative information sets, including the requirement that the physical nature of these spatial displacement event trajectories are all fully and permanently represented by physically existent Fact Set continuums.

So, while you can look further into this surprising perspective on the true nature of open space in Section III's speculation *"Dark Matter: How the Change/Spatial Trajectory Serves the URC-Determined Macro-System"* I did want to introduce the inescapable inference (permanent physical Fact Set continuums that fully and accurately represent all volume displacement occurrences exactly as they each existed from quantum instant to quantum instant, and the fact that information sets — not being physically interactive with material photons — must be inherently imperceptible to material observation) that this entire perspective presents as one ponders the true physical nature of open space.

After all, if Reality itself is to exist, it must *stand out* with its own inimitable Identity. That Identity must be established and preserved as relentlessly inimitable, ensuring its resistance to duplication. And this is what the Informational Continuum does, as countless material Change/Event Trajectories entangle into holon structural matrices (each bringing unimaginable flurries of contextually dense information sets into permanent existence) in service of Reality's own pursuit of Identity Survival by way of contextual complexity increases that grind on endlessly at blinding speeds.

And in service to this blistering ID Survival pursuit, it's the Informational Continuum that not only establishes and enforces the Identity parameters of the Contextual Environment as a whole, it also preserves precedent, all system precedence, continuity, association specifics, and everything that has to do with the progressive emergence of organization and default material and informational structure within the whole of that environment.

As the permanent record of all that's ever won, lost, survived and ceased to exist, the Informational Continuum provides the URC-Determined Environmental Confine with an evolving survival super structure that consists of an entire labyrinth of open avenues of development potential (each based on what has already proven to be successful) that (combined with the only existential imperative that exists; Survival) transforms raw activity into effective and efficient progressive development. Maybe a good way to imagine this in action is to picture Reality's pursuit of Identity Survival (as an allegorical characterization) reaching back through openings in a wall to pull all ongoing progressive development (as if fastened to a rope) forward toward those openings.

Concerning Creators and Gods and Such

Many theists point to organizational structure (this extremely fundamental response to the universal demand of Identity Survival) as being evidence of a divine (or even simply intelligent) creator, but the truth is that between the Residual IC, as a full and permanent representation of all that's ever occurred within a URC-Determined Environmental Confine, and the relentless drive of all that occurs to simply occur yet again from quantum instant to quantum instant (and in that sense, continue to survive and — as a direct result — serve Reality's own Identity Survival pursuit), no intelligent involvement is require to bring what has become an incredibly dense and sophisticated physical structure into existence.

The truth is that no intelligent actor/initiator would be capable of competing with the absolute fury of this extremely simple and completely natural confluence, even if such an entity could avoid being swept along with the dynamic flow of historical and emerging relationships as a result of also being physically existent (and therefore integral to that seething contextual confluence). After all, such an entity (if one were to exist) would have to be physically associable with the entire environment in order to have any capacity to affect it. Yet Reality itself is logically defined as the full and integral relationship between everything that exists as physically associable. You can go ahead and run that conundrum down whichever rabbit hole you choose, but I'm confident that regardless of how you massage the specifics, the logical failure of the existence of an intelligent creator will eventually become obvious.

To some, the very existence of default progressive development (a universal survival imperative combined with a ramification structure that's based on simple success/failure precedent and evolving system survival preferences) may seem like a notion that's built on pure conjecture, but the evidence for its existence is all around us. Evolutionary biology is only one evidential indicator of this *natural selection* process. Beyond the obvious biological system development examples, we constantly deal with the fact that even the most fleeting physical confluences are capable of spontaneously launching completely original emergent systems if such systems have been previously brought into existence as a result of similar confluences (proving the existence of even the most fleeting of system precedent *memory*). It's widely accepted that storms, and even naturally occurring environmental anomalies (like tornados), spontaneously organize without any help from divine or intelligent sources.

And yet, it's these very same basic factors that set up the natural laws and logical defaults that have literally everyone passing responsibility off to either gods, primordial conscious singularities, or asterisks. But it's a very simple and scalable system of default establishment of environmental order, and without it, the most basic level of progressive development would have been impossible to even initiate.

The Emergent System

This brings us to one of the most fascinating bits of Reality that I've run into during the years I've spent qualifying and verifying the specific of this unique Theory of Everything; the Emergent System. The reason I bring this up here is because the same dynamics of contextual confluence that define environments also create emergent systems all the time, and you'd be hard-pressed to locate a human being on this planet who hasn't encountered or even been integral to one of these mysterious manifestations at one time in their life.

Instead of trying to limp my way through a dry technical physics definition of the emergent system, I think that I can make this a lot easier on us if I simply give you an example that you can probably recognize and immediately relate to. This one's a good example, even if the truth is that this is only one type of emergent system. At least it'll get us started on the topic in a manner that's general enough and obvious enough to keep everyone together and moving forward. That said, it'll eventually become clear enough that not all emergent systems are created equal.

The most dramatic emergent system common to the continental United States is the tornado. What makes it an emergent system is that when examined relative to its contributing component systems, a tornado is completely unlike any of them, or even a sum of them as a unified collective. A tornado is more than a low barometric pressure, a warm air current, a clashing cold air current, a wall cloud tossed in to provide a visual ceiling for the funnel, or even a gathering of all of these in most cases. That said, once a tornado has formed, it exists as a unique and transcendent emergence with a defined *personality* that is immediately recognizable.

What's also true about a tornado (unlike many emergent systems) is that it is entirely dependent on the total confluence that brought it into existence; making it a particularly good example as we examine the unique nature of emergent systems in general. What this means is that if any single contributing factor is eliminated, or even altered in a way that changes what constitutes the necessary relationship balance that exists between all constituents, a tornado will immediately lose its structural organization. This instantaneous structural collapse often happens throughout the emergent life of tornados, causing them to seem to *hop* over structures located along the path of destruction they leave behind. The truth is that tornados don't hop. What happens is that they suddenly lose strength, and even fall apart, only to instantly emerge yet again with violent power; all as a result of the ongoing relationship between contributing factors adjusting as each factor's influence shifts in relative balance.

The warm air might persist, the storm cloud may endure, a strong updraft might continue to drag water droplets up and transform them into hail stones, but the tornado will be gone forever once the required confluence [the necessary relationship between all of the contributing factors relative to one another] has ceased to exist. This suggests that the relationship structure itself is as much a principal component as any of the physical factors within that relationship structure, and this is critical to understand about emergent systems. Not every confluence of necessary factors will result in an emergent system. The proper relationship structure must also be present.

Then there are those emergent systems that unexpectedly spring from material-environmental confluences that — as purely material factors — are otherwise incapable of such emergences, regardless of the relationship structure. In these cases, the sudden introduction of one or more non-material constituents can suddenly replace what was initially a reducible collective with an overwhelmingly obvious emergent system. Again, to make this easier to explain, I'll use an example instead of slogging through a technical description of what I mean by this.

A crowd of people can be reduced [factor by factor] until the crowd becomes less than the number of people that can reasonably be considered a crowd; say four people, constituting several as opposed to a crowd. However, if you introduce a noumenal factor as profoundly integral to the entire collective [fear, outrage, fervor] what was a crowd can become a very different entity altogether.

With this non-material factor added, in a specific contextual balance and blend, to what was an already established relationship structure, what you'll have is an emergent system that we refer to as a mob; a crowd, possessing its own unique and inimitable personality, longevity, and strength of cohesion, that cannot be reduced without being completely destroyed as the system that it has become. In fact, the mob is probably the best known example of an emergent system that is primarily dependent on the proper relationship balance of material and non-material factors due to its impact on the fates and fortunes of so many throughout the history of humankind.

Once the relationship between the noumenal factor [fear, outrage, patriotic/religious fervor] and the rest of the confluence has been significantly altered, the mob immediately disappears and a crowd takes its place. And, this happens without the elimination or alteration of any other material factor; people, location, or any other aspect of the given environment. The mysterious impact of relationship dynamics on spontaneous emergence can be just that obvious and readily examined. However, it can also be much more subtle, as in the case of the tornado, where they're believed to hop over one house only to completely shred the property just across the street, as if directed by the invisible hand of faith.

It's also important to note that the most significant emergent systems go on to persist once they've emerged, with their instant of physical genesis launching their own relentless pursuit of Identity Survival as novel systems in their own right. Biological life is easily the most conspicuous example of this form of emergent system, even if some believe that life will be successfully reduced to its component parts someday.

As we get further into this examination of Reality, you'll be seeing a lot more examples of how the emergent system fits into the overall nature of progressive development and into the ongoing battle for raw survival that defines what it means to physically exist. In each case, we'll note the contributing factors and examine the plausibility of the relationship between the contributive confluence and the system that has emerged, in the same general manner that researchers approached the emergent natures of the two examples we looked at above.

For a fuller understanding of the ongoing debate over emergence and the many complexities [philosophical and as a result of other means of examination] that persist within that debate, **http://en.wikipedia.org/wiki/Emergence** offers a point of entry. Yes, it's Wikipedia, but the specific references are accurate, and from there you can run down most of the larger notions that have surfaced and survived over the years.

For the purposes of specificity and increased clarity, the perspective that I'll be using within this examination is *strong emergence*, which features an *"emergent property that is irreducible to its individual constituents"* (quoted from the above linked Wiki page).

It is emergence that provides the magic that obviously exists within the cause-effect drudgery of simple progressive development, and until you get a handle on the validity and wide variety of those emergence systems that populate your own life from day to day, their impact on what it means to be human and aware will continue to seem like God reaching down from on high with purpose and power; leaving you helpless to whomever or whatever it might be that offers the least implausible explanation for why things are what they are and do what they do.

Just be aware that existential staples like the sub-environment, the spatial trajectory, and even life itself, are the kinds of novel systems that will prove to be examples of emergence, with each of them critical to the successful survival of physical Reality; itself, an emergent system.

The Real You That You Are

Note — I need you to keep in mind that Section I is limited to the introduction of widely accepted existential basics (like the quantization of physical Reality) and the major points of departure that Auto-G takes relative to every other philosophical or scientific approach to the subject

AutoGenesism: A Theory of Everything

of Reality (departures like defining material structure as entangled densities of activity quanta, information existing as one of two basic forms of physical existence, the existence of system precedence, and the pursuit of Identity Survival as the lone primordial imperative). In Section II and Section III, I will address the larger question of how all of these staples work together to present what we've all become familiar with and grown to depend on as reliably real. And yes, this will include how the human being fits in and how it departs from all that's preceded it within every URC-Determined Environmental Confine that this unique manifestation calls home. That said, we've still got a few accepted fundamentals and major departures to get through before that, especially concerning the nature of the human being. Again, be advised that these notions are only being introduced in this section. Sections II and III will serve to more fully flesh these notions out.

So, we've gone over the concept of Identity, context, and how context establishes and provides Identity to and within the URC-Determined Environmental Confine. We've touched on Identity Survival, and how it is Reality's lone primordial requirement [all that exists either seeks to remain existent or is used by that which pursues existence], defining what it means to exist. We've just touched on the hierarchical structure's quantum class of holons — the emergent system — and how a precisely balanced contextual confluence of otherwise disassociated factors can create these completely novel and irreducible existential wholes. In fact, keep that emergent system subsection handy, since referring back to it might help as we now move ahead to quickly touch on how the human being emerges as a result of the amazing emergence confluence created by system precedent, system Identity Survival, and the miraculous material survival system that we all know as the human brain.

Yes, I do realize that I'm not the first to suggest that the human mind is an emergent system, and as we get into this, I'll certainly alert you to some highly regarded researchers who labor in this very promising field of study. But, let's get the headline out of the way before we dive into the specifics.

A HUMAN BEING IS CREATED BY EACH HOMO SAPIENS BRAIN

Kevin Brian Carroll

This will be the first issue to address; this false notion that the human being is a material manifestation. I suppose I will end up beating this issue to death, but it is probably the most insidious fallacy of all. Unless I can help you to allow your corporeal body to take its rightful place within your own development process, I'll never be able to teach you the truth of what you actually are. I will also be reiterating that this corporeal life (the one that you're living) is actually a 2nd phase of developmental gestation, since this fact will also be crucial for you to understand and internalize if you're ever going to get to the truth about the nature of human existence. First, a quick overview of what you are as an emerging human being.

When you think, respond, react, initiate, emote or express, your material brain actually configures and releases information sets, and just like the residual information sets we've been examining, they share physical existence with everything else that exists. Like the music that is generated by the vibrations of the violin strings as the violinist draws the bow, your thoughts have physical substance. You can call it energy if you like. It's not energy. It's information. But, like released energy potential, it is imperceptible to material observation; only observable via the effect it has on the Material Realm. Of course, there will always be those who reject anything they can't examine, manipulate, or replicate within their chosen theaters of observation, but even they have to admit that as they embrace or dismiss whatever it is that they confront, they are producing thoughts as they do so. And, those thoughts do exist.

Digression Alert — Yes, this does sound like philosophy but, let's face it; the notion that information physically exists isn't a philosophical stretch. In fact, you'd have to be unreasonably strict in your interpretation of the word *exist* to deny that information exists. And, after all we've learned in the last 300 years about the constantly expanding definition of physical existence [think nuclear radiation, gravity, electromagnetism, laws of physics, and other invisible physical forces] by what authority could you ever deny the physical existence of information?

And what constitutes a full description of physical existence anyway? Certainly the definition of physical cannot be restricted to that which is material. The fact that every emergent system that exists possess its own unique trigger (from the *spark of life* to the obvious and often deadly difference between a crowd and a mob) that cannot be materially identified or reproduced should be evidence enough of the intellectual irresponsibility inherent within those strident calls to produce the particles [or *waves*] responsible for Reality's most common, yet immaterial manifestations.

Most emergent properties cannot be explained by examining the system's list of contributing factors, and this is powerful evidence that an observation can only reveal to us what is materially observable. An observation [alone, and without our own capacity to immediately arrive at its proper interpretation] cannot reveal to us what that observation actually suggests relative to Reality as a whole. A data set can only provide what it can provide.

Observation is an important step toward getting to the truth, but the Scientific Method [data collection, analysis, and even experimentation] is only one part of the investigative process. Sadly, what's become of the Scientific Method (see *"The Preface"* for a pretty stark example) has been elevated to the extent that modern scientism is a dog that's chasing a car being driven by whatever happens to be the moment's most widely-embraced conjecture, and if scientism has proven anything, it's that it won't know what to do with that car if it ever actually catches it.

Throughout human history, we've struggled with the fact that we live in a world that obviously extends well beyond our five senses; inventing gods, demons and impossibly fortunate serendipities, depending on the philosophy being promoted. I love to toss out the line *"400 years ago viruses and bacteria were spiritual"* whenever I'm challenged on this notion that there is more before us, behind us, and within us than meets the eye. Yes, it's a clever riff, but it's also a very important truth to keep at hand at all times when examining the world and how we relate to it.

The best aspect of the Scientific Method is that it acknowledges that the nature of physical existence is an ever evolving revelation, and as we move along here, we'll be giving that acknowledgement a solid workout. But for now, I'm simply going to declare that at this moment, you are the indivisible, contextually entangled mass of information sets that your brain has produced to this point over what has, so far, been the course of your life. And that is the whole of what you are.

You aren't that material structure of flesh and bone any more than a violin and its strings are the music that is created through their use. The circumstances in your life that shaped you and inspired your reaction to their impact, are like the hands of that violinist in my previous analogy and the physical effort he contributed to creating that music note through the physical tone generating structure of the violin itself. And the ever evolving impact of every bit of residual information that still exists within this environment (giving your thoughts the historical context they each require to form as the unique creations that they are) is like each note and rest, written by the composer of that music piece, guiding the efforts of the violinist within a defined parameter, and providing him the platform from which to create the music that lifted the hearts and minds of those in the concert hall.

And you? The real you? You are like that music, that first C#, then that second pure, clean note in the piece, and the three-hundred and twenty-first note; all those notes gathered as that unique and inimitable performance, with your own clarity, power and singular identity. You are an eternal creative expression that came into physical existence as a result of a very specific and inimitable confluence of many contributions that can never be duplicated. Please take a moment to consider this one critical fact of who and what you are. This will be the basis of everything that you'll learn about yourself as we go forward.

The Isolated You

I suggested in the last subsection that in response to every instant of ongoing material survival your brain's unique organizational structure actually creates information sets that can be likened to a form of dynamic energy. The reason I likened what is actually a form of information to energy is because (like energy) each quantum unit physically emerges as the result of a confluence that includes the presence of a specific requirement for its emergence [similar, in its own way, to what an energy potential field provides], and in that (like energy) this information also *releases* in quantum bursts to inflict a dynamic impact upon the environment that contains it.

Obviously, this is not the same kind of information that emerges as a default factual representation of each change/event within a URC-Determined Environmental Confine. This isn't residual information. The physical nature of this information is very different due to how and why it is created.

In fact, the creation of this specific form of information can cause a suite of entangled residual Fact Set continuums to emerge to represent its *generation* by the brain. This is because, while that generation is a simple change/event in its own right, the generated information set itself is inherently dynamic. Its generation sets it into active existence. That means that its generation is actually the first Change/Event Unit in what can end up being an enormously significant

AutoGenesism: A Theory of Everything

Change/Event Trajectory that will include that information set's ongoing dynamic impact upon the larger environment that contains the brain that *launched* it.

This is especially true at the highest levels of Material Realm developmental sophistication [Homo Sapiens is a good example], because while each generation change/event creates only a precisely configured burst of information that is designed to actively assist the corporeal body of the organism possessing this brain in responding to a survival requirement, the Homo Sapiens survival system [our human brain] has the potential to actively and dynamically address survival requirements that have proven — again and again — to feature wide-ranging implications that guarantee enormous and seemingly endless ramifications.

Yes, the human brain has achieved the capacity to generate information sets that possess dynamic and progressive time-line awareness, providing the corporeal human a powerful leg-up within the battle for raw material structure survival [abstraction, planning, and an incredibly high-speed capacity for on-the-fly response adjustment], but as you'll learn, the human brain's ultimate impact on the whole of physical Reality extends far beyond the simple survivability of any one corporeal species. And each Change/Event Trajectory that is launched (or is even just an incidental result of a specifically launched trajectory's impact as it continues on elsewhere) carries on in pursuit of Identity Survival until it no longer exists as a chain of events, leaving behind a residual Fact Set continuum that fully represents every quantum of *Now* that it spanned during its existence as a unique entanglement of change/event quanta. Yes, Reality actually is that relentlessly extensive.

The reason I likened what your own brain produces to dynamic energy in that opening sentence is to also make sure you understand that even though it is information, what your brain generates has an actual physical presence and substance. To you, it may seem like thoughts are fleeting and formless, but in Reality, they are more concrete than anything you can see, touch, smell, taste, or hear. All information, even the simplest residual Fact Set, has physical presence, and as such, it affects all that exists around it; albeit, residual Fact Sets affect Reality passively and collectively.

Also, as I just did yet again, I'll be referring to the brain as *generating* or *launching* these information sets, even though the true process is less like a generation than a natural physical emergence process that can be observed with the help of modern brain scanning and fMRI equipment in the same way that a tornado's vortex emergence can be examined with the use of video technology and high-end Doppler radar systems.

In this Section I, I'll be using a variety of descriptive terms to reinforce the fact that this form of information is actively authored by a material brain, that it's not a default ramification [as is the case with residual information sets], and that, as a result of not being environmentally produced, these sets gather in a profoundly entangled mass that is rigidly associated with the material brain that brought them into existence. For now, that's more important than emphasizing the subtle difference between the term *generation* and what the brain actually engages in.

Also, in this Section I, we will be primarily referring to the dynamic information sets that are generated by the human brain [be it the brain of Earth's Homo Sapiens hominid or otherwise], even though all material/corporeal brains generate dynamic information. This is to keep the digressions in this section to a minimum, as I try to keep the focus as much on you as I can. The information sets that are generated by the human brain are unique (possessing very specific emergent properties that nonhuman brains do not possess) and in Section II, I will detail those properties that makes this form of dynamic information special, so don't distress over the cursory treatment I've decided to give this topic at this stage of our examination. Believe me, you'll have plenty to feast on long before we've finished with what the material brain has loosed upon Reality.

We'll call the dynamic information that's generated by corporeal human brains *Intellect*, and that's because while all higher functioning brains produce dynamic awareness [sentience], the human brain produces dynamic awareness that is profoundly unique. Sentience is sensory awareness and the sense of presence. Intellect involves sapience; the ability to conceptualize, engage in abstraction, and to employ inference to the degree that wisdom is possible. Yes, the human brain also produces sentience and instinctive survival responses. Still, the capacity for the inclusion of sapience within that ongoing wash of survival response makes the human brain's Intellect output unique.

Each developing Intellect mass possesses a definite [and also developing] Identity that is integral to, and affected by, each and every dynamic **Burst Set** [the quantum unit of one brain's dynamic information response to the survival requirement] generated by one and only one material brain. Each Intellect mass is physically and contextually isolated, meaning that it *presents* to the

AutoGenesism: A Theory of Everything

URC-Determined Environmental Confine as an indivisible solid throughout its entire existence.

As each brain continues to produce additional **Intellect Burst Sets (IBS)**, its gathering Intellect mass actually works on developing its own unique and inimitable Identity through an ongoing process that involves that entangled IBS mass purposely affecting how the brain itself operates as the survival system that it is [remember, this is dynamic information that is still dynamic, even after it's accomplished what the brain originally generated it to accomplish]. We call this process the development of personality, and every human brain's growing and developing Intellect mass is engaged in defining and refining its own unique and inimitable personality [its Identity - more on this shortly]. Like I said, most of this is stuff that you already know about.

This interaction between the human brain and the gathering Intellect mass that it is generating may seem unique, but as you'll learn in Section II, it's just a modified version of the same symbiotic relationship that the change/event and residual information have always had. In fact, the only reason that our atoms and cells and the bits and parts of our bodies behave in the way that they do is because of the effect that information (in the form of DNA) has on these bits and parts.

Information's partnership with physical activity is the reason why structure exists and why it maintains such rigid consistency. So, when you think of information (even the simplest of Fact Sets) remember that it has physical presence, and that it affects how things behave. It's like the wind, and how even if we can't see it, it's there and making a difference.

So, let's take a quick nontechnical look at the Intellect Burst Set for a moment. First off, it must be stated that each IBS is generated, and exists, in relative sync with the Unit Rate of Change (URC) of the URC-Determined Environmental Confine (remember, I am actually referring to what is commonly called Reality or the universe). That IBS generation rate is definitely slower (much slower in most cases) but it's in sync with the URC, and that's important to understand. In fact, here's a diagram from an earlier sub-section — *"Extra Dimensions and Stuff"* — that illustrates this pretty effectively:

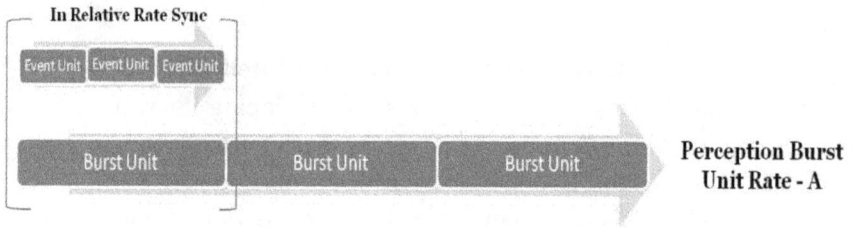

In Relative Rate Sync

Event Unit | Event Unit | Event Unit

Burst Unit | Burst Unit | Burst Unit

**Perception Burst
Unit Rate - A**

URC and Change Progression Perception Synchronization
Define a Permanent Physical Environment

Figure 1-F

What's also important to understand is that regardless of the true duration of *Now* [the environmental URC] each brain's experience of *Now* is the generation and launch of one Intellect Burst Set. Still, a full conscious thought or even the most fleeting experience can be comprised of a very hard to determine quantity of these burst sets that were generated as a definitive segment of what we'll be referring to as an **Intellect Burst Set Trajectory (IBST)** — which is literally the entire Intellect mass that a single human brain will ever produce during its life span. Okay, with that settled, let's look at the internal contextual structure of a defined IBS segment that's been generated by your own brain.

Being the Isolated You

When you think of human generated thoughts and emotions, you have to look at them as a physically dense form of information. Remember the analogy of the violinist? Remember how complicated the C# note actually was when we took the time to examine everything that was included within the identity of that one single note as it was played on that one specific evening? Well, when you think of a single thought or emotion springing from your mind, try to imagine everything that exists as contextually included within that thought as it comes into physical existence.

Here's a short and very incomplete breakdown of the internal and relative contextual Identity structure that defines that one thought, and allows it to *stand out* apart from any and all other thoughts:

- The complete set structure [circumstance, impetus, relevance, specific details] of the actual thought itself

AutoGenesism: A Theory of Everything

- The historical fact that your brain generated a thought
- The historical fact that your brain generated that specific thought
- The precise moment within your life that the thought was generated
- The precise moment within the entire progression of time [from the very first instant of *Now*] that the thought was generated
- The relative position of all the material elements within your body at the exact instant the thought was initiated
- All relative positions of all the material elements within your body during the entire span of each contributing IBS generation process
- The full contextual Identity presented by the entire material structure of the brain and body at that instant of each contributing IBS generation.
- The precise hierarchical relationship between all material elements and sub-structures within your body at the exact instant the thought [a string of contributing IBS events] as a defined whole was generated
- The relative context between all prior generated thoughts, emotions and reaction, within the whole of all gathered information [the IBST] generated by your brain at that exact moment that the generation as a defined process whole was initiated
- The precise contextual relationship between this thought and all other defined information sets that had already been generated by your brain at the exact moment that the generation, as a defined whole, was completed
- The contextual nature of this generation relative to the physical state of total Reality — as a whole — enveloping the brain that produced that generation and the structure that directly supported the brain that produced that generation, as well as the relative contextual status between the brain and that support structure at the precise instant of that generation per contributing IBS and per the defined generation event as a whole.

Of course it continues, but I think you get the drift. The short version of this is that when you generate a thought, the internal context makes that thought and every single IBS that collected within that thought impossible to duplicate, and almost impossible to associate with any other form of information. But then, that thought is immediately followed by another thought, and then another, until you have an entire train of thought — emerging in perfect synchronicity [even if not sharing URC velocity] with the rest of the environment's reconfiguration frequency — with each thought unique in many ways, while being quite similar in other more pervasive ways.

The most pervasive commonality that any generated thought shares with its contextual cohorts is not on my list of identifying contextual aspects. Remember how I stated that:

> All things (be they incidental or permanent) that share environmental origin, also share permanent informational representation within the same Informational Continuum. This means that regardless of all other factors, no residual Fact Set continuum can ever become separated from the originating continuum *"trunk"* that established the historical precedent responsible for its eventual existence. Keep this very specific fact in the front of your mind as we progress with this examination, because eventually we'll be looking at developments where the environmental origin of an Informational Continuum will rigidly determine how it reacts to those developments. It'll be good if you begin preparing your understanding of how historical context affects permanent existence.

Well, here's where I'm going to explain what I was foreshadowing with that specific statement.

Information is ultimately defined by the circumstances that brought it into existence. There's no way to overstate this, and even the URC (which generally unites all physical existence into one Contextual Environment) must ultimately defer if there is an Identity clash between what it provides [quantized existential synchronization] and the authoring circumstance suite that literally defines the specific Fact Set or Burst Set in question. This is because of the permanent nature of information sets, and the requirement that all historical [internal context] identification specifics be preserved in direct service of preserving the contextual Identity of the URC-Determined Environmental Confine as the inimitable universal system that it is and will always seek to remain.

This does not mean that an internal contextual attribute of a residual Fact Set (such as the URC that it represents) or a Burst Set can change as a result of such a clash, but it does determine the permanent contextual hierarchy that the information set *belongs* within if there is a clash between URC-Determined environmental systems that can each be viewed as possessing a potential contextual claim to the information set in question. This will become very important to fully understand once we get into Track#2 of Section II, but for now, all we want to establish is that authoring circumstance trumps all other contextual considerations when assigning information sets, be they residual Fact Sets or generated Burst Sets.

AutoGenesism: A Theory of Everything

When your brain does what it does, all your thoughts [Intellect Burst Sets (IBS)] string out in the same general manner as residual Fact Sets collect within a URC-Determined Environmental Confine. In a sense, you create your own personal Informational Continuum, of sorts. Your brain authors each thought, and as a result it supplies each thought with the lion's share of its contextual composition, since most of each IBS is historically entangled with what has already come together [circumstantially and as a result of progressive development] over time to form the distinct Identity of your brain as it does what it does. All previous thoughts that have been generated; your brain's specific electro-chemical balances, carbon elemental structures, all the shifts and developments of both since you came into existence, and all the experiences and circumstances that caused your brain to progress and develop as it did, come together to form the foundation upon which the very precise aspects of each instant of IBS generation are gathered as additional context. This foundation establishes the authoring context of each thought, and causes each IBS to physically gather as yet another unit of Intellect with all previous Intellect Burst Sets that have been generated by the same author source; your brain.

This solid contextual foundation requires all similarly authored Intellect to collect as an actual physical mass of information that is literally and permanently indivisible. Over the centuries, people have referred to this physical mass as the human spirit, the soul, the divine essence, and probably other terms that I'm not aware of. This information mass is in direct and ongoing physical association with the brain during your entire lifetime, increasing in quantity and complexity as the result of all the perception and response information sets your brain generates, right up until the moment your brain stops generating.

As you sit there and read this, you're feeding your own Intellect mass with these information sets, and all that these information sets contain will be there, within that physical mass of Intellect, forever. In fact, you can never unlearn something, since brain-generated Intellect (like all information) is eternal. This is a good thing, but I want to take a moment and allow you to experience the generation of this unique form of information for yourself.

Close your eyes and stop thinking about anything at all. Clear your mind, in that way they tell you to while meditating. Just be in the moment as much as possible and experience yourself as being alive and aware of yourself, of your place in the room, of your place in the progression of moments that have come to pass during your life, and of your entire fullness of being. This is what it feels like to generate your eternal self. That awareness, that sense of unique individual

Identity within the entirety of physical existence; this is what it feels like to be eternal and to transcend the corporeal realm.

Now, that instant of transcendent awareness you just experienced was immediately replaced by the next instant of transcendent awareness, and that's because your brain is generating Intellect in unique quantum burst sets. Your experience of the generation of the Burst Sets that address cognitive interpretation and response [a very specific survival functionality suite] is what you know as conscious awareness. These bursts launch [and are replaced by your next instant of conscious awareness] at an incredible rate that you experience as a seamless flow of sentience and, at times, sapience. Your unique brain's burst rate is perfectly in sync with our Reality's URC, and because it is, what you experience is a constant *Now* that immediately becomes the past as soon as it occurs.

It also causes you to move ahead in sync with all the other events that are happening at the blistering pace of our universe's URC, and this causes you to perceive Reality as still and solid, even though everything that exists as material is structurally changing at that quantized rate. Remember the space-station analogy? Your awareness is changing at a rate that is in sync with everything else that is structurally reconfiguring. That's you, tethered to the mother-ship and rocketing through the motionless void. Your slice of immediate conscious awareness is replaced with your next slice of conscious awareness at a rate that is in perfect sync with the quantum rate of change, so it all feels stable, solid and motionless.

Section III's *"From Here to There: The Crossing Over Event"* thoroughly explains the nature of corporeal conscious awareness, and I strongly encourage you to take a moment (once you've become a bit more knowledgeable concerning this theory) to check out what this very important digression suggests. I can't overstate the impact that this knowledge will ultimately have on your ability to gel this entire premise as a recognizable and thoroughly plausible theory, and it could even be the key to helping you manage the biggest events of your own physical existence.

And Then, There's the *'Lizard Brain'*

So, what about the brain-generated information that contains awareness, but is not human Intellect? Not every brain is a human brain. In fact, most information generating brains on this planet aren't human brains. And yet, these brains also create information that is different than the residual Fact Sets that make up the Informational Continuum. And, yes, some of it is aware, even if that awareness is strictly limited to sentience.

For starters, this information is just as dynamic as Intellect. It was configured as Burst Sets and set into action to address a survival requirement, just like the Intellect Burst Sets that we've been discussing. After all, this is brain-generated information. The Homo Sapiens brain is just a brain, and while it does produce a very unique form of dynamic information, it's not the only kind of brain that produces dynamic information. All brains produce dynamic information.

The generated Burst Sets that each animal brain produces are also just as contextually isolated from all other information sets as those we've examined that emerge from your own Homo Sapiens brain. And why wouldn't they be? The beast responsible for them has a whole physical/structural/contextual history of its own, just like you have. And, it has its own reasons for doing what it does (providing that additional level of internal context). Its motivations might be much simpler, and more rooted in raw survival, but the thing has a brain, and that brain is generating Burst Sets that help it immediately respond to its own immediate and fluctuating survival requirements.

And like the Intellect that you're responsible for, that animal brain's Burst Set generation initiates Material Realm activities that go on to be represented as residual Fact Set continuum threads within the URC-Determined Environment's Informational Continuum. These trajectories might not reach out to impact as large a swath of the Material Realm as those initiated by human brains, but the URC-Determined Environment is ultimately defined by all such trajectories, large or small. From an environmental perspective, both Burst Set trajectories are physically similar.

That said, the animal brain's generated information is not Intellect. There's no capacity to abstract or to conceptualize contained within these Dynamic Burst Sets. What these Burst Sets contain is reaction to external stimulation and rote adherence to those very specific survival directives (provided by DNA) that are shared by all members of a particular species. These brains are certainly capable of managing the material survival requirements of the beast being served, and in most cases, these requirements are met with brilliant consistency and efficiency. That said, there are inherent limitations imposed upon a brain that is incapable of placing itself within an ongoing time-line; i.e., the abstraction of now versus then. Planning and plotting, and, with such capacity, the transcendence of *Now* in a deliberate and purposeful manner is a survival capacity that only the human brain possesses. Obviously, it is very different dynamic information that the human brain releases into the permanent confines of the **Informational Realm** than what these lesser brains are producing.

In Section II, I'll be getting deeper into how radically different human and nonhuman Burst Sets are, how the pursuit of Identity Survival is central to what constitutes the line of demarcation between the two, and why it's been the existence of time itself that's responsible such a profound delineation. By the end of Section II, you'll know everything you could ever want to know about what makes a human being *human*, but for now I want to show you something that might really help you nail down the difference between residual Fact Sets and generated Burst Sets, using manifestations of each of these forms of information that have been globally embraced, cross-cultural staples for centuries.

Concerning Ghosts, Demons and Other Monsters

So, if this generated Intellect is information, and residual Fact Set continuums are also information, and both exist as physical masses that can (and do) directly affect how the Material Realm operates, how could you tell the difference between free-roaming Intellect and a segment of a residual Fact Set continuum if you were confronted with either as a perceptible manifestation? There was a time when this question would have been a lot more difficult to answer succinctly, but recently there has been a lot of popular media interest in paranormal research, and people are learning a lot about the things that have traditionally gone bump in the night. Even better, these bumping things have become less associated with folklore and more associated with the sort of video and audio evidence that can make a strong case for the claim that there may be more out there than is dreamt of in anyone's philosophy.

While I'm not a fan of anyone chasing down unhappy or disturbed people [be they alive or dead] we have gained a lot of insight into the physical nature of information through the paranormal investigation community and the work they do.

> ***Note*** — the notion that paranormal activity is the result of a manifestation of residual and/or dynamic information sets is not a conclusion that is embraced by this community in any manner whatsoever. That said, the evidence that's been collected by this community has been very valuable in progressing the specifics of this notion regardless of the mindset and intent of the field teams collecting it.

AutoGenesism: A Theory of Everything

Being scientists, the more established researchers work with defined categories that have emerged as a result of the fact that there are very specific types of paranormal manifestations that they run into in the field, and that these types are obvious and easy to differentiate [one from another] when examined with the technology that these researchers use. I'm not a paranormal researcher, but I've discovered that their typing of these forms of manifestations helps me to more effectively and graphically summarize the differences between the various forms that information can take.

These categories are based on the three primary ways that paranormal activity manifests within a haunted location. This really makes it easy to describe the physical differences between residual Fact Sets information, free-roaming Intellect, and the gathering Intellect mass that our material brains continue to feed with Burst Sets as we go about living our lives. I've found that if I use these categories of paranormal manifestation as examples, these differences end up being pretty easy to picture in your mind since who doesn't know at least one ghost story.

Acknowledging that many people don't believe in ghosts, what is true is that the following still does a really good job of detailing the differences between the two basic forms that information can take, and the difference between Intellect Burst Sets that are still massing versus the Intellect mass that's completed its development process. According to professional ghost hunters [for the most part, anyway] authentic paranormal activity is initiated as a result of only one of three possible manifesting sources.

The Residual Haunting — The residual haunting is the classic *"Gray Lady"* type spectral anomaly that features a ghost that presents as if it is still the living person going about their business during the time they were alive. This apparition glides down a hall, or stands at a window, has no conscious awareness, and doesn't even seem to physically relate to the actual surroundings. These images are often seen walking through walls that had once been open walkways, and there is even a case of a squad of ghostly Civil War troops being marched through a hotel lobby as witnesses reported seeing only the top half of the men. Research later revealed that the original floor's surface had been raised 3 ½ feet since that squad had originally marched through, and the ghosts were simply not aware of that fact.

These apparitions, or noises [footsteps, voices, even machinery] are manifestations of residual information that emerge as perceivable impressions projected onto a specific spatial environment [in the same manner as a *placeholder* residual Fact Set will persist to fully represent a volume displacement event that occurred relative to other contextually associated proximity positions]. A specific location [we know that all material structures are matrices of contextually entangled Change/Event Trajectories] where either an event or a personal reaction [also an event] took place that was contextually profound enough to defined that location as integral to that event can affect the human mind's perception at times, physically reflecting the moment, or a person's self-image with that moment. Still, this is only a snapshot of a moment in time [a segment within an event's representative Fact Set continuum — albeit, a contextually significant segment, for whatever reason], and it is devoid of all deeper context other than physical appearance, sound, smell, relative proximity, or however the informational representation manifests.

This common type of paranormal manifestation is a human brain perceiving a finite segment of a residual Fact Set continuum. Not to ruin the fun here, but it's just an informational representation of a Change/Event Trajectory that occurred that was (for some reason) contextually significant enough [relative to the rest of the location — which, as we've already learned, is a persisting Change/Event Trajectory structure] to continue to define the relative identity of the location as a whole thing [a holon] in its own right. This is why some locations are perpetually *haunted* and it takes a more significant change/event (like a ritual *cleansing* or even a religious ceremony that focuses the minds of many people) to overwhelm that definition with a new definition that won't manifest as *haunted*. Yes, even this rote residual stuff can get complicated.

I do like the term that ghost hunters use for this type of haunting. *Residual* is a very effective term for this kind of information. As you've likely noticed, I even decided to use the word *Residual* to refer to Fact Sets and Fact Set continuums.

The Intelligent Haunting — A full-blown intelligent haunting involves a post-corporeal, fully gestated human being who has decided (for whatever reason) to pursue a presence within the Material Realm. Large displays of this kind of haunting are much rarer due to the sheer effort it takes for the *spirit* in question to effectively interact with the Material Realm in general, let alone with the extremely specific Change/Event Trajectories these

AutoGenesism: A Theory of Everything

folks pursue in most cases. When people think of being haunted, this is the kind of spirit that they think of. Mostly, because this is the kind of spook that books and movies feature due to the fact that this one is focused on purposeful activity (which, let's face it, is just scarier than a mindless phantom wandering around).

Now, it's important to always remember that the intelligent haunting is inflicted upon the Material Realm by a someone or *something* [our own interpretation of a human being that was not *generated* by a Homo Sapiens brain] that once lived as a material organism, even if it doesn't seem like this could be the case. It's also important to remember that this being is laboring under a variety of technical limitations as it works to affect our realm, although humans have always been known for being resourceful. It is through the ability to manipulate material objects that such an entity is even discovered to exist [remember that object manipulation — for the dynamic informational being — is actually the intersection and redirection of an entangled matrix of Change/Event Trajectories, but we'll deal with that subject a bit later].

Some of these folks have gotten extremely good at working around their inherent limitations. One brilliant means of interacting with the human that is still *under construction* (like you and me) is through directly affecting their brain's sensory processing centers [each is just an entangled Change/Event Trajectory matrix after all]. Sight, sound, smell, touch, taste; if a *spirit* has become adept at Change/Event Trajectory redirection and manipulation, then introducing a vision [as real as the manipulator is capable of producing] is possible, as is a touch on the shoulder, or a scratch on the back [even leaving marks or breaking the skin by directly manipulating the skin surface as yet another contextually entangled mass of Change/Event Trajectories].

As you can imagine, the longer the post-corporeal individual has been perfecting Change/Event Trajectory manipulation, the more *powerful* they will seem to the person who still experiences Reality through the lens provided by their brain's Material Realm structure. This can cause the *spirit* to seem omnipotent, or even demonic [by being particularly nasty, or even simply choosing to project that specific persona]. In Section II's Track#2, I'll get more specific, but a lot of traditional wisdom is based on the antics of those involved in this kind of activity. The key to the intelligent haunting is that it features someone who knows you are there, and is focused on you for whatever reason.

In the case of disturbing or destructive hauntings, the individual involved is emotionally or psychologically unbalanced, and his/her capacity for mayhem is limited only by their knowledge of their own range of options. What is clear is that these types of ghosts have fully developed personalities, and it illustrates how generated Intellect is different from simple residual Fact Set information. This form of information can physically interact with the Material Realm, and possesses active awareness within all realms of physical Reality. This is very important to remember when thinking about this form of information.

The Poltergeist Haunting — This version of paranormal activity is dynamic and purposeful, but does not involve free-roaming Intellect that has an intelligent awareness of purpose. While this does involve dynamic Intellect, and it does feature Change/Event Trajectory manipulation (often in spectacular displays), the nature of this activity is reactive, animalistic, even spontaneously disjointed in many cases. It doesn't seem to have a conscious human mind attached to it.

In the other two types of hauntings, the information was either a residual Fact Set continuum [The Residual Haunting] or a person whose corporeal phase of overall development has completed [The Intelligent Haunting]. In the Poltergeist haunting, a gathered Intellect mass is intermittently manipulating the Material Realm while it is still actively associated with and being *fed* new Burst Sets by its authoring human brain. In these cases, the Change/Event Trajectory manipulation is much more powerfully effective in impacting the corporeal realm. This is likely due to the specific electro-chemical or hormonal malfunction that is directing immediately generated Burst Sets to actively affect these Change/Event Trajectories so precisely [perhaps an intermittent form of savantism, although there's no research in this area focused on this possibility].

This activity is generally very aggressive, and more often than not, the target of the aggression is the generating author of these dynamic Burst Sets. The statistics vary, but most suggest that around 95% of these spectacular cases involve a pubescent girl whose brain chemistry is in transitional flux, and they last only a handful of months while the hormone balances are in transition. Why the aggressive targeting of the host? Could be self-image issues, or any of a number of possible reasons, but the girls involved never have conscious control over the phenomena, and are just as

AutoGenesism: A Theory of Everything

terrified as anyone else around them.

What is happening here are temporary misfires of the brain's response generation process, as is the case with so many other forms of mental illness. Other examples of this sort of Burst Set generation havoc feature seizures, psychosis, compulsive behavior, autism, savantism, and all kinds of examples of dynamic Burst Set trajectories being improperly directed at initiating activities within the Material Realm. Of course, we don't see anything paranormal about these initiated activities because they are confined to the apical holon structure that includes the brain that generated these Burst Sets. What's *paranormal* about these Burst Set trajectories is that they are directed at [and they affect] apical holon structures that are not directly associated with the brain, and while that's not normal by any means, the only reason it's seen as paranormal is because the ancient and traditional wisdom has always been that this activity is otherworldly.

In the normal relationship between the human brain and the emerging human being, the focus is primarily on managing the Burst Set generation process through the **Personality Development Trajectory (PDT)** [we'll definitely get deep into this in Section II, Track#1]. This is a complicated and surprisingly delicate process, and as has been well-documented, it doesn't take much — either mechanical [brain damage] or electro-chemical [shifting hormone balances] — to disrupt it, causing quite a variety of really evident Burst Set malfunctions. In Poltergeist cases, these sporadic episodes of psychokinesis are dysfunctional Burst Sets that are not much different than the remarkable Burst Sets generated by the brains of Savants as they perfectly replicate extraordinary pieces of music after hearing them only once. In fact, replicating complex musical compositions from memory alone is not very different than examining precisely isolated ongoing Change/Event Trajectories, calculating their precise potential involvements with other entangled trajectories, and redirecting them to cause havoc within the rest of the Material Realm. Not really. A bit more removed from what constitutes our own version of conscious awareness, but no more extraordinary when viewed from a learned perspective. Certainly not the way that Intellect Burst Sets normally manifest within the Material Realm, but not supernatural.

In Section II, I will detail how everything came into existence. That will include what caused the emergence of fully conscious, self-aware Intellect, since that account is an amazing story in its own right and deserves its own space to breathe and develop. Still, as we wrap up this section on the existential staples that set the stage for (and affect the ongoing development of) what has become Reality, I want to make a very specific statement concerning consciousness, and I want this statement to sit all by itself, since it's a really important point. It's an especially important point, given the recent efforts to blend what's always been the basis of traditional wisdom with what's become of popular science, with the nature of consciousness as the primary elixir to allow that blending to occur.

Human Intellect [nothing else is capable of what the metaphysics and popular science folks refers to as *"Big C" Consciousness*] is the result of an unimaginable level of relentless activity, focused solely on the pursuit of raw survival in all possible expressions of what *survival* means, and at all levels of holon structure. Constant and unwavering, the onslaught has been mindless and brutally efficient. It's been precedent creating system preferences — each win setting the stage for more wins — with Reality itself pulling everything forward in the sheer pursuit of Identity Survival via quantity of successes and for no other reason. And on it goes, even now, as the inevitable epitome expression of survival success in all realms discovers its capacity for observation, takes a look around, and begins trying to make sense of itself relative to the rest of Reality.

What I'm trying to say is that the idea that physical Reality was launched by even the most brilliantly crafted definition of primordial Consciousness is an amazing example of putting the cart before the horse. Human Intellect [and regardless of the material nature of the authoring brain] is the only version of creative consciousness that exists. It is an epitome accomplishment of physical existence. It's not the primordial author of physical existence. There is no Creator and there never has been a Creator; godly or otherwise. No primordial Consciousness whatsoever. I hope that I'm being clear about this. To be capable of understanding the truth concerning Reality and your own place within it, this is a fundamental realization that you must accept. If this is not possible for you, then the rest of this reveal will also be impossible for you to accept.

Let's Summarize What's Been Covered

This section focused on the fundamentals of physical Reality, and those emergent systems that present their own inimitable contribution to what is, and what can possibly become, as a result of what is.

AutoGenesism: A Theory of Everything

The Quantum of Everything

After starting off with a little basic physics, we applied what we determined, concerning the nature of a quantum manifestation, to the question of what can be known about the true quantum of material existence. Quarks were quickly ruled out, as it's clear that the quantum of anything is necessarily identical in all properties to quanta of the same thing. There are several families of quarks, so that eliminates the quark from consideration. In fact, it became pretty clear that the particle, in general, was not going to qualify as the Material Realm's ultimate quantum.

The fact that the activity of an atom's electrons determines the identity of that specific atom [i.e., its Atomic Radius] suggested that activity [the quantum of action] might be responsibly considered when pursuing the identity of the material quantum. This brought us to the realization that material structure is anything but material in physical nature, which got us thinking about simple existence, and the duration of a scientific measurement called Planck Time. Naturally, this reminded us that all of Reality exists as uniform, quantized bits [this is the basis of Quantum Physics] and that got us considering the physical existence of the quantum that we call *Now* (which is what Planck Time conceptually represents within the field of Quantum Physics). Clearly, nothing could be more primitive than the quantum of *Now*. So, is the material quantum actually the instant of *Now*? As we discovered, there is certainly a strong argument for suggesting that to be a lot more than likely.

Time's Arrow

We then took the quantum of *Now* and examined how each *Now* replaces the previous *Now* in a rigid quantized lockstep progression that sure seems a lot like the *Arrow of Time* when you stop and really examine it. But, could Time be as simple and obvious as one Planck time unit replacing the last? Perhaps. What *is* true is that within our own quantized Reality [again, it has repeatedly been proven to be true that physical Reality is structurally quantized], the quantum of *Now* is a uniform span of existence (whether that span lasts Planck Time's 5.4×10^{-44} sec or not) which means that *Now* is *Now* everywhere and at the exact same instant, since this is what quantization specifically requires. But what about other areas of our universe? Areas that are much too far away to even perceive?

By definition, a macro-system (like our universe) requires structural coherence within the whole of that system. This coherence, especially concerning something that is as structurally defining as quantization of existence, establishes a system and isolates it from other systems. Perhaps it will help us connect quantization with Time if we look at the official definition of Time that relates directly to this specific question.

> a. the continuous passage of existence in which events pass from a state of potentiality in the future, through the present, to a state of finality in the past
>
> **Collins English Dictionary - 2012 Digital Edition**

As obvious as it might seem, given all the deep reflection and years spent by so many brilliant minds on the nature of Time, the progressive exchange of one *Now* quantum for the next does fully satisfy that definition, while providing an inalterable physical development structure for all that also exists [check out the Planck Time-Planck Length relationship to get a sense of the connection between the quantum of *Now* and the quantum of everything else that exists] in the exact manner that we also experience development as a result of Time's Arrow as fellow constituents within this quantized Reality.

What also appears obvious is that Time [the universal exchange of *Now* quanta] cannot be the result of kinetic energy release, given the progressive development requirements for a kinetic energy field of potential to emerge. Besides, Big Bang or otherwise, spatial movement itself requires spatial proximity (regardless of the overwrought arguments to the contrary), and spatial proximity doesn't just exist as a primordial constant. Unless you embrace a static universe theory, you have to agree to the fact that spatial proximity must exist as a result of a much more primitive existential activity of some kind. I promised that in Section II I will reveal exactly how the difference between here and there [spatial proximity] comes into physical existence as a direct result of Time and the quantum of *Now*.

The Existential *"It"*.

From there, we ventured into the subject of Identity, and the actual nature of physical existence. Identity was determined to be the one essential property concerning existence, with the loss of inimitable Identity resulting in the cessation of physical existence. This determination was coupled with the presence of the sole existential imperative [Survival] to suggest that Identity Survival [the

AutoGenesism: A Theory of Everything

establishment and preservation of inimitable Identity] is physical survival for whatever it is that exists (and that must, therefore, pursue ongoing existence).

The next issue we tackled was the controversy over whether Reality, as a physical system, is at all capable of progressive development. Yes, when stated in that manner, the claim that progressive development is impossible does seem like a ludicrous assertion; given that we can point to ample evidence [ourselves amongst that evidence] that progressive development is not only possible, but relentlessly ongoing. Still, the existence of system precedence is a controversial notion within the physics and cosmology communities, and since it set us up for the examination of context to follow, we took it on and established that all biological sciences are predicated on the examination of the impact of system precedence, and that all experimental physics involves the management [or elimination] of the physical influence of naturally evolving precedence on even the most pristine and primitive systems under examination. And with that, we moved into the subject of internal and relative context, the net ramification of precedent within a given system.

We enjoyed a few analogy narratives that established the relationship between internal and relative context and how together they establish and define inimitable Identity within each system and on behalf of the system as a whole. Then, we established the existence of the macro-system, which we referred to as the Contextual Environment. It was here that the quantum of *Now*, in the form of the Unit Rate of Change (URC), emerged as the Contextual Environment's sub-structural contextual commonality, establishing the most primordial level of possible physical association as being via united change synchronicity.

Now that we were dealing with precedent, context and environments, the topic of Information seemed ready to be addressed. The primordial form that information takes — the residual Fact Set — was the first to be examined, and the Fact Set was fully associated with what it is that brings it into physical existence; the Change/Event Unit. We examined why each Fact Set comes into physical existence [when something changes or happens, it's a fact that it changed or happened], and what is served as a direct result of its physical existence [Reality — the Contextual Environment — pursues its own Identity Survival, and each Fact Set further clarifies that Identity with increasing contextual density and complexity, thereby ensuring its unique and inimitable nature against any possible pretender].

As with all that exists, Identity Survival is the fundamental impetus for all that happens and the reason why all that exists progressively develops as it does. With the emergence of the residual Fact Set continuum, and the permanent existence of historically entangled residual Fact Set continuums in the form of a Reality-defining Informational Continuum, we can now see the logic behind precedent; providing material system definition. And, with the realization that the URC-Determined Environmental Confine's own Identity Survival is promoted and ensured as a result of more and more residual Fact Set continuums adding definition and density to that Identity, the existence of precedence; providing material system preservation through the default promotion of successful Change/Event Trajectory structure [thereby ensuring the emergence of as many residual Fact Set continuums as possible] suddenly becomes easy to justify as well. Again, from the least to the greatest, it's all and only about the raw survival of Identity for that which possesses it.

Humanity: The Epitome Fundamental

After establishing the true basis of Reality, we took a moment to look at the only example of high-level progressive development that I featured in this Section I; the human being. I singled this one out mainly because . . . well . . . because we're human. But, I also wanted to take a quick look at us because the emergence of the human mind [the brain authored dynamic Intellect Burst Set mass] was an existential game-changer of the highest order. Yes, the emergence of simple dynamic brain-generated Burst Set information was an Identity Survival accomplishment for every single Change/Event Trajectory that was ever involved in the development of the brain and the generation of each permanent Burst Set, and we'll get deeper into this later. But, the moment that a brain-generated Burst Set became aware of its own existence relative to *now versus then*, the entire definition of physical existence changed forever. That fact cannot be overstated, and therefore I felt that it was critical that I acknowledge human Intellect as a staple in its own right, and include a quick overview of its unique and unprecedented physical nature within this, our section concerning existential basics.

There, I think that about sums things up, and brings us to the subject of how all of this came about in the first place. In this next section, I'll start at the very beginning of everything, and to keep things moving along I'll be keeping the digressions to a minimum; referring larger explanation requirements to the more

AutoGenesism: A Theory of Everything

expansive digressions featured in Section III. I'll also be structuring this next section a bit differently; laying things out in more of a narrative format. You'll want to keep what we covered in this section handy, since all of this stuff is featured within what we'll be examining in the next section.

That said, there's no possible way to make this next section easy, even if the difficulty you encounter is just keeping the ramification structure straight. Reality is not complicated, but there's no way to simplify the way that this structure is allowed and required; even if the basics of it are simple and efficient. The truth is that it just gets exhaustingly dense and it does so quickly. But, as I just explained to you, Reality has its own agenda, and structural complexity is fundamental to that agenda.

Just don't get intimidated by any of it. Hell, I figured it out and (after years of effort) finally figured out how to explain it all, so it's not impossible to grasp by any means. Just remember what we just covered, and feel free to check back to this Section if something just doesn't seem right [such as Change/Event Trajectories actually existing as fundamental to the Material Realm, or emergence systems being capable of spontaneously emerging when the right combination of factors come together]. I'll be further defining and explaining things as I go along, but I can't litigate every item again and again throughout this entire presentation. Believe me, there's way too much being revealed here for that to be a workable strategy. Besides, as we move along, it'll get more and more recognizable, and more immediately associable with what you've always known to be true about what sits right there in front of you. And that's because it's about what real and ultimately recognizable. Just as you'd expect from a Theory of Everything that's actually about the nature of everything.

Kevin Brian Carroll

Section II

A
Theory
of
Everything

In Section I, we took a good look at what sits at the foundation of pretty much everything. I say *"pretty much everything"* because there are those fundamental staples that exist due to the coming together of those basics we covered, and while they are fundamental [technically, all emergent systems are fundamental], they're the result of even more primordial fundamentals. It's complicated, but as we examine the circumstantial journey that a typical URC-Determined Environmental Confine takes from initiation to full-blown maturity, we'll be focusing a lot on those kinds of higher-end emergent staples, since it's the ramifications that these periodic emergences inflict upon each **URC-DCE** [I've officially had it with typing that entire descriptive label out each time] that cause each one to progressively develop into an inimitable Reality that is capable of pursuing and securing its own Identity Survival.

In short, I'll be explaining how progressive development necessarily works in general. In fact, I'll be focusing on the original URC-DEC and how it progressed from that one instant of required emergence into what it had to ultimately become; keeping this overview applicable to as many versions of URC-entangled Reality as can possibly exist. It won't be easy to do, but I've got a plan that I think will get the job done. Of course, I don't know that my strategy will work to perfectly answer all questions in all minds, but I do know that when we're finished with this Section, most of you will have a much more realistic and comprehensive understanding of why our own universe works as it does.

Yes, we'll be taking this Theory of Everything for a spin in the way that such a theory should be; the way that they've been taking such notions out and putting them through their paces since humanity started cobbling them together thousands of years ago. I'm going to start at the beginning and explain how everything came about and why it came about the way that it did. And when we get to the part of the story where human beings start showing up, I'm going to explain how and why it came about that they're so clearly different from their closest cousins, and what that difference means to everything else that exists and why.

I won't be leaning on anyone else's work here. No Sacred Geometry. No inscrutable mathematics or sketchy new-science hypothetical inferences that are based on experimental indications that show up only in a vacuum environment at absolute zero and with gravity *"turned off"*. None of the usual stuff that suggests everything but doesn't physically link up to anything that actually exists. Also, I won't be referring to any ancient scrolls or hidden manuscripts, or anything that demands life-altering adherence to any impossible-to-define psycho-spiritual transformation as the price you must pay for achieving full *gnosis* [which means knowing something without knowing how or why you know whatever it is that you know] concerning other stuff that's just as removed from your own experience of Reality as a chalkboard full of messy squiggles.

And, above all, I won't be attempting to change the applicable definitions of words like *nothing* or *existence* or *Reality* or *physical* or even *genesis* for that matter, in any effort to slip through a semantics work-around in those places where they've shown up again and again in other efforts of this nature.

I'm going to take you on a journey that starts with the absolute absence of physical existence. In fact, I'm going to kick it off before the **Relative Being State** emerged to allow this to be separate from that, and I'm going to work without a net as I lead you right back to where you sit and where you'll be employing your own inimitable version of sapience as you struggle to figure out how it was that the human race got so turned around on all of this when the clues were always right there in front of us. And then I'm going to explain a lot more than you'd expect concerning who and what you (as a human being) are, and why it is that the human being, in general, is what it is.

AutoGenesism: A Theory of Everything

This is a true Theory of Everything. And, that everything includes the human being as the complex (and often bewildering) epitome of progressive development that it is. That everything also includes the natural, fundamental basis for why our own version of human being (emerging from the lives of the Homo Sapiens hominid of Planet Earth) believes itself to be an eternal, spiritual being with an afterlife and (as far as most of us are concerned) a supreme deific creator god-being awaiting its individual arrival with either reward or punishment, as a direct result of how it behaved and the life choices it made. After all, how can any ToE ignore such a universal human predilection, even if it's just a predilection. The truth is that it can't. And we won't. We're taking it all on, and when we're done, you'll be amazed at how sensible the whole thing actually is.

In The Beginning . . .

The genesis of physical existence, as a whole, seems like the right place to start when laying out a theory that explains how everything came to be what it is. The bible makes the case that God brought it all into existence over a period of six very specific units of time. It uses the term days, but most scholars suggest that the term is used figuratively. That might ease some of the burden that literalists bear when this timetable is contrasted with the scientific evidence that insists on lingering across the entire planet, but the larger issue isn't the timetable itself. The real problem with this theory involves the genesis of God, and the Contextual Environment that contains this God. As in: *Who or what brought God and everything godly into existence?* To date, this problem remains intractable.

The secularists smile when this infinite-reduction conundrum is placed before the panel, but the elimination of God doesn't let these folks off that same hook as the question concerning the genesis of physical existence stubbornly lingers, no matter what big bang string theory they try to hide behind. There's no way around dealing with the fact that since we've got full blown intelligent, self-aware physical existence, it had to initiate somehow, even if it was, then, drop shipped in from the ninety-third dimension with a fleet of plasma starships.

Now if we were only examining the specific origin of Earth's human species, or even the launch of what contains the Earth and its contents, then the following verses featured in the Book of Genesis 1:1-2 could be part of the debate over whose theory of genesis is more reasonable.

Kevin Brian Carroll

> ¹ *In the beginning God created the heaven and the earth.* ²
> *And the earth was without form, and void; and darkness was upon*
> *the face of the deep. And the Spirit of God moved upon the face*
> *of the waters.*

Genesis 1:1-2

Okay, so this hypothesis probably wouldn't hold up to scientific scrutiny, but you can't dismiss it as irrelevant, since it was the gold standard for hundreds of years. But, if we're going to dig into how everything that exists came into existence, we'll need to go back a lot farther than that. And this is what we'll do.

In this section, we're going all the way back to the beginning of everything. Before physical existence, before information, before anything was there to reach its hand out and impose its will on anything else. We're going back to when there was nothing at all, and that fact (of there being nothing at all) might have been the only thing that existed if an existent-nonexistent juxtaposition had been possible — making that fact's existence possible. Yes, when I say: *the beginning*, that is exactly what I mean.

You see, the instant of true existential genesis inflicts the same intractable conundrum on every theological, philosophical, and scientific ToE narrative that's ever been successfully promoted. All theological narratives (as well as the wide variety of spiritual/mystical versions of deism that preceded them) begin only after the established existence of what amounts to a conscious, sapient entity that is already whole and perfected. In fact, while each of these narratives features a being with its own unique need (that only humanity can satisfy), everything else that pertains to this god is completely and absolutely supreme, and all of it to the fullest expression imaginable. In most modern versions of this notion, the human imagination can't even approach a means of conceptualizing the magnitude of supremacy and fullness of perfection that the deity in question contains within itself.

Heck, in some theologies, this god is a singularity (already containing all that exists — that can ever exist — within itself as a form of intellectual manifestation) with the existence of humanity merely its own effort to manufacture a form of relative contextual juxtaposition (within the non-relative existential whole of itself, of course) so that it can finally get to experience itself as intellectually conscious within any contextual framework whatsoever — even if this

AutoGenesism: A Theory of Everything

god knows that this framework is nothing more than an artificial contextual juxtaposition of its own creation. Better that, than the frustrated loneliness of being an absolute manifestation of perfect wholeness unto itself. Or so it must seem.

In another highly developed iteration of one of the more traditional theologies, this god is obsessively engaged in the moment-to-moment micro-management of the world it's created; skillfully walking each and every human being around what constitutes a game board without allowing anyone or anything its own room to act or react. In this bizarre dramedy, not only is the result a foregone conclusion, but each instant has been predetermined; an insanely elaborate ballet with a purpose served that can never be comprehended, nor should the comprehension of that purpose ever be pursued.

I do have to admit that this specific narrative beats an earlier iteration where this particular omnipotent, omniscient and omnipresent deity is stuck having to repair the damage inflicted by humanity after losing its original master plan to complete chaos. In that traumatic debacle, this god is finally forced to become human itself so that it can be brutally slaughtered by other humans in order that it can pay for the sins that those humans committed as the necessary result of the fact that it (this poor god) screwed the whole thing up in the first place. And even then, the vast majority of that god's human beings end up screaming forever in a lake of fire in spite of its best efforts.

Yeah, that narrative's a bit disturbing (to say the least) even if it does present the most compelling cast of characters featured in any of the more successful story lines. Still, who can honestly imagine a supreme being that's been reduced to tossing most of its most cherished creations into eternal horror and suffering as a result of its own stubborn incompetence? A middle manager? Sure, I could see that happening to a middle manager, but not the Alpha and Omega of existence itself. The omniscience of this beast would immediately expose it (especially to itself) as the most miserable and odious demon of them all, and it takes heroically strenuous philosophical gymnastics to come to any other conclusion. Then again, faith does do amazing things for people.

Maybe the most self-satisfying ToE narrative is the one that declares that we are each God (and all at the same time, no less), and that we're putting ourselves through all of this . . . this struggle-through-life business . . . for reasons that we need to strive to somehow relearn, so that we can be God again, and finally experience the coming home to our rightful selves, and true eternal bliss. That's a fascinating premise, and maybe in some social circles it could even be seen as intellectually debatable. But, if you walk into one of those dark, narrow old-guy bars downtown, on a Wednesday afternoon, the entire premise collapses completely and can't seem to get up off the wet floor to grab a proper seat.

Looking for that divine spark in the dull eyes that stare back at you from the regulars in that place is like looking for (to misappropriate a clever lyric) a *"Coupe de Ville, hiding at the bottom of a Cracker Jacks box"*. If it's there, it's perfectly disguised, and it doesn't feel like being bothered right now. At least not while it's still got a cigarette burning and a beer in front of it.

There are more religious notions out there than I care to dive into, and I'm sure there are many more that have never been honored with the effort to scribble them down for publication. What I haven't found, however, is an attempt to take a theological premise and follow it back to the instant where this almighty being comes into conscious and dynamic physical existence.

And, Concerning Those Damn Atheists . . .

It seems as if the secular agnostic/atheist community is just as resistant to taking on such a challenge, with their Big Bang-Chaos-String-Gauge theories, and all that whatever-it-is launching from wherever-it-was into whatever-it-is, as it makes its way to wherever-its-going for whatever-reason it's going there. Of course, they see their trump card as being that they don't believe that anything is in charge or that anything has any reason for existing. As if what's been proven to exist (and existence itself, for that matter) doesn't require an explanation.

And as far as all the rest of it, maybe it's easy to state that unless you can replicate it in a wind-tunnel or a supercollider, or prove it out in on a blackboard with white chalk, it just plain can't exist. But, that kind of broad dismissal is nothing more than an intellectual punt on the whole question of initial existential emergence, and the philosophical equivalent of grabbing a beer and turning on the Cartoon Network.

Hell, even the most productive metaphysicists are unwilling to take on the question about what preceded the very beginning of physical existence. As in, what happened to initiate existence, and what requirement pulled that instant forward? Probably for fear of having to admit that they have no idea, and not even a presentable guess, concerning why anything exists at all.

AutoGenesism: A Theory of Everything

And yet, all sides of this great cultural divide are demanding that we anchor our definition of Reality itself on their wildly conflicting declarations concerning unassailable truths that contain no formative basis whatsoever; not even an attempt to tie any of these certainties to anything more substantial than an eternal always that requires no more explanation than it requires existential context. As if a perpetual now is the same as a beginning-less/endless always. Which, by the way, it's not.

So, why is it that both Atheists and Religionists embrace the very same notion concerning an infinite and always presence, while arguing only over what its name is? Is it really only a clash over what to label this infinite presence and whether to assign it a conscious personality or not? Let's take a moment to look at the infinite-always notion itself, and see just how realistic it is. We'll examine it from both sides, giving weighted examination to both sides relative to how important this notion is to the basis of the belief system as a whole.

Do You Think They Know This About Each Other?

One popular scientific axiom is that *energy can be neither created nor destroyed*, and while it's a sophomoric misappropriation of one phrase taken from the law of Conservation of Energy, it still gets tossed out there as if it's a basis to start building extrapolations upon. And yet, as it relates to Reality as a macro-system, just how logical is that statement anyway?

This *forever-and-ever-and-always* energy assertion is especially important to address in light of our original issue with the timeless, intelligent, and all-powerful God claim. An *always-was and always-will-be* presence of this energy (in whatever form, or forms, it takes) is essentially the same thing as a timeless, *"everything-and-nothing"* God that always was, always is, and always will be, as a whole and unchanging, perfected, all-powerful, dynamic expression. These two assertions [all-existent energy and the all-powerful, all-existent intellect] depend upon each other as acceptable premises, and the reason they do is because they both require the complete dismissal of the logical requirement that, for something to physically exist, it must go through a physical emergence of some kind.

And that is the primary issue here. Not whether the *always something* is raw energy or a fully developed, powerfully active, and deeply contemplative being with an agenda of its own. The issue is the requirement of physical emergence (via a logically plausible emergence process — i.e., ramification or factor confluence *strong emergence*), regardless of whether one's all-mighty god consists of energy, or is made of some other substance that allows it physical form and dynamic presence. It's this claim of a physical *always* [as a basic attribute of the effectible, contextually applicable anything] that needs to be determined as being either logically viable, or a weak intellectual device that is meant to push aside all challenges to an otherwise useful suite of traditional assertions.

It's pretty easy to just state that God (or energy, for that matter) exists, has always existed, and will always exist. In fact, it's extremely easy to make that statement. It's even easier if you follow it up with the claim that human beings can't know the truth about the beginning-less and endless nature of God (or energy), and are foolish to even approach the subject. Or better yet, you can declare that humans are defiant of God's authority when they approach this subject, and that it's a mystery that no human can ever know. This approach wraps it all up nicely.

However, if we take a good look at what else has been stated about (for instance) one of these always and forever gods, we begin to see some real problems with the notion of an always God who has a specific timetable for humanity, and who actually adjusts His approach and attitude toward humanity as time moves forward within the relationship between the two. Let me explain.

In the larger narrative of at least one of these timeless Gods, we have a spectacularly brilliant, conscious being that has simply always existed. In fact, time doesn't even exist in the realm of this being. He experiences a forever *Now*; with all that was, all that is, and all that ever will be, existing as a permanent *Now*. Not only does He experience this *Now*, He experiences it as an all-knowing, and all-experiencing hyper-awareness that is expressed as a dynamic and unique personage. This suggests that what *Began* for humanity, what *Is* for humanity and what *Will Be* for humanity, *Always Is* for God. This, logically speaking, suggests that God and humanity occupy two completely incompatible being states that can never become reconciled. Or so it would seem.

In fact, there is one issue that presents itself immediately when conceiving of a relationship between that which *Is*, and that which *Becomes As Time Progresses*. In His physical involvement with humanity, which *Now* would this God deal with? If this God selected a *Now* for physical interaction, how would He separate that specific slice of *Now* out from the entire equal and logically indivisible *Now* that is always present in this timeless God's perception of the human's ongoing trajectory and then resulting [God sees all] Fact Set continuum?

AutoGenesism: A Theory of Everything

How would this God even perceive (let alone, respond to) this trajectory/contin-uum structure if progressive change does not exist in His realm? Or is it a case where this God can become immersed [changing the fully expressed and funda-mental basis of what He is] within a URC-Determined Environmental Confine's evolving relationship matrix at will, but if so, how does He establish His own individual historical context [back-dating Himself as integral to what has al-ready evolved within the URC-DEC to that instant without obliterating the pre-cise Identity of that URC-DEC] in order to fit His own inimitable and histori-cally viable contextual Identity properly into a relative contextual relationship with each previously established continuum that permanently represents those very specific Change/Event Trajectory matrices that He seeks to impact or to even communicate with?

Or is it a case of God being able to do whatever the hell He wants to, and just doing it in spite of all that's come into being within this intricately woven, causally evolving, physical solid that consists of us and everything else that ex-ists? But then, if that's the case, why does each religion have its god focused on (let's face it) petty dramas that are obviously designed to engage humans in ac-tivities that are meant solely to satisfy some clearly self-indulgent whims, re-gardless of the god in question? Or am I in danger of losing my eternal existence by even bothering to puzzle any of this out?

And, as far as a beginning-less, limitless, always existent energy source is concerned, are you kidding me? Infinitely vast dynamic existence exploding from a physical microdot that's been squeezed into becoming a limitless kinetic potential by nothing whatsoever? That miracle microdot couldn't have been squeezed by gravity since gravity is a net impact and not a force [check out General Relativity]. This is science? From this microdot [no explanation offered or considered concerning where this microdot came from] to infinite expansion without anything added? All-in-one everything, from nothing [we have to as-sume]? The complete absence of physical existence — with nothing beneath absolutely nothing — pushing such a fully self-contained *something* to the sur-face, and then that *something* launching into spontaneous existence to become all forms of physical energy? Not only all forms of physical energy, but all the energy, in all forms, that will ever exist? Energy that can't be created or de-stroyed? Never created, and never destroyed? And this is the theory of what eventually developed [by way of sheer chaotic causal mayhem, no less] into the rational, deliberative intellect that is sitting in your chair and reading this sen-tence?

That's just as impossible as the all-in-one, super-deluxe god thingy that needs nothing to be absolutely the epitome of everything — well, except for what it seems to really, *really*, **really** need from me and from everyone else on this planet, and is willing to viciously rip each of us limb from limb for all eternity if we don't come across with whatever the hell it is.

And didn't Max Planck debunk the notion of physical infinity when he presented the lowly Quantum, and thereby stabilized the electron orbit by obliterating a full one half of the infinite trajectory potential? Seriously. Isn't anyone in the physics department paying attention to the defaults that exist within their own slice of science? You can't have infinity extending in only an outward direction. That doesn't make any sense whatsoever. If there is infinity going outward, then there has to be infinity collapsing inward, and yet, Planck's Constant, and the quantum itself, have proven that this does not exist, and cannot exist relative to physical action. Nor with proximity, since the two are interrelated; and as a result, nor with time. The logic is simple and definitive, and yet, science is still offering energy as its own god of genesis.

What seems to be missing from both narratives is the emergence of an initial contextual framework for all of this drama and brute activity. You see, as we've already established, Identity-providing contextual juxtaposition is required for physical existence, and devoid of that, there isn't even the fact that there is nothing at all to provide existential delineation. Now this is the kind of primitive thinking that can eventually bring you to the simplest notion possible, the true genesis of physical existence.

Remember, this will be a two-track presentation. The Track#1 narrative is going to focus only on the natural process that initiated all by itself, becoming the very first URC-Determined Environmental Confine. This eventually progresses to the point of this URC-DEC's own fully recognizable human beings emerging to take a look around and begin trying to make sense of it all, as happened within our own Reality. And all the result of pure, natural progressive development, and nothing more. But as you'll see, that's always been enough.

In fact, you'll discover in the Track#2 presentation [as we examine, within the wildly speculative confines of what I've devised as the only plausible scenario that fully explains how the concept of gods and spirits could have emerged and so precisely developed into what it is today] that even then, the process itself isn't and can't be messed with. It's just intentionally initiated, and while that

AutoGenesism: A Theory of Everything

may not seem like it'd be sufficient to make anything intentional actually happen, you'll discover that intent carries its own arrangement of developmental implications around with it.

I expect Track#2's speculative overview to be pretty difficult for most folks to accept due to reasons that I will detail in the next sub-section. What I will say here is that while fundamental Reality itself [the original URC-DEC] is the result of a very fundamental and natural initiation response to a primordial requirement, there actually is compelling logical, empirical, and historical evidence that suggests that our own universe [atheists are going to really hate this] is a Reality confine (perhaps just one of many) that was deliberately initiated to achieve a very specific net result that (when finally achieved) will serve a very natural existential requirement that we're each familiar with and that we actually celebrate (each in our own way) as being a fundamental aspect of life itself. And that this [possible] fact of our own Reality's physical initiation is why that bizarre and otherwise inexplicable concept of gods and such was at all possible. Oh, and of course I will detail exactly how it works out; tying it all securely to the primordial staples that we acknowledged in Section I.

That said, [theists are going to really hate this] the evidence is overwhelming that the original progressive development process initiated and evolved without any external influence whatsoever. So, of course, that original process will be the focus of Track#1 so that you won't be left imagining that I'm suggesting that some supreme something-or-other was behind it all.

Yes, there's going to be plenty to hate here for everyone; not that it matters to Reality . . . or to me, for that matter.

AutoGenesism — A Rose by Any Other Name

When I suddenly realized that I had successfully determined the only plausible means by which physical Reality could have naturally emerged from a true physical void [*void* meaning: no physical existence whatsoever], and that the basic mechanism behind that initial instant of physical genesis can readily be shown to still turn up again and again at all levels of physical existence [proving system coherence], I knew that I had to come up with a moniker for what I'd realized if I was going to be able to put it all together as an accessible explanation. Of course, the extremely comprehensive nature of this hypothesis made the job of coming up with a descriptive label really difficult. After all, by the time the dust settled, what I actually had was a full Theory of Everything, and one that was unlike anything that exists or has ever existed. And, the truth is that there is no other theory that's this overwhelming in its breadth, or this revolutionary in its many fundamental determinations. There's also no theoretical precedent that exists for it, and this fact also needed to be properly reflected in its moniker.

I'm not a scientist, and while I am fairly conversational in the jargon of each applicable discipline, I had to respect the fact that, as an outsider to these communities, I couldn't toss together something too focused on the core technical specifics of this extremely definite process. I knew that I had to acknowledge my lack of formal education within the label itself, if only out of respect for those whose lives have been defined by their dedication to effort and their personal resilience within the hyper-competitive environs of professional academia. So, I decided to take a look at my hypothesis, to see what its most revolutionary assertion was. Perhaps my moniker would simply reflect the nature or implication of that claim.

I eventually came back to that determination that was the most unprecedented of them all; the autogenous emergence of Reality.

Yes, this realization is the one that clearly defines and delineates this ToE from everything that's ever been offered by anyone on this topic. And by quite a margin, I might add. And, the fact that (as you'll soon see) I can succinctly detail the exact process itself, and (as you'll also see) link that exact process up to what occurs on a moment by moment basis across every arena of interaction from one end of our universe to the other, makes this one realization the cornerstone of this notion, and again, by a wide margin.

The autogenous emergence of Reality. The word *autogenous* — meaning *"produced by or within oneself"* [Scott, Foresman Advanced Dictionary - 1979 Scotts, Foresman and Company] — reflects exactly how Reality emerged; all on its own and without any help whatsoever. The moniker I went with was *AutoGenesism* and I guess it was a pretty obvious decision, especially considering the process I went through. That said, it wasn't an easy decision, since the term *Autogenesis* is often associated with an evolutionary theory — *Orthogenesis* — that directly took on *Natural Selection* and failed. Still, the combination of *auto* and *genesis* seems to perfectly sum up the primary determination; that physical Reality came about on its own, and without any *outside* help.

I did sort of short-blend in the suffix *ism*, since I am offering this as a distinctive theory (like Darwin*ism*, for instance), and not an assertion that is, in any way, associated with any other implication suggested by anyone else's previous

AutoGenesism: A Theory of Everything

usage of the term Autogenesis. Okay, so *AutoGenesism* doesn't roll off the tongue as well as I'd hoped, but it is immediately descriptive. It does make it clear that this very specific theory is founded on the idea that all of Reality is based on instances of *Strong Emergence*, including the initial genesis of physical Reality itself.

As for building this entire notion on periodic emergence, there's an axiom that I've always embraced. And, it's one that really served me well back when I was still trying to *be somebody* in a world of so many people trying to also be somebody (and by any means necessary in most cases). That axiom is *"Nothing comes from nowhere"*, and while the grammar itself is likely suspect, the basic truth of what it suggests isn't assailable.

Regardless of whether you're looking at a star on the silver screen or looking for the existential foundation of every star in the night sky, everything that is, became what it's become, by way of a progression of circumstance that can be traced back to at least one point of emergence; an instant of initial genesis. And that instant of initial genesis can be examined to successfully determine the very specific confluence responsible for its seemingly miraculous contribution to the concept of transcendence. The truth is that nothing comes from nowhere, and as you'll see, that's no play on words.

As we established in Section I, all of Reality is littered with emergent systems, and while no one has been able to detail exactly why emergence occurs, no one can insist that emergent systems do not exist. I see the nature of emergent systems as an important clue to how Reality works, and I see no restriction on placing emergence at development junctures where it's clear that no other explanation exists. As long as the basics of existential requirement are served, and without clashes in logic or system coherence, then I am in good company with a large number of professional theorists toiling in much more siloed fields of endeavor, as I reject strict reductionism and embrace sporadic Strong Emergence as the physics staple that it is.

AutoGenesism is a Descriptive Term

What AutoGenesism describes is a 100% natural progressive development process that all URC-Determined Environmental Confines go through by rote default. All it is, is a description of what's always existed. There's nothing deterministic about it, other than the raw fact that basic emergence stages inevitably show up, and that they result in novel systems that, then, go on to redefine

159

the nature of physical Reality through the simple fact that these novel systems now exist, causing Fact Set continuums to emerge to permanently represent their existence. Basically, it's a case of things progressing within a clearly defined fundamental structure, driven by a universal imperative, with the results being a fairly obvious range of plausible variations in the ramification structure as that progressive development progressively develops.

Still, the fact is that I have chosen to address a lot more with this Theory of Everything than any other that's ever been published, and that does include some of our own human race's most enduring mysteries. And this could present a challenge to many folks concerning how to view Auto-G. In fact, I have struggled with how to effectively present some discoveries that I've stumbled onto as a result of vetting and challenging the logic structure and overall *reach* of AutoGenesism as a true ToE. Especially one unexpected ramification structure that powerfully exposes what's most likely behind our uniquely human belief in mysticism, spiritual realms and deific personalities, and why such logically impossible certainties could have become fundamental to the Reality view of the average person. It's really hard to explain, yes, but it's twice as hard to explain without that explanation sounding like yet another weak attempt at combining science and religion.

In **Track#2**, I'll get very deep into this startling determination, and you'll certainly get all you could ever need or want concerning the nuts and bolts of how it works and why it emerged to affect Earth's Homo Sapiens human race so profoundly. Still, I want to make it clear that AutoGenesism is the complete description of only the purely natural process of existential emergence, logical causal ramification, and how the universal imperative *Identity Survival* drives all that exists to be what it is and do what it does. Yes, there is plenty of conscious and reactive activity to examine once you get to those epitome systems that are fully capable of that sort of activity, and yes, Auto-G is a description of what drives those epitome systems to do and be what they do and are. That said, this theory encompasses all of it as a truly natural and inevitable macro-system that is always defined by the active-reactive-representative whole that is in endless evolutionary development.

With that settled yet again, I think it's time to take a good look at the original URC-Determined Environmental Confine. This **Track#1** will lay out exactly how physical existence initiated from a true absence of anything at all, and how the defaults took Reality from that instant of existential genesis to the inevitable emergence of full-blown intelligent self-awareness.

Track I

From
Nothing
To
Everything

So, what I'm going to do is hit the highlights of how a typical URC-Determined physical Reality environment evolves as a progressive development process. What will be unique about this description is that I'll be starting from scratch, which means that I'll be using the original URC-DEC as my model. After all, if I'm going to make a point of the fact that all other Theories of Everything avoid the question of initial genesis, then I certainly can't avoid that question myself.

To be honest, I wish that I had been able to find someone — hell, anyone (preferably someone with an advanced degree, or at least some level of professional profile, within an applicable field) — that had already done work that I could have offered to supplement with my own. I wanted to hook in with a pro who was publicly searching for the fundamentals of existential genesis in a manner that flatly rejected any traditionalist *just-so* stories or similarly irresponsible secular assumptions, but after five years of searching unsuccessfully for such a theorist, I finally decided that I'd go ahead and show what it is that I've got in my pail.

It being the case that there has never been a shortage of highly developed and rigidly disciplined research that has focused on the many siloed bits and stages of progressive development that have been clearly available for observation (for instance; the variety of ways that systems take advantage of their established places within the larger systems that contain them, as they do what it takes to maintain their material structures), I see no value in doing more than revealing how AutoGenesism naturally aligns with what has already become thoroughly established within the various scientific disciplines that are associated with questions concerning Reality and its natural development process. I won't be challenging the work that's already proven itself well beyond a few experiment indications here and there — fundamentals, like the system stabilizing impact of Natural Law and the Laws of Physics, natural selection and the evolution of biological systems, and intra-system developmental divergences created by progressing environmental changes. I'll be merely placing solid, defensible staples like these within a proper context. In fact, what you'll soon discover is that Auto-G — as a theoretical structure — succeeds brilliantly as a rigidly predictable contextual framework that embraces all of the obviously rational science that we've depended upon to lift human civilization out of those dark ages of mysticism and magic, defining it all as thoroughly natural, and while not deterministically required, certainly reasonably inevitable; given the sub-structural requirements that Auto-G reveals.

As we move through Section II, there will also be some amount of assuming that you've remembered the stuff we covered in Section I [the ongoing existence and nature of those existential staples] since I wrote Section I to reveal and established the staples that all progressive development depends on as the whole of Reality acts, reacts, progresses and becomes what it's become. I'll probably be more inclined to reiterate than not, but there may be those spots where beating something into the ground could have a negative impact on what it is that I'm trying to introduce. It'll be there, that I'll need you to either remember the fundamental nature of what we're examining, or be able to turn back and find that applicable staple in Section I and make the necessary intellectual association between what we're examining, and the existential basics involved. I guess that what I'm trying to say is that this is a presentation that is going to get increasingly complicated, and I need you to be aware of that and be ready for it.

So, with that established, I guess we'll start at the beginning, and then try to let the whole thing roll out as if it's a story of some sort.

AutoGenesism: A Theory of Everything

Existential Genesis

Before I get into this, I'm going to admit that I feel a bit intimidated here as I begin this attempt to accurately describe the instant of existential genesis in the way that I envision it. I made some diagrams, and hope that they will help, but I know that this has never been successfully accomplished. Still, regardless of how successful this effort comes off, I have sworn an oath (to myself, I suppose) that I will not allow any of this description to devolve into yet another worthless display of poetic esotericism.

Metaphor has its value, and having been primarily a songwriter and poet throughout my life, I'm as fluent as anyone in the art of linguistic abstraction. However, this topic has already been thoroughly butchered by poets, allegorists, philosophers, religionists, songwriters, and most recently, shameless professional semanticists; with the result being that no one has any idea how to even define a proper evaluation of the question: *What happened that resulted in the existence of physical Reality?*.

I believe that the only real way to approach the question of initial genesis is as an investigation of something that happened. That probably seems like an obvious statement, but when was the last time you read or watched an actual examination of the transitional event that brought physical Reality into existence? Most people might point to a program about the Big Bang they watched on The Discovery Channel. However, the many examinations and explanations of the theoretical Big Bang have nothing to do with that singular and unprecedented instant of existential genesis. Here, let me explain.

The Big Bang theory starts with whatever the hell it was that exploded already physically existent. In fact, extremely existent; with the entire universe that exists right now compressed into the size of an atom (perhaps even smaller). I defy anyone to suggest anything more physically existent than this entire universe compressed into the size of an atom. And then there's the physical environment (the necessarily relative state of being) that this explosion occurred within. Since a physical release of anything at all (and definitely so much that's been compressed so tightly) must exist relative to that which is not physically it, how can anyone declare that it [this Big Bang's hosting environment] did not physically exist before that whatever-it-was exploded? Unless you want to declare that the Big Bang created the Relative Being State (which makes no sense at all, since that atom-size universe had to exist *relative* to, at least, nothing, for it to exist as an identifiable *something*), then you cannot declare that the Big

Bang created the entire universal environment that contains the ongoing ramifications of itself as an explosion.

Sure, anyone can declare anything, and yes, there have been similar declarations made for centuries (albeit; with somewhat different labels and specifics — like God — associated with those declarations). However, other than offering flippant linguistic convolutions or math equations that seek to balance sets that have no connection at all with what's been proven to be even vaguely existent, no one can back up such a declaration, and it doesn't take much effort at all to prove that conceptual schisms like these are obviously and inarguably impossible; in spite of the math. I could go on and on, but those two issues alone [the preexisting *atom-universe* and the preexisting relative state that the *atom-universe* existed within] eliminate the Big Bang as a plausible explanation for how physical Reality came into existence. So, what about a universe-birthing multiverse; one that's complete with black holes that burp entire universes into parallel dimensional existence by way of Big Bang events?

I don't think so. Again, let me explain.

Even if there is a universe-birthing multiverse with burping black holes that Big-Bang whole universes into physical existence, the presence of that multiverse has still got to be explained. Attributing our own universe's genesis to a trans-dimensional cosmic production facility doesn't answer the question concerning what happened that brought physical Reality into existence. If anything, it distracts from the very simple nature of the original question itself, by pointing at a suite of much more impossible (as well as unnecessary) questions concerning the structural nature of, and reason for, something as physically overwhelming as a universe-birthing multiverse that possesses black holes that do what these black holes have been described as allegedly doing. Not that it isn't fun to let your imagination run wild with these sorts of questions, and if all you want to do is have fun with wild, meaningless questions . . . well, then have at it, I guess. I probably wouldn't pay anyone to waste their time on such obvious dead-ends, and I certainly wouldn't spend billions on the technology that's become required for one to continue that pursuit.

At any rate, this will be the first attempt to actually detail the genesis of physical Reality in terms that realistically connect that singular event with everything that exists, and even the stuff that sits right in front of us. That being the case, I've decided to strictly isolate this segment from the rest of Track#1 by fully detailing how I came about what seems to me to be the only plausible ex-

AutoGenesism: A Theory of Everything

planation of how the Relative Being State (which is the being state that is required for anything to physically exist) initiated; with permanent physical Reality as the default ramification of that very unique and singular event. Without this one aspect of Auto-G fully fleshed out, there's no reason to proceed any further; therefore, I'm going to treat this subsection special.

Now, I will state ahead of this that, unlike much of what's been confidently declared within the myths, legends, allegorical constructions, and poetic expressions associated with this topic, it is possible to successfully determine and detail the genesis of physical Reality as a real and relatable emergence event. And, there's a really important reason why this is, and why it must be, possible to achieve. That is because complete system coherence must exist as a foundation of any full and functional Theory of Everything.

The requirement of system coherence demands that from the least to the greatest, and from the most primordial to the most sophisticated, the fundamental nature of everything that comprises a system must share a readily appreciable familiarity. The whole of it must be coherent. In this case, the presented definition of everything must reflect the fact that physical Reality is one relationship matrix, and only one relationship matrix, regardless of how many contextually distinct holon structures exist within that one, apical relationship matrix.

In many scientific theories concerning the nature of physical Reality, we're told that Reality is a lot weirder than we can imagine. Of course, one definition of *weird* can be a lot more structurally isolative that another definition of *weird*, and the nature of normal is certainly a progressing revelation. However, there are limits to how different two things can actually be while physically adhering to a natural level of system coherence; certainly when dealing with a structural coherence that exists as an ongoing default ramification.

> ***For instance*** — Can anything possess absolute properties (an infinite mass density, for instance) while it exists relative to the rest of physical Reality? Not unless other absolute properties are relatively commonplace within what would seem to be a being state that cannot permit such properties to exist. It's not the extreme density of the mass that's in question. It's the absolute, infinite property attribute that's been theoretically assigned to that density. Immediately, all system coherence has been compromised by a clear violation of the Relative Being State by the introduction of a mass density that cannot physically exist relative to any other amount of mass density. By this application of the requirement of system coherence, Black Holes cannot be structured in the manner that theorists believe them to be structured. And yes, it gets even worse

when the Big Bang is slipped under the same microscope and hit with a few probes.

As you can see, there are definite limits to just how weird Reality can get, and it's not a case of anyone attempting to impose limits. It's about acknowledging the default consistency of what's real as opposed to trying to impose the contradictory nature of adventurous intellectual abstractions on a definition of that which simply isn't even remotely associated with that sort of thing. Reality is a factual relationship structure that's constantly evolving as a default ramification of changes and events. It is what it is, and it's much too relentlessly dynamic to structurally tolerate any true contradictions.

What I want to do now is lay out exactly what kind of thinking led me to believe that I had accurately determined, and could successfully detail, what occurred to bring physical Reality into existence. It won't be a linear presentation of this-following-that-and-on-to-that, since the instant that we're dealing with here didn't spring from a this-following-that kind of state. Still, by the time I get done here, I'm pretty sure that you'll understand what I see as having occurred, and you'll have more than a vague notion concerning how I came to see it as having occurred as it did. At the very least, you'll have a good appreciation for how my mind works when addressing historically intractable conundrums such as this.

Determining the Instant of Genesis

The very first thing that I made sure of was that I knew that my terminology was going to be consistent, and that each primary term was going to represent a quantity, a quality, or a state that does, in fact, exist in the manner that the term suggests. Yes, this is about language, but it's also about accurate attribution. When I refer to Identity, I need to know that I am referring to something that's been thoroughly examined and determined to be a fundamental aspect of logical thought. After all, the word itself is used in a variety of manners, even though one of those uses has been fundamental to the stabilization of conceptualization for centuries.

The classical *"Three Laws of Thought"* are the three fundamental linguistic principles without which there could be no intelligible communication. Their formal expression is generally attributed to Aristotle, and they were foundational in later scholastic logic. The law of identity is the most fundamental of the three, the law of non-contradiction and the law of excluded middle being corollaries.

AutoGenesism: A Theory of Everything

http://en.wikipedia.org/wiki/Law_of_thought#The_three_classical_laws

As we've already seen throughout this examination, conceptual stabilization is critical, and accurate terminology is key to that stabilization. None of this has been easy, but working to get this one notion correct, and then to accurately communicate that fully determined notion in a fixed format was a truly harrowing endeavor. Still, I always knew that it was possible to connect Reality, at its most mundane and commonplace, to this one seemingly impossible transition from nothing to something, and to accurately communicate how that transition occurred. Like I already stated, system coherence demands that whatever it was that occurred, it must be thoroughly relatable to what has developed as a result of that occurrence. In other words, nothing that was involved in that transition can be at all alien to the fundamental nature of what occurs all the time. Knowing this to be true [and required] eliminated a lot of guesswork and overly adventurous musings.

Since this is an investigation into something that did, in fact, occur, I decided to employ deductive reasoning [deductive logic] and to remain strict in that usage. I realize that many modern theorists freely depend on inductive logic, but that's not something that investigators allow themselves to fall prey to. If they did, the prisons would be packed with innocent people whose only crimes were based on statistical predilection and nothing else. Obviously, since the instant of physical genesis did happen as a singular and non-recurrent event, a subtractive approach to establishing the nature of that event (in the same manner that the pros approach those one-off occurrences of criminality that they deal with all the time) is the most effective approach. So, that's the approach I took.

Once I determined that deduction [*a process of reasoning in which a conclusion follows necessarily from the premises presented, so that the conclusion cannot be false if the premises are true — Random House Dictionary, 2014*] was going to be the key to solving this mystery, I began listing the premises that I knew to be true, or that I had excellent cause to believe to be accurate as a direct inferential result of what I knew to be true.

This is the list of what I know to be true:

- Reality is the relationship matrix consisting of all physically existent holons
- The Change/Event Unit (C/EU) is the quantized [identical duration] causal foundation of emerging Reality
- The residual Fact Set (RFS) is the primary holon that bases Reality's

relationship matrix

- An RFS physically emerges in default response to every C/EU's occurrence, accurately and permanently representing that C/EU as having factually occurred
- Each C/EU occurs within a trajectory of C/EU quanta
- Each C/EU trajectory is accurately and permanently represented by an RFS continuum
- A Reality confine is determined by the quantum duration of its foundational Change/Event Units — the Unit Rate of Change (URC), — establishing and enforcing a contextual substructure based on quantized synchronization.
- The URC is the physical basis of linear Time.
- We refer to our own Reality as The Universe
- The Relative Being State exists [this relative to that]
- The Relative Being State is the being state of physical Reality
- An Absolute Being State [required for physical existence possessing infinite properties of any kind] cannot exist if the Relative Being State exists
- The existence of the Relative Being State confirms that the concept of infinite regression [beginning-less physical existence] is a logical fallacy
- The impossibility of beginning-less physical existence proves that the genesis of physical Reality [the emergence of the Relative Being State] did occur

This is the list of what I have excellent cause to believe to be accurate as a direct inferential result of what I know to be true:

- There is no such thing as absolute or infinite physical existence [it's an imaginary conceptual construct that is logically impossible]
- The Change/Event Unit is the only candidate available when one searches for the very first physically existent something
- The C/EU only lasts long enough to cause a residual Fact Set to emerge as a permanent representative of the fact that it (the C/EU) occurred.
- The residual Fact Set is the only physically existent something that can persist long enough to exist relative to whatever it is that is NOT it.
- The RFS established the Relative Being State as a result of its permanent physicality.

AutoGenesism: A Theory of Everything

- The key to solving the mystery of existential genesis is determining the nature of the change/event that launched Reality and the Relative Being State.

So, this is where I started my investigation, and to be honest, it's taken several years of developing AutoGenesism as a fully fleshed out Theory of Everything to even allow me the perspective that makes approaching this conundrum in a realistic manner possible. And, as I stated above, this is due to the requirement that Reality, as a macro-system in its own right, possess full structural coherence; most critically, with that coherence defining its instant of genesis. As tempting as it is to craft an ingenious solution that can compete with the brilliant narratives that have populated the minds and cultures of our human race, my goal has been to get it right. Even if that means that I'm forced to strip every bit of mystery and majesty out of that one instant in order to do so.

I realized early on that whatever it was that *changed*, it could not have been something that already existed as a physically expressed something. That said, it had to have been existent in its own sense of what that might suggest. Not necessarily capable of existing in ongoing Association with what is physically existent, and perhaps not even something that survived the instant of physical genesis itself, since any Change/Event Unit would have left a residual Fact Set in its place as permanently existent; thereby satisfying the Relative Being State's need for the persisting existence of a physical *something* to provide the necessary contextual juxtaposition. That said, the state of existence that the changeling would have possessed would have to be quite commonplace even now, since system coherence would demand this of every participant within this once-ever instance of transformation.

This increasing definition of what could and could not have been the subject of change (thereby providing the single Change/Event Unit that launched the whole of physical Reality) channeled my investigation into the nature of Potentiality and Actuality. After all, what is change but the transition from Potential to Actual? Besides, it's a fact that if something does exist [and physical Reality certainly does exist] then it was preceded by the potential that it can exist. This seemed to be a promising direction.

I dug into what was readily available concerning the science and philosophy of Potentiality and Actuality [Aristotle, Leibniz, Sachs, Kosman, Coope and even St. Thomas of Aquinas] and quickly learned just how complex and nuanced something so seemingly simple can be. What I also realized was that for something to transition from Potentiality to Actuality, there must be a trigger of some sort, and this suggested the requirement of an agent that provides that trigger [much in the same way that a specific confluence of contributing factors reaches a contextual balance that triggers the launch of an emergent system]. Obviously, this wasn't going to make sense if what I was trying to determine was the initiation of physical Reality itself. In fact, no trigger could have existed to transform that Potential for the emergence of physical Reality into the Actual emergence of physical Reality.

So, this is what it looks like in general, with all the actors in this drama onstage at the same time.

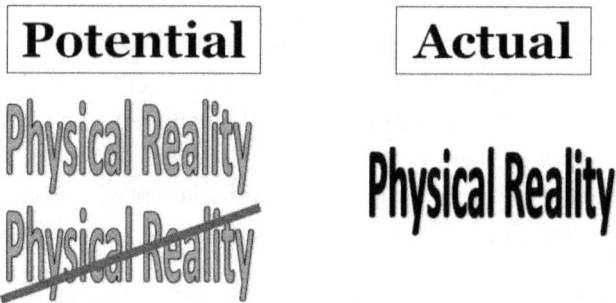

Potential   **Actual**

Physical Reality

~~Physical Reality~~   **Physical Reality**

Figure 2:1-A
As you can see, both Potentials (for and against the realization of physical Reality) existed until one or the other became Actual

But, this [Figure 2:1-B] is closer to what it actually was like . . .

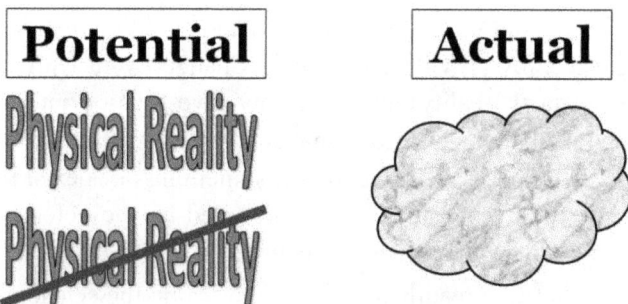

Potential   **Actual**

Physical Reality

~~Physical Reality~~

Figure 2:1-B
As long as the Potential continues to exist in its own state, the Actual doesn't, and cannot, exist at all.

. . . and I might add, what this same process looks like when it occurs countless times, each and every moment, across our entire universe. Of course, once the Actual emerges, both Potentials (since they are both precursors of only that one emergent Actuality) must necessarily cease to exist.

Potential   Actual

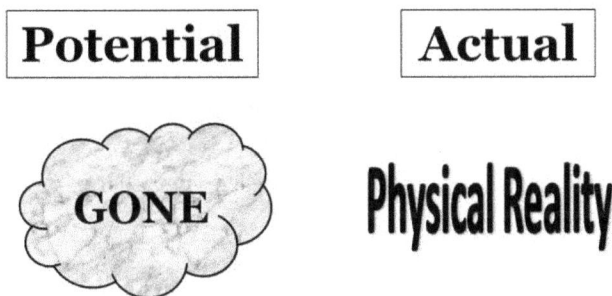

GONE

Physical Reality

Figure 2:1-C
The existence of both Potentials ceases as soon as either emerges as Actual

I remember getting up from my desk and walking into the living room at that point, and deciding that it was a good time to lay back and rest my mind a little. Hell, for all I knew, there was no possible way for the potential for physical Reality to ever be realized, in spite of the fact that it clearly was realized [look at all the physical Reality that does, in fact, exist].

Just as I laid down, it hit me. The simplest of thoughts. Not fancy and certainly not anything that could be defined as genius. I remember saying to myself *"Yeah, some Potentiality that was. I'm surprised that it ever got it together at all."* — and it was at that instant that the most primitive of all possible notions walked right up . . . slipped right up behind that quick bit of frustrated internal dialog . . . and the damn thing stood there and smiled right in my face. I didn't get a chance to rest my mind or anything else for the rest of that afternoon. I now had the answer, and I needed to get it sketched out before the startling simplicity of it all intimidated me into dismissing it altogether. As you'll see, this realization is so simple that . . . well, all I can say is that even after sketching it out and aggressively vetting it relative to its coherence with the rest of Auto-G, I required some time alone with it before I could feel sure that I actually had something there.

Kevin Brian Carroll

The Emergence of the Relative Being State

The first thing I want to say is that the reason I spent so much time and effort chasing down the nature of the change/event that started it all is because Reality is a literal chain reaction that started with just that one Change/Event Unit (as you'll discover as soon as I get done with this issue of physical genesis.) From that first ever Change/Event Unit, Reality has whipped forward and has never stopped progressing and developing and defining itself, so it seemed obvious to me that the target of this investigation into that instance of existential genesis was going to be one simple and unprecedented change from what *was* to what *had never been.*

What I didn't consider, until that afternoon of digging into Potentiality and Actuality, was that for the emergence of physical Reality to occur, the existing potential (for the emergence of physical existence) didn't have to be triggered to change. Yes, once physical Reality emerged, that specific state of Potential would no longer exist (since it was a realized potential; having just become actual), but I realized that something else could have affected that Potential state without having acted upon that potential, or having had any impact on it whatsoever.

When I said, *"Yeah, some Potentiality that was. I'm surprised that it ever got it together at all."*, what became existent was my own intellectual realization that while the potential for the emergence of physical Reality obviously did exist, at some point so did the counter potential that the emergence of physical Reality would never occur [in whatever manner it is that Potentiality continues to exist even now, within that being state that does not feature the progressive change duality of now and then]. What is inescapable is that as soon as that counter Potential came into being, each existing Potential (each a potential that — if realized — would be replaced by a qualitatively different net result; assigning each its own relative presence) created a true and actual juxtaposition between itself and the other. For that instant, those two distinct and propertied Potentialities did exist relative to one another. The default ramification of that juxtaposition was the immediate emergence of the Relative Being State — which was the 1st ever Change/Event Unit. And you'll see that this is what launched physical Reality into permanent existence.

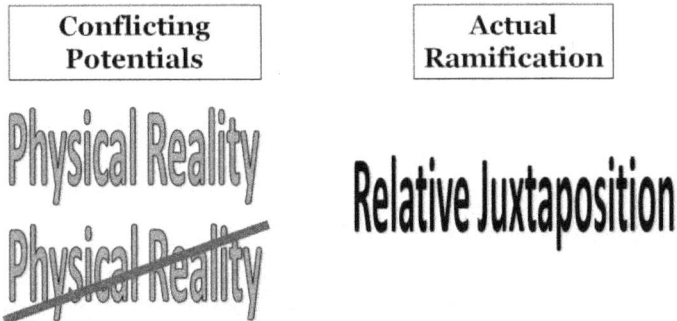

| Conflicting Potentials | Actual Ramification |

Figure 2:1-E
What really emerged as a result of that first clash of Potential vs Counter Potential was the first-ever instance of *relative* juxtaposition.

Of course, both opposing Potentials ceased to exist as soon as the one was realized as Actual and the other relegated to oblivion, but as physical Reality has persisted, so has this relationship between the Potential and the Actual, with the Actual erasing the Potential as soon as it emerges to replace it. So, is the Potential physically existent? No, it's not, but it does exist in a nonphysical state until the Actual emerges as physically existent, and that's important to note here.

> ***Note*** — Certainly the Heisenberg Uncertainty Principle has cemented the concept of potential versus counter potential within the field of Quantum Mechanics, with all existing potentials evaporating the instant that the actual emerges as physically existent [they call it a collapsing wave]. The fact that some theorists insist that each potential be physically existent is unfortunate, but then some theorists take Heisenberg's principle and "generate" infinite numbers of entire universes with it. Obviously there's more (and/or less) to Reality than most will ever agree on, but as I've stated already, Reality isn't something that requires human agreement. It simply is what it is.

What I finally remembered — as I searched in vain for the trigger that had to have transformed the Potential for physical Reality into the Actuality of physical Reality — was that I actually needed to successfully determine the 1st-ever change/event; not run down a Potential-to-Actual trigger agent. That 1st-ever change/event (as I'll begin to detail in the next sub-section, any change/event would suffice) would kick off all that's occurred and developed and progressed ever since (which, in a nutshell is a really apt definition of physical Reality). Upon that realization, I immediately noticed [just look to the left side of Figure 2:1-E and there they are] that any Potential for the existence of physical Reality would have had to have been, at some point, challenged with the counter Potential that physical Reality would never exist at all, with both competing Potentials creating an unprecedented instance of relative juxtaposition.

Remember that relative juxtaposition can only occur within the Relative Being State, which could not have existed at all up to that instant. That being the case, the Relative Being State had to suddenly exist [by default ramification] as soon as that relative juxtaposition occurred. Also, keep in mind that the emergence of an unprecedented being state would certainly constitute a true change/event. Each Change/Event Unit causes a permanently existent Fact Set to immediately emerge [by default ramification, as you'll recall from Section I], to forever represent the fact that the Change/Event Unit did (in fact) occur. That permanent, physically existent Fact Set would always (and forever) provide at least one *something* to exist relative to *something* that isn't it [as well as a relative absence]; forever cementing the default reign of the Relative Being State. As trite as it sounds, this would jump-start the chain reaction that is physical Reality, and it would do so from a complete absence of physical existence.

Since this is a really critical bit of information, here's a somewhat bulleted rundown for those of you that prefer that sort of thing. To make it easier to follow, I'll even structure it out as sort of a logic proof.

Premise #1:

The notion of Infinite Regression has been proven to be a logical fallacy

This means that:

At some point, that which exists as Actual did not exist.

Physical Reality is a relationship matrix of that which exists as Actual.

This means that:

At some point physical Reality did not exist.

Premise #2:

If something exists as Actual, it exists relative to that which is not it

This means that:

The Relative Being State is the being state of physical Reality

At some point, physical Reality did not exist.

This means that:

AutoGenesism: A Theory of Everything

At some point, the Relative Being State did not exist.

Premise #3

The physical manifestation of the Actual is always preceded by an existing Potential

The Potential's existence ends when the physical emergence of the Actual is realized

This means that:

The Potential and the realized Actual do not share being state

That which exists as Potential doesn't always manifest as Actual

The failure of a specific Potential to actualize [its opposing Potential actualizes] will terminate that Potential's existence

This means that:

The Potential exists solely as a precursor to the Actual

Premise #4

Each Potential for success is balanced by a Potential for failure

That balance can shift until one or the other Potential is realized

Devoid of system precedent, either Potential is realizable

This means that:

Novel emergence is a real crapshoot.

Conclusions:

Physical Reality was necessarily preceded by the Potential that it would become Actual

That specific Potential was necessarily the first Potential to ever exist

At some point, the Potential that Physical Reality would not become Actual existed

These competing Potentials existed relative to one another

Ramifications:

The existence of this relative juxtaposition created the Relative Being State

The creation of the Relative Being State was the 1st-ever change/event

That change/event caused the 1st-ever residual Fact Set's default emergence

That residual Fact Set's default physical permanence cemented the Actualization of Physical Reality.

The Actualization of Physical Reality ended the existence of both competing Potentials.

So, that's as good as I see this explanation ever getting. Now, keep in mind that this genesis theory does fully satisfy every requirement, and sets everything up nicely for what lies ahead for Reality. The truth is that while no one can flatly declare the precise steps that took place in that very singular instant, it is instructive to remember that this event did happen, that whatever happened must have involved existential staples that persist even now, and that the entire thing was ridiculously simple in structural requirement.

This is my own take on the instant of existential genesis, and if you've got a better take, then by all means, let's have it out in the market place of intellectual discourse. Just leave the chalk and blackboard home. Seriously. Math [zeros and ones and prime numbers and all that] could not have been involved in that one extremely primitive incident, and I really hope that we can all agree on at least that one overwhelmingly obvious fact. Beyond that, I'd be fascinated by any and all theories concerning how Reality appeared from nowhere, just before it got up on all fours and started its journey to where it sits today. As for my own take on where Reality went forward from here, read on.

. . . and Away We Go!

This 1st ever change/event resulted in the fact of that change to physically emerge (by direct default response) as a Fact Set. Let's take a look at all that occurred when that 1st ever change/event took place, so we can examine the Fact Set itself and what it permanently represents as having changed when it emerged.

The first-ever change/event established that:

- If a something physically emerges, it is preceded by the potential that it will physically emerge
- All potential for the realization of physical emergence is countered by the potential against the realization of physical emergence

AutoGenesism: A Theory of Everything

- The emergence of the Relative Being State [this exists relative to that which is not it] had to occur upon the incident of relative juxtaposition

The default emergence of this Fact Set was also an event; the second-ever change/event. There were several very important and permanent ramifications of this first-ever Fact Set emergence. Let's take a look at a quick bulleted list.

The first-ever default emergence of a Fact Set established that:

- Change/events cause Fact Sets to physically exist as a default ramification [something happens, the fact that it happened comes into existence]
- When something happens, it can never NOT have happened [each Fact Set therefore possesses permanent physical existence]
- The permanence of each Fact Set establishes a relative contextual juxtaposition between itself and anything else that also physically exists, as well as between itself and the absence of physical existence
    - The permanence of each Fact Set assures the permanence of the Relative Being State

Something else happened when that first-ever Fact Set emerged as a result of that first-ever change/event. Actually, a lot of stuff happened. It's probably best that I simply bullet it all out here initially and then take some time to wade through the specifics once that's been done.

As a result of the default emergence of Fact Sets, the following were established:

- The physical emergence of any information set — in any form or configuration — constitutes a change/event
    - This set emergence results in yet another information Fact Set to physically emerge
    - and again, this physical Fact Set emergence brings yet another Fact Set into physical existence
- This constitutes a very real chain reaction of physical emergence as each Fact Set's emergence event causes a representing Fact Set to emerge
- The relative existence of all Fact Sets (as well as the ongoing emergence of a new Fact Set per each subsequent change/event) causes each Fact Set to possess a definite, yet ever evolving, contextual relationship between itself and all other Fact Sets

- This contextual relationship that exists and develops between all Fact Sets, as a constantly emerging whole, establishes the structure and identity of a URC-Determined Environmental Confine — we call this constantly emerging relationship matrix *Reality*

Yes, these were some heady moments, and a lot was being determined and established. Now, I fully realize how incredibly crude and simplistic these initial achievements might seem when viewed from where we stand as Reality's epitome of developmental sophistication, but when examining the factual nature of Reality, our human point of perspective is always a challenge that must be overcome. I know that I could have loaded this reveal with jargon that I grabbed from a physics dissertation, or perhaps some mystical sounding medieval references in an attempt to better showcase its relative significance, but what good would that have done? I want you to fully understand what I've discovered. I want you to know what I know, even when it's really obvious and pedestrian.

What started everything rolling was the same as everything that's sitting right in front of you right now. And the reason it was, is because it never stopped being what it is. It's still the basis of everything that occurs and reoccurs all the time. What started physical Reality is what makes everything real, and this is how it is from the quantum of Now right on up to the entire universe as a whole. This hasn't changed and it won't change. The fundamentals are fundamental and they will always be fundamental. And that will always be true because they're fundamental to what is real.

I do understand that we all have been raised to demand that *The Unknowable* be a lot more unknowable than what I just described to you, but I think we can all agree that plenty of what we were raised to believe has turned out to be untrue. That said, the real question is whether I can successfully (and clearly) connect my description of this inauspicious beginning to the world that we all see, hear, touch, taste and smell, while adhering to the rigid requirements [default ramification, system coherence, universal pursuit of the meta-law Identity Survival, and periodic system emergence via readily apparent factor confluence] that I am holding all other Theories of Everything to, and the truth is, I think that you'll be surprised at how well I can.

AutoGenesism: A Theory of Everything

Wash, Rinse, Repeat

Note — do you remember that segment within Section I concerning Identity Survival and how I detailed why it is the sole primordial existential imperative for that which has become physically existent? If not, then go ahead and take another look at it while I wait.

All set? Good. This part is going to have a lot to do with Identity and what it means to survive in the physical confines of the Relative Being State. It can get pretty complicated, but I'm going to work to keep it as simple in this segment as possible, since I've got a whole extended segment on it in Section III's Digressions area.

What I want to let you in on is the fact that there are several ways that Identity Survival is pursued by things that physically exist (and that therefore have Identity). These include *Isolation* and *Competition*, which we'll refer to as **Masculine Survival Expressions** (because they are based on the active elimination of threats) and *Increase, Association* and *Symbiosis*, which we'll refer to as **Feminine Survival Expressions** (because they are based on the passive inclusion and creation of contextual similarity between things trying to survive).

Note — You can look at gender any way you wish on your own, but here, I need to keep the word count to a manageable level, so I've adopted a traditional (and therefore fairly intuitive, and regardless of culture) pursuit-behavior labeling system when it comes to Identity Survival Expressions and the qualifications that are assigned to information wholes as a result (yes, there will be much more on this later).

What I want to reiterate here is that literally every structural advancement that has occurred within the Material Realm, especially raw complexity, is the result of the pursuit of Identity Survival by that which exists. This is true regardless of what level of material structure is being noted as having progressed. Now, this does not mean that the survival being achieved is physical or material survival, even though this is also being pursued and for obvious reasons. What this means is that the physically existent *something's* Identity — the combination of its internal context (its history) and relative context (what it is relative to everything else that also exists) — must persist as contextually integral to the Identity of something that physically persists if at all possible. This can get complicated, but it doesn't have to.

Digression Alert — There's a concept called Holon Theory that was invented by Arthur Koestler and later reinvented by Ken Wilber to ultimately describe existential wholes that combine to create larger, more complex existential wholes. In Section I, I used the Boston Red Sox baseball team as my holon example, since the hierarchy is pretty obvious (players, the team, the Eastern Conference, the American League, and finally, MLB as a whole) and laid it all out in fairly good detail.

That said, what I want to lay out now is how Identity Survival is accomplished by way of leveraging the holon hierarchical structure, and at even the most primitive levels of physical Reality. What we've covered so far is the initial flurry of Change/Event Units, and how each unit's occurrence caused a residual Fact Set to emerge as a default response before being replaced by the next Change/Event Unit's occurrence. What I want to detail now is why, after these initial Change/Event Units occurred, more have continued to occur (obviously they still occur, since they're occurring right now) and what the larger implications are. And I want to do this as quickly and efficiently as possible, so as to not lose your interest while I do. To that end, this digression may involve some bullet points, but I guess we'll just have to see if that turns out to be the case.

In Lee Smolin's 2013 book *"Time Reborn: From the Crisis in Physics to the Future of the Universe"*, he lobbies for the existence of what he calls a meta-law; *"a law that governs how the laws (of physics) evolve"*. I agree with Prof. Smolin, and my candidate for this universal meta-law is Identity Survival's *"first, survive"* existential imperative. It does govern how all subsequent laws evolve and have evolved, but it does even more than that. It literally compels physical and contextual isolations and associations to develop and persist between what would otherwise be separate and disparate holons with no real follow-on connection. This was especially obvious when the whole of Reality itself was just beginning to coalesce into something tangible.

While it is true that the emergence of Fact Sets, and the establishment of existential basics (like the fact that a Fact Set emerges as a direct default ramification of each Change/Event Unit's occurrence) did keep the event chain going for a while, at some point the nature of physical Reality's progressive development process obviously progressed to include more effective and more robust ways of progressively developing Reality as a physically expanding whole. Since it did [let's just all agree that the evidence for this assumption is overwhelming] we've got to determine why it did and

AutoGenesism: A Theory of Everything

propose a plausible theory concerning how it did; well, initially, how it did. I've compiled a much more thorough effort in Section III's Digressions area of this book, but for this initial genesis overview, I'm going to lay out why one Change/Event Unit would be compelled to replace the last Change/Event Unit, and why the rinse-repeat chain reaction might even become a much more expansive and complicated affair before long.

What Arthur Koestler and Ken Wilber discovered and developed concerning holon structure changed the way that many of us view societal and biological matrices, but what they didn't realize is how the holon structure serves the meta-law Identity Survival. They also didn't realize that holon structuring was the initial survival strategy and was employed by the Change/Event Unit in its own struggle for Identity Survival in those earliest moments of physical Reality. Let's see if I can briefly encapsulate how this worked as a survival strategy. Keep in mind that the duration of all Change/Event Units are quantized, as has been proven over the last 100 years or so by Einstein, Planck, Bohr and others.

- Change/Event Unit (C/EU)#1 happens
- Change/Event Unit #2 (C/EU#1's Fact Set emergence) happens as a direct ramification of the occurrence of C/EU#1.
- A trajectory of Change/Event Units is created as a result of C/EU#1's immediate causal connection to C/EU#2's occurrence.
- The creation of this first-ever C/EU trajectory results in C/EU#1's Identity being contextually integral to the Identity of C/EU#2 (C/EU#1 persists as internal/historical context of C/EU#2) and both C/EU#1 and C/EU#2 being integral to the Identity of this first-ever C/EU trajectory (or simply C/ET#1), which is now a physically existent holon in its own right
- C/EU#1's Identity Survival — as a result — has been prolonged by a full 100%, due to the fact of C/EU#2's Identity being contextually defined by the physical occurrence of C/EU#1, with both C/EU#1 and C/EU#2's Identities being further prolonged as the holon C/ET#1 (it's the first-ever after all) persists (as new C/EUs emerge at the Unit Rate of Change) with both C/EU#1 and C/EU#2 continuing to be contextually integral to its own Identity

And it's just that simple. Yes, C/EU#1 did not physically survive longer than the quantum rate of change, but C/EU#1's Identity did persist

181

longer, and it is survival of Identity that is what's at stake.

Now, to better connect all of this to what continues to occur even now, let's take a quick look at the pursuit of Identity Survival at a more readily accessible level of progressive development and see if it doesn't begin to get really obvious that ID Survival is what drives everything to do and be what it does and is.

In Section I, I showed you the various ways that most humans on this planet pursue Identity Survival from day to day. In nature, Identity Survival is also being pursued as each species and subspecies naturally responds to the span of existence it's been allowed by adding more of itself to its kind. In fact, replication and procreation are easily the most obvious examples of a high-level life form Identity Survival strategy based on holon structuring. Obviously, the replicating or procreating *something* is only pursuing ID Survival (survival of its unique biological identity specifics) and certainly not the survival of its material structure, since the passing of the procreative phase of a biological holon's lifespan generally initiates a very deliberate structural decline process that culminates in the natural death of the organism.

So, let's look at holon hierarchical structuring as an ID Survival strategy (we can use pine trees as an example), and see how the dropping of pines cones onto the forest floor and the possible seeding of that floor with a new generation of pine trees serves a pine tree's natural pursuit of Identity Survival.

> Again, in a holon hierarchical structure, holons combine in common cause to create a larger holon (I used the Boston Red Sox and their players as an example). Each player is a holon and the team of all the players combined is a greater holon. In that example the Identity of the team has certainly lasted longer than the Identity of any one player, and yet each player who's ever been a member of that team has contributed to the ongoing Identity of the team to the degree that the team itself would not at all exist if not for each and every individual player who has, at one point in its long and storied history, been a player member of it.

When we take this example and apply it to the Identity Survival of a non-specific pine tree, we exchange the Boston Red Sox team holon for the genus *Pinus* holon, since the genus holon sits just above the species holon, and we didn't specify a specific species of pine tree (making the species level the lowest level of holon referenced; the referred equivalent of the

AutoGenesism: A Theory of Everything

Red Sox player holon). Easy enough.

Let's now examine this hierarchical structure relative to the Identity Survival pursuit of a single Japanese Red Pine tree. Since this is one tree, we've got to acknowledge that the next-higher holon tier (just above that one Japanese Red Pine tree) within that specific hierarchical structure is the species *Pinus Densiflora* holon. Each Japanese Red Pine tree seeds the next generation, doing its part to contribute to the material survival of the species holon that is Pinus Densiflora. In turn, that species holon provides each Red Japanese Pine tree's inimitable Identity a real and actual contextual preservation [as historically integral to the species' contextual Identity] for as long as there are any Japanese Red Pine trees that exist on Planet Earth. And it's the fact of this default reciprocity that compels biological holons to contribute to the survival of their species through replication or procreation.

So, how does any of this relate to the simple Change/Event Unit, and how the structure of physical Reality clearly progressed to the point where there are sentient/sapient minds puzzling over the relationship between holon structure and Identity Survival? To get there, we'll need to briefly encapsulate Section III's digression *"Our Emergent Universe: How the Event Became Spatial"*, and begin that journey by introducing the first really significant post-genesis instance of true system emergence.

"This general hypothesis concerns the transition from simple chain-of-event existence to what can be truly considered material existence. I intend to make the case that this involves the progressive development of the URC-Determined Environmental Confine as a whole (universe, if you like) to include the emergence of the Change/Spatial Unit trajectory (or simply *spatial trajectory*) as a critical contributing factor to the survival of its (our universe's) inimitable contextual Identity, and to detail the spatial trajectory's part in the creation of physical space, physical distance and relative proximity. I also intend to show that physical existence does make this transition the only way that anything develops; as a result of Identity Survival (the lone existential requirement) specifically pulling that transition forward."

This is — in essence — how *"Our Emergent Universe: How the Event Became Spatial"* starts, and as you can see, it's no small feat being attempted here. In fact, to date, this hasn't been accomplished by anyone else, so I will need you to be sympathetic to the fact that connecting the quantum of Now to the quantum of action does take a lot more than a quick overview to fully flesh out exactly how that connection initially took place. I do cover it fully within that specific digression, but as a result of a need to preserve room for much more to cover in this section, you'll get the crib notes here.

My understanding of how this initially took place is that it involved (yet again) the presentation of a requirement, and the physical emergence of a unique and novel manifestation that satisfied that requirement. This is the same potential-expenditure build/release paradigm that we encounter when any emergent system becomes physically existent as a result of a confluence of factors and requirement. Of course, there were differences present when this specific emergence occurred, but the process basis has always been pretty much the same. After all, with system coherence serving as a fundamental requirement, why would the basic nature of it fundamentally change?

> "Now, I've made the case that Identity Survival is the sole existential imperative, and provided plenty of evidence to that effect. That means that if I'm to remain consistent here, I need to show that the emergence of the spatial trajectory can only occur (or have ever occurred) if it serves that specific requirement (Identity Survival) for something that already exists. In this case, I'll be declaring that the existence of the spatial trajectory serves the Identity Survival requirement of both, the Change/Event Unit Trajectory (or simply *event trajectory*) and the relationship matrix involving all that physically existed at that instant (both change/event and information) that we refer to physical Reality."

Yes, we're going to introduce the spatial trajectory, and we're going to quickly detail how the spatial trajectory emerged (and still emerges) from the event trajectory — or, as some rogue physicist might suggest, that *time is not a product of movement, but that movement is a product of time*. I realize that this notion of the universal primacy of time runs counter to Einstein's Relativity theories, but if that's going to throw you, then you may as well stop now, since much of what we'll be examining going forward is counter to what has been scientific scripture during the last 100 years. The truth is that Einstein's Relativity (specifically GR) does work if you've built your mock-up of Reality using very specific mathematical sets and adventurous assumptions, but the net result has sent theorists of all kinds on a decades-long bender involving being-state clashes, multiverses containing indeterminable quantities of constantly sprouting universes, and any number of impossible-to-verify spatial dimensions in their efforts to make any of its default ramifications sync up with what's real and universally verifiable. I'm not troubled by the idea that Einstein might have inspired so many others to put this specific carriage before this specific horse.

At any rate, here's the event-to-spatial emergence confluence as it coalesced with the relentless requirement that something change so that the URC-Determined Environmental Confine's own unique and inimitable Identity could be further defined and therefore protected.

The Initial Confluence Suite

- The Universal Imperative — Identity Survival
  - possession of inimitable Identity = physical existence
- A Change/Event Trajectory (C/ET#1) seeking Identity Survival
- A Successful Resolution Precedent
  - A residual Fact Set Continuum
    - Holon collaboration (Increase) results in C/EU Identity survival
    - Contextual Association (entanglement) results in C/ET Identity survival

As we've established, for emergence to occur, there must be a very specific confluence of factors (specific to that particular emergence, of course) that causes that emergence. We see here that there are three factors . . .

- ID Survival requirement,
- something trying to satisfy that requirement (C/ET#1, for instance),
- and the existence of a Fact Set continuum detailing how that requirement has already been satisfied [A Success Precedent]

. . . that have coalesced into an emergence confluence. But is this the only confluence configuration that was possible?

I suppose that anyone can suggest otherwise, but the fact is that at this stage of physical progressive development, what I've listed here is all that existed as available to coalesce. Well, Reality existed, but the confluence itself was an aspect of Reality, since Reality is only the complete whole of all relationships and confluences that exist. So, no, you couldn't include Reality on the list of coalescing factors.

This confluence included the requirement, the physically existent item with that requirement, and information concerning how that requirement had already been successfully satisfied, and as emergence confluences go, this one literally had it all sewn up. Still, what was needed was a unique and unprecedented physical solution, and as we've witnessed time and time again, physical emergence is the means by which these unique and unprecedented physical solutions become part of the whole of reliably repeatable Reality without the requirement of a *"particle"* of some sort to make the blackboard math balance out.

In this case (and who knows if there were misfires or what-have-you before a win was finally registered) what happened was a simple broadening of what constitutes a true change from Now and Then (as a system-altering change/event) to include Here and There (a change in relative proximity — definitely a system-altering paradigm transformation) with the emergence of Change/Spatial Unit #1 (or C/SU#1), ultimately launching Change/Spatial Trajectory #1 (C/ST#1) with a mother lode of macro-system Identity Survival benefits immediately obvious for the URC-Determined Environmental Confine (URC-DEC) and its ongoing need for Identity Survival ensuring contextual complexity. Of course, this locked this specific emergence in as a *"do this again"* priority preference within the affected URC-DEC relationship matrix. And how can we be sure that such a translation did occur? Let's bullet it out and see what we have as certainties.

- Again, spatial proximity and spatial trajectories exist.
- The quantum of action (based solely on the release of kinetic energy, C/S units) and the quantum of Now (based solely on the progression of C/E Units) are inextricably linked to the degree that the first cannot exist apart from the manifestation of the second.
- The denial of an initial emergence of either creates an infinite regression logical dilemma, since both do exist and both do persist to this day.
- Nature continues to feature common examples of exactly the kinds of physical emergence and emergent systems that the transformation of these three confluence factors into the Change/Spatial Trajectory suggest.

Considering the complete absence of any other plausible alternative explanation for the existence of both movement and spatial proximity, I'm very comfortable with suggesting that this is how both the URC-DEC's Identity Survival requirement and C/ET#1's Identity Survival requirement were greatly enhanced with the existence of this one emergent system.

It is important to note here that any and all variations of the Change/Event Trajectory (spatial or otherwise) are factually represented by the Informational Continuum (IC) as Change/Event Trajectories (C/ET) with the specifics (whether it is a spatial change, a Fact Set emergence change, or any other sort of change) included as part of the contextual Identity of the C/ET being physically represented. As far as the URC-DEC is concerned (to anthropomorphize it all for just a moment) a change is a change is a change, and the Identity specifics are the only delineating factors that exist between one C/E Trajectory and the next.

So, what were some of those ID Survival benefiting ramifications that locked the emergence of the Change/Spatial Trajectory in as part of the structural basis of Reality?

- A change from one proximity position, relative to all else that exists within each quantum of Now, to another proximity position (eventually resulting in **C/ST#1**) is registered within the URC-DEC's Informational Continuum (IC) as the launch of a unique Change/Event Trajectory (**C/ET#2**) that will serve the ID Survival of **C/ET#1** (since **C/ET#1** was integral to the emergence confluence that brought **C/ST#1** into existence) and all C/E Units that were ever part of the contextual history of **C/ET#1**.

- Even though **C/ST#1** (again, each Change/Spatial Trajectory is permanently represented within the Residual IC as just another Change/Event Trajectory — **C/ET#2**, in this case) will be physically distinct from the "authoring" **C/ET#1** (the C/E Trajectory that contributed to its emergence) **C/ET#2** will always be profoundly contextually entangled with **C/ET#1** as a result of **C/ET#1**'s direct involvement in its physical emergence. (thereby enhancing **C/ET#1's** ID survival potential).

- This default contextual entanglement result establishes the survival benefit of physical diversification as a successful precedent.

- The fact that the precedent/precedence structure that serves the

URC-Determined Environmental Confine's ID Survival pursuit *"sees"* each Change/Spatial Unit as just another Change/Event Unit means that — as a ramification of the C/E Unit's successful contribution to the ID Survival of the URC-DEC — each C/S Unit's survival will, by default, also be pursued within a trajectory comprised of Change/Spatial Units (creating **C/ST#1**).

- This established the transferability of preferred survival precedent (precedence) from one system to a similar, but more robust, system.
- A spatial change launches a Fact Set that fully and permanently represents the contextual ramifications of that spatial change as a change/event; establishing that all forms of change/events bring Fact Sets into existence as a default ramification.
- The emergence of each residual Fact Set (concerning the emergence and establishment of each C/S Unit's contribution to — in this case — **C/ST#1**) is also a change/event, with the emergence of each new associated Fact Set (in this case, representing the emergence of each quantum constituent within **C/ST#1**) occurring as a follow-on (and contextually entangled) Change/Event Trajectory (to become **CE/T#3** in this case)
  - Due to the specific reason for the emergence of this new Change/Event Trajectory (in this case, **C/ET#3**) [al-though it is a continuum of residual Fact Sets concerning the factual existence of a spatial trajectory — **C/ST#1** in this case — its physical emergence does constitute a default impact on the contextual relationship composition within the URC-DEC after all, making it a Change/Event Trajectory in its own right] **C/ET#3** will be contextually entangled with the C/E Trajectory (**C/ET#1**) that was part of the **C/ST#1**'s originating emergent system confluence suite.
  - This physically distinct, yet contextually entangled C/E Trajectory (**C/ET#3**) now serves to further assist the ID Survival pursuit of that original C/E Trajectory (**C/ET#1**) and the original C/S Trajectory (**C/ST#1** — represented within the URC-DEC's Informational Continuum as **C/ET#2**) as they each continue to physically persist.

AutoGenesism: A Theory of Everything

- The net survival win here is already obvious and profound.
- This new C/E Trajectory (**C/ET#3**) is also available (as are all C/E Trajectories with the same primordial requirement to independently pursue Identity Survival by any and all means possible) to be part of a similar emergent system confluence suite (along with Success Precedent and the Identity Survival imperative, since these factors are perpetually available) that can, and will, cause yet another kinetic energy potential field to emerge to launch yet another spatial trajectory (**C/ST#2** for instance).
- This specific confluence is simple and readily available to produce this specific emergent system, and with each C/S Trajectory succeeding in exponentially extending the C/E Trajectory's ID Survival, it is repeated by URC-DEC ID Survival pursuit directed rote default (in this example, launching **C/ET#4**, **#5**, **#6**, and so on)

As you can see, the mindless pursuit of this lone existential imperative, Identity Survival, was sufficient to establish the literal basis of physical Reality, and to set the table for all that succeeded these earliest of instants. From here on, while it does get more complex, the basic requirement never changes, and this is going to be extremely critical to keep in the front of your mind, since the manner with which that requirement is addressed fluctuates considerably at times.

So, that was one hell of a digression, and while it was necessary, I think it's pretty obvious why repeatedly indulging that sort of thing could negatively impact the cohesion of a complicated presentation. That's why I decided to include an entire section [Section III] devoted to expanding the specifics concerning how some of the bits and pieces of progressive development work.

The truth is that a lot happened in really quick succession, and all of it permanently established how the rest of progressive development would ultimately roll out going forward. And this is something that I really want to stress before moving on past this very early stage of our Reality emergence narrative. The laws of physics, for the most part, are based on very fundamental wins that were achieved very early on. I do realize that some theorists seem to feel the need to suggest that our universe was *fine-tuned* by external forces to be uniquely capable of supporting the kind of life that it features. However, I hope that with this specific digression I've illustrated that:

- when you combine the very simple *"first, survive"* existential imperative
- with the notion that Identity Survival is the only true survival being universally pursued,
- and then realize that the unique nature of holon hierarchy grants that survival through contextual entanglement,
- that it's not very difficult to then factor in the precedent/precedence impact of residual Fact Sets and RFS continuums on any progressive development process
- and come up with an extremely plausible default means by which the basis of the Material Realm, the laws of physics, and literally all that we know to exist, would have had no alternative but to eventually become what it's become,
- and, without anything more than Time itself providing the unitary before and after that this relentless progression needed to do what it's done.

And, while entire libraries of books could be dedicated to just this facet of Reality, we're going to be moving on now, and simply allow for the obvious wash-rinse-repeat that's now been loosed upon the whole of Reality.

The Quantum of Now

I want to quickly address a point that I will be subtly and not-so-subtly reiterating throughout this entire section. That point is that regardless of whatever it is, and regardless of how whatever-it-is manifests, the physical basis of it is either information or the change/event. Even when we get into hybrids [emergent forms that feature properties of both of these basic forms] the physical basis will either be information or Change/Event Units, and there are no exceptions within the whole of physical Reality.

As we established, the first form of physical existence was the Change/Event Unit, which doesn't so much exist as occur. And as soon as it happens, it ceases to physically exist once the next event unit initiates to replace it. This replacement process proceeds as a Change/Event Trajectory, and since the very first Change/Event Unit, there's been no pause whatsoever in that very first Change/Event Trajectory.

We've also established (within that extended digression we just made our way through) that many subsequent Change/Event Trajectories have been

AutoGenesism: A Theory of Everything

launched as a result of the variety of ramifications and ID Survival tactics that were employed as a result of that very first C/E Trajectory, featuring residual Fact Set continuums and even C/S Trajectories establishing proximity, distance, spatial context and all kinds of successful survival precedents that will affect the nature of Reality forever.

What I want to flesh out just a little before we go any further is the absolute core of Reality, and why it is what it is.

When the first Change/Event Unit occurred, it lasted for however long it lasted before being replaced by that second C/E Unit (the system change that was caused by the default physical emergence of the very first residual Fact Set concerning that first C/E Unit's occurrence). That second C/E Unit lasted exactly as long as that first C/E Unit before being replaced by the third C/E Unit [yes, the physical emergence of the residual Fact Set representing the change/event ramification inflicted upon Reality by the emergence of that first-ever residual Fact Set also inflicted its own change/event ramification upon Reality when it emerged] and the point I need to stress here is that, within that Reality, every C/E Unit — from that instant forward — has always been of the exact same duration. We know that this is true, since it was established as true nearly 100 years ago by Planck, Einstein and Bohr, and the field of Quantum Physics became the difference between the 20th Century and all other centuries for the human race.

What Einstein and Bohr and the others didn't extrapolate from their discovery and development of Quantum Theory is that the Quantum of Action is the unit survival strategy of the Quantum of *Now* (as I detailed in the above digression). What they also didn't realize is that this Quantum of *Now* is the unitary basis of Time itself [with all units of Time progression rigidly quantized] and that it is this quantization of Time that forces the quantization of literally all other forms of physical existence.

What becomes obvious, as one fleshes out the ramification structure associated with progressive unitary quantization, is that this quantization of Time also establishes and enforces what can and what cannot share physical existence. This will require a small amount of explanation, but I think I can get this done without resorting to yet another digression.

As has been thoroughly established by Quantum Physics, the quantum itself is indivisible, uniform, and there's no *"space"* between one quantum and the next. This is true regardless of whatever sort of quantum it is that's being referred to. The Quantum of *Now* is yet another quantum unit of physical exist-ence, but as we've now learned, it determines how all other quanta (of any sort) come into physical existence, since all physics agrees that the entire Material Realm [matter] is based on movement/action quanta [C/S Trajectories], and we've just seen that movement/action quanta are created by Time quanta [C/E Trajectories].

Now, with the relationship between Time and matter defined, what's im-portant to bring in is the nature of quantum synchronization, and how this pri-mordial aspect of physical structure affects the relationships that exist between everything that exists, both material and informational. Specifically, the fact that stuff that shares quantum synchronization can have a relationship, and stuff that doesn't share quantum synchronization can't have a relationship. And it's just that simple. In Section I we covered this and there are even diagrams in that section that can help if need be.

Quantum synchronization is based on two *"things"* having the same C/E Unit rate of progression as their quantum basis. We've been referring to this quantum basis as the Unit Rate of Change (URC) and as we stated in Section I, all residual Fact Sets are in default synchronization with the C/E Units that cause them to emerge. This being the case, the URC itself is the *quantum rate*, and it is the literal determination concerning whether something exists within the same Reality as something else. In other words, what exists as real is based on shared Unit Rate of Change, with quantum synchronization serving as the physical unit-ing/isolating property.

As we get into epitome levels of developmental sophistication, this fact of structural cohesion will become a lot more of a player than it is at this juncture. Still, I wanted to bring up this quantization topic again, and perhaps bake it in a little more as I do, while we're getting so much other stuff nailed down. Believe me, we'll be returning to this again and again, so just be aware of the fact that Time synchronization is key to what can be contextually associated — and there-fore physically interact — regardless of what anyone claims about multiverses, superposition, transdimensional human ascendency, and whatever else it might be that's getting ready to come into ToE fashion.

The Push for Reliable Survival

From here, the C/S Unit's primary survival strategy [C/S Trajectories] pur-sues ID Survival in the only way possible, by establishing trajectory entangle-ments and introducing elements of pre-structural diversification [likely a variety

Autogenesism: A Theory of Everything

of oscillation forms and frequencies]. Eventually, the C/ST registers its first major survival achievement with a stable, organized trajectory with no discernible end point — **the orbit**. This definable C/ST manifestation is a true structure of prolonged contextually-related change, with its own holon Identity defined by each C/E Unit (which is what C/S Units actually are) that has contributed to its on-going existence [historical context]. This structural breakthrough significantly expands the role of *Increase* [the Feminine ID Survival expression that is based on contextual entanglement] as a primary ID Survival go-to strategy.

As far as the nuts and bolts of the simple orbit, as Newton 1st Law of Motion suggests, a kinetic trajectory keeps progressing at a steady rate until it stops for whatever reason. Friction, collision, whatever causes it to stop, it stops due to a cause, but this fact of the orbit's cyclical potential for ongoing manifestation is extremely important to the primordial requirement *"first, survive"* that always faces the C/ET, since its primary survival strategy is the spatial trajectory. The reliably predictable proximity parameters of the orbital trajectory are a definite advancement over the C/ST's freshman accomplishment, best illustrated by the linear trajectory that a ball takes as it rolls across a flat, smooth surface. Simple, predictable, and possessing a definite (if not uniform) relative dimensional property set, the orbital trajectory makes the next breakthrough in structural complexity possible.

As more orbital C/STs develop, their unique properties begin to interact and become affected by each trajectory's historical provenance and resulting contextual entanglements [again, the natural emergence of ID Survival strategies]. They begin developing unique and novel ways to coalesce into densely packed holon matrices that are based on both historical and tangential contextual associations; even the emergence of oscillation frequencies serving to harmonically unite what would otherwise be disparate collectives. In turn, each C/E Unit that persists as part of the internal context of these larger, more complex Change/Spatial Trajectory structures is achieving prolonged ID Survival. Of course, the longevity of the physical structure itself (not even considering the ID Survival achievement here) is exponentially extended as a result of this increase in sheer complexity, making this a real win for the change/event half of the physical realm.

Physicists refer to these emerging structures as **particles**, and due to the very specific macro-system developmental preferences that emerged as a result of established C/ST entanglement successes, there are only a relative handful of uniquely identifiable particle configurations that are known to exist [quarks, photons, electrons, to name a few] After all, once a unique *"lineage"* of C/ST entanglement successes has become established, that specific particle configuration will be sought by subsequent C/S Trajectories that are defined by a common historical point of origin within that specific lineage. As it is the macrosystem's primary means of ID Survival, the *"do this again"* default response to success (for the most part) sets rote development protocols in stone for each C/ST as it emerges, per the definitional requirements established by its unique historical context. This can also prevent any subsequent entanglements from occurring.

I'm not going to beat this phase of progressive development to death. Especially since there's an entire field of physics that is devoted to examining and detailing the specifics concerning particles, their properties, and how they all get along with one another. As I stated early on, AutoGenesism is focused on the larger questions concerning Reality as a whole, why we exist in the unique manner that we exist, and how we fit into the whole of Reality itself. Most of the stuff from this point forward has been fairly well fleshed out over the last 100 years or so. That said, there are still a few whys here and there to deal with before we get to the next major ID Survival breakthrough, even if the minute mechanics that cause one particle to emerge as opposed to another aren't going to be part of this overview narrative.

Serving the Whole

By now, there's been enough ramification diversity that linear, orbital, and vibrational C/ST lineages are all in full flower, with plenty of possibilities in development from one end of Reality to the other. And, this hand-in-glove symbiosis between the C/E Trajectory and the Informational Continuum is really making a difference; at least for the C/E Unit and its survival prospects. But what, if anything, is each residual Fact Set getting out of this arrangement? Isn't all naturally occurring progressive development a reciprocal arrangement? Well, it is, but like I've stated, not everything that pursues ID Survival pursues it in the same manner.

Residual Fact Sets (RFS) and RFS continuums can't do anything but fully, factually, and permanently represent change and occurrence. Residual information is completely passive and once it comes into physical existence, it's like furniture placed in a room; affecting that room by simply being there and taking up space. That being the case, the collective presence of those Fact Sets and RFS continuums (populating the Informational Continuum as an emerging whole)

AutoGenesism: A Theory of Everything

establishes and then progressively develops the *floor plan* of the URC-Determined Environmental Confine in the same way that furniture in a room establishes and then continues to affect the floor plan of that room. The furniture literally defines the Identity of a room, as anyone who's ever moved to a new apartment with all their own furniture will tell you, and Reality is literally becoming what it is as a direct result of the emergence of all this Information.

Now, the URC-DEC does pursue inimitable Identity, which, in its case, it does by promoting the relentless establishment of material diversity and novel complexity. Since Reality is the result of contextual relationships involving permanently existing information wholes, it can't cease to physically exist. However, the threat in its case could be (although very unlikely) a challenge to the uniqueness of its Identity. Its *Isolation* strategy [keeping all that it is, physically intact and permanently possessed] is the Unit Rate of Change [Time synchronization], but it also depends on the Informational Continuum's endless representation of all change and occurrence (and all the contextual ramifications that emerge as a result) for its primary defense against any possibility of its loss of inimitable Identity to a potential pretender. And as an ID Survival strategy, it's hard to imagine how such a relentless increase in diversity and complexity could ever be successfully overcome. So, the default emergence of each residual Fact Set is a survival win that Reality achieves as every C/E Unit establishes that one step forward, and this closes the loop on existential reciprocity at this most primordial level because Reality is the relationship whole that exists between all permanent information sets that exist as a result of activity that occurs at a common Unit Rate of Change.

As C/S Trajectories feature structure that is more and more reliably durable, and as increasingly diversified matrices become commonplace, the prospect of more and more residual Fact Sets becomes increasingly certain. And as we established, Reality's contextual density is amplified and diversified by every residual Fact Set and RFS continuum that is brought into existence. Pretty simple, but it does explain the universal *"do this again"* dictate, concerning why such a dictate exists. In evolutionary biology, it's referred to as Natural Selection, yet that label does nothing to explain the why of such a default. At this extremely primitive level, the reason for the existence of a naturally emergent success/failure system preference that serves as a progressive development basis, become a lot more obvious.

As this symbiotic relationship matures, the nature of activity begins to change. Ramification, system precedence, and the impact of Survival imperative expressions on C/E holon structure, results in the emergence of more progressive redundancies, and increasingly durable C/ST configurations. Of course, this new evolution in trajectory structure radically improves the depth, the quality, and the sophistication of each residual Fact Set that emerges if what's changing is an intricate matrix of holons [multiple linear C/E Trajectories and layers of entangled C/ST configurations] moving from one *"Now"* to the next as one apical holon structure.

For the C/ST, inclusion within these increasingly complex trajectory matrices provide enhanced survival potential through holon Identity Association within any larger matrix structure that achieves prolonged survival as a C/E Trajectory holon in its own right. Once the full survival benefit of the holon matrix is established, structure and the concept of multiple C/ST assemblies that are contextually entangled [matter] emerges. A rock is a pretty impressive example of a contextually entangled C/ST matrix of multiple holon assemblies. Extending the ID Survival of each historically entangled C/E Unit from the URC to millions of years is a pretty good trick, but there are apical holon C/E Trajectories that we know of that have lasted billions of years (Earth, for instance).

When you realize that Identity (and the survival of Identity) is determined by a blend of both internal contextual structure and evolving relative contextual relationships, it becomes obvious why the C/ET also pushes for C/ST *Increase*. It's not forever, but with a robust C/ST matrix that features a lot of structural diversity and redundancy, the apical holon C/ET can accomplish a lot on behalf of the ID Survival of each unit involved.

Suddenly, the C/E Unit possesses something akin to a durable state — as opposed to merely initiating the emergence of information quanta concerning its fleeting instant of physical existence. This changes everything for both the Quantum of *Now* and the URC-Determined Environmental Confine that it brought into physical existence, with both benefiting from the prolonged physical existence of the C/S Trajectory and its ability to physically create matrix entanglements. After all, (yes I will be reiterating this a lot) Reality's ongoing development depends on the structure building activity of the C/S Trajectory, and the more complex and sophisticated each C/E Unit (each deeply structured apical holon's quantum of ongoing existence), the more robust the representing residual Fact Sets become. And they gather as RFS continuums within Reality's ID defining Informational Continuum. And the Residual IC continues to define and solidify ramification and successful precedent, which provides proven channels of stable success potential (an emerging progressive development structure) for an increasingly complex development frenzy, with incredible C/ST matrix structures emerging as a result. And yet, while both are profiting, the truth is that the Change/Event Unit can only postpone oblivion.

Residual Fact Sets and RFS continuums possess permanent existence, and with ID Survival the only driver that exists, finding a way to effectively pass along Identity representation (prolonging ID Survival) from one inherently finite C/ST matrix holon to a brand new C/ST matrix holon that's been brought into physical existence for the sole purpose of carrying that original holon's historical context forward, by leveraging the way that Reality itself uses the RFS continuum to define and ensure its own ID Survival, would seem to be a good next step for any ultra-sophisticated manifestation of C/ST structural development.

It's Alive!!!

So, here's where it all starts getting really clever. As any high school kid knows, life exists as a result of yet another emergence confluence of very specific factors. It's pretty complicated, but there's a lot of good science being pursued on the specifics, so I see no reason to get into any of that here. I do, however, want to examine why such a progressive development step was taken, and why it ended up becoming such a success.

Again, it's the pursuit of Identity Survival, as is the case with all that occurs and has ever occurred. When the molecular components came together to initially create the emergent system that we call life, it was the Identity Survival requirement — within that confluence — that brought the intangible extra that scientists have been puzzling over ever since they began their own effort to replicate this seemingly miraculous feat. What researchers have also failed to address in their own laboratory processes is the impact of historical context, and how complex that history can be for even the most primitive molecular structures.

Under a microscope, a protein is a protein is a protein. You can't see the historical context that defines the Identity of a protein by simply observing it, or even measuring it. Two seemingly identical proteins can bring remarkably different forms of life into emergent existence. When such a protein is placed within what's been artificially constructed to replicate a successful emergence confluence configurations, yet its historical provenance clashes with that of any other confluence constituent, no emergence is at all possible. Why? Because the Identity Survival of the confluence itself — as is the case with a historically

entangled system — is not being pursued, since this confluence is not a historically entangled system. It may list out as comprising all the necessary constituents, each constituent might appear to be precisely appropriate and required, and
the staging of the emergence process itself can be perfectly replicated, but if
there are any internal contextual clashes within the confluence then no emergence can possibly occur.

While life's emergence may come across as a frustrating mystery when
viewed from a strict materialist/reductionist perspective, when viewed from the
perspective gained through a full understanding of the role of information [re-
sidual Fact Sets and RFS continuums] within each physical system's relentless
pursuit of ID survival, it becomes yet another deceptively simple rote ramification process. Not that this perspective makes the artificial creation of life any
easier. Even before you start getting into ultra-sophisticated life form configurations, the historical specificity and complexity of any constituent can be pretty
hard to quantify, and certainly impossible to reverse engineer, even for the brilliant minds that are working these issues today in labs all over the world.

The point here is that this mysterious emergence confluence process isn't
just bits and pieces that come together to create new and unique bits and pieces.
Each bit and piece presents a full and often complicated suite of contextual implications that will be weighted and factored as it combines and coalesces with
other bits and pieces that also present their own complicated suites of contextual
implications, with the established precedent of any and all previous wins tossed
in (in general) as a blend of environmentally imposed weights and factors that
will affect the nature of the system that emerges from such a confluence.

Artificially engineering such a dynamic process would require a lot more
data, and a lot more environmental control over the isolated system presenting
that artificially constructed confluence, than is (at the moment) technically plausible. Replicating the focused complexity that we observe in life is not impossible, since it's nothing more than satisfying macro-system preferences through
accurately combining the proper contextually defined constituent sets within an
environment that is sufficiently isolated, but unless the full extent of such processes is completely understood, the puzzle of how to intentionally engineer life
in a controlled environment will continue to elude researchers.

As to why the progressive development process moved from inanimate objects (like rock and water) to life forms (like bacteria, microbes, and plant matter), the impetus was (wait for it) Identity Survival, yet again. This part of the
overview concerning life is actually pretty simple. Well, definitely a lot simpler

than the specific process that brings any one form of life into emergent existence. The why of anything is generally simpler than the how of it, especially when you start getting into advanced stages of progressive development.

To fully grasp the survival win that life gave the Change/Event Unit, we'll have to refer yet again to the holon hierarchical structure and how it facilitates ID Survival by way of contextual entanglement between otherwise dissimilar items.

Once again, let's bullet point what a C/E Trajectory holon gives each C/E Unit holon.

- That C/E Trajectory itself is a holon, and
- each C/E Unit that was ever a part of that C/E Trajectory is also a holon.
- Each C/E Unit's historical contribution to the physical existence of that C/E Trajectory has (by default) made that C/E Unit an integral part of the internal context of that C/E Trajectory,
- which has, in turn, preserved the existential Identity of that C/E Unit as integral to the existential Identity of the C/E Trajectory.
- This inclusion literally extends the Identity Survival of that C/E Unit beyond the URC-DEC's Unit Rate of Change (URC) duration,
- from that specific duration to the actual duration of that C/E Trajectory as a whole.

That's a hell of an improvement, and when you start looking at how the Change/Spatial Trajectory drastically extends that duration with the orbital trajectory, and then with matter-producing entanglements and the building of complex material structures through the matrixing of these entanglements, you have to be impressed with how resourceful even the most primitive expressions of raw ID Survival actually are. However, it's nothing in comparison to the sheer genius of will that we encounter when we examine the phenomenon of life, and how it has revolutionized the battle against existential oblivion that the C/E Unit has always faced, and will always face, from instant to instant.

In our last digression, we used the Japanese Red Pine tree as an example of how holon hierarchical structure provides the most basic means of achieving Identity Survival;

Let's now examine this hierarchical structure relative to the Identity Survival pursuit of a single Japanese Red Pine tree. Since this is one tree, we've got to acknowledge that the next-higher holon tier (just above

that one Japanese Red Pine tree) within that specific hierarchical structure is the species *Pinus Densiflora* holon. Each Japanese Red Pine tree
seeds the next generation, doing its part to contribute to the material
survival of the species holon that is Pinus Densiflora. In turn, that species
holon provides each Red Japanese Pine tree's inimitable Identity a real
and actual contextual preservation [as historically integral to the species'
contextual Identity] for as long as there are any Japanese Red Pine trees
that exist on Planet Earth. And it's the fact of this default reciprocity that
compels biological holons to contribute to the survival of their species
through replication or procreation.

What I didn't get into was how each Japanese Red Pine tree (if it were
capable of intellectually considering such a thing) would view its own act of
seeding the forest floor; its own act of replication of self. If it were in possession
of both sapience and a full understanding of what was at stake, it would know
that it was seeding that forest floor with biological *ID packets* containing ready-
to-grow replications of itself that will most likely survive as living material trees
long after it [the seeding tree] has already lived its normal life span.

Of course, this same ID Survival strategy adjusts with the sophistication of
the species. Our species engages in procreation, which involves inviting a level
of ID diffusion into the process. Yes, this does lessen the degree of material
structure ID Survival being pursued, but procreation dramatically improves the
potential for material system survival of ultra-sophisticated C/ST matrix manifestations. As structures get more complex, there are all sorts of trade-offs that
must be embraced. That said, there are also ways that such ID Survival trade-
offs are balanced by other means of pursuing Identity Survival, but we'll get
into that shortly.

What life brings to the table is the capacity for multi-generational Identity
representation, and the definite ID Survival benefit of next-higher holon structure inclusion (as detailed within the Japanese Red Pine example, above) for
each contributing holon within the lineage itself. The procreating/replicating holon is now able to spread its Identity as far and as wide, and through as many
subsequent lines of further generational progression, as opportunity allows for
as long as it survives.

Of course, the downside [there's always a downside if there's an upside] is
that, unlike a rock, the living holon will die, and when it does, it will decay as a
system into nonexistence. Still, Identity Survival is the only true survival, and
the externalization of the living holon's ID to other living (and procreating/rep-
licating) holons is far superior to the rock holon's material resilience. Especially

when one compares the Identity presence of trees as compared to the Identity presence of a single rock, regardless of how enormous that rock might be. The initial tree holon wins the Identity Survival contest hands down.

So, we've reached the point in our narrative where we've got rocks, water, grass, shrubs, flowers, trees, and all kinds of microbes and single cell creatures moving about within it all, and it's all coming along nicely, but it's just not enough. It's too quiet.

It Thinks, Therefore, It Is

Okay, now here's where everything really changes, and changes forever. By now, the Contextual Environment has hosted a pretty impressive variety of matrixed C/S Trajectories, and it's benefitted nicely as a result of all that complexity emerging as Identity-assuring, densely packed residual Fact Sets, but it's not the only thing working to survive here. Also, Identity Survival might be the only true existential survival, but that doesn't mean that what is alive and functional isn't in a cage match against corporeal death at all times, because it is. And the key to understanding progressive development is that it is progressive in how it develops, which means that if something that exists can improve, it will. And it will improve relative to simple survivability; material survivability as well as Identity survivability . . . well, for the most part . . . but as with all exceptions, we'll get into the specifics shortly.

As we've established, **Increase** [the Feminine ID Survival imperative expression] is and has always been the primary strategy of the C/ET (by way of its principal agent, the C/ST and its capacity to build structure and material complexity by way of holon hierarchical matrixing). When the C/ST matrix achieved life, it wasn't long before the inherent sophistication of the life process itself hit a point where a simple DNA survival protocol, [basically success-precedent focused residual information Fact Sets uniquely tailored to a species] physically translated and implemented at the cell unit level, was not going to be a sufficient survival response strategy; and a central survival processing sub-system [a central nervous system] developed in reaction to necessity. This helped, but let's face it, we all know what's coming next; **the brain**.

Yes, the brain was a true game-changer in the realm of living material things, and there's no way to overstate the impact of that kind of central data processing on the compete-survive-thrive effort that is central to material existence. That said, what the brain really revolutionized was the larger battle that is

Identity Survival, and this is what I want to take some time with. After all, any science text book can fill in the open holes for you concerning the progressive development of the corporeal brain.

So, I'm thinking that the best way to approach the ID Survival benefits that the brain brought to the table is to digress a moment and detail how the general operation of a typical higher-functioning brain impacts the URC-DEC structure as a whole, with a special emphasis on the hybridization of the two primordial forms of physical existence; the information Fact Set and the C/E Unit.

Digression Alert — So, we're all aware of what the brain does for whatever it is that possesses a brain. It manages the larger biological processes that serve the system whole, and in those higher functioning brain-equipped things, it gives a distinct advantage by enabling it to learn how to do what is required for whatever-it-is to survive and even thrive as a corporeal/material whole. I don't expect to have to defend that statement, so let's move on to examine how a brain works to enable a higher life form to learn or even remember (at even the most instinctive level) what it takes for it to function as a normal version of what it is.

In the more primitive species, the DNA predilection [instinct] is still in charge of managing all external survival responses, and the brain simply translates those predilections into full system action items. Feeding, hunting/foraging, mating, offspring management, and self-preservation/protection response are based on inherited dictates. Pretty simple, and very predictable as long as everything is working properly within the brain. As is the case with all C/ST matrices (which the brain definitely is), what creates all available *avenues of trajectory potential* is a suite of Residual Information Fact Sets that is contextually entangled (and therefore permanently assigned) to that specific C/ST matrix. In the case of primitive brain-equipped species, this suite of Fact Sets is supplied within its DNA configuration. Due to this, a primitive species member is *hard wired* to do what it does and be what it is regardless of what confronts it throughout its span of material existence.

Higher life forms have more sophisticated brains, and along with the DNA suite, these creatures share what I refer to as a residual Fact Set *memory cloud* [each is a contextually entangled and highly specialized RFS cluster collective that is culled from what is otherwise a common RFS continuum] with other members of their species. Access is physically restricted to allow only the brain that is sufficiently entangled (biologically and circumstantially) quicker and more accurate access to those "memory" data sets that have collected within the framework of what has been established as the most likely range of potential survival scenarios.

This efficiency-promoting structural development, over long periods of time, has resulted in obvious evolutionary behavioral diversity that exists even within species; a result of climate and other environmental constants and their differing effects on the survival needs of the creatures in question. Not to the extent of creating new species, but definitely to the extent of instinctive response specializations relative to unique environmental demands that are consistent, while being only significant enough to warrant periodic group-level response.

Still, this shared memory cloud does give these higher life forms the capacity to learn and add to that community cloud in a more dynamic and flexible manner than is possible via DNA evolutionary adjustments. And this is important to note, since there is a pretty impressive range that exists between the simplest and the most sophisticated manifestations of this relationship between the brain and the contextually assigned residual information cloud. We've labeled this unique capacity to upload Fact Sets [gained by way of the brain's dynamic reactions to external stimuli — each reaction a definite C/ET that causes a contextually entangled Fact Set continuum to emerge as part of that species memory cloud] and to then access them in service of survival requirements *intelligence*, and we all know what intelligence looks like in animals when we encounter it.

Now, as to what the brain does, relative to serving the *"first survive"* meta-law requirement, the most obvious answer is that it serves the immediate survival needs of the thing itself. But there's something else that is happening here that is a lot more profound and so completely revolutionary that I had to digress this segment in order to make sure it was given its proper emphasis. You see, what the brain does (and what only the brain can do) is create a unique and thoroughly original form of physical existence that is a literal blend of the C/E Unit and the information Fact Set. This emergent system is a true existential hybrid that I call the **Dynamic Burst Set (DBS).**

First, a little about the DBS, and what's so revolutionary about it. As an information set, it's eternal, and that's critical to always keep in mind when thinking about the revolutionary nature of the DBS, but the most novel property that the DBS possesses is that it dynamically responds to its own existence relative to other things that also exist without having to be contextually entangled with them; something that is absolutely unique among quantum wholes. Now that statement probably seems a little vague, and I know it probably does because I really struggled over how to encapsulate the difference between the DBS and the other two fundamental existential quanta — the C/E Unit and the residual Fact Set (RFS) — in a quick and definitive phrase, and I just know that I didn't nail it with that. The problem is that it might be impossible to construct a definitive statement that covers the whole of what the DBS is and how it has radically altered the contextual nature of Reality itself. Maybe a quick sketch of how it comes into physical existence will help.

When the brain encounters an external threat or opportunity [either or] it receives the heads-up by way of its suite of sensory systems. This launches an analysis/response process that happens both concurrently and consecutively, with the brain accessing pertinent residual Fact Sets embedded within its memory cloud and processing DNA predilections/directives in reference to both the incoming stimuli and those memory data sets that are relative to that stimuli. What happens next is yet another example of Reality's miraculous process of novel transcendence [the Emergent System confluence] with the launch of an activity directive in the form of a **DBS trajectory (DBST)** that literally sets a physical system response into action.

The creature fights, flees, pounces, mates or whatever it is that has been initiated as the proper survival response action item. But as far as Reality is concerned, something far more important, and permanently significant, has just occurred. A dynamic form of information has just emerged, and it came into existence in the form of a Change/Event Trajectory, whose tailing edge remained existent, immediately extending in the form of an informational continuum that (unlike an RFS continuum) presents itself as a contextually indivisible whole to the rest of Reality. This caused a normal RFS continuum to emerge that fully represents its factual and relative contextual nature, as well as the factual and ramification impact that it (as a C/E Trajectory) had on the system it served and the larger contextual environment. Basically, the Residual IC reacts to the DBST as it does to any C/E Trajectory.

The emergence of a form of physical information that initiates and imposes dynamic change is a revolutionary development, but that's not the headline here. The fact that the individual burst sets within this new form of informational continuum are contextually isolated from the rest of Reality is nothing short of a paradigm shift. With the launch of the first-ever Dynamic Burst Set Trajectory, what's just become a factual precedent is the existence of a contextually defined sub-environment that physically exists within the URC-determined confines of a macro-system *parent* environment. The ramifications of this have profound and far reaching implications, as we'll see in Track#2 of this section.

What's most important is that you understand that this dynamic form of information launches as a Change/Event Trajectory, yet persists as an informational continuum that (as a contextually united whole) remains as active and capable of physically affecting Reality as any other Change/Event Trajectory, with residual Fact Sets emerging whenever it does. In a minute, we'll be taking a look at when such a trajectory is free to go ahead and do just that, but for now, I think that closing this digression is in order.

And that's why the development of the corporeal brain was such a breakthrough for the C/ST's drive for Identity-extending complexity, the Informational Continuum's role in providing the URC-DEC with denser and more contextually inimitable Fact Sets, and (as a result of all that novel activity) for Reality's ID Survival as an inimitable whole. It may have evolved as a survival tool for making increasingly complex C/ST matrices possible, but the net impact of the brain redefined what it means to exist as physical. It also redefined what it means to persist, which brings me to the material brain's most significant achievement (well, as far as that brain matrix's own survival is concerned) — the permanent Identity Survival of the Change/Event Unit.

Again, the natural fate of the C/E Unit has always been that it is doomed, and no matter what its trajectory expressions have ever done, at some point, the last C/E Trajectory was going to fail, and there was never anything that could be done about it. Well, that was how it was until the very first brain launched its first Dynamic Burst Set Trajectory.

The Change/Event Unit Achieves Permanent ID Survival

If you didn't see this coming (especially after that whole digression concerning how the brain creates what it creates as it does what it does) then you really have to do something about your capacity for connecting inference dots. The fact that the DBST acts like a C/ST [affecting the Material Realm in the same manner] while physically existing as an informational continuum, should have had you wondering when I was going to get to announcing that the Change/Event Unit had finally found its ultimate survival strategy. Well, I held back until I'd detailed all the other breakthroughs that the brain's responsible for so that I could spend a little time on this, its most overwhelming achievement.

The headline here is that the physical process of configuring and launching each Dynamic Burst Set directly connects the resulting DBST to every C/ST structure and associated C/ET to ever give its all to the material whole whose brain built that DBST and put it into action; providing each with true Identity Survival in its purest form. No replication inductance or procreative proxy percentage blends shared with other Identity contributions, this survival win is direct and therefore fully realized.

Now, I do realize that suggesting that the brain launches dynamic information bursts will clash with the beliefs of most folks, and when we get to the segment that details the difference between human beings and the rest of those other brain-equipped creatures out there, there will be plenty more to cause some folks real difficulty. I'm not oblivious of the traditional array of viewpoints concerning human consciousness, so I want to suggest that if you have a problem with the notion that conscious awareness is an informational emergent system, that you do some looking into other — more authoritative — sources that will help you better understand why I'm comfortable suggesting such a thing.

My favorite examination of the notion that consciousness (in humans) is an emergent system is Prof. Michael S. Gazzaniga's *"Who's In Charge? Free Will and the Science of the Brain"*. This excerpt from his Wiki bio states that he

> "is a professor of psychology at the University of California, Santa Barbara, where he heads the new SAGE Center for the Study of the Mind. He is one of the leading researchers in cognitive neuroscience, the study of the neural basis of mind. He is a member of the American Academy of Arts & Sciences, the Institute of Medicine, and the National Academy of Sciences."

I felt that I was in good hands as I checked in with his explanation of the way that the brain functions, and while he and I have undoubtedly arrived at different conclusions concerning the ultimate impact of the human brain as it relates to the whole of Reality, I did find a level of agreement on the notion of the brain's material structure contributing to the unique confluence required to launch thought and response as an authentic emergent system. If you're interested in further information concerning exactly how this occurs, then Prof. Gazzaniga's book is a brilliant place to initiate that research.

What I wanted to announce here is that the C/E Unit (in general) has finally achieved what seemed as if it should have been literally impossible. It has actually established a reliable and repeatable means of achieving permanent Identity Survival within the internal contextual structure [historical provenance] of a form of information that was purposely configured and generated to dynamically affect the Material Realm; a hybrid informational trajectory that is inherently dynamic and permanently existent. Even with all the other immediate precedent-altering transformations within the progressive development process, this ID Survival achievement stands alone. It has redefined what dynamic physical existence means and forever expanded the parameters of Reality in the process.

The Sentient Brain and Its Sapient Mind

It is here, once the brain has become sophisticated enough to add awareness to its cache of survival tools, that the line between physics, biology, and philosophy begins to get grainy and less distinct. Of course, sentience is merely the capacity to sense that which is outside, that which exists as *other than* the brain itself. It's not what we think of when we consider the human mind and its ability to abstract and conceptualize. Still, it's light-years beyond any previous capacity that's ever existed; material or informational.

Regardless of so many books, video clips, and documentaries proclaiming the infinite presence of a primordial sea of pure consciousness, the truth is that until the sentient brain went online, nothing was consciously aware of anything else, and certainly nothing was conscious of itself. I know that I've made this statement in several previous areas of this book, but it's one of those issues that we'll be revisiting off and on, especially once we get into the physical emergence of the human being.

Consciousness is not an existential staple. It's not foundational in any sense of what that term suggests. Consciousness is a survival capacity achievement, and only a corporeal brain (whether that brain is carbon based or however its material structure is configured) can produce consciousness. Also, it needs to be said that consciousness can only exist as the property of a contextually indivisible Dynamic Burst Set Trajectory whole, a DBST, and it can't physically exist as a capacity property of any other structural form, regardless of how the brain that produced it as a survival capability was formed in material structure.

Sentience, the basis of consciousness, is the capacity to sense the environment that contains the brain, and that's the long and short of it. Of course, there are degrees and magnitudes that vary from brain to brain, and whatever the brain itself is capable of, its DBST will also be capable of; regarding the level and sophistication of sentience. To make it easier to internalize the relationship between the sentient brain and its Dynamic Burst Set Trajectory, I'll be referring to the conscious DBST as the mind, since this is already the most popular term that's in use.

Yes, the brain that is capable of sentience produces the mind, and the mind is a conscious DBS Trajectory. And yes, even animals have minds. Well, the more intelligent animals do. However, as you'll learn, this is not to suggest that animals have human-like sapiential minds. They don't, and we'll be getting deep into what makes the human mind very different than the animal mind. But first I want to go over a very important aspect of this new Reality paradigm that the corporeal brain has initiated as a result of its emergent mind; what happens when that corporeal brain ceases to exist.

Information does not cease to physically exist, and that includes all forms and manifestations of information. This means that once the corporeal brain dies, all that dynamic information it *generated* remains. This is the ultimate survival win for every C/ET that has ever been lucky enough to be integral to the material existence of any brain, whether it's a brain that's capable of producing full sentience or simply spending its entire life span translating DNA survival dictates. As soon as that brain's first burst set led off that dynamic hybrid trajectory/continuum, that C/ET's eternal Identity Survival was assured. The concept itself is easy enough to understand, but what does a mass of contextually indivisible dynamic information look like? How would we recognize it if we encountered such a thing?

That's a question that probably has as many different answers as there are physically existent DBST manifestations within any URC-DEC, multiplied by the number of ways that such a variety of manifestations can possibly be perceived by a sentient/sapient observer. In other words, that's not a question that has an answer. That said, all DBST wholes that have been loosed upon Reality share some common property specifics. Here's a bullet point list:

AutoGenesism: A Theory of Everything

DBST Wholes:

- *present* to the rest of Reality as inimitable, indivisible physical wholes
- act on and react to their physical surroundings in a dynamic manner
- are literally indestructible
- possess only those intelligence capacities that their authoring brains possessed
- are only capable of what they believe they are capable of — in higher levels of sentience and sapience, this can result in a DBST that is involved in an evolving developmental progression

And that's about all there is that is common among DBST wholes. From there, the differences can be staggering. Especially when the human DBST joins in with its own version of unique and inimitable expression. From insects to fish to your own dog, each brain leaves a DBST whole behind when it loses its hold on life, and if you think that this makes the Informational Realm a complex and thoroughly dynamic environment that's teeming with all kinds of informational *"life"*, in one sense you'd be right, but in the sense of what can be consciously experienced or observed, you'd be surprised at how empty the Informational Realm can be for some. But, more on this in a minute. Right now I want to sew this segment up with just one more statement about the relationship between the brain and its DBST whole.

In Section I, I stated that the contextual property that most defines the existent something — relative to anything else that also exists — is how that something came into existence; its authoring source. Yes, Reality's URC unites everything within its confines [forcing all of it to remain systemically integral] but since the URC is universal, the primary delineating identifier (long before other specifics emerge to create additional contextual density) is historical context; the provenance of whatever it is that is being identified.

This is extremely significant when addressing the nature of the dynamic informational whole, since it is physically authored by an enormous historical C/E Trajectory of C/ST matrices that contain countless C/E Units whose ID Survival is directly linked to the contextual Identity of the DBST that ultimately emerges as the literal salvation of them all after such a long and dedicated struggle for ID Survival. So, the bottom line is that one brain creates one DBST — one eternal mind — and once that one brain has died, that DBST is fully developed. It has physically matured, and is now (structurally) all that it will ever be. It's done, and that's that.

The universal battle for ID Survival that rages at all levels of physical Reality is too primordial and too obviously omnipresent for there to be any legitimate question concerning the *one-brain-equals-one-mind* rule regardless of the talking points that have been tossed against it. As I stated before, Reality doesn't have a lawyer because it doesn't need one. Reality is what it is, and it can't be convinced to be any other way than the way it is. The human mind can imagine just about anything, but it can't insist on anything simply because it finds it preferable.

Now, speaking of human minds, it's time for us to take a quick look at what it is that makes the human being *human,* and what happened to the rest of Reality as a result.

"I Am Not an Animal"

This is going to take a while, and it's not going to be easy, but if you can get this part internalized, you're going to be well on your way to understanding everything that I have to teach you. This is due to the fact that until the human being showed up, Reality itself was fairly simple (in a witheringly dense matrix of C/ST structures and contextually isolated DBST wholes, represented by incalculable quantities of divergent Informational Continuum trunks, branches and twigs, version of being fairly simple).

When the human mind reached out with its own expressive sense of self, the complexity of Reality as a whole literally erupted in sophistication and progressive nuance. In fact, the concept of Reality was forced to change as a direct result of this new and overwhelming manifestation of the sheer will to achieve and defend unique and inimitable Identity, and we'll get very deep into that transformation in Track#2 of this section. But first, let's look at what makes the human being different from everything else that exists or has ever existed.

On Planet Earth, we (the members of the Homo Sapiens species) are the only corporeal human race that we're aware of. This may mean that we're the only human species that exists on this planet, but as you'll see, what it is that makes the human brain different from other brains (thereby defining that human brain as being human) allows for the possibility that the Homo Sapiens hominid is NOT the only corporeal human race native to Planet Earth. And as I reach for such a conclusion, I'm not leaning on Bigfoot or any other cryptids for support. The truth is that we could very well be sharing this distinction with whales and dolphins, with the only real difference being that we decided to define brilliance and wisdom relative to our ability to successfully battle Reality instead of our

AutoGenesism: A Theory of Everything

ability to successfully work with it. We could just be the loudest and most competitive of Earth's human species, as well as its most belligerently delusional.

You see, what makes a human *'human'* is not an opposable thumb. It's not two eyes, a nose and a mouth. It's not a larynx, buttocks, or the ability to build tools, weapons, houses, and subjugate the rest of the world. What makes a human *'human'* is how the brain processes survival responses on behalf of the corporeal whole that it serves. That's it in a nutshell. The rest of what makes the Homo Sapiens hominid unique is just the degree of *humanness* that it's achieved relative to whatever else it might be (on this planet) that's also human.

As you'll see, *humanness* is very much a divergent progressive development path when compared to all other progressive development paths that exist within the larger whole that is progressive development. This is due to the fact that what is being pursued by the human brain is not C/E Unit Identity Survival. Well, it is, but that's not all that's being pursued, or achieved. Let's see if I can first clarify the conceptual aspects of this, with the hope that that will help clarify the nuts and bolts of the actual process that results in the emergence of the human being when we get to detailing it. Like I said, Reality got a lot more complicated as soon as the human being showed up.

We've touched on the fact that Reality itself [the URC-DEC] pursues Identity Survival in its own inimitable way by ensuring that it remains . . . well . . . inimitable. After all, existential oblivion isn't the threat that it is for the C/E Unit, since Reality is the established and developing contextual relationship between all informational wholes that share the same Unit Rate of Change, as activity feeds that relationship with C/E Units that appear and replace one another at that common URC. Information is permanent, therefore so is Reality.

That said, Identity Survival is about being identified as unique and inimitable; possessing identity that is not and cannot be duplicated. For the URC-DEC, this is its pursuit as it compels all that exists as integral to the whole of itself to pursue new and novel expressions of holon survival and structural complexity. It's a very similar survival pursuit for each human mind, and yet, the mind has only got the corporeal lifespan of the human brain to achieve this goal before it's released into the wilds of the Informational Realm, never to be granted the opportunity to physically develop and refine that inimitable Identity again.

Remember, the mind is the Dynamic Burst Set Trajectory [the DBST] that's produced by the corporeal brain. The mind is permanently existent. What

211

makes the human mind unique is that it not only realizes that it exists, it develops a plan for its permanent existence while still in developmental gestation. There's no possible way to overstate the significance of this difference when comparing the human mind to all other brain generations.

So, what happened to lift the human mind out of the rest of simple act/react progressive development and place it on this road toward . . . toward what? . . . toward authentic transcendence? What's transcendence? Who's to say what is transcendent? The Change/Event Unit? The Change/Spatial Trajectory? The URC-Determined Environmental Confine, or its servant, the Informational Continuum? This notion of transcendence is a human notion. A human mind invented it. Love, hate, good, evil, honor, disgrace; all invented by the human mind. Nuance and subjective interpretation; invented by the human mind.

Now and *then* did exist, but the *future*; another human invention. The concept of *anticipation* and its darker half, *foreboding*; human, through and through.

So, what did cause the human mind to evolve in such a peculiar direction? It noticed that Time [the difference between now and then] exists. The human brain/mind survival system gained the revolutionary capacity to intellectually place itself within a timeline; the primordial genesis of conceptual abstraction. From that point on, nothing would ever be the same for it or for everything else that shares Reality with it.

The progression from *"What should I do?"* to *"What will happen to me?"* to *"Who am I?"* should be fairly obvious, but what's important to understand is that this kind of thinking places the mind's experience of existence *outside* of the brain; setting the mind up for the inevitable *"I am not my brain"* conclusion that started what has become the human being on its road toward unprecedented levels of intellectual sophistication. It also created the developmental distinction that ultimately qualifies any such brain/mind survival system as being human.

The Soul of Man

Before we go any further into the unique nature of the human being, I need to clear something up. Now, I know that there's no way to subtly slip this assertion through without upsetting a wide arrangement of cultural sensibilities as a direct result of having done so, so I'll just come out with it: — **you don't have a soul, and neither does anyone else**. At least, not the sort of soul that was physically (or *spiritually*) existent before your baby brain began its life of configuring Dynamic Burst Sets and sending them out within a trajectory on behalf of the survival of you as a whole.

I hate being the piss in the punchbowl here, but when I decided to write this book, I also decided to be completely honest with all of it (yes, even if it meant millions of unsold units as a direct result of that honesty). Hell, if you look into it, you'll discover that the *always-and-forever* version of the human soul was largely invented by the Greeks, but that's beside the point. The point is that you haven't got a soul, and there's nothing that I can do about that.

You do, however, have the equivalent of a human spirit, and the difference between the fictional soul and the actual human spirit [I probably won't be calling it this, though] will need to be established and enforced if you're going to fully understand the complications that await. Maybe some bullet points will help?

The Fictional Soul:

1. is preexistent
2. is part of a conscious singularity that some call God
3. engages in multiple human corporeal incarnations
4. sheds predilections between incarnations
5. starts each new incarnation as a *clean slate*
6. ultimately blends back into the conscious singularity

The Actual Human 'Spirit':

1. is created by the corporeal human brain
2. is unique, inimitable, and presents to the rest of Reality as an indivisible physical solid
3. is the result of one brain's physical lifespan
4. is the entirety of the thoughts, feelings, experiences, and reactions of that one human brain
5. is the permanent personality expression of the corporeal human being in the physical form of a dynamic information mass
6. persists indefinitely as a contextually indivisible and physically indestructible informational whole with the capacity to interact with and impact the whole of Reality in an active and proactive manner.

213

I realize that there are many subtle differences between one religion's definition of the human soul versus another's but I wanted to cover as much territory as possible while remaining as general as possible. The main point was to make it clear that the traditional *"soul"* does not exist, and if you've been paying attention to the existential basics that have been constantly in play since that first ever Change/Event Unit happened to start everything off, then you shouldn't need any further clarification concerning why the soul doesn't and simply cannot exist. Still, in the spirit of keeping everyone in class on the same page in our text book, here's a bulleted rundown of why the soul is literally an impossible manifestation within this or any other Reality confine.

The Fictional Soul:

1. is preexistent

As we've established, Reality didn't even exist until the juxtaposition between the potential *for* and the potential *against* the emergence of physical Reality created the very first instance of duality, which caused the default emergence of the Relative Being State

2. is part of a conscious singularity that some call God

If there is anything at all that isn't that singularity, and at any level of physical distinction, then that singularity does not exist. I exist and so do you, therefore, there is no singularity and there never has been such a thing.

3. engages in multiple human corporeal incarnations

One mind emerges as the result of one brain, making each brain's mind a permanent and contextually isolated informational being that (like everything else that exists) pursues unique and inimitable Identity Survival. Attempting multiple human corporeal incarnations would involve hijacking the PDT process of a newly born human brain, but the result would still be a different (albeit; severely damaged) human mind that would eventually pursue its own inimitable Identity, leaving the *hijacker* no more or less than it was when it began its assault on that young, vulnerable brain. Traditionalists refer to this sort of nonsense as *spirit possession*.

4. sheds predilections between incarnations

One brain creates one mind, and when that brain dies, that mind becomes a human being. Try as it might, that fully gestated human being *is what it is* and cannot physically alter its structural composition. Think of each predilection as *like part of the DNA embedded within each cell that makes up the body* of the permanently completed human being, doing its part to provide that human being with a unique and inimitable Identity that cannot be duplicated; thereby ensuring its Identity Survival.

5. starts each new incarnation with a *clean slate*

see 3 and 4 above

6. ultimately blends back into the conscious singularity

see 2, 3 and 4 above

Yes, it ultimately comes down to whether the existence of the soul makes sense [remember the requirement of system coherence] as part of the URC-Determined Environmental Confine that it supposedly operates within. It doesn't.

Keep in mind that the URC-DEC is the relationship matrix that has naturally developed between everything that exists as real. By default, this matrix provides each dynamic item that can ever operate within its physical confines with the necessary relative context that ultimately defines it.

Conceptually, the soul exists contextually and literally isolated from all of physical Reality, as if it's an observer that's watching the whole thing on a remote video feed, while (in some versions) directing a developing human mind in the fulfillment of specific requirements that it sketched out (sometimes in great detail) prior to injecting its own fully and independently developed Identity into this physical Reality [an airtight relationship matrix of unfathomable complexity] in any of a variety of manners on behalf of its own independent version of progressive development. Basically, coming from its own *nowhere* to lease a human being's corporeal lifespan until it's gotten whatever it is that it needs (experience, perhaps) from that lifespan and then trading it in for a new model, or maybe ditching the whole physical Reality thing altogether and heading back to its nonphysical source and calling it a forever.

I understand the philosophy behind the soul's *existence*, but there's no Reality hosting its existence. Reality is a relationship matrix of physically existent wholes. Nothing can exist relative to that which is undeniably physical if it, itself, doesn't physically exist. Claiming that the soul is capable of existing *beyond* the contextual/structural requirements of the URC-DEC that hosts the human brain that it [the soul] is associated with, is admitting that the soul only exists within the imagination of the human mind, since the DBST [which is what the mind is] possesses the only constituent structure that is contextually isolated from the rest of the URC-DEC that it inhabits. In short, that claim defines the soul as an intellectual construct.

So, now that we've laid the conceptual soul to rest, it's time to examine what caused the concept of the soul to emerge and wreak such cultural havoc for so many centuries. What I want to do is introduce you to the one single differentiation between the human and nonhuman mind. This one process — noted as being significant by those magnificent minds that ruled their day so long ago — ultimately laid the groundwork for what's been embraced as Reality for the last few thousand years.

Plato was the first to really write extensively about the soul, and he got Aristotle working on it and putting his own spin on the concept, with the obvious crossroads cultural impact of Greece's Hellenistic period firmly establishing the soul across a wide cross section of both Eastern and Western spiritual traditions as a result. But, there was, and still is, something unique about the human experience that allows for the conceptual soul to exist and persist as plausible (perhaps even necessary) for most minds that confront an otherwise materially reducible world from day to day.

This unique something is what some have labeled *"the observer"*; the unique capacity for the human brain to observe itself exist and to ponder that existence in an intellectually detached manner. It's this capacity that set the stage for the appearance of the soul, and it's this breakthrough in the relationship between the brain and the mind that we're going to take a good long look at right now.

The Personality Development Trajectory

So, now that we've briefly dealt with the soul as the pretender that it's always been, I want to detail why it is that you can examine your own self, look back over your own life, and actually work to achieve a better perspective on exactly who you are and why it is that you are the way you are. And if you think that this capacity is a pain in the ass, then you're confronting the give and take that exists at the relative stratosphere of developmental ultra-sophistication. Identity Survival, for you, one of Reality's most elite developmental manifestations, features opportunities and risks that nothing else has ever dealt with or can ever deal with. You face the best and the worst and every possible gradient point between the two, and this is what it means to sit at the apex of both the

AutoGenesism: A Theory of Everything

Material and the Informational realms. And how it all shakes out for you in the end depends solely on how you manage your personal pursuit of Identity Survival. It all depends on your mind's **Personality Development Trajectory (PDT)**.

The nonhuman brain's DBS Trajectory was a thoroughly spectacular developmental breakthrough, and as we've seen, it revolutionized the material pursuit of Identity Survival, but the human mind's development of the PDT took the pursuit of Identity Survival in a whole new direction. While it's a lot more complicated than this, the headline is that the human mind's capacity for observation-of-self introduced the Information Set [the human mind is comprised of Dynamic Information Sets] to the pursuit of Identity Survival. The PDT is the human mind's primary Identity Survival pursuit strategy.

Until the emergence of the human mind, Information had always been a survival strategy [DNA and the nonhuman DBST] or a default means of preserving inimitable Identity [the URC-DEC Informational Continuum]. The human mind is (basically) a DBST that's taken the reins of its own generation process and has begun actively shaping its own progressive development in an effort to ensure that its ultimate Identity will not only be inimitable, but that it'll be comparatively attractive (in whatever way it determines attractive to exist). Yes, this is starting to sound as if I'm devolving into blatant anthropomorphism here, but what we're now examining *is* human, so I don't know that I can anthropomorphize any of it. It's human after all.

What I will do, over the next few subsections, is sketch out how it all works, and why it all works as it works. In the Section III digression *"Human Consciousness and the Personality Development Trajectory"*, I get deeper into the subject, and I present what I see as compelling inference evidence (leaves waving in the breeze, so to speak) that the PDT does exist. Here, as with all previous stages of Reality's development progression so far, I'll be struggling to hit the important points without stalling this Track#1 narrative over details that can be better addressed in Section III. But first, I want to preemptively address any possible misinterpretation of the term *trajectory* as it pertains to the PDT as a physical manifestation (as opposed to what this term might suggest).

Digression Alert — To really understand the physical nature of the DBS Trajectory and especially the Personality Development Trajectory (PDT) what's important to establish is the actual nature of the kinds of trajectories we're dealing with here. I did make a quick note of this issue within Section

I, but it's worth reiterating here, since we're going to be working with two very different trajectory variations that are extremely integral to one another as I detail how the PDT serves the ID Survival pursuit of the human DBST. Believe me, you'll be glad that we took the time to revisit this.

So, let's take a look at the physical structure of a Dynamic Burst Set Trajectory first. We've all observed the spatial trajectory, and it's easy to describe. Baseball provides us with a good example: a fly ball that's hit to the outfield, with the ball rising into the center of the stadium and then arcing evenly into a glove, or the seats, or wherever it ends up landing when that arc is completed. That's a classic spatial trajectory, and it progresses as the ball (in this case) physically moves forward, leading the way and establishing that trajectory's direction, distance, and relative positional proximity as it does so. Maybe not the most technical explanation, but since we've all witnessed this sort of trajectory, it'll do for now.

We've all experienced the Change/Event Trajectory as well, but none of us has ever watched one physically launch, progress and resolve as a defined and identified trajectory. This is because we each exist within a myriad of contextually entangled C/E Trajectories that are both ongoing and intermittent and existing within layers upon layers of shared and isolated C/E Trajectory entanglements, to the degree that it'd be literally impossible for any one of us to accurately separate even one such trajectory out from the airtight matrix that they all comprise, as each instant of material structure [each corporeal life is an apical C/E Trajectory holon, after all] is replaced by the next instant.

To suggest that the C/E Trajectory arcs, or races from here to there, or orbits, as is the case with the spatial trajectory, is to completely misunderstand the physical nature of the C/E Trajectory. Obviously, one quantum of *Now* replacing the next quantum of *Now* is the basic description of the *event trajectory* [yes, this is shorthand for the C/E Trajectory] but maybe a better illustration is the baseball game that featured the fly ball spatial trajectory that arced into the outfield.

Each pitch to the plate, each play, and each inning existed as its own identified event trajectory, with all of them contextually entangled to form the event trajectory that was the game itself. That's easy enough if you visualize each of those event trajectories as akin to drops of water within a stream of water. However, every instant involving the physical participation, or just the focused observation, of each and every person at the ball-park also existed within its own event trajectory, with each of them contextually entangled within the whole that was the game event trajectory. Of course, there was a lot more complexity within that game matrix than it'll serve this discussion to indulge, but you get the idea. That said, the complexity that develops as a result of all of these contextually entangled trajectories is not what's important here. What's important is how each one of these trajectories progresses.

If you snap your fingers *Now*, and then snap them again *Now*, you've sort of concocted a brief event trajectory that consisted of C/E Units that were contextually entangled within your own larger life event trajectory by the simple, yet deliberate, decision you made to consciously delineate that specific span of time as an observed stretch of quantum existence units occurring between the act of one finger snap and the act of another finger snap. And just like that, you intellectually identified that quick several seconds or so as being unique and inimitable within the matrix whole that is your ongoing corporeal existence. It might've been limited solely to your own isolated perspective [therefore not a true C/E Trajectory, relative to Reality as a whole] but for our purposes, it'll do the job as an illustration that is accurately representative.

So, did anything arc? Did the C/E Units scoot across the floor as one followed the other within that very specific trajectory? Of course not. It wasn't a spatial trajectory, and only spatial trajectories arc or scoot across the floor. Change/Event Trajectories don't move at all. That said, spatial trajectories are C/E Trajectories. They are in the same way that all women are human beings. Not all human beings are women, but all women are human beings. All spatial trajectories are event trajectories, but not all event trajectories are spatial trajectories.

Event trajectories consist of quantum units of *Now* that are all tightly entangled as a result of a contextual similarity that is more primordial than any other similarity that any of them can have with any other physical item of any kind. The newest C/E Unit is historically defined by the C/E Unit that it replaced, and that goes for every C/E Unit that came before that one, and for every C/E Unit that will come after the next, with the resulting event trajectory's Identity becoming more and more contextually defined and — therefore — increasingly inimitable with each C/E Unit's addition to that evolving history.

In that sense, an event trajectory as a whole *"gathers forward"* in relative contextual development, with each new C/E Unit increasing in relative environmental presence from its source of trajectory initiation as a result of each prior C/E Unit's pursuit of Identity Survival. Yes, this contextual *presence* is established and defined by one RFS continuum that emerges — one residual Fact Set in default response to the occurrence of each C/E Unit within one event trajectory's ongoing manifestation — physically representing this contextual development, but let's try not to lose the bottom line impact here over details.

The Dynamic Burst Set Trajectory is more similar to an event trajectory than it is to a spatial trajectory, in that it also *gathers forward* from a source of trajectory initiation; being pushed from behind, as opposed to being a product of leading edge momentum. That said, the DBST (unlike both the event and the spatial trajectories) consists of every burst set that's ever emerged as part of that trajectory (in permanent physical existence and not merely integral as Identity-definitional historical context) gathering as an ever emerging physical mass of information sets. While this may end up being hard to describe, I'm going to see if I can find some common trajectory examples that are not DBS Trajectories, but still sort of illustrate this *gathering forward* in actual physical development that the DBS Trajectory employs, as opposed to the C/E Trajectory's contextual-gathering-forward historical environmental impact or the leading-edge-kinetic-energy-release relative environmental impact that the spatial trajectory displays.

Maybe a seed that pushes a plant stem outward, and how that stem keeps adding more and more plant cells to its leading edge as it grows could be an example? Or, perhaps how a quiet pool of water grows and expands as a spring feeds it from underneath. It's growing, not arcing or scooting, and as it grows, it's increasing in uniqueness internally and therefore relative to everything else that also exists.

Yes, I think that when you picture the DBST emerging from the active, proactive and reactive brain as relentless burst sets of action oriented information, it would be helpful to visualize either a tree growing from a seed, or a pool slowly filling with molecules of water. You'll be a lot less likely to be imagining the human being as a rocket streaking across the sky, on its way to who knows where. Believe me, this moment spent on correcting such a mental image will pay off in a big way once we get further into the nature of the human being and its impact on Reality at large.

Now, concerning the PDT; again, this trajectory is the difference between the human mind and all other kinds of minds. It's the PDT that makes a human mind *human*. Seems clear and definite enough, but what it implies is anything but simple. In fact, there's nothing at all simple about the Personality Development Trajectory, and the very first complication we encounter concerning the PDT is the fact that — in spite of its intimate relationship with the growing, massing DBS Trajectory — it is, physically, more like a basic C/E Trajectory than a branch of the DBST that launched it. It doesn't gather as a continuum of burst sets like the DBST does. It's an activity that the human mind pursues from the instant that it achieves the level of intellectual sophistication that defines that mind as being *human*.

Remember, the DBST is a dynamic hybrid. That means that it might be informational in physical structure, but it's as dynamic as any spatial trajectory. And, since the human DBST is comprised of self-aware burst sets, it carries with it its own source of initiating impetus. It can turn on a dime, and that's really important to keep in mind; even as each of us already knows this about ourselves without anyone having to point it out.

The PDT is the DBST engaged in a very specific and highly focused activity, a true event trajectory that is ongoing and contextually entangled from one C/E Unit to the next. Then again, the typing that I'm doing right now is also a true event trajectory, so it's not as if I'm inventing a new form of physical existence here. It's just the DBST being what it is; a dynamic environmental influence with its own agenda. The only thing unique about the PDT is that it targets and profoundly affects the brain's DBS generation process while that brain is still generating the DBST that has launched that PDT activity. Basically, the PDT is the human DBST reaching back to proactively shape the nature of each DBS that gathers within it before that DBS is launched by that brain.

Stumbling Into Maturity

I'm going to try out a 2nd person narrative voice for a moment to try and help you become a little more intimate with how the PDT works by detailing how your own PDT likely operates. Maybe it'll help, but if not, then you can simply substitute you with he, she or it, and it'll all end up being essentially the same overview.

So, you're brain has been pushing out Dynamic Burst Sets for at least a couple decades, and as a result, your own Personality Development Trajectory has been up and on the job for quite some time now. Most professional estimates have the PDT starting to get its land legs together around 4-5 years into the brain's career as a survival data processing center for the average Homo Sapiens hominid, but the truth is that it doesn't really kick in until the rest of the body starts getting with the Identity Survival program as a full-on distraction. That would be puberty in most cases.

What I mean by puberty being the time when your entire body started getting serious about Identity Survival is that this is when your procreative developmental shift started shifting, and your brain started being affected by hormones and the more obvious physical changes that some of the other kids were going through. Now, there's a very sophisticated and dynamic relationship between your brain and your mind. Each profoundly affects the other. When the hormones started adjusting your body and brain in a wholesale manner, there was no way that your mind was going to avoid being swept along with all that transformation that was under way. And this is what I want to cover as we address the Personality Development Trajectory, and the role that the PDT takes on as a result of the maturation process that the entire body and brain is engaged in.

Until the sexual maturity transition process launched, your PDT was primarily engaged in stabilizing the experience of ongoing existence for your brain. By managing the residual Fact Sets [actually, these sets are perception-based, but they are factual concerning what you perceive] that were allowed into your individual *memory cloud* your PDT established your unique version of what's real, what's not real, what's important, what's trivial, what's possible, impossible, right, wrong, good, bad, ugly, and sad, and how the whole of Reality fits together as an ongoing and stable progression that you could, then, operate reasonably well within from moment to moment. And, until your body alerted your mind that there was such a concern as Identity Survival, with the production of hormones that were designed to transform your body into a procreating vessel bent on either producing or fertilizing the eggs of a new generation, your mind had no idea that such a concern existed. That all changed once the puberty transition hit a tipping point.

Suddenly, the members of the opposite sex became *"members of the opposite sex"* and being attractive to them became an issue. But that's not all that happened. It was then that your mind began to feel its own need to establish its own version of *human* and maybe even feel the initial stirrings of a unique definition of what that version might ultimately feature as details and nuanced refinements.

Yes, it can be argued that the mating urge drives much of what begins to coalesce as inimitable personality development specifics, but there is too much distance in most cases (although not in your case, I'm sure) between what could ever be considered effective developmental response to simple mating/courtship competitive preparations, and what emerges as the pubescent mind grinds through its bewildering teenage years in search of who it is that will be coming out on the other end of it all.

It can also be argued that in all competitions there are winners and losers, but again, this notion only manages to diminish the human being by assuming the authority to declare a strict and narrow definition for what it means to win in the human procreation game. As if a cop is more attractive than an athlete than a rock star than a con man than a woodsman than a politician than just a sweet guy who listens to a girl's thoughts, and more likely to be successful when it comes to planting his seed within a willing partner. Seriously. Since when has it ever been that simple and rudimentary to be human? No, winning in this case goes way beyond the splashing of genetic material within a receptive vessel. For the human being, winning means full Identity Survival, and this is survival that is much more comprehensive than littering the planet with babies.

In the same way that the URC-DEC serves the *"first survive"* meta-law by establishing and ensuring that its own Identity remains inimitable, and so densely packed with contextual complexity that its uniqueness remains unchallenged, your own human mind launched a mission to establish its own inimitable Identity as soon as it realized that such a requirement exists. And that mission persists, and will persist for as long as your mind is in physical gestation.

Generally, a common archetype is chosen by the teenage mind after some struggle to determine what is available and plausible (given a variety of cultural, economic and physical factors). During this period of time, your young mind probably tried on several archetype personas before ultimately settling on one as a usable template upon which to then go about the business of crafting your own unique interpretation of that archetype. Often, family members are chosen, especially if the culture specifically encourages such a choice, but in the modern developed world, it is increasingly common for public figures to provide the emerging mind a much broader choice of attractive Identity archetypes from which to choose. Maybe this was where you found your template?

I know that I found my archetype within the troubled (and troubling) world of late 60s early 70s rock and roll and wild excess, and while I crafted a version that survived into middle age, my personal history speaks for itself as testimony to the powerful influence of one's primary archetype on how that person develops as a mature and fully viable human being regardless of all efforts to redirect that specific developmental trajectory.

Of course, the inherent vulnerability of perception has to be acknowledged whenever such a process is being examined, and especially when it involves young, emerging minds that possess precious little judgment or applicable life experience. Negative and self-destructive archetypes are too often presented as sexually attractive within media-driven cultures, and the brain's procreative drive can cause the mind's choice of archetype to clash significantly with what should have been a positive or even plausible Identity template decision.

The truth is that we've all seen the mayhem that can result when the choice of archetype has been overtly affected by the grinding urge to serve the *"first, survive"* imperative as presented by the body's DNA. In such a case, the cultural definition of powerful, alluring, alpha, and desirable can take on amusing proportions as a result of the relative naiveté of the mind in transition from childhood to adulthood. The whole thing can get pretty absurd before the mind finally settles on a reasonable variation of the grossly caricatured archetype it chose to emulate.

Tragically, there are those archetypes that provide no material survival alternative to the young mind that has chosen it for its template. Self-destruction and/or suicide (even murder) is central to the Identity of these archetypes, and if no intervention is staged, the results are pretty much what you'd expect them to be. Does this mean that all acts of self-destruction, suicides and murders committed by teenagers are archetype-driven efforts to establish Identity? Not at all. Such tragedies are the result of a complex confluence of factors, but too many of these terrible results do not share similar, let alone identical, causal factors. Also, the factors themselves are common to too many results that are not similarly tragic. Obviously, there is a noumenal component that must be considered, but given what we've already established about the sub-structure of physical Reality, *"the Devil made me do it"* is no such noumenal component.

So, what was the point of this examination of the hell of puberty? I wanted to take a moment to present what is probably (at least for most adults) the most obvious example of the PDT and what it does on behalf of the emerging human being.

Building the Ultimate You

As difficult as those teen years can be, it's during this transition that the mind itself discovers what it really means to be human. It's then when the realization hits the emerging sapient mind that Identity Survival will be predicated on that mind's Identity becoming as unique and inimitable as possible, while remaining socially accessible enough to ensure that the corporeal system's own pursuit of ID Survival (procreation) is not negatively affected in the process. This is extremely complicated stuff. And this is why those years are so traumatic for so many.

In fact, deliberately choosing an appropriate persona template and then doing what it takes to turn that basic caricature into a true-to-life, multidimensional human being is a serious challenge for even the most seasoned professional fiction writer. This is what the young human mind is suddenly presented with as its authoring brain is flailing helplessly with hormonal surges and neural pathway transformations, and its entire body is changing in ways that no kid could really anticipate, or, in most cases, appreciate.

And it's not as if this is just a temporary phase that passes by; leaving the poor confused mind to recover and get back to what's been the normal stuff of life. No, this explosion of emotional and psychological turmoil marks the permanent end of what it's always meant to be human, and the beginning of what it will always mean (from then on) to be a human being. This mind's struggle to successfully craft an Identity that it can accept and embrace will not end until its authoring brain has died, and it (this often beleaguered mind) has been finally released into the wilds of the eternal Informational Realm as a fully developed and viable human being.

And this often harrowing process is the primary difference between the human mind and any Dynamic Burst Set Trajectory that emerges as a result of the lifespan of a nonhuman brain. It's not the actual burst generation process itself, since all highly functional brains work basically the same. It's the mind's seizure of that process, and the resulting transformation of the ultimate goal of that process, that makes the human mind/brain relationship different. I often refer to this mind-initiated/directed Identity development process as the human being's 2nd stage of physical gestation, and as you'll see, I have good reason to describe the corporeal lifespan of the human being in this manner.

As to how the PDT Identity sculpting process works, let's see if I can make this sound as uncomplicated as possible. A bit earlier (within the *"It Thinks, Therefore, It Is"* subsection) I introduced the *memory cloud* and detailed how some higher functioning brain-equipped creatures share a species memory cloud that literally provides residual Fact Set clusters that have become contextually isolated (relative to all other general residual Fact Sets within the Informational Continuum) as specific to the survival predilections and requirements developed by generations within the historical lineage of regional subsets of certain species. Well, it's time that we look a little closer into what a memory cloud is and how it's formed so that you can better appreciate just how unique the human being is when compared to whatever else it is that's dynamic and intelligent.

> ***Note*** — The first thing to clarify here is that the term memory cloud is the best I can do as I struggle to physically describe what it is that we're getting ready to examine at a much deeper level. The truth is that, metaphors aside, RFS continuums are what they are, and they emerge — RFS by RFS — as a default ramification of the progression — one C/E Unit on the heels of the last C/E Unit — of any kind of C/E Trajectory until it inevitably ends. And since they are brought into existence through event occurrences that happen within the URC-Determined Environmental Confine, they *"belong"* to that Environment.
>
> This means that each RFS is universally accessible within the environment, since everything that exists within the environment (dynamic as well as residual) is inherently integral to the full definition of the environment. Of course, this means that the contextual relationships between residual Fact Sets and RFS continuums are constantly being affected by dynamic activity and dynamic actors, with a constant flow of new residual Facts Sets and RFS continuums emerging as a default ramification of those changes.
>
> What I've termed a *memory cloud* is a subset of RFS clusters that has become affected by a Dynamic Burst Set Trajectory (or by a species subset of historically entangled DBS Trajectories) in a manner resulting in the contextual entanglement of these RFS clusters with a material brain as integral to a specific suite of structural or Identity survival expressions. These entangled "memory clusters" can exist within one RFS continuum [entangled with the generating brain of one DBST] or they can become associated with any number of mind/brain survival systems within a species subset [creating herd/flock/pack behavior] depending on the nature of the survival strategy being pursued. These RFS clusters are more responsive to ongoing and immediate survival requirements

than DNA directives, and they can range somewhat within a species, affecting only the stimuli-referencing processes of the animal brains that are historically associated within a specific region or even localized territory.

I bring this up due to the fact that the memory cloud is a major component of the emerging human being's Identity Survival strategy, and is literally built — cluster by cluster — by the Personality Development Trajectory. I also bring this up because it is this PDT-constructed memory cloud that contains the whole of a human being's conscious experience of self-aware material existence. If it's not in there, then it may have been initially perceived, but it wasn't ultimately experienced by the corporeal human as a moment of conscious awareness. The net impact, of the PDT's aggressively specific management, on this very unique memory cloud makes it obvious that — compared to nonhuman, species memory clouds — it is being built to serve a completely different survival strategy.

So, perhaps this is a good spot to declare that there is no communal memory cloud that is shared amongst members of the Homo Sapiens hominid species. It doesn't exist, and no amount of belief in a one hundredth monkey washing its food in the surf will ever create a species memory cloud for the Homo Sapiens hominid. No such thing as a *collective consciousness* suddenly emerging as a result of a critical mass acceptance of peace, or love, or even the realization that chocolate tastes a lot better if you mix in a little vanilla. The Homo Sapiens species will always be a seething, roiling cacophony of divergent views and predilections, and let's see if I can effectively explain why.

Of course, the simple reason is because no two Homo Sapiens creatures share a common memory cloud, but that statement isn't going to suffice. I realize that what I need to do is explain exactly why no two Homo Sapiens creatures are capable of sharing a common memory cloud. The hell of it is that it takes a deep dive into the ramification structure that rolls out in default response to what constitutes the primary difference between the human mind and all versions and iterations of nonhuman minds, while detailing how that ramification structure is integral to why the human mind is ultimately so different from all versions and iterations of nonhuman minds. Damn, I already don't like how this is sounding. I'm going to try a digression. Maybe a few digressions.

Digression Alert — As I covered within the animal brain/mind relationship segment, when the brain itself configures and launches each Dynamic Burst Set (DBS) as yet another link in that brain's single, relentless DBS trajectory (DBST), that activity is immediately reflected within the URC-Determined Environmental Confine (URC-DEC) as a change that requires a residual Fact Set (RFS) to emerge; as is the case when anything happens within the URC-DEC. This is also how it works when the human brain configures and launches each DBS, but it's here where all similarities end.

The animal brain/mind relationship isn't all that sophisticated, and the animal mind (if it's even sophisticated enough to sense that it does exist relative to what surrounds it) diligently serves the brain's mission to prolong the survival of the corporeal whole for as long as possible. Therefore, the memory cloud that a higher functioning animal brain shares with others of its own kind will only consist of broadly attributed survival adjustments that relate to the species in general. The human survival system is very different, since each human brain possesses its own contextually isolated memory cloud. And that extremely precise and highly detailed data resource is deliberately formed and managed by the mind that is being developed by that human brain.

While the brain is still alive and functioning, the PDT has its hands full, carefully selecting and processing what is allowing to become part of its brain's memory cloud. For some, this might seem like the most logical and elegant means by which such an end result (control over the nature of each DBS that emerges from the authoring brain) is achieved, but for others, it might still seem a bit vague, so please allow me a moment or two of reiteration so I can make sure that everyone thoroughly understands what's going on here and why.

Memory cloud control and development is the primary focus of the PDT, since each mind eventually realizes [this is not anthropomorphism, since the human mind is human] that the only way it can manage its own ongoing development is by way of precisely manipulating its authoring brain's Dynamic Burst Set configuration process. And if not handled properly, this could end up being a really laborious and complicated effort (to say the very least). Let me see if I can list some of the main processes that the PDT must control if it is to successfully manage the mind's own ongoing development.

To manage the mind's progressive development, the PDT must:

- Fully stabilize the perception experience that the brain relies on for survival initiation/reaction responses

AutoGenesism: A Theory of Everything

- Establish and promote a broad contextual framework that contains Reality specifics that will give the brain its best chance at successfully responding to a wide variety of challenges and opportunities that exist within its own theater of operations, while keeping the entire system as open to novelty and new experience as reasonably possible.
- Establish and promote an increasingly defined character expression (Identity) that is unique, inimitable, and above all, accurately representative of the self; to the extent that the PDT has actually determined what the self consists of as a suite of definable characteristics, which is a large part of this particular task.
- Perform these functions as a holistic process, with no perception schisms as each DBS follows the last in response to incoming and internally generated stimuli.

It's a hell of a job, and if tackled incorrectly, one that is pretty much impossible to accomplish. But, the human mind is brilliantly capable of learning from those minds that surround it, and what each young mind eventually learns is that there's an extremely efficient and effective way to get it all done with just one highly focused effort; processing what makes it into the brain's memory cloud (stacking the deck, so to speak) and only giving the brain carefully attributed data sets to work with as it configures and launches each DBS. After all, these data sets are what the brain will use to compare and contrast with what it confronts (the incoming data wash from its sensor systems) from moment to moment, and to then use as its go-to interpretation/response DBS configuration basis. These data sets will become the basis of the brain's (and ultimately, the mind's) entire relationship with the rest of Reality.

So, this is what the PDT is all about. The mind *reaching back* and grabbing onto the steering wheel (so to speak) in order to have control over how it (the mind itself) is going to emerge from the ongoing C/E Trajectory that is the life span of the brain. In the 70's, a book called *Bio-Feedback* introduced a method of consciously taking control of the PDT and sculpting a winner out of the emerging you, and while I have no idea just how well that all turned out for folks, I do want to point out that this concept was based on targeting a process that does exist and is ongoing within all human beings. In fact, the basis of behavioral modification is also predicated on the existence of the PDT and what it

229

does on behalf of the human mind's development. In this next quick digression, I want to focus specifically on that part of our PDT overview.

Digression Alert — If you mix grape juice and apple juice in a single glass, you can never decrease or eliminate the amount of grape juice you mixed in with the apple juice in that glass. You can add more apple juice, and dilute the impact of the grape juice within the resulting mixture. Maybe you can even add enough apple juice to make the mixture look and taste as if the grape juice had never been added to the mixture, but the truth is that the amount of grape juice will always remain the same. What this has to do with the PDT's job of crafting the human mind will become apparent.

What a person does becomes integral to who that person is. What a person thinks becomes integral to who that person is. What a person believes becomes integral to who that person is. This is because what the PDT allows the brain to focus on as fundamental and (as a result) to fill its DBST with (becoming its emerging definition of normality) becomes integral to the Identity of the human mind. This process has its similarities with another environmental development process. It's not exactly the same, but not that different as to be absolutely unprecedented either. Let's take a look.

Just as each emerging RFS and RFS continuum within the Informational Continuum (IC) further defines and solidifies the Identity of the URC-DEC, the Identity of the human mind is defined and solidified with each DBS that is generated by its authoring brain. The PDT's promotion of what it sees as desirable response predilections (causing dominant personality traits to emerge over time) is definitely comparable to the IC's promotion of successful survival precedent (establishing a range of fundamental constants, predictable laws of physics, and material structure that is increasingly reliable, complex, and diversified). Each serves the primary ID Survival pursuit strategy of an evolving environmental whole; one ensuring a definite Identity that is as resilient as it is unique, and the other ensuring an endless supply of contextually dense, Identity protecting, RFS continuums. The impact of the PDT's relentless ID sculpting process is something that we notice on those people who are important in our own lives. The personality traits that emerge as a result of this steadily evolving promotion of beliefs, likes, and dislikes are what bring us closer to or distance us from those friends and family members we started with.

As this process continues and the PDT becomes more and more focused on the definition and solidification of inimitable Identity, the properties of the Dynamic Burst Sets that are being generated are becoming increasingly *human* and incredibly contextually dense. This ever increasing fixation on the Identity development of the collecting/emerging DBST makes it impossible — fairly early on, in fact — for the human mind to engage in even the most tangential of flock/herd entanglements with other human minds. This is why there is no species memory cloud for any organism that features a human-generating brain, and why I see the presence of this specific gestation process as creating a definitive line of demarcation between what emerges as either a human or a nonhuman DBS Trajectory whole.

Due to what is — at the very least — a clear and identifiable break from what constitutes a common mind/brain developmental relationship, I will be referring to these *human* burst sets as **Intellect Burst Sets (IBS)** as I continue to describe this process. I will also be referring to the data sets that are selected and processed by the PDT for inclusion within its human memory cloud as Perception Fact Sets (PFS) since these are factual representations of human perception, and not factual representations of what actually occurred beyond that perception interpretation.

Note — Okay, a quick explanation is in order here. The act of perception interpretation/translation [conscious awareness] is as much a C/E Trajectory as any other activity. That means that it causes an RFS continuum to emerge (which, like any RFS continuum, is contextually entangled with the consciously aware system that caused its emergence by making sense of what's been perceived). The dynamic PDT (launched by that same consciously aware system) further isolates *"set clusters"* within this very specific RFS continuum by intentionally linking them to precise data retrieval sub-assemblies [memory cells within the brain] - creating a quick reference "data cloud" that is profoundly entangled with the brain's IBS configuration process. The data sets within this RFS continuum are factual (as are all RFS continuum data sets) but they are only factual concerning the nature of the ongoing stream of conscious awareness. Due to this degree of separation between an environmental occurrence RFS continuum and an RFS continuum that emerges as a result of the subjective experience (involving perception interpretation-translation) of conscious awareness, I have given these unique data sets the term **Perception Fact Sets (PFS)**.

Each IBS is configured by the brain as it reacts to what it's presented with as conscious and unconscious stimuli that is both internally generated [rumination] and externally received [perception]. Since the brain reaches for the PFS clusters that populate its memory cloud and uses them as reference data sets during its IBS configuration process, obviously the PDT's best shot at influencing what the brain configures and launches involves controlling which PFS clusters will be most readily available for referencing by the brain during that process. And this is exactly what the PDT does to ensure that each IBS that the brain configures and issues is in relative sync with the mind's already established and prevailing contextual blend. It carefully controls what is allowed into the brain's memory cloud, and how each cluster within the entire cloud is attributed.

Taking all of this into consideration it's not surprising that the mind's PDT intercepts each Perception Fact Set as soon as it emerges, and immediately acts to ensure a level of perception stability; ignoring some within the continuum and carefully coding the rest before even allowing them to be referenced as immediate short term memory [putting them into the memory cloud] which is what we remember as conscious awareness. Often the experience of awareness doesn't align with Reality, but what is of primary importance is that the mind's ongoing Identity development effort progresses in a stable and predictable manner. Isolating the brain's memory cloud and stacking it with carefully selected and processed Perception Fact Set clusters — as opposed to allowing the brain access to environmental data sets — has emerged as an effective and highly efficient Identity sculpting strategy, since all brains rely on data sets (residual or otherwise) as they configure and launch Dynamic Burst Sets in response to the business of corporeal survival.

As I stated above, not all perception translation events result in PFS clusters that are attributed for inclusion within the human brain's memory cloud. This can happen due to any number of reasons, or for no real reason other than relative insignificance versus the need to focus on much higher priority data set clusters. We refer to the impact of the PDT's *discard* of a Perception Fact Set cluster as cognitive bias, and its rejection is due to the PDT's inability to quickly fit it into the mind's prevailing paradigm in an effective manner.

During instances of extreme focus requirement, the PDT's aggressive avoidance of otherwise usable PFS clusters is why some people experience *tunnel vision* during high stress moments, and why instances of extreme

AutoGenesism: A Theory of Everything

chaos can literally freeze a person's cognitive functionality. Raw physical survival of the brain and body will naturally emerge as the primary mission of the entire system in these instances, with primitive DNA dictates over-riding the PDT's data management process. The PDT process can be halted completely in favor of keeping the brain's more primitive sensory translation systems free should DNA-dispatched survival act/react burst sets become required. This is why police and military training focuses on repeated stress exposure combined with behavioral modification therapy. The goal here is to prevent any instinctive survival responses (to keep trained responses in constant control) during moments of extreme stress and sensory overload.

Under normal circumstances, each PFS cluster that is allowed into the memory cloud is *coded* by the PDT with contextual attributes concerning importance, usable accuracy as it relates to established factuality, degree of Identity relevance, and contextual relevance as definitional support for otherwise unrelated determinations, among many other detailed and precise contextual identifiers that rigidly prepare the brain's compare/contrast data cluster reference library in such a way as to control that brain's intellectual response as tightly as possible in support of the Identity profile that the mind has been working to establish and define all along.

Some clusters can't be ignored, even when they've been determined by the PDT to be in direct opposition to the mind's preferred Reality paradigm. This can be the case due to a variety of naturally occurring reasons, including repeated encounters, contextual relevance to high value reference items, and the sheer weight in balance between the offending information and other, more supportive PFS clusters within a necessary larger informational whole, among a much wider range of possible scenarios.

When this occurs, the PDT will code the cluster in such a way that alters its contextual relationship with the PFS clusters that historically support it within the memory cloud, thereby changing its overall application to the degree where it can then be used by the brain, perhaps as an example of flawed perspective, erroneous perception, or any of a host of easy-to-dismiss perception failures that are common to the average human thought process. Some PFS clusters can even be entangled with unrelated clusters that serve to redefine them just enough to become data sets with acceptable implications, as the PDT does what it must to allow a pesky, but unavoidable, perception schism a place within the memory cloud.

Such translation defaults are not all that mysterious, and we each encounter such determination instances all the time. Of course, the great majority of them are in response to errors in perception, perspective, or interpretation, and have nothing to do with our PDT's effort to protect our emerging Identity from factual challenges to what's been established as a necessary Reality paradigm. Still, the system does exist, and it is a very real reason why so many people are literally incapable of comprehending that which is so obvious and commonplace as ongoing experience for other people who actually share what should be a common Reality sphere with them on a daily basis.

This denial system serves the amplification of whatever has been promoted as real and true within the mind as a whole; offsetting the mixture percentage of grape juice with additional apple juice, if you will. Over the course of the brain's life, this blend of *truths* and *realities* becomes more and more defined and solidified, until the contextual balance becomes literally unalterable due to the impossibility of new PFS clusters significantly affecting the established percentages to any degree. *"Old dog, new tricks"* is another way to put it, I guess. By the time the brain finally dies, the human being is fully developed, and *"it is what it is"*, for better or worse.

And this is how the Personality Development Trajectory builds the human being. One IBS at a time, and by manipulating the brain's data vault so that all it has to work with are carefully controlled and prepped reference set clusters as it scrambles to configure and launch the next burst set and keep up with the demand that's piling up in its own in-box from instant to instant. Pretty ingenious, and according to one large study conducted in 2008, the prepping process takes anywhere from a half a second to a full seven seconds to complete (depending, I would imagine, on the complexity of the IBS configuration being processed and a variety of external factors, as well as the intellectual capacity of the brain/mind system that's doing the work). Here's a web link to the study, in case you want more information. However, be advised that the researchers did not connect the same dots, as a result of their findings, as I did.

http://www.nature.com/neuro/jounal/v11/n5/abs/nn.2112.html

If this relationship between the mind and brain intrigues you, in *"From Here to There: The Crossing Over Event"* [Section III: Digressions] I go into detail concerning the human mind's corporeal Point of Perspective (POP), and

AutoGenesism: A Theory of Everything

how (as a manufactured perspective) the POP of the 2nd stage gestating human being (which is what you and I are) is specifically positioned to ensure the survival of the brain and body, even though the conscious human being itself [the human mind, as it develops and matures] is NOT a material manifestation.

Of course, the human brain (as is true about everything else that materially exists) is a densely packed matrix of contextually entangled spatial trajectories, with each level of similarly structured matrices devoted to its own part of bringing the brain as a functioning whole into manifestation. Neurons, Synapses, and all the perceptible structures of the brain and nervous system serve as established IBS targeting pathways, since this has obviously proven to be the most reliable and efficient means of targeting critical movement directives to the appropriate parts of the body. If a major pathway is destroyed, then no IBS is capable of immediately connecting with the part of the body that was once served by that pathway, and paralysis results.

There is also the powerful influence of the body's own DNA survival dictates to consider when balancing everything together as the dynamic confluence of factors that cause the human mind to exist as the emergent system that it actually is. Often the PDT is in direct conflict with the DNA's very simple and common sense approach to material survival, and it doesn't take much imagination to visualize those instances where the outcome of that conflict has for the moment been decisively in favor of one version of survival over the other [Homo Sapiens versus human being] and with permanent ramifications for both.

This is not to suggest that the human mind is inherently at odds with its corporeal Intellect generation system, but it is a powerful indication that the mind's primary focus (while in physical gestation as the brain feeds it with Intellect Burst Sets) is the definition and development of the human being. In effect, the material brain and body (as a result of the PDT's primary devotion to the ID Survival requirements of the gestating human being) are ultimately expendable if this is what the Identity of the emerging human being requires.

This is what's radically different about the human brain/mind relationship when compared to all other brain/mind survival systems. But there is a very natural reason for this. You see, (and I hope this has become painfully obvious by now) the human mind is the physically gestating human being, and if the human brain and body have any *mission* whatsoever, it is the successful production of a capable human being.

Kevin Brian Carroll

The Eternal Human Being

When the human brain dies, the human being is born. Yes, that sounds like religious philosophy, but if you've been reading along to this point and comprehending what you've been reading, then you know exactly what I mean by that statement. For a much deeper and more comprehensive examination of what the human being's birth event entails, check out Section III's *"From Here to There: The Crossing-Over Event"*. As with many such topic digressions, there's just too much that requires additional explanation and referencing for it to be dropped in here.

In fact, the fully developed human being is much too complex and as a physical manifestation, much too unlike the rest of physical Reality to be quickly overviewed. It's also true that a lot of what we can determine about the physical nature of our own eternal selves can come as a result of properly interpreting direct and indirect inferences concerning what's come to us from some very unscientific sources. But, that's an entirely different level of extreme complexity; one that has resulted in centuries of devoted effort by the world's greatest minds, without the composition of a single declarative statement that's free of some level of faith in the possession of an impossible knowledge. The bitch is that there's no quick, easy list of bullet points that can encapsulate the fully realized human being.

I'm going to go ahead and admit to the fact that a complete examination of the physically eternal human being is beyond the scope of this section, and set up for our look at one extremely important (and remarkably revealing) aspect of the physical nature of the human being. And when that's done, we'll be through with Track#1's description of Reality's rise from nothing whatsoever to its hosting the emergence of the human being.

In Section II's Track#2 we'll examine a very common frame of reference from an unexpected perspective as we look at how some human beings carry on after their authoring brains have shut down forever. As we get into it, you'll understand the relevance of this examination, and why it has the level of importance that it does within this larger presentation of AutoGenesism.

As for the whole of progressive development, while it continues and will continue without end, its pinnacle of achievement has been reached with the emergence of the self-aware Intellect Burst Set Trajectory. The human being (regardless of how its emergence is materially accomplished) is as complex and

AutoGenesism: A Theory of Everything

sophisticated as progressive development gets. That said, there are and will always be many progressing ramifications as a result of the human being's ongoing presence, so it's not a case of Reality ceasing to be a dynamic contextual matrix.

Still, if there are developments that push the expression of Identity Survival further forward in a real sense, they won't initiate as a default progressive development response. The truth is that there's nowhere further for naturally occurring default progressive development to progress toward now that a dynamic, self-aware form of Information has become focused on what no form of Information has even been capable of; a true and relentless pursuit of its own Identity Survival.

I hope that you've remembered that the only requirement that's driving whatever it is that exists to become what it becomes or to persist as being what it's become, is the meta-law *"first survive"*, with Identity Survival as its bottom line definition of what it means to survive. If not, then you need to go back and get that straight in your head before you read on, because it's going to matter just as much here as it did back when each Change/Event Unit was replacing the last one as the resulting C/E Trajectory was fighting for its very existence. At this epitome level of developmental sophistication, Identity Survival might look different, but it's the same universal impetus that's been responsible for everything all along.

So, the human being has finally been loosed upon the Universe [yes, it's okay to refer to the URC-Determined Environmental Confine — physical Reality, as it were — as the Universe, since that's sort of what the word *universe* means] and if I was writing this story, I would toss in the *"And they lived happily ever after"* tagline and call it a wrap. And why not? The human being is physically eternal, fully aware, as dynamic and proactive as any C/E Trajectory that's ever existed, and completely free and invulnerable. There are no restrictions on its capacity to experience whatever it wishes to experience; well, as long as it can convince itself that what it is experiencing is real and actual, of course. In my own definition of *"happily ever after"* it doesn't get any better than this.

However, each human being is also allowed to define *"happily ever after"* for itself, and let's face it, if we've each learned anything at all by this stage in our own gestational development process, it's that happiness doesn't look the same when viewed through the eyes of two different people. The real kicker here is that people don't change all that much once they've finished the 2nd phase of their gestation. In fact, you could say that by the time they've slipped the surly bonds of Earth, they have been defining and refining their core personality, and who they've become is who they'll always be. And, for better or worse, I might add.

What's also present and not as easy to dismiss for some folks as it is for others, is the meta-law's relentless demand that all that exists continue to ensure and/or promote its unique and inimitable Identity at all costs.

While the human being is in gestation, this urge manifests in a variety of ways, and each evolving person addresses it in whatever manner is most agreeable and most readily available. Some work to gain relative notoriety [either positive or negative] to ensure that their Identity has a shot at extending beyond their immediate vicinity. Fame has always meant much more than the potential for associated wealth and privilege to those who've pursued it.

Some work to gain power, and it's easy to see how great power feeds the innate drive to extend one's Identity presence beyond all common parameters. There are those who create art, literature, and music, as well as those who reach out to change the world with their ideas and dedications. Soldiers, who have inspired us all with their heroics, cement their Identities as transcendent within the societies they sacrificed it all for.

However, for most humans, Identity Survival comes down to one very simple and natural drive; leaving behind at least one human that genetically represents them, with the expectation that this person will leave others behind to keep their biological lineage going far into the future. We call it the *Biological Imperative*, and while many people don't indulge, most do. Most people who work and strive for other versions of Identity Survival have also done what's needed to ensure that their 2nd stage gestational placenta will be represented going forward.

Identity Survival; nothing more and certainly nothing less. But what happens to this urge once the human being has been fully developed and it has walked off on the Material Realm? I can assure you that Identity Survival doesn't cease to be the driver that it was. Other than that, the ramifications can be as divergent as they were when the person was still hooked up to the generating brain. That said, we can assume a few things.

The first thing we can assume is that due to the fact that people don't radically change as a result of being freed from the gestational development system that brought them into existence, what they pursued in life to satisfy their own

AutoGenesism: A Theory of Everything

Identity Survival requirement will probably be similarly expressed as they go about their afterlife. Sure, some may explore alternative methods (especially if they were stymied along those lines during gestation due to intractable circumstances) but for the most part, a person eventually resorts to being that individual that they've created.

Of course, this suggests all kinds of dramas and complex arrangements are ongoing within the eternal realm, and why not? If the eternal realm is packed with people, then it's going to be like any place that's packed with people; with every bit of drama and complication you'd expect from such a place. That said, for reasons that will eventually become clear and compelling, what I really want to do is focus on the people who primarily addressed their Identity Survival imperative urge by procreating while existing as corporeal manifestations. The breeders. Those folks whose entire 2nd stage gestation centered on mating, producing offspring, and raising their offspring to also become breeders so that they could be certain that their own genetic lines would be continued. I want to take a good look at what full human existence might look like for these folks.

I Breed, Therefore I Am

I don't have anything against breeders. I really don't. My mom was a breeder and God bless her for it, since I wouldn't exist if not for her need to breed. I also have a daughter, and she's got two children of her own, so regardless of how irreverent I seem to be concerning the sacred act of leaving babies to the world, I'm a big fan of the whole thing. Still, when I began looking hard at which traditional promises can possibly await the fully viable, post-gestational human being, the only severe clash between what is claimed and what makes any sense whatsoever turned out to be (and this is after acknowledging the miracles allowed by human perception's absolute dominion once the Material Realm is in the rear view mirror) the *heaven* that awaits the breeders once they've walked off on the DNA thing and woke up to the fact of being informational in physical structure.

Now bear with me, since this is where the human race really splits with the program as a whole, and the truth is that I'm only going to be able to introduce the basic dilemma facing the fully gestated breeder human being before I'll be forced to stumble noisily into the pure speculation of this Section II's Track #2. Once we get there, it's all going to get a lot more wide open and I won't be insisting on a damn thing, but for the moment, what I want to suggest is that by all responsible interpretation of available data concerning everything that I've carefully laid out for you (from the very beginning of this book until this point in my presentation) as far as I can tell, once the breeder human being is done with its own 2nd stage gestation, if it insists on continuing to address the meta-law's *"first, survive"* in the manner with which it has grown accustomed, then it's personal forever is going to feel like a very, very long time, and not in a good way. This is due to the physical structure of the eternal human being.

Now, back in Section I, I covered how internal and relative context blends to define and ultimately establish the Identity of literally every single thing that exists. I also introduced the role that origin [internal context] plays in establishing whether entanglement is possible between holons, be they permanent [information] or tangential [material structures]. Basically, shared or sympathetic origin [depending on the nature of the entanglement] will allow for that entanglement, whereas origins that feature authors or circumstances that are contextually isolated from one another cannot result in holons that are capable of entanglement. This is more thoroughly examined in *"Entanglement: The Laws and Dynamics of Contextual Association"*; one of a variety of in-depth digressions located in Section III of this book.

As to how the fully gestated human being is affected by all of this, due to the fact that a material brain creates the Intellect Burst Sets that make up its IBST in direct response to survival requirements (as opposed to these data sets emerging on their own as a default result of environmental occurrence) the IBST that the brain creates [remember, this is the human being as a physical structure] ends up being literally indivisible as far as the rest of Reality itself is concerned. Not only indivisible, but physically incapable of ever shedding or acquiring bits to increase or otherwise adjust the structure of itself. In fact (and I want to reiterate this here because it is critical that you fully understand this) to the rest of physical Reality, each permanently existent DBST is literally its own contextually isolated (and therefore impenetrable) sub-environment, and it always will be.

Now, as I also made clear in Section I, this works out just fine for the kind of DBST that is a simple collective of Dynamic Burst Sets whose primary goal was to actively ensure the ongoing structural survival of that DBST's authoring brain/body material matrix; the *mindless* result of translating DNA survival dictates.

It's also okay if the permanent and discarnate DBST is the response-reaction *mind* of a nonhuman brain-equipped creature of some sort. It might even

AutoGenesism: A Theory of Everything

work out wonderfully for those human minds who were never much for expressing themselves in terms of creating more of themselves for the world to enjoy and appreciate while they were incarnate. However, for the human breeder, the fact that it can't ever physically *spread out*, as it did on Earth with kids, grandkids, and entire family trees to fixate on, is going to be an immediate problem — well, it will be for those who have come upon that realization, of course.

For those breeders who are ignorant about such things, the stress could feel like loneliness or even *love starvation*, since that's what the denial of physical procreation feels like for such a person while still being fed by the living brain. After all, the *"first survive"* meta-law doesn't disappear regardless of the level of developmental sophistication. All it does is *hide* within plans and concerns of a more sophisticated nature.

And the truth is that, within the URC-determined physical confines of any Contextual Environment, there's no possible means of addressing the Identity Survival grind for the fully viable, post-gestational breeder human being in the manner that this human has grown to prefer. Traditional sexual procreation is a literal impossibility for the eternal informational human being, and yet, as you'll discover in Track#2, there's a logical and technically plausible means by which such a breeder human being can — in fact — fully satisfy that procreative drive.

Now, I will state here, and for the record, that what I've discovered here may very well be nothing more than my own brilliant solution to this inevitable existential dilemma for the billions and billions of denied human beings that are presently *loveless* within the Informational Realm; having no way to seed the future with their own ongoing need to procreate. And if this is true, then I'm declaring myself this planet's most visionary genius, and I defy anyone to challenge that declaration, since as a solution, it actually works.

That said, I've also found some pretty compelling evidence that suggests that I haven't invented anything at all; that this fascinatingly complicated, yet wonderfully elegant, hands-off solution is real, and that it is this remarkable solution that drove Earth's Homo Sapiens hominid to eventually create gods, demons, heavens and hells out of what should have been a whole cloth consisting of nothing whatsoever.

And this is why we'll be taking a good long look at the plight of the post-gestational breeder in this next track, as representing just one aspect (yet obviously an aspect that's made an enormous impact on our own development as a sapient species) of the human being's reaching out to arrange the furniture, and make a home for itself within the Informational Realm.

Track II

A
Divine
Gestation

Before we even start here, I want to make it clear that this entire Track#2 is speculative, and that it's not even an actual theory. A theory can be tested at some level, either by experiments, or forensic evidence, or even with a rigid examination of the logical and empirical inference structure to see if there's any correlation between it [the theory] and what's been conclusively proven to be true and reliable. The stuff I'm about to lay out for you can't be conclusively proven to be true and it can't be disproven either. This means that it can't ever be presented as a theory.

That stated, and without any caveats or qualifications whatsoever, I do want to take a moment to explain why I included this extremely ambitious overview, and why I elevated it to a shared status [it's Track#2, after all] with what I believe can be, and will eventually be, proven true about the actual physical structure of Reality [that would be Track#1]. It comes down to the extremely unlikely definition of what it means to be human, as opposed to being anything else, and to exist as mortal on Planet Earth.

If there was any evidence of chimps building altars, or gorillas holding worship services, then I would not have seen any need to continue in my examination of the human being after it finally made its appearance at the end of Track#1's climb from a literal void of physical existence. Still, I think that it's important to once again make it clear that I am an atheist, and have no intention of slipping in some half-baked *scientific* concoction that pulls God out of a magic top hat on you.

I admit that I've already broken whatever atheistic code there seems to be that insists that when the corporeal human brain dies, the human mind dies with it, but the eternal survival of the human mind has nothing at all to do with the existence of a creator god thingy, and I absolutely reject the dogma that insists that the two notions are intrinsically interwoven. Reality is a lot different than any of our centuries-old human invented narratives have declared it to be. I've already proven that much.

I kicked all dogmas to the curb before starting this adventure, and that goes for the tousled hair, leather elbow patch crowd's dogmas as well. No one gets to define Reality for me. If the evidence clashes with even the most appealing and elegant solution, then that solution is just plain wrong, and I have no qualms with finding room in the dumpster for it and moving on. But, I did explain up front that I was not going to summarily dismiss anything that could stand on its own, even if I was not going to accept any traditional or nontraditional interpretation of what it is or what it means without doing the hard work it takes to really challenge it.

I also admitted that if I ran into anything clearly improbable that refuses to be readily explained away while persisting as axiomatic across divergent cultures and societal structures, that I would have to indulge the possible existence of whatever it is to the point of establishing its failure as an accurately interpreted aspect of physical Reality. And that in such a case, I would then move to uncover why such an erroneous interpretation could've become so axiomatic, and perhaps — as a result of that effort — offer a more plausible interpretation of whatever the hell it is that's persisted as so culturally fundamental while being so obviously impossible as traditionally depicted.

Well, this Track#2 narrative is the net result of such a case, and I want to share it with you. By leveraging every imperative, protocol, and qualifier that I've presented as fundamental to the way that physical Reality operates, and in an honest effort to try and figure out how the fully viable, dynamically informational human being [specifically the breeder human being] might ultimately pursue its own procreative fulfillment of the meta-law's *"first, survive"* imperative, I was actually forced to successfully construct a very plausible (and surprisingly practical) interpretation to replace what is perhaps the greatest example of flawed empiricism that Earth's human race has ever universally embraced. And,

Autogenesism: A Theory of Everything

to be perfectly frank about it, this interpretation fits the forensics as if it'd been revealed in hindsight.

What I was going to do is lay it all out for you in the same narrative style I used in Track#1; as if it were a progressively developing process. I saw no harm in doing so, since I was going to point out again and again, here and there, that this entire track is nothing more than an exercise in informed speculation. That didn't work out as I'd hoped, so I took this presentation in a very different direction, with distinct sections focused on important factors that simply couldn't be properly covered in a narrative style. After all, this is not the result of a naturally spontaneous emergence. It's the result of human intervention.

Still, as you read on, keep track of the rigid structure that is established and how every minute impetus, initiation and ramification adheres precisely to what I've already established as physical Reality's natural progressive development structure, and how it does so while logically defaulting accurately in the specific manner that one would anticipate a human initiated process of this nature to logically default. It's really pretty spectacular, and like I said, if it's not true, then I might have concocted something here that the post-corporeal human breeders are going to really appreciate. That's because, as a solution to the procreative urge that persists for the contextually isolated human breeder, this very simple process works, and it resolves beautifully without anyone having to lift a finger to micromanage it.

Section I

Why the Ethereal Must Be Examined

In Track#1 we examined the natural development chain that started with a very simple change-event, and followed the relentless pursuit of Identity Survival, as every possible version of the Change/Event Trajectory leveraged ramification and contextual entanglement to progress the whole of physical Reality from being no more than a realized potential to hosting the emergence of the

245

fully developed human being. And the one fact that's been present at every step, every stage, and every emergence along the way has been that nothing simply exists without having been brought into existence as a result of a requirement that it exist; whether by ramification or emergence.

All that exists, does so in service of the meta-law *"first, survive"* and this relentless Homo Sapiens fixation on the divine exists. In fact, it literally defines Earth's human being in a way that nothing else does or ever has. Regardless of the time period or specific culture, a majority of Earth's humans embrace the existence, if not the authority, of celestial beings, and this has been the sole anthropological constant for thousands of years.

The net result of the meta-law as basis for all progressive development is that there are forensic fingerprints on everything that exists, and while that's an obvious metaphor, you know what I mean by that statement. All that has become can be linked to what came before it, and this goes for the creations of the human mind as well. Conceptual creativity is about reconfiguration. Taking an idea and transforming it, or reapplying it. Maybe combining it with another notion. Thesis + antithesis = synthesis. Like tossing stuff in a blender and hitting all the buttons to see what comes of it. It's about creating something new, but it's about creating something new from stuff that's already there and available.

Creativity is not about bringing something into existence that is comprised of no preexisting ingredients at all. It's also not about creating something that can't be logically connected to anything that already exists. The mysterious nature of physical emergence notwithstanding, the act of creativity (even conceptual creativity) always leaves fingerprints on what has been created, and this is really important to understand as we begin this examination.

As I've already stated, when I began to take apart the Creator God concept, it wasn't long before I ran into a wall between the fundamental concept itself and where that very specific concept connects with an actual Reality paradigm that is creatively possible for any Material Realm corporeal brain; human or otherwise. There have been plenty of proposals to account for the logical emergence of an imaginary infrastructure [based on a progressing suite of intellectual capacities and cultural predilections] that is capable of hosting a celestial god being, and yet — to date — no one has directly connected this imagination-crafted infrastructure to the clearly defined material infrastructure that sits immediately before the sight, sound, smell, taste and touch of the corporeal human sensory system. And, this is the specific connection that must be revealed before

AutoGenesism: A Theory of Everything

I can walk off on what is such a deeply affective and broadly pervasive delineator between what's human and the rest of what exists, and declare that delineator to be a product of the naturally evolving human imagination.

After all, even emergence requires a full confluence of contributing factors, and if we compare the invention of an imperceptible, yet fully existent, sapient personality (let alone one with superhuman qualities) with other natural examples of physical or conceptual emergence, we're left with some serious vacancies within its required confluence structure, and no means of responsibly filling those vacancies. While I realize that if approached in a cursory manner, it's easy to dismiss it all as either wishful thinking or ignorant indulgence of the *observer* dichotomy that's created by the cognition schism between the brain and the mind, when all available evidence is examined [biological, empirical, historical, and otherwise] the initial invention of imperceptible people requires a leap that a material brain is specifically protected against making. In fact, such a conceptual creation directly violates the primary cognitive structure that bases the brain/mind relationship, and while insanity can cause that relationship to become damaged, there's no means available for explaining the existence of the conceptual germ that would be needed for such an empirically resistant paradigm to even initiate, let alone become so virulently axiomatic.

And it's not as if the effort hasn't been made. A week spent buried within the pages of Robert Bellah's excellent *"Religion in Human Evolution: From the Paleolithic to the Axial Age"*, (required reading for anyone attempting this sort of endeavor) erases all doubt that the specific link between the material human brain and the raw notion of impossible-to-perceive intelligent life is a link that has never been established, even if the evolutionary development of the mind/brain relationship did progress through thoroughly natural stages as a result of the Homo Sapiens creature clearly wrestling with the ramifications of that notion.

I know that most folks assume that the human mind can imagine anything to exist, but that's actually not true. It can only imagine what can be possibly inferred by what it already suspects to be true or existent as a result of what it has been physically presented through its authoring brain and its IBS configuration activities. Even the most outrageous flight of fantasy reveals intellectual trajectory linkage to other, more pedestrian notions. And as anyone who's ever worked with creativity knows, nothing imagined is ultimately original. You can always find linkage if you run an idea back far enough.

That said, if you follow the notion of an invisible, non-physical, super-powerful creator being back far enough, it becomes clear that (as an original concept created solely as a result of sheer imagination) it has no fingerprints on it. Certainly not if its invention was originally accomplished by a corporeal human that was in search of an imaginary protector, struggling to make sense of a natural phenomenon, or trying to invent a means of refuting the inevitability of its own demise. Hell, it's not as if every form of struggle confronting the Homo Sapiens creature hadn't always existed for as long as they'd been part of the animal kingdom. The threat of existential oblivion was not something new, and neither was the human mind's realization of the inevitability of death.

Of course, the most common explanations involve ancient, ignorant people somehow transforming their fixation on dreams, the sun, or a volcano, into a superstitious fixation on a host of invisible superheroes that are much more available to be bargained with, and maybe in a bar (or a freshman philosophy class) that sort of banal assertion can be suggested before the talk moves on to more manageable aspects of human evolution. But, we're addressing aspects of Reality at their fundamental levels here, and in Reality, the human brain/mind creative process just doesn't work like that. In Reality, the brain produces ideas and perception translations that have a direct connection to what it already knows to be either real or at least plausible.

That's because every Intellect Burst Set that is configured and launched within the IBS Trajectory is conceptually linked to at least one Perception Fact Set that already exists within the brain's memory cloud. Remember our examination of the brain's IBS configuration process? Remember the role of the PDT and how it inflicts cognitive dissonance on the perception interpretation process if it encounters a PFS that severely challenges what it has established to be true and reliable? Well, here's a primary example of why it's important to definitively establish exactly how cognitive functionality occurs and is protected from extreme threats to the mind's carefully developed version of what's real.

Even after thousands of years of the human race's exposure to the general idea, the actual existence of a person who cannot be materially perceived is tough enough for a human mind to allow in as experienced perception. Even if (and often, especially if) that imperceptible person's nonphysical existence is being intellectually or empirically imposed upon that human mind as a result of a real and undeniable external introduction. To insist that such a completely counterintuitive premise would (or even could) be spontaneously available as an existent PFS rumination basis for a human brain without the notion itself having

AutoGenesism: A Theory of Everything

ever been specifically introduced and initially defined as required survival data within its memory cloud, seems to be a bit more than is possible for even the most creative genius who's ever lived.

If the primary concept that literally defines what's radically unprecedented about a novel thought can't possibly be connected directly to any Perception Fact Set that already exists within the memory cloud of a human brain, then that novel thought simply can't ever be part of an Intellect Burst Set that's been produced by that brain. There's a difference between being able to entertain such a counterintuitive notion, and being capable of spontaneously originating it — even considering the many surprising capacities of the human mind that have been given credit for making such a creative leap possible. Those capacities made the notion possible to entertain, and even embraced, but the notion itself has no linkage to what the brain's own perception systems are capable of introducing as novel data sets to the brain's memory cloud, and this has to be considered when running down the origins of anything that is inherently imperceptible, yet accepted as existent and culturally central to the world of prehistoric Homo Sapiens.

And yet, I fully expect to be challenged on the idea that the first human brain to ever have such a notion available within its memory cloud was physically presented with the idea as external perception that came with its own presented interpretation, and that this occurred with enough relative *authority* that the PDT's natural discard response was overcome. And I'm okay with that, since we're all poking around in the dark when it comes to how this original concept actually developed into what's clearly the most unlikely and unsupportable certainty that the human mind can possibly embrace as fact.

In addition to this attribute-free conceptual leap dilemma is the fact that regardless of the specifics involved (be they based on ancient theological assertion or the latest in secular cutting edge scientific theory) the largest notions concerning the fundamental nature of Reality itself are each based on the same very specific fundamental paradigm; that this one Reality confine that we all share, the only Reality that can be objectively proven to exist, is only one such Reality confine that exists, with other similar (or dissimilar) Reality confines fully capable of containing intelligent human life. Heavens, hells, dimensional spaces, or multiverses; it seems that no one who's serious about chasing down the true framework of physical Reality is immune to that visceral certainty that just beyond our senses lies at least one realm that we can't physically perceive, with specific labels and ramifications existing as the only real areas of controversy.

Now, I cannot actually settle this debate, since an impossible-to-perceive realm that's populated by impossible-to-perceive intelligent life is inherently impossible to perceive; therefore impossible to prove as being existent or nonexistent. What I can offer is the most plausible explanation for the existence of such a realm or arrangement of realms, if based on the AutoGenesism progressive development structure detailed in Track#1. To be honest, if such a realm (or multiple realms) is not based on AutoGenesism, then there's no plausible narrative that successfully explains how a realm (or multiple realms) of this kind could exist as imperceptible, while existing as such a widely shared, yet integral Identity staple for such an overwhelming majority of humans, even if only on this one planet.

Yes, this is speculation, but as you'll discover, it's speculation that adheres rigidly to the very real imperative expressions, ramification structure, and existential protocols that we've established throughout this examination. In short, since no one can factually determine whether the human mind dreamed up the invisible god, heaven, hell, sheep-to-the-right and goats-to-the-left, higher-versus-lower-vibration Reality paradigm on its own (and out of whole cloth) then what I'm about to share with you certainly deserves to be included within the established suite of theological-philosophical explanations as to where the human mind originally got such a completely unexpected idea.

At best, it explains how such an impossible assumption could have originated, and at worst, it's some pretty entertaining stuff that puts all the concepts in AutoGenesism to work on behalf of those poor frustrated breeder humans and their need to carry on with the procreation thing.

As to why I'm presenting what is (essentially) no more mystical than a procreation process as central to the myths and theologies that have shaped the hereafter for every major culture on our own planet; the allegories, metaphors, and analogies associated with these traditional narratives are much too specific for anyone who is serious about figuring this stuff out to not look into such a process while looking into other explanations for where the notion of divinity came from. How many references to familial characters does it take before you begin to associate the whole thing with gestation? Father, mother, son, children, child, wife, husband; the list is pretty insistent, and every major theology either employs these references or describes deity-humanity relationships in parent-child terms.

AutoGenesism: A Theory of Everything

Even those mystical interpretations that are presented with more esoteric treatments imply a nurturing parent-like predisposition toward the enlightened seeker. In the end, even if a specific human being is considered unworthy of being invited to sit at the table for any of a thousand reasons, humanity itself is family to the deity in one sense or another. Procreation is how families become families, so that's where I started. The amazing thing is that it worked out much better than I could've ever expected it to.

Section II

Labels and Quick References

This Track#2 narrative is going to get really complicated really fast, so I feel that it's important to quickly review some of the basics that we established in Section I. Believe me, you're going to be working with every single bit of that stuff here, and this quick bullet point overview of the staples will really help out. In fact, I'm going to just list each fundamental as a blurb so that if you run into a snag later, you can flip back to this page and these crib notes will be here waiting for you.

Internal and Relative Contextual Identity: If something exists, it has a contextual relationship with everything else that exists and has ever existed. That relationship defines it, and gives it Identity. Once it ceases to maintain full material existence, if it has established a contributing presence within the internal contextual Identity of something that possesses full material existence, then its contextual Identity persists. This historical presence, making the once material thing integral to the internal context of an existent material something, constitutes Identity Survival for the former materially existent thing.

The URC-Determined Environmental Confine (URC-DEC or simply, Environment): You can call it Reality, The Universe, or even The World, but when you're referring to the complete relationship matrix of all

251

Change/Event Trajectories that share a common Unit Rate of Change, and every Fact Set and Burst Set that has ever come into being as a result of any and all C/E Trajectories that share that very same exact URC, then you're referring to the URC-Determined Environmental Confine. It is a permanent relationship matrix, and most folks call the one that we are part of *The Universe*. There's no way in from the outside, and no way out from the inside. This is because the relationship itself is based on in-sync progression of quantized Change/Event Units. This progression of in-sync unitary change is what we call Time, and while it may be perceived by the human mind as malleable, in truth, it's not malleable at all. Its quantum structure literally defines what is physically inclusive and exclusive relative to our own and any other universe that may exist.

Identity Survival: This is what it's all about. Physical existence is defined by possessing unique, inimitable Identity, and Survival is maintaining physical existence at all costs. The Change/Event Unit survives as a contributing holon within the Change/Event Trajectory [a holon itself] as historical, internal context, with adherence to the meta-law *"first, survive"* forcing the Environment itself to establish the system preference [natural law] that brings the next Change/Event Unit into existence. Change/Spatial Trajectories [a specific form of Change/Event Trajectory] survive by becoming entangled with other Change/Spatial Trajectories as holon matrix structures, thereby surviving as contextually integral to the next larger holon's internal contextual Identity [again, serving the Environment's own pursuit of ID Survival with increasing structural complexity and diversity]. These trajectory matrices become so densely layered and dependably entangled that they are perceived by us as matter and material structure. The fact is that everything that is physically dynamic is driven to extend its contextual identity within a larger, more durable holon, as its primary means of Identity Survival.

A Trajectory is a Trajectory is a Trajectory: This is probably the hardest notion to hold onto when dealing with the enormous range of material holon sizes and structural designs. You will be challenged in this section with trajectory concepts that, while logically correct, will seem to clash with the simple definition of a classic event trajectory. This is because the DBST hybrid is physically informational [per burst and as a contextually isolated whole] while being materially driven, due to how it came into physical existence; as an event trajectory that leverages holon structure to pursue Identity Survival in the same manner as all versions of Change/Event Trajectories. That said, the gathering of contextually associated Dynamic Burst Sets into a contextually entangled collective is a true informational continuum.

AutoGenesism: A Theory of Everything

And yes, that is a very unexpected way of describing what hits the *Environment* [I may use this term to shorthand my reference to the URC-Determined Environmental Confine from time to time] like a dynamic activity trajectory, but as you'll see, the net impact of the dynamic information hybrid has been and continues to be unexpected.

Not All Context Is Created Equal: In Section III's Digressions section [*"Entanglement: The Laws and Dynamics of Contextual Association"*] this is fleshed out pretty well, but to put it in a nutshell, what exists is a pecking order between relative contextual properties and relationship dynamics that I call *The Hierarchy of Kind*. What's important for our purposes in Track#2 is that we want to keep in mind that the historical origin of a specific mass of information [its permanent relationship with the event or process that brought it into existence] trumps all other internal contextual Identifiers. This is because a residual Fact Set continuum's historical context contributes directly to the Identity of the Environment (and therefore its ID Survival) by default.

Identifiers like Unit Rate of Change, for instance, lock all such physical existence into one Environment, but only historical context [provided by residual Fact Sets and RFS continuums] defines that Environment. Not that such a significant incompatibility like out-of-sync URC can persist unresolved, but when such a clear incompatibility exists, a resolution is reached that is based on an established hierarchy of weighted contextual attributes that all permanent forms of physical existence naturally possess.

Masculine versus Feminine Gender Expressions: Whatever exists as permanent [information sets and/or environmental confines] is precisely identified as a result of a very specific suite of existential qualifications that exist in a balanced blend of often shifting percentages. The relative gender expression of the pursuit of ID Survival [we'll shorthand this as simply *gender expression*] is the most primordial of those qualification subsets [preempted only by historical origin which is not malleable at all] when Identity qualifications are listed out. Therefore, relative gender directly determines how each permanent holon responds to the ID Survival imperative, whether passively or aggressively (depending on the physical nature of the holon in question).

- Masculine survival expressions compete and isolate against *rival* existential wholes. Masculine expressions include Competition and Isolation.

- Feminine survival expressions gather and associate with other wholes in pursuit of common benefit. Feminine expressions include Increase, Association [entanglement], and Symbiosis.

Nothing exists as purely Masculine or purely Feminine in gender expression. There is always a relative balance between the two that defines the gender expression of each contextual environment and information mass. If qualified as being relatively Masculine in gender expression, the permanent whole [environment or information mass] will respond to all other wholes that exist as Identity threats and immediately Isolate against that threat. If qualified as being relatively Feminine in gender expression, that isolation response won't occur. In all cases, a 50%-50% balance in relative gender expression must be crossed to initiate a change in gender survival response.

I think I'm comfortable with that, and if you need more, the deeper analyses are in both Section I and Section III's Digressions section, depending on what the concern is. As we move into this narrative, you may notice developmental responses that are default combinations of more than one of these existential basics, and some issues may have to be detailed when we're confronted with them on the spot. Still, this short list of blurbs will go a long way toward covering most of what we'll be dealing with.

Labels

In this track, the complexities can become pretty dense, and there are several new *players* that emerge as critical components, even though most have been part of the existential whole all along. One of these players is the Intellect Burst Set Trajectory (IBST) that is still physically attached to and being fed Burst Sets by the Homo Sapiens brain. Let's see if I can offer it as an example of why I've decided to employ a unique labeling system for use in this Track#2 narrative.

In this Track#2 narrative I'll refer to the developing IBST of the living corporeal human as the Gestating Dynamic Intellect (GDI) being, and while it seems like I'm inventing a new character here, it's just a new label for the human mind that exists while the human brain is still alive. Obviously, I'm not inventing anything new, since what I'm labeling the GDI is what you yourself are; the conscious and aware human mind that's still being developed by the material brain as it continues to exist and do what the brain does.

To this point in our examination, it's been easy enough to make the distinction between the GDI and the human being that has already survived the death of the human material body and brain to carry on with existence within the Informational Realm. However, in this Track#2 overview, there will be important interaction between *gestating* human beings [those human minds that are still intrinsically rooted to the Material Realm and choosing which PFS to attribute as part of their brain's memory cloud] and those human beings that have completed their own gestational phase of existence. Obviously, providing labels to specify which of these two kinds of humans I'm referring to will help prevent confusion, since both players are human, even if they possess very different goals, perspectives and physical capacities.

Below is a list of the specific labels that I'll be using in this Track#2 narrative, and the basic definitions that apply. These labels will only be used within this overview, and it is conceded that some of these specific items are speculative in nature.

- **THE PROCESS** — AutoGenesism is the all-natural, spontaneous progressive development process that we examined in Track#1. THE PROCESS is different than AutoGenesism in that THE PROCESS is initiated intentionally with the specific purpose of serving as a post-corporeal human procreation process, and in that it creates a URC-Determined Environmental Confine (URC-DEC) that is historically linked [internal context] to the URC-DEC that is the home of the post-corporeal human (IDI) breeder that initiated THE PROCESS.

- **Procreating Entity (PE)** — The post-corporeal human who initiates THE PROCESS. This is an IDI that has authored a Gestational Sub-Environmental Confine.

- **Parent Environmental Confine (PEC)** — The URC-Determined Environmental Confine that is home for the Procreating Entity (PE).

- **Gestational Sub-Environmental Confine (GS-EC)** — The URC-Determined Environmental Confine that serves as THE PROCESS, naturally evolving in the same manner as any URC-DEC once it has been intentionally initiated, even though it historically *belongs* to the PEC as a result of how it is physically initiated. This URC-DEC remains a

GS-EC until its gender survival expression becomes relatively Masculine, at which time it will physically isolate from the PEC with a gender specific survival expression response that I refer to as the Move-To-Isolate Event. Until that moment, it serves as the developmental placenta for the SDI (see below)

- **Intellect Burst Set (IBS)** — Introduced in Section II's Track#1, this is a Dynamic Burst Set that is configured and set into existence by a human brain. It is a hybrid that is Information in structure while possessing the dynamic characteristics of a Change/Event Unit. The primary feature that sets it apart from other forms of brain-generated information sets is that it contains a unique manifestation of full self-awareness that is contextually tied to the instant and circumstances of its original generation.
- **Intellect Burst Set Trajectory (IBST)** — A Dynamic Burst Set Trajectory that is launched and fed by a human brain. This is the term we'll be using to refer to the physical structure of the human mind.
- **Personality Development Trajectory (PDT)** — As detailed in Track#1, the PDT is the activity that the IBST (in its role as the developing human mind) is engaged in as it carefully selects which Perception Fact Sets (PFS) are allowed into the brain's memory cloud, and assigns contextual attributes to each PFS relative to significance, accuracy, and immediate survival relevance. Once the brain has died, the PDT naturally takes on the mind's self-governance activity and continues to manage awareness and perception. It is the IBST's focus of intelligent personality, proactive and reactive sapience, and full self-awareness.
- **Primary Expression** — This is the contextual recipe, the inimitable Identity, of the human being. It exists within every IBS and permanently locks all Intellect Burst Sets created by one single human brain into one indivisible IBST. Its dense structure, featuring an incomprehensible balancing of internal (historical) contextual predilections and restrictions, is what the PDT works to craft over the lifespan of the human brain. It's the precise and permanent Identity of the fully realized human being relative to the rest of Reality, and in THE PROCESS, any environmentally based requirements and protocols affect each human being specifically on the basis of that being's Primary Expression.
- **Gestating Dynamic Intellect (GDI) being** — The human mind (IBST) that exists and is in ongoing gestation as the human brain is

alive and feeding it with Intellect Burst Sets. I will refer to this trajectory as the GDI in reference to it as an intelligent and proactive entity in its own right, as opposed to when I'm solely referring to its physical structure.

- **Isolated Dynamic Intellect (IDI) being** — The fully developed and physically independent human being that has become freed of the material authoring brain upon the death of that brain. I note its contextual isolation in this label, but the IDI is fully capable of perceiving and interacting with the rest of the Environment. It is the IDI seeking to express its *"need to breed"* in service of the meta-law *"first, survive"* that initiates THE PROCESS as a procreation effort. That said, most IDIs find other means of pursuing Identity Survival (than launching a GS-EC) once they've graduated from the Material Realm.

- **Symbiotic Dynamic Intellect (SDI) being** — The intelligent, fully dynamic, and consciously aware "offspring" of an IDI that has chosen to become a Procreating Entity. This is the procreative goal of THE PROCESS, and while it is physically different than the IDI that initiated its gestation process, it is definitely "related" to that IDI, thereby fulfilling the overwhelming procreative urge that has so profoundly defined the personality of such an IDI. This label suggests that the SDI possesses a physically symbiotic, and therefore, contextually accessible external structure, but Symbiotic actually refers to the internal physical structure of the SDI, and not to any external difference between the SDI and the IDI. To the rest of the Environment, the SDI is just as contextually isolated and physically indivisible as the IDI is.

I realize that this new list of labels may end up being a challenge to some of you, but believe me, it won't be as challenging for you as laying this complete process out for you would be for me without these labels. The complexities are really unexpected, since what's happening in THE PROCESS is that naturally occurring defaults are being intentionally leveraged, and while the actual progressive development process is no different than the process I detailed in Track#1, the ramifications of an Environment's having been intentionally initiated are extremely different, and could have deeply affected the way that human beings in this Environment (at least here on Earth) view themselves and the nature of Reality itself.

The possibility that our own Universe is a GS-EC, and the net impact that it (if true) would've had on us and our own evolving Reality view, is the point of this Track#2 narrative. That said, what's also useful about Track#2's detailed analysis of how an artificial initiation of a URC-Determined Environmental Confine affects the net result of what is otherwise natural default progressive development is that it opens up AutoGenesism for deep examination in a way that Track#1 simply doesn't. And yes, it will get complicated. This being the case, having these labels in place will really make it easier for you to immediately tell what aspect or role of each and every *player* [i.e. IDI versus IBST or GDI versus PDT] I'm referring to within any given scenario.

Section III

Impetus and Obstacles

THE PROCESS involves the literal creation of an entire physical universe that serves as a gestational placenta that will eventually produce only one intelligent, sapient being, and yes, I agree that such a venture does seem a bit over-the-top, given the limited scope of the results. But, the human being is nothing if not notoriously prone to such extravagance in its pursuit of Identity Survival. Our own planet is littered with the evidence that no monument is too large or too magnificent to serve as one man's ode to his own lasting legacy. And there's no reason to believe that such men (or women) become less fixated on their own lasting impact on the world around them as a result of death or any other quick perspective adjustment.

The reason why some IDIs would have been driven to pursue Identity Survival in such an elaborate (and Masculine) manner has been answered again and again from one end of our own planet to the other. What's harder, and ultimately more important to determine is how any such human mind could have imagined such an extreme means of spreading their Identity within the eternal Informational Realm. On the face of it, the venture seems cartoonish in its ambition, but as you'll discover, there's a lot more and a lot less than meets the eye here.

It might seem that a gestational procreation process result should be achievable without employing such extraordinary measures, but in this section I'll reveal why this specific process is the only plausible means of post-corporeal procreation that is available to the informational human being. I will also suggest a reasonable explanation for how such an elaborate notion might have emerged as a solution worth pursuing by the very first IDIs who pursued it and ultimately realized its viability. Finally, I will take a look at what some of the challenges might've been, as the very first Environment's fully developed human beings [the first IDIs] worked to deal with this extremely specific and deeply innate Identity Survival urge response that is still so central to the Primary Expressions of most corporeal, and therefore gestating, human beings.

The Biology of Creation

It's just not the same within the Informational Realm as it is within the Material Realm, and there's nothing that can be done about it. Information comes into existence as a result of change and activity, and once it comes into existence, it lingers . . . well . . . forever.

The Material Realm is the realm of activity, and it only physically exists as the quantum duration of Now, regardless of which quantum unit of *Now* you choose to focus on. Yes, there are an immeasurable number of changes and distinct activity trajectories that are part of each instant of Now, but they all happen at exactly the same instant and cease to happen at the same instant, from one end of the Material Realm to the other. Even the brain's generation process of Dynamic Burst Sets (occurring at a much slower, yet quantized rate) consists of actual change/event quanta that initiate and resolve in sync with this environment-wide Unit Rate of Change.

The entire realm can be imagined as an incredibly wide span of physically existing Reality that is, at the same time, unimaginably thin from leading to tailing edge. I see it as if every quantum of *Now* that's establishing the leading edge of every ongoing, quantized Change/Event Trajectory is marching — arm in arm in arm in arm, as one solitary, united row of identical units — in lock-step forward progression. It's quite a visualization that can be pretty tough to hold onto in your mind's eye.

Kevin Brian Carroll

The Informational Realm is the permanent collection of residual Fact Sets that connect as the incalculable number of tentacles [long and short, momentous and miniscule in significance and implication] of the URC-DEC's enormous Informational Continuum that reaches from the literal dawn of Reality itself to provide complete and accurate historical context and identity defining relevance to all aspects of the present quantum instant of Now. This massive web of factual structure persists in contextual balance with those brain-created Dynamic Burst Set Trajectories that are either still in gestation or already set loose within the Environment (each an impregnable whole unto itself) to do and be what they are; existential hybrids that can literally project their presence as C/E Trajectories, each equipped with their own internal initiation/response management systems.

What is important to note is that information wholes [residual Fact Sets, RFS continuums, Dynamic Burst Sets] cannot structurally transform or be structurally transformed once they have emerged. Even the most sophisticated IBST (IDI) is incapable of transforming its own physical structure once its authoring material brain has ceased to exist. Besides the havoc that such widespread reconfiguration would inflict on the Environment's own pursuit of Identity Survival, the physical nature of information sets simply makes any such effort impossible.

For our own (human) purposes, this rigid structure also makes direct post-corporeal procreation or replication of self completely impossible. After all, the Primary Expression of the IDI is its relative Identity within the Informational Realm, and it took the PDT an entire lifetime to craft that Primary Expression. It is so amazingly dense in contextual specificity that there's literally no way of replicating it, and, of course, information sets that are units within an informational mass cannot ever be externally accessed or affected once that mass has achieved contextual isolation, so the breeder IDI is physically stymied if it tries to pursue a traditional satisfaction of the Biological Imperative that drove it while in its GDI development stage.

One thing you have to remember is that the procreative urge is not unknown to the breeder IDI. After a lifetime of being primarily driven by this biological imperative, these IDIs know what it feels like to have this need to breed. They've felt it before. It'd been the lone constant requirement droning in the background as they'd otherwise picked their way through the material phase of their existence.

AutoGenesism: A Theory of Everything

For some of these souls, I suppose that it might have been experienced as simple love-sickness; a yearning for love and all the traditional trappings that accompany it. For others, procreation was better described as their way of addressing a deep visceral need to literally inflict more of themselves upon the rest of the world. For whatever reason it might have been that procreation was the cure, these IDIs would certainly recognize that same gnawing emptiness — and that same need to address it — once the confines of the Informational Realm became familiar enough to no longer be a distraction; the apparent impossibility of satisfying that need notwithstanding.

So, it's not as if, as a result of hitting what would seem to be a brick wall, the concept of producing an offspring (and for the same reason that offspring are produced on this side of the divide) would have then become a non-issue for such an IDI. Also, keep in mind that if the history of humankind on Planet Earth is any indication, the very existence of such an intractable problem would have provided its own requirement for resolution to any number of similarly driven IDIs. After all, each IDI is no less human than each of us will be once we've graduated into their ranks. Some folks are simply in love with solving problems, and corporeal death certainly won't change that aspect of who they are.

All in all, the central position that species procreation occupies within the Material Realm, and the dedication that so many corporeal humans have to procreation, insists that it will remain important (at the very least) to a significant percentage of IDIs once they've crossed into the Informational Realm. Definitely important enough for any barrier to procreation to be seen as a problem worthy of resolving for those so inclined as a result of how their own PDTs managed their cognitive development.

As to how the *breeder* IDI might experience this powerful urge, it stands to reason that he or she would feel it in the same manner that it manifested as an urgency while dominant within their corporeal phase of physical development. After all, the human mind experiences perception, and only perception. The basic drives might become translated differently within a different environment, but they'd still *"feel"* the same. The Biological Imperative would tug at the heart strings, just as it always has. For some, it could be sublimated, but there are those who could only be satisfied with the real deal. Again, it's reasonable to suspect that this drive persists if the human mind itself persists.

Kevin Brian Carroll

Coming Upon the Notion

As for a plausible explanation concerning how the idea emerged that the physical initiation of the kind of chain-reaction that ultimately brought such an IDI's own physical Reality into existence could be leveraged into a gestational placenta that would successfully produce an intelligent, sapient offspring, what I'll need to do is return to one of the earlier statements I made in Section I concerning how a URC-Determined Environmental Confine [or Environment] is defined.

The Residual IC (Informational Continuum) literally defines the whole of its environment, and there is only one Informational Continuum within each Environment, even if developmental complexity results in countless branches reaching off that one trunk. No matter how many limbs, or how convoluted the contextual associations get, the Informational Continuum includes every branch, every budding twig, even as it physically gathers as one dense, indivisible mass of residual information.

This information literally belongs to the Environment as a whole (since it defines it) with the net result being that all Fact Sets that exist within the Environment are completely available to whomever might be capable of retrieving them and examining them for whatever purpose they have to access them.

Then, as a result of being fully capable of determining (from the Fact Sets alone) precisely how the Environment itself evolved (after all, I figured it out — right?), it's certainly conceivable that any one or more of the researching IDIs could realize that such an Environment could be intentionally launched by manipulating an initiating event based on a URC that clashes with their own Environment's fundamental rate of change. Again, I figured out the same thing without being freed to fully access the Informational Continuum directly, so why should it be assumed that such a revelation is unachievable for others?

From there, why would it be inconceivable for any one of those IDIs to make the conceptual leap from simply initiating such an Environment to the realization that if one does initiate such an Environment, that the net result will be the emergence, within their own Environment, of a fully dynamic, fully sapient, being with human qualities, that possesses significant capacities that the naturally occurring IDI doesn't possess? Hell, if I could realize that, then why not any one of them? Of course, if our Universe is a GS-EC, then I probably benefited from the existence of the Fact Sets that emerged to represent the intent behind that purposely created alternate-URC event that brought our own Universe into existence.

As far as THE PROCESS being difficult to achieve, the entire technical challenge is limited to bringing that one event instant that features an incompatible URC into existence. That lone contribution is the full requirement and involvement of an IDI that is seeking to procreate in this manner. So, it's actually about creating that alternate URC event instant, and that's all it's about.

I would imagine that the alternate URC event's duration would need to be shorter than that of the authoring IDI's own Environmental URC, but beyond that I wouldn't even pretend to know how to make it happen. That said, if the human being has proven anything, it is that once a seemingly intractable problem has graduated to being only about the development of an effective technical solution, that solution is inevitable. Once that lone technical issue has been resolved (as you'll discover) the rest of THE PROCESS is completely hands-off and naturally evolving, and it simply cannot fail to deliver the breeder IDI's offspring as a fully capable, wholly relatable and intellectually superior version of human being that freely and fully exists within the universe of its *parent* IDI.

As to how the notion of THE PROCESS first entered the realm of human consideration, the very first Environment's IDIs could very well have (for reasons of simply seeing if it could actually be done) launched an intentionally initiated URC-Determined Environmental Confine only to ultimately discover that when purposely launched, the net result of such a confine's initiation is the physical emergence of a fully developed, cognizant, human-like informational being within their own Environment. Of course, if this was how THE PROCESS became THE PROCESS, then no real genius solution meant to address the stymied Identity Survival urge of breeder IDIs was actually accomplished at all.

After all, this intellectually cognizant, human-like informational being [this would be the Symbiotic Dynamic Intellect — SDI — being described earlier in this Track#2] that ultimately emerged would have been fully knowledgeable of exactly how it had come into existence. The SDI would have easily found its *parent* IDI [I'll explain exactly why that would have been easily accomplished shortly] and simply taught its *parent* what its alternative URC event creation act had accomplished.

The Identity Survival implications of this SDI's existence would have been immediately overwhelming (especially for that *parent* IDI who actually performed the alternative URC event that launched that SDI's GS-EC) and this dis-covery would have probably been news that breeder IDIs would have taken pro-found interest in. The rest almost doesn't even need to be explained, since these IDI folks are as human as everyone here on Planet Earth. Of course, we can only speculate as to how the notion developed, but if we simply apply what we know about human nature, we can probably reduce the plausible scenarios down to a very short list.

This is the hardest part of this Track#2 narrative; responsibly suggesting how the first-ever GS-EC became recognized as an effective human procreation process, since humanity is anything but limited in its movements from point A to point Z. That said, it would be fairly easy for a scientifically bent IDI to dis-cover the exact Unit Rate of Change duration of its own home Environment. That Fact Set would be as freely available as every other bit of the Environ-ment's Residual IC. From there, I'm going to have to admit that, as just another Material Realm inhabitant, I'm completely ignorant concerning the steps in-volved in creating an event unit that's of a shorter duration than the URC that sits at the substructure of all that brings me into physical existence.

Maybe it's not even possible for a Material Realm inhabitant to do such a thing, whereas the different physical properties of those who are aware and con-templative within the Informational Realm allow them a different degree of lat-itude when it comes to very small and finite schisms like that? Obviously, there's still a lot that we don't understand about our own Material Realm, let alone the whole of Reality.

Naturally, I have no idea how I happened upon this notion, but then, as a corporeal human being with absolutely no extraordinary perception capabilities, my own experience of conscious existence is delayed somewhat, so I can only guess as to how such a counterintuitive concept might've slipped through my own PDT's management system and into my memory cloud. Perhaps it's true that many IDIs already know about this, and perhaps it's also true that many other corporeal human minds (GDIs) have already been *inspired* by IDIs to con-sider exactly what I am sharing with you here?

Perhaps most of them let the notion pass right through without considering it to be significant or anything more than a moment of runaway imagination. Then again, perhaps there have been others that felt as I do about this infor-mation, and who proceeded to translate it into any one of a myriad of theological and mystical concepts; some that have changed the actual trajectory of human civilization from time to time? We do know that these people did exist, even if we can only speculate as to how they came upon the specific notions that were used to change the course of human history.

After all, how did the corporeal human brain initially conceive of the inconceivable? It's conjecture, and that's all it'll ever be. Maybe it was dreams, but maybe they were dreams that were *fed* to them by people [fully gestated human beings — IDIs] that saw a value in alerting their fellow human beings (albeit, still in gestational development) about what their world is really all about? After all, why wouldn't they? Even now, those GDIs that are devoting their 2nd stage of gestational development to pondering these ultimate questions are fellow searchers (kindred spirits, I suppose) in the view of those IDIs that had worked so hard to ferret out the actual Fact Sets associated with this Environment's initiating instances and carefully translate them. These are people, after all, regardless of which side of the divide they inhabit.

The Power to Connect

So, what is the mechanism that allows the discarnate IDI to get information through to the memory cloud of the corporeal human brain? They call it telepathy, but if you're anything like me, that word doesn't explain a damn thing. It took a little bit of taking what I've learned as a result of this Auto-G research project and applying the staples to the issue of non-material communication, but I think I might just have the method that intelligent, consciously aware humans (who are only missing the material body) use to communicate with one another, as well as with those of us who are still anchored to the Material Realm for the time being. I'll employ a digression, since this will definitely take us off track for a moment or two.

Digression Alert — As we've seen, the IDI has the capacity, as dynamic information, to inform the momentary, ongoing bursts of consciousness that emerge from the corporeal brain. But the how of it is not as simple as finding a faulty PDT process, and chatting up that conscious mind during a momentary lapse in corporeal survival focus. In fact, it's not easy at all. Especially since there's no actual direct exchange of information between dynamic information wholes. Yes, that sounds ridiculous, but let me try and lay it out for you here.

Now, we know that IDIs can't physically mass with other IDIs, but we need to realize that this also means that they can't exchange dynamic information directly, since direct acquisition of this form of information by an

IDI would be a form of Intellect massing. That seems counterintuitive — the notion that beings of pure information can't communicate directly with one another — but the fact is that the IDI is 100% dynamic information as an isolated physical mass, and communication is the exchange of information. Isolated dynamic masses of Intellect (all Dynamic Information masses for that matter) are contextually prohibited from shedding or adding mass within the Environment of their origin.

The fractal nature of their physical structure makes that sort of activity impossible, with every unit burst of their structure flush with the full contextual recipe of the whole itself. This recipe is called the Primary Expression, and it serves as its permanent informational fingerprint or DNA identifier, once the authoring brain has stopped adding new bursts to it. This Primary Expression is extremely precise, and just like all existential identifiers, it isolates the units within the whole against all Identity threats that might challenge that whole. Again, this is a primordial Survival response of dynamic Masculine physical existence once it has emerged and achieved Identity.

What the IDIs can do, however, is directly perceive and add to the Environment's Informational Continuum. This is because the Residual IC [comprised of RFS continuums representing every bit of change and activity that's ever occurred within the Environment] shares the same URC with everything else that exists within that Environment while presenting no contextual barriers whatsoever that prevent tangential association.

Of course, all this information is available to the entire Material Realm as Reality-defining contextual precedent, but it's also available to each dynamic informational holon and [in select subset clusters] to each corporeal brain as PDT-attributed Perception Fact Sets. After all, this symbiosis between the Residual IC and all dynamic activity has been the basis of progressive development since the instance of existential genesis itself.

If an IDI causes anything to occur, or even actively considers causing anything to occur [an occurrence in its own right], the facts concerning that occurrence emerge by default as a RFS continuum within the Residual IC. As soon as it emerges, that factual information is immediately available to everything that exists within the entire environment.

Now, if an IDI knows how to target one of its expression events toward a specific IDI, using the emergent RFS continuum [associated with that expression event] as a communication medium [perhaps like a post on an

Autogenesism: A Theory of Everything

Internet forum], and if that targeted IDI knows how and where to find that specific RFS continuum *post*, the sending IDI will be able to communicate with the receiving IDI on an effective level. We refer to this sort of communication as *telepathy*.

In most cases, the communicators aren't aware of how they're using the Residual IC and its vast network of informational continuums. This is due to the fact that by the time the GDI has been freed to become the IDI [as is also the case concerning the amazing complexities that comprise the PDT's survival/ID development management process], it has become pretty familiar with most of this sort of post-corporeal day-to-day routine stuff, having learned by watching/mimicking others [the way people generally learned most everything when they were getting acquainted with daily life within the Material Realm].

That said, in spite of the GDI and its natural affinity with the workings of the Informational Realm, the corporeal human being's progressively emerging experience of conscious awareness is not generally capable of this sort of communication [instinctively or otherwise]. The PDT's management of the brain's emerging memory cloud isn't designed to include data sets that clash with what's generally available within the ongoing wash coming in from the body's sensory systems. Even the intermittently distracted PDT is still primarily focused on material survival and personality development, and it takes deliberate effort to make IDI-to-material brain communication possible. This effort, for the most part, features the IDI doing the heavy lifting.

When it comes down to an IDI reaching out in direct communication with a corporeal human brain via the PDT's memory cloud management, we have to assume that the approach is a bit different than IDI-to-IDI or IDI-to-GDI communication, since these communicators inhabit separate and incompatible physical realms. Now, in Section III *"From Here to There: The Crossing-Over Event"*, there is an explanation of what I've termed the human mind's **Point of Perspective**, or **POP**, and the impact that moments of intermittent shifts in POP focus have had on the beliefs and cultures of people for thousands of years within our own Reality confine. In that digression, I refer to the two very specific POPs that the human being [as corporeal and then as the post-corporeal IDI] experiences during the course of its overall existence; **Corporeal Conscious Awareness (CCA)** and **Post-Corporeal Conscious Awareness (P-CCA)** respectively.

267

Note — Keep these acronyms [POP, CCA and P-CCA] in the front of your mind for the time being, as I'll be using them quite a bit during this digression.

The terms are pretty self-explanatory, but the important thing to make note of is that both terms describe the same discrete conscious mind. They do not refer to a transformation that ends the physical existence of one specific event trajectory of conscious awareness to launch a new event trajectory in replacement. In fact, the awareness being described never changes at all. What changes is the POP of that seamless event trajectory of dynamic awareness, with the mind's CCA rigidly focused on the experience of the PDT's connection of PFS clusters to its authoring brain's memory retrieval *circuitry*, and its P-CCA refocused upon the death of the brain to the view of the entire Intellect mass relative to itself as a unique identified whole within the URC-DEC. Of course, these two POPs are very different experiences for the one conscious mind.

What focuses the mind's conscious awareness at the brain's memory cloud *inbox* is the experience of activating those *memory circuits* in the brain as the PDT links each to a Perception Fact Set cluster (I cover this in *"Building the Ultimate You"*, back in Track#1). As I explained in that subsection, the PDT selects these PFS clusters from the residual Fact Set continuum that naturally emerges in default response to the ongoing C/E Trajectory that is the brain's lifelong effort to make sense of the constant wash of data sets coming in from each sensory system by referencing PFS clusters that the PDT has already linked to material *memory circuits*. The PDT then attributes these new PFS clusters, selects an available *memory circuit* assembly, and when the assignment connection is made, the corporeal mind experiences that PFS cluster as conscious awareness.

This is how it's supposed to work, but since this is Reality, glitches exist here and there. In most cases, the kinds of glitches that exist tend to be fairly random, inconsequential, and tend to appear in relative isolation. This is not the case with glitches involving the human mind's experience of conscious awareness. In fact, these are glitches that have clearly had an overwhelming impact on the way that Earth's Homo Sapiens human race has continued to evolve, with every major culture developing as it has as a direct result of how these glitches have been interpreted. So, what's the glitch here, and why is it so influential? Actually, there are two kinds of glitches here, but they each involve an errant PDT.

AutoGenesism: A Theory of Everything

There are people whose mind-brain generation processes are unique to the extent that their PDT process is much less rigidly focused on the business of PFS cluster selection and attribution than what might be considered normal, or at least average. Not that their experience of perception vacates their CCA Point of Perspective altogether, and races off to take the P-CCA helm of the GDI as the brain is left to carry on without any perception generation management process whatsoever. No, it's more of a slip of focus than a full break-away, making random residual Fact Sets or even dynamic information holons potentially experienced as conscious perception (which, will be how the mind will be focused once it has permanently settled into its P-CCA POP position).

Of course, the PDT then manages this errant data as it does the data that's gathered by the corporeal sensory systems [since the focus slip isn't total, making these P-CCA and the CCA inputs merge as one data wash], and tries to fit it into the ongoing Reality narrative it has worked so hard to craft over the years. This sort of focus slip is noticeable within the Informational Realm, and naturally, some IDIs will take advantage of these episodes as an opportunity to connect with the old neighborhood through these people by intentionally slipping their own carefully crafted and attributed residual Fact Set clusters in with the PFS clusters that are lined up to be linked to the brain's *memory circuitry* by the PDT. Just as you'd expect.

These folks with the wandering focus are called either mediums or psychics, depending on the form of information it is [dynamic or residual, respectively] that their PDTs allow through as processed perception during these focus slips from time to time. Due to a certain amount of demographic evidence, some suggest that this specific condition is generally inherited, which would suggest that the glitch is in the brain's structure. That said, the predilection could very well be environmentally induced, with family being highly influential in that sense as well. As with all brain/mind relationship dynamics, the truth is often a blend of every potential, with percentages that are unique in each specific case.

Now, this ability to refocus one's POP (or inability to prevent one's POP from drifting in focus; a matter of individual perspective here, I suppose) may seem like a flaw in engineering, but we're not talking about divine creation here. This is natural progressive development, and there's slop in natural development. Then again, all slop in the system serves its own useful function, as we'll continue to note throughout this entire examination. And yes, this is exactly that advantageous sort of slop that occurs in all progressive development, often resulting in evolutionary progress. Now that we've detailed how the memory cloud of a human brain can be breached as a result of glitches in the PDT process, I'd like to focus on the mediums, since these are the folks who see, hear, and talk to dead people.

What seems reasonable (and is also widely reported) is that IDIs are capable of noticing these mediums, and they use these folks to get word back to the Material Realm. After all, every IDI did gestate as part of the Material Realm, and that realm's existence isn't a source of debate among them [as is the existence of the Informational Realm among those future IDIs who still reside in the Material Realm]. As to why such communication might be desirable, one speculation is as good as the next. The important point here is that the means to communicate directly from the Informational Realm to the Material Realm is physically possible; with the process I just described certainly plausible, given what we've established thus far in our examination.

It's pretty apparent that there are practical and reasonably mundane ways for discarnate human beings to communicate with corporeal human beings, even if you have a hard time dealing with the concept of the existence of discarnate human beings; be they communicative or otherwise. I'm going to consider this inter-realm communication issue settled, and invite you, if need be, to do some further research on the subject if you're still stuck over the idea of post-corporeal human existence and its ability to interact with our Material Realm. For now, I need to get back to THE PROCESS and my own process of explaining what it is and how it works.

Defining the Goal

As to how the GS-EC actually produces a single intellectually superior human-like being, and how this satisfies the breeder IDI's gnawing urge to procreate, we're going to need to [yet again] reiterate a few specifics concerning Identity Survival, with a special emphasis on the method of achieving that survival that THE PROCESS pursues. And yes, this is going to get increasingly complicated.

The IDI remains the direct physically surviving holon continuation of the entire Change/Event Trajectory that was (at one time) its own corporeal brain and body while that system was still alive and functional. Yes, the IDI is an Informational being, but as the C/E-Information hybrid that it is, it's got an entire lifetime of survival pursuit that doesn't simply vanish as soon as the brain dies. Remember the Section I analogy about the C# note that the violinist played? Identity-defining internal context doesn't ever simply vanish. This means that the urge to pursue ID Survival remains, as does the capacity to address that urge in new and surprisingly innovative ways.

This ID Survival dilemma might be something that residual Fact Set continuums never encounter, but for the C/E Trajectory, it's old hat. Highly sophisticated Change/Spatial Trajectory matrices have been solving the ID Survival dilemma for a long time through replication and procreation, so it would be *"instinctive"* [not a bad term to use here, actually] for this to be a resolution strategy that a breeder IDI would pursue, once it became aware of its potential. It would immediately view the intentionally-initiated URC-Determined Sub-Environmental Confine as a gestational placenta, and only a gestational placenta, as soon as the net result of such an initiation [the SDI] became apparent. THE PROCESS would immediately become the breeder IDI's primary survival expression, resulting in who knows how many Procreating Entities (PE) responsible for who knows how many Gestational Sub-Environmental Confines (GS-EC) launched from the original Contextual Environment alone.

Building on a Need to Succeed

To recap the situation before proceeding, what each IDI faces [as a hybrid blend of an information continuum and a survival-driven C/E Trajectory] is a complete roadblock to certain ways of pursuing Identity Survival, while still possessing the primordial urge to pursue it in whatever manner it individually chose to pursue it during its 2nd stage of developmental gestation. As an aware and conscious being, this can become absolutely unacceptable; depending, of course, on the particular IDI, its basic character, and the specific manner of ID Survival pursuit it learned to embrace as a GDI.

As we learned in Track#1, the emergence of Dynamic Burst Sets (DBS) and the Dynamic Burst Set Trajectory (DBST) was a C/ET breakthrough survival achievement in its own right [the ultimate dynamic survival expression] due to the fact that every contextually entangled Change/Event Unit's Identity is permanently assured as soon as the apical matrix holon's brain generates its first Burst Set. No plan ever existed for the IDI's own Identity Survival urge fulfillment. It wasn't until its authoring brain advanced in sophistication to the point of generating a permanent self-awareness that the human being and any such thing as a plan for anything whatsoever came into existence. Such a thing as an ID Survival strategy requirement for a dynamic informational being could never have been anticipated. Especially since human Dynamic Intellect was the first [and still, the only] form of physical existence capable of anticipating anything at all.

Then again, there's never been an actual plan for any of this. It's all been driven by the C/E Trajectory's immediate survival requirements as they've emerged along the way. Even humanity's breakthrough Intellect, with its revolutionary realization of self, was no more than a natural progression from the relatively simple development of the capacity to plan; a skill set improvement meant to give the human brain survival system a leg up over competitors that don't have that capacity.

That ability to dynamically abstract the concept of placement within a much larger ongoing Change/Event Trajectory results in a full recognition by the human mind as having a past and a future, even as it addresses the present instant, and this is what drives the GDI to develop an interest in its own Identity development as the future emerges. We've already covered the net impact of that change in the relationship between the brain and the emerging Gestational Intellect mass, and how it causes the corporeal brain to serve as an IDI placenta. The point here is that there never was a plan for any of this natural progressive development process to do or be anything as a result of whatever initiates, responds to, or is, as a result of the raw pursuit of Identity Survival.

That this natural process would eventually be intelligently leveraged as integral to IDI procreation [THE PROCESS] is no different than the fact that electronics engineers leverage the natural chain reaction *flow* of electrical current to make their circuits do what they do. Good engineering always uses the natural process flow to its advantage.

So, as we've also established, once it's been freed from the deceased brain, any mass of dynamic information becomes contextually isolated; basically an event trajectory that physically presents to the rest of the URC-Determined Environmental Confine as an indivisible sub-environment. And that's fine for a DBST in general, since its physical survival is assured, and not at all threatened by developmental stagnation. But the IBST is sophisticated enough to realize the full nature of itself as an existent entity, and fully contemplative in response to the specifics of its nature (with all the pluses and minuses inherent within that

AutoGenesism: A Theory of Everything

capacity). For it, raw survival isn't going to be enough. That intrinsic C/E drive to *"spread itself as far and wide as possible"* — especially for those breeder IDIs — could end up being akin to an itch that can't be reached.

After all, even though it does not result in the same sort of direct Identity Survival pursuit achievement as that of the material brain's Dynamic Burst Set Trajectory [permanent ID Survival for every C/E Trajectory connected to that brain's C/S Trajectory matrix structure], the human PDT is a proactive, purposeful Identity Survival expression effort; the only ID Survival pursuit that originates from within the Informational Realm. The PDT's development of inimitable human identity has been a true Identity Survival pursuit all along, so when the brain dies, this cessation of IBS Trajectory progression can create a palpable angst within the IDI's internal rumination process, since it's still managed by what had been that mind's Personality Development Trajectory. And as I've been emphasizing, this angst [based on the IDI's unique perception] is more excruciating for those IDIs who only ever focused on material Identity Survival [procreation] as they gestated.

> ***Note*** — Before we get into the nuts and bolts of THE PROCESS, I want to, again, make the statement that this entire Track#2 is entirely speculative, and if you wish, you can consider it as just a *"using it in a sentence"* treatment of AutoGenesism concepts and logic structure, and nothing more than that. That said, I do want to point out that the process specifics that I've introduced — those that are still technically intractable for me, and I would imagine everyone else who lives on our planet, [the purposeful initiation of a Change/Event Unit that is out of sync with this Reality confine's URC is probably the most obvious of these process specifics] — could be reasonably presented as proof of the impossibility of THE PROCESS [regardless of how stable the internal logic is] if it were not the case that human flight had been a technically intractable specific, and one that humanity firmly believed to be equally impossible to overcome, until it was overcome by the genius of human intellect. The truth is that no one knows enough about something like Unit Rate of Change [Quantum Rate] to actually be qualified to make any determination concerning the plausibility or even possibility of achieving a one-unit manifestation that could not continue to be in sync with the rest of our own Environment as a whole.
>
> If the alternative URC Change/Event Unit is of a shorter duration, it would exist within the initiator's own URC-Determined Reality confine until the residual Fact Set concerning that one Change/Event Unit's occurrence emerged (as C/E Unit #2) and the entire launched C/E Trajectory (as well as the accompanying Informational Continuum) becomes

273

out of sync with the initiator's own Quantum of Now, and *"vanishes"* forever. But, as we've already learned, all it takes to launch an entire *"universe"* is one Change/Event Unit, so it's not as if that C/E Trajectory actually ceases to exist. It simply launches an Environment of its own. One that is based on that alternative Unit Rate of Change.

That said, there will be profound and permanent implications due to the fact that this new Environment was physically initiated within the confines of a different and incompatible URC-Determined Environmental Confine by an inhabitant of that Environment. Some of those implications [perhaps] having profoundly affected the way that our own human race has defined itself, and Reality as a whole, for thousands of years. And we'll get to all that shortly, I promise.

So, I think I really beat this intro stuff to death here, even though I know that there will be some reiterations and further clarifications to deal with. The main point is that there have always been breeder IDIs with their own unique requirements, and that permanent existence can easily feel as if it *"drags on forever"* if a requirement is intensely perceived while remaining unresolved. The pursuit of Identity Survival persists for the sentient/sapient informational being, and for some of them, that pursuit is solely defined as procreation, and the procreation of their offspring.

The sad truth is that a dynamic informational being can't naturally procreate or replicate, and for some breeder IDIs this can place them in their own version of eternal torment after spending an entire corporeal life span focusing solely on procreation as the definition of ID Survival. What I want to now detail is how THE PROCESS allows these breeder IDIs to have a small slice of heaven along with the rest of us after they've left their bodies, brains, and reproductive organs behind.

Autogenesism: A Theory of Everything

Section IV

THE PROCESS

This part of the premise — THE PROCESS — is brutally complicated in only one sense, and that is in how difficult it is to effectively explain it. It's not complicated in any other sense. In fact, it's completely natural, and requires nothing whatsoever from the author once the process has been initiated. But, correctly detailing how all those natural default responses come together, and making sure that you won't be left scratching your head over how and why what happens, happens when it happens is extremely difficult.

I'll sketch out how THE PROCESS works, but the truth is that it takes this entire book to fully explain why this unique process works as it does, and I'm going to suggest that you approach this Track#2 segment in that manner. What I also want to suggest is that my earlier notion concerning how this process was initially discovered to actually be gestational, [the specifics revealed by the first-ever SDI that inevitably emerged from the first-ever intentionally initiated URC-Determined Environmental Confine] while impossible to verify, will be the explanation I'll always feel to be most plausible. Not that THE PROCESS itself is all that impossible to understand in hindsight, but that it seems most plausible that such a revolutionary notion is the kind that would've been initially realized in hindsight, with the process specifics revealed by the SDI itself.

Yes, I figured it out, but as far as I'm concerned, that's strong evidence that our own universe is such a gestational placenta, and that the details already exist as residual Fact Sets that are freely accessible to any one of us. Of course, that first-ever SDI would have also had free access to those residual Fact Sets as they pertained to that first-ever GS-EC's role as its own placenta. After all, (as you'll learn) that entire GS-EC's original Residual IC would then serve as that SDI's own memory cloud. Yes, there's a lot to explain here, and we're getting to it in the best and most accessible way I can come up with.

All that said, I'm going to describe THE PROCESS in its role as a deliberate procreative process that's been initiated by an IDI who is driven by the same existential imperative that drives all dynamic activity, since ultimately that's

275

what it's become. Each topic we've covered so far is integral to the stuff that affects the utility of this process, and while I won't litter this relatively concise overview with reiterations concerning everything that contributes to its success, I will require you to keep in mind all of what we've covered to this point. I can assure you that as the whole of this premise gels together in the end, you'll definitely feel it was worth the effort.

The Sub-Environment as a Placenta

Since any procreation process inherently expresses the being that initiates it, the first thing to note here is the issue of scale. In Mary Shelley's horror classic Frankenstein, Victor Frankenstein realizes that increasing the size of the parts would make his own job of fitting the parts together that much easier. Well, there wasn't any impetus for the massive increase in the scale of this gestational process [not that there is any actual means of affecting scale] but I would imagine that an IDI's reason for wholeheartedly embracing such scale increase isn't that much different than another of Frankenstein's reasons for going big (so to speak). Victor envisioned a super-man emerging from his own bizarre procreation process, and why not? If such a thing could be accomplished, then why not go for the most powerful and magnificent result?

As we know, in Victor Frankenstein's case, the whole thing went horribly wrong, but not so for our procreating IDI (we'll start using the term Procreating Entity, or PE here). In fact, it's hard to imagine a more astounding result. And yet, when you examine the direct alignment of each principal process aspect between the GDI and the SDI's gestation process, it is clear and obvious that this offspring is an easily recognizable member of our extended human family. As we progress, I will make a concerted effort to emphasize this alignment as each process aspect becomes the focus of this examination. For now, I will post a quick chart to make sure this part of the process is fully introduced, with an eye on preventing those who skim from missing anything really important.

The PE's reproductive process definitely increases the scale of the component parts. The following is a list of direct linkages between the components of a gestating IDI and the components of the SDI's gestational process. On the left is the GDI. On the right is the SDI's gestation process.

AutoGenesism: A Theory of Everything

The IDI's Gestation Process	The SDI's Gestation Process
Each Dynamic Unit = One IBS	Each Dynamic Unit = One IDI
One Brain's PFS Memory Cloud	One GS-EC's original Residual IC
Result of One Brain	Result of One GS-EC

As you know, the IDI is the term I'm using for the Intellect Burst Set Trajectory (IBST) that persists after the generating brain has died. The IDI is a dynamic entity in its own right; an informational holon with a sense of self. That said, it's also a physical, structural composite of every Intellect Burst Set that its authoring brain ever configured and *launched* to actively address a survival requirement. This means that each IBS ends up being akin to a dynamic *cell* in the *body* of the IDI when all is said and done.

Now, the IDI's composite nature doesn't mean that there's no central focus of intent or response; every IBS for itself, or anything like that. The mind's PDT managed the definition and development of this composite whole, and with that task successfully completed, this relentless and deeply experienced aspect of the human mind pivots to keep all those *cells* working as a cohesive team. In fact, the IDI's experience of conscious awareness is pretty recognizable when it is compared to that of its PDT-managed corporeal perspective; taking all factors into consideration, of course.

The SDI is definitely different than the IDI, but it's recognizable in most aspects. Its own version of the IDI's IBS *cells* are uniquely gestated IDIs that are fully viable and fully conscious, and who each possess a full sense of personal history and inimitable self. In the same way that the Intellect Burst Set collective provides the *dynamic* in Isolated Dynamic Intellect, the SDI's IDI community provides its active/proactive physical nature. Of course, being a true dynamic intellectually conscious holon in its own right, and not merely a gathering of independent constituent items, the SDI possesses its own collective sense of self and Identity. While it may seem odd to the average human mind that the SDI's constituent IDIs can be brought into functional agreement to the degree that it [the SDI] can actually possess a true sense of self, it will become obvious, as we move deeper into this description of THE PROCESS, that the average human mind is not appropriate for inclusion within the community of IDIs that comprise an SDI. And, we'll get to that soon.

Also, remember the way that the human brain uses its memory cloud to create the IDI's emerging IBST component structure, as that structure, in turn, proactively refines the effective utility of that memory cloud, with all of it occurring as the brain simply does what it does to ensure its own material survival? Well, the Gestational Sub-Environmental Confine (GS-EC) sort of works with its residual Informational Continuum in a somewhat similar manner. It relies upon the Residual IC's default capacity to establish an accurate success/failure precedent structure to ensure that its universal *"do this again"* ID Survival default effectively promotes successful progressive development, as that progressive development process [which ultimately produces the SDI's dynamic component structure; the constituent IDI community] — in turn — further refines the uniqueness and complexity of that Residual IC one C/E Unit at a time, with all of it occurring as the principal way that the GS-EC ensures its own Identity Survival.

The point here is that the gestation processes for both are strikingly similar, even if the scale and detailed specifics are necessarily unique to each process. In fact, the only really significant difference between the two is that the SDI gets to keep its memory cloud — the GS-EC's entire Residual IC — after the SDI has completed its gestation.

And finally, it should be clear by now that, in the same way that each material brain can only produce one IDI, each GS-EC can only produce one SDI. As to what happens to the entire GS-EC once the SDI has emerged from THE PROCESS, we'll get to that as well. Just be assured that none of this will violate any of what we've already established as the bedrock of progressive development, and that nothing will drop out of a closet onto the table [not even in the form of yet another example of physical emergence] to allow this entire miracle of simple default ramification to bring what is an amazing version of humanity into full physical existence.

As to why THE PROCESS features such a massive scaling increase, the easiest way to explain it is to refer back to that brief analogy in Section I featuring you, your company coworker, and that lunch lady that you teamed up with while on vacation in Germany. In that analogy, all three of you, as you labored within the physical and occupational confines of your company, were relatively dissimilar (and therefore not contextually entangled) due to your jobs. Kind of like how it is for dynamic information holons (IDIs, for instance) that share the same URC-Determined Environmental Confine, and their inability to mass together or physically contribute to the emergence of a new dynamic informational holon (like an offspring IDI).

AutoGenesism: A Theory of Everything

So, back to that Section I analogy. You'll recall that once you all found each other within the foreign confines of a Hamburg bar, the fact that you each work at the same company created an immediate *environmentally-induced contextual entanglement* that was immediately palpable. In fact, the company that imposed a contextual isolation upon each of you (relative to each other) as a result of your specific jobs, now imposed a contextual entanglement upon each of you (relative to each other) as a default ramification of those same jobs and the fact of your having encountered one another outside of the company's environmental confines within an environmental confine that is equally foreign to each of you.

I'm going to refer to this common and reliable contextual default as an **Environmentally-Imposed Contextual Entanglement**, and abbreviate it with **E-ICE**, since that's a lot of typing that I'd rather spare myself if I can. What I want you to note is that it took a complete and shared change in environment to grant you, your coworker, and the lunch lady the capacity to become contextually entangled in that manner. Relative context works this way at all levels of physical reality. For the prospects of any version of contextual entanglement between dynamic informational holons (the IDI, for instance), the URC-DEC of shared origin is kind of like the company workplace was for you folks in that analogy, only there are no vacations for an IDI; no escaping the physical confines of a *mature and isolated* URC-DEC. That said, for an IDI to be able to extend its Identity by way of contextual entanglement with another IDI of any sort whatsoever, that necessary change in prospects would seem to require that a similar shared change in Environment be featured at some point along the process. For the breeder IDI, this would be the technical dilemma it faces.

Note — In Section III's digression, *"Entanglement: The Laws and Dynamics of Contextual Association"*, I detail a Reality default that I call **The Hierarchy of Kind**. It is the priority structure that kicks in when information masses that have a contextual connection at some level or other [a potential for some sort of in-kind association] affect one another within the same Environment.

You might imagine that fully conscious and dynamic IDIs [human beings] that are engaged in these relationship dynamics could somehow transcend the confines of this rigid structure (as can be the case with C/E holons as they navigate their freewheeling battlefield of competitive survival) but information masses are not like C/E holons [C/E Trajectories and C/ET matrices]. Once brought into existence, information masses are physically permanent, and the evolving relationships between residual Fact Set continuums [for instance] establish contextual precedents [and many system preferences] which directly affect progressive development at all levels of evolving Reality.

The bottom line is that the relationships that exists between information masses ultimately define and protect the Identity of the entire URC-Determined Environmental Confine. So, yeah, the way that Information masses affect one another is definitely important enough to require a rigid logic structure governing contextual entanglements.

As you'd expect, it doesn't take long for an IDI to get a feel for the Hierarchy of Kind. After all, it's pretty simple and it's not as if this yes/no logical structure can be ignored or overcome. It's the law of the land; a default environmental response that is absolutely predictable, relentlessly dependable, and that's imposed immediately as a direct result of any change in relative context between information and everything else that it shares physical Reality with. And while it is restrictive, the Hierarchy of Kind (just like any rule or regulation) can be put to good use if properly leveraged.

> ***Note*** — Again, keep in mind that what replication/procreation does is extend the replicating/procreating holon's Identity presence beyond the physical confines of that holon's physical presence; ensuring a degree of extended Identity survival as a result. This is the achievement being pursued in this case. Also, remember that an information set permanently *"belongs"* to its authoring source, as does whatever that information set becomes profoundly and permanently entangled with if that entanglement results in a newly emergent information set due to the nature of that entanglement.

Yes, this is going to get increasingly complicated from here on, but for now, let's get back to how the breeder IDI leverages The Hierarchy of Kind in its pursuit of the only form of procreation available to it.

When the IDI realizes that . . .

- each *mature* Environment is physically isolated by a rigidly quantized Unit Rate of Change, and that
- if that URC environmental isolation can be overcome, that an E-ICE between information wholes that are otherwise contextually prohibited from permanent entanglement with one another can be achieved,

. . . the requirement of creating a URC-Determined Sub-Environment that can be leveraged to create an E-ICE response of some sort between dynamic information holons (like IDIs) becomes pretty obvious. And basically, this is

AutoGenesism: A Theory of Everything

what THE PROCESS is all about; a *breeder* IDI initiating a URC-Determined Sub-Environmental Confine that will host the progressive development of a very specific collective of sentient/sapient dynamic information components [IDIs] that will, at some point, emerge from that sub-environment, fully coalesce as one viable sentient/sapient being [due to the very specific nature of the default E-ICE response that will trigger when it does emerge], and ultimately join that *breeder* IDI within its own URC-Determined Environmental Confine as that IDI's offspring. And yes, I know exactly how crazy this is starting to sound.

Now, I've got a number of rough diagrams coming up that I hope will help you conceptualize the Gestational Sub-Environmental Confine (GS-EC) and how it physically relates to its *parent* Environment. I'm going to assume that you know that these abstractions are not meant to be viewed as accurate depictions, or even artist renditions of the actual physical nature of these incompatible Environments. As I've noted, concerning the nature of Environments, the separation between any two such confines is their respective Unit Rates of Change. Again, the whole gist of THE PROCESS is that this difference in URC is leveraged.

Now, like you, I'm a human being that is still undergoing gestational development. I haven't the capacity to physically initiate such an Environment, nor have I the technical knowledge of how such a thing is done, but it seems obvious that it should involve the production of a Change/Event Unit that features a URC that is of a lesser duration than the URC of the Environment that this C/EU has occurred within. That one Change/Event Unit's resulting trajectory would become contextually isolated from the authoring Environment as soon as the follow-on C/EU [the default physical emergence of the residual Fact Set, C/E#2] occurs. And from this one instant a GS-EC would then progressively develop in the same manner as the very first URC-Determined Environmental Confine developed [detailed in Track#1 of this Section II].

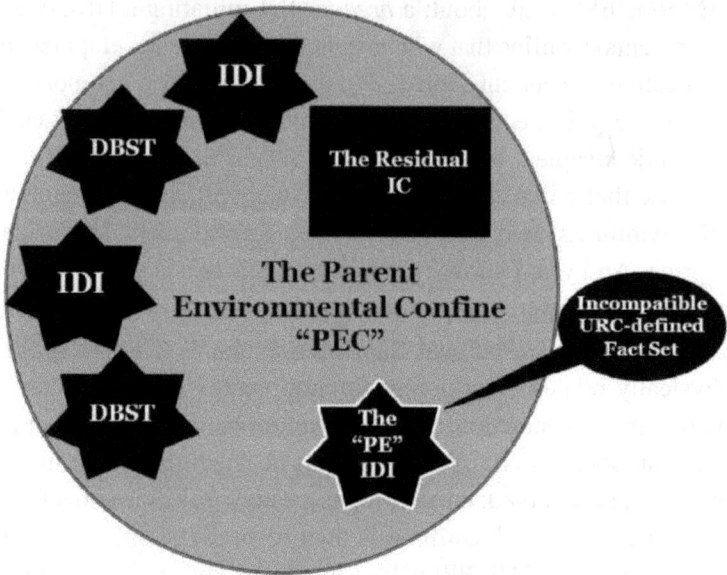

Figure 2:2-A.
The Procreating Entity launches the GS-EC
with a Change/Event Unit featuring an incompatible URC

Now, it's important to keep in mind that all further GS-EC progressive development would be affected by the specific intent that existed within the mind of the Procreating Entity as it produced this out-of-sync Change/Event Unit, since that GS-EC initiating C/EU would be an uninterrupted continuation of an already established C/E Trajectory that includes that PE's intent as historical precedent. As a result of this historical precedent, an intentionally initiated URC-Determined Environmental Confine isn't quite the same as that one and only original URC-Determined Environment that launched as a default ramification of that first-ever C/E Unit [the default emergence of the Relative Being State].

This means that the Procreating Entity's intent — since it is central to that GS-EC initiating C/E Unit's Identity-defining historical context — sets a foundational precedent within that GS-EC's otherwise contextually-pristine residual Informational Continuum, and since the Residual IC manages all activity via contextual precedent [in general], this intent will broadly inform the GS-EC's progressive development structure as a primordial influence going forward. Of course, naturally emergent mitigating factors and evolving system preferences will always ensure that each GS-EC develops in its own inimitable manner.

AutoGenesism: A Theory of Everything

Digression Alert — I'm going to digress my reiteration of this explanation concerning the PE's residual influence within the developing GS-EC, since I need to make sure that you see it as significant. It's not a true digression, but if you skim over this, you'll have some serious challenges with why the intentionally-initiated GS-EC naturally serves as a gestational *placenta* for the Procreating Entity's *offspring*, and does so as a natural response default.

Before the PE initiates the GS-EC with a C/E Unit that features an out-of-sync URC, the PE's intent and preparations occur. Like it goes with any activity trajectory, the residual Fact Sets representing that intent and those preparatory events immediately gather as a branch of the Informational Continuum within the PE's own Environment [the Parent Environmental Confine - PEC].

Once that GS-EC initiating C/E Unit occurs, its default residual Fact Set also emerges [that RFS emergence is a follow-on Change/Event Unit within that C/E Trajectory] and its URC [in quantized lock-step with the out-of-sync URC of the Change/Event Unit that it emerged to factually represent] makes it, and every follow-on C/E Unit within that ongoing C/E Trajectory, immediately out of sync with the PEC's URC. That, of course, causes these gathering residual Fact Sets to form the first ever Residual IC to feature this new Unit Rate of Change — which will ultimately become the new GS-EC's own Reality-defining Residual IC. After all, the very first URC-Determined Environmental Confine's Residual IC was *born* as a result of its own initial Fact Set having emerged to factually represent the first-ever Change/Event Unit featuring its own unique URC.

But in the case of an intentionally initiated URC-DEC, the environmental isolation imposed by the new URC cannot overcome the historical context of that initiating C/E Unit. Nor does it eliminate the PEC's permanent default contextual entanglement with the residual Fact Set that represents that initiating C/EU [as well as all subsequent RFS continuums that will emerge to represent every resulting C/E Trajectory that occurs within the GS-EC going forward].

When comparing the Identity impact of *URC* versus *author*, the more primordial Identity qualifier is *author* [source of origin], and common author will require that a URC-incompatible, yet historically unbreakable, Residual IC branch always *belong* to the Parent Environmental Confine [acknowledging the GS-EC initiating C/E Unit's occurrence as being planned and its execution imminent]. And this contextual entanglement will persist even when that new Residual IC continues to literally define the GS-EC as a URC-Determined Environmental Confine in its own right. In fact, the emerging GS-EC's Residual IC is — and can only ever be — just one more branch of the Parent Environmental Confine's Residual IC, even though it physically bridges two separate and incompatible URC-Determined Reality confines. If it seems that this situation creates a logical dilemma, it does, but only concerning the issue of Environmental Identity. And only if the GS-EC ever *sees* Identity Survival as an issue.

It's important to note that this environmental Identity linkage issue is what makes an intentionally initiated URC-DEC serve as a gestational *placenta*. Also, this unique logical schism can be leveraged [with a carefully embedded suite of intents during the initiating event] to craft the nature of the offspring that emerges from this gestation process. It's all pretty ingenious, and we'll get into that aspect of this shortly.

Here is a quick diagram showing the inter-Environmental Identity linkage that's caused by the author's intentional initiation of the GS-EC.

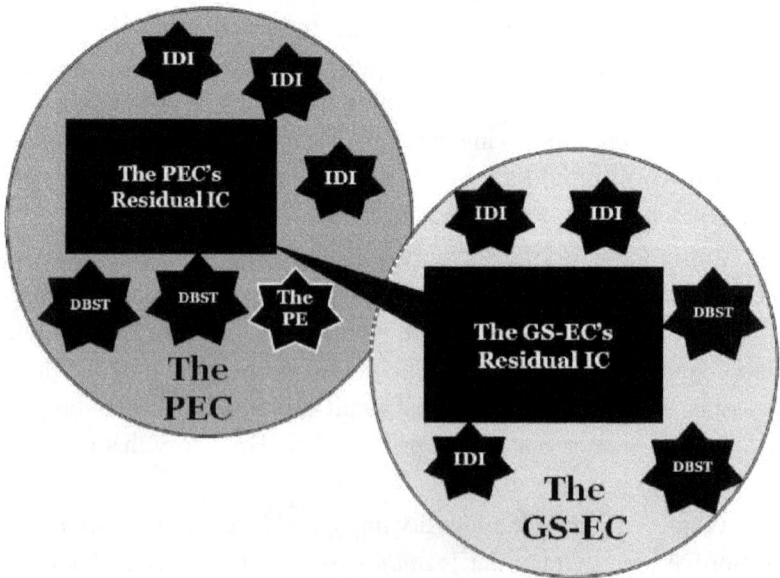

Figure 2:2-B.
The Relationship between the PEC and the GS-EC
[note the IC linkage and the *"porous"* border between the two]

AutoGenesism: A Theory of Everything

For as long as this original Residual IC continues to grow within that sub-Environment and continues to define it, the GS-EC will continue to be the *"child"* of the PE's home Environment (the PEC). At some point, however, that GS-EC will be driven to shed that contextual linkage so it can establish its own full and inimitable Identity and become a *mature* Environment. And that's something that I want you to keep in mind as we go forward.

Now, I will need to digress yet again, so that I can explain why the GS-EC itself will eventually need to become a *mature* URC-Determined Environmental Confine, and go through what it takes to become such an Environment. The reason is pretty complicated, but in short, it has to do with relative gender.

Yeah, gender.

Well, it also involves the pursuit of Identity Survival (like everything else that happens) but the specifics, they have to do with gender. Believe me, this is much harder to explain than it is to learn.

Sheep to the Right — Goats to the Left

Note — Before you go any further, I'll need you to turn back to this track's sub-section *"Labels and Quick References"* and read the descriptions of my usage of the terms *Masculine* and *Feminine* and how they will relate in this examination; specifically concerning the issue of Identity Survival expressions. As usual, I'll be applying these two terms in a very strict manner, and I don't want you wandering off once we get into the meat of what's coming up.

Once you've finished this quick overview, you should be fully aware that our use of the term **Masculine** refers to those ID Survival pursuit expressions that involve the resistance of Identity diffusion, the competition for advantage, the struggle for Identity dominance, and the aggressive advancement of *kind*. You'll also know that we'll be using the term *Feminine* to refer to those Identity Survival pursuit expressions that feature receptive expansion of kind, Identity development through physical association [entanglement], advancement through mutual advantage, and general symbiosis. Your quick glance should have also introduced the fact that relative gender serves as an existential qualifier, and how relative gender [percentage of Masculine versus Feminine] expression affects how permanent holons [information masses and environments] respond to one another.

Now, to see what these two gender-specific ID Survival expressions have to do with THE PROCESS, let's examine the gender expression [shorthand for *gender-specific Identity Survival pursuit expression*] of a typical URC-Define Contextual Environment, but let's do so at two distinct stages of its overall development.

It's critical to understand that what defines an Environment is what exists as permanent within that Environment. As human minds that are being created by material brains, we consider our corporeal bodies and this Material Realm to be the only real and physically tangible stuff that exists within our slice of Reality, but in truth, the entire Material Realm only exists at the Unit Rate of Change before ceasing to exist altogether. Of course, this quantum unit of *Now* is replaced by the next *Now* within the ongoing trajectory it exists within, but since every C/E Trajectory is ultimately doomed (even if its contextual Identity does survive within the internal historical context of the next larger C/E Trajectory holon) the Environment itself isn't defined by what's happening. It's defined by what has already happened. As we've already established, Reality is the relationship matrix that exists between every residual Fact Set continuum and Dynamic Burst Set Trajectory that shares a common URC.

So, what does this mean relative to the gender expression of an entire URC-Determined Reality Confine? It means that such an Environment's gender balance equals whatever the total gender balance (of all informational masses gathered together) is. Fairly straightforward actually. For a younger URC-DEC that hasn't yet become host to brain-generated DBS Trajectories, this gender expression ends up being pretty easy to determine, since the only information that exists within its confines is its Residual IC.

Regardless of the circumstances, any Residual IC is inherently passive [Feminine] in gender expression. Information is eternal and since the Residual IC consists of only residual Fact Sets, it has no ID Survival pursuit expression whatsoever. In fact, the entire Residual IC is completely open and available since its only attribute that is potentially isolative is URC, which it shares with everything else that exists within the entire Environment. Its contribution to the Environment's pursuit of ID Survival is its collective depth and complexity, and its passive establishment of a success/failure precedent. When determining gender expression, the Residual IC is as relatively *Feminine* as an expression gets.

So, it seems obvious that the entire Environment can only ever possess a Feminine survival expression until the emergence of DBST and IBST information wholes [of course, these show up much further along the progressive

Autogenesism: A Theory of Everything

development chain within an Environment] begins to directly challenge that Feminine gender balance with contextually massive primarily Masculine information set collectives. Of course, the reason why these dynamic Information masses are primarily Masculine is due to the fact that each is a hybrid Change/Event-information trajectory that is launched by an entire hyper-masculine C/E matrix trajectory that's in a literal battle for moment-to-moment survival. Yep, it doesn't get much more Masculine than that.

The DBST (and especially the IBST) can be amazingly dense, since internal contextual Identity is informational and a Burst Set is all about dense layers of internal contextual Identity. Even with the Residual IC's constantly emerging Fact Sets gathering in countless continuum branches and limbs, it will eventually come to pass that the sheer informational *weight* of the increasingly complex and sophisticated brain-generated Burst Set Trajectories [becoming denser and denser as a result of that progressing contextual sophistication] will overwhelm the Residual IC's much larger number of much simpler data sets. And when it does, the Environment's gender expression — as determined by the total gender balance of the information relationship matrix that defines it — will finally tilt Masculine.

When that happens, the newly-Masculine GS-EC will immediately respond with a standard ID Survival expression response to competing Environmental wholes; it will Isolate against all such directly competing wholes. To this point in its development, the GS-EC has been Feminine in its pursuit of Identity Survival, allowing the Residual IC to contribute (by default) to that survival with increasing complexity, density and diversity. Yes, the Environment imposes its *"do this again"* success/failure precedence, but it does so within the confines of what it is; a URC-Determined contextual relationship matrix. All that it has directed to this point is what is integral to itself. This sudden Isolation response is its first-ever direct reaction to that which may exist as a potential threat or competitor.

Note — While Isolation is the default ID Survival expression response of anything that is capable of evolving in a dynamic manner, in this dichotomy — where the GS-EC's own ID-defining Residual IC is historically [and therefore permanently] identified as just another branch of the PEC's Residual IC — the impact of what the *breeder* IDI has initiated [an inevitable Identity definitional schism] is extremely important to fully understand and appreciate. As long the GS-EC's gender was defined by its Feminine Residual IC, the incompatible URCs that separated these two environments [even as their shared Residual IC permanently defined them as contextually inseparable] hadn't really presented itself as a survival issue for either environment. After all, a Feminine gender expression does not establish and defend against potential threats to inimitable Identity. This being the case, until the GS-EC's Masculine shift in relative gender, it hadn't possessed any Identity Survival response at all in connection with its role as the PEC's sub-Environment.

What occurs, as soon as the GS-EC's relative gender expression tips past the 50/50 relative Feminine-Masculine gender balance, is what I've termed the *Move-to-Isolate Event*. And this is what the physical initiation of the GS-EC has been all about since that first out-of-sync URC C/E Unit occurred. This is what the authoring Procreating Entity had in mind all along.

When the Move-to-Isolate Event occurs, it immediately becomes obvious that something must be done about the GS-EC's Residual IC and its permanent historical linkage with the PEC's own Residual IC. The newly Masculine gender expression of the GS-EC requires that the Identity threat of this linkage be immediately eliminated. Yes, its entire Residual IC initiated as the direct result of a C/E Trajectory that started within the PEC, even if the incompatible URC of that one Change/Event Unit caused the resulting residual Fact Set to initiate a completely incompatible environment with that same URC. The historical context can't be overcome since all residual information establishes and defines Reality through historical context. It's intrinsic to what residual information is and what it does.

When this Move-to-Isolate Event occurs, a couple very significant simultaneous changes occur as an immediate result. To make this easier to digest, I'm going to detail them both separately. In truth, however, these two responses occur simultaneously. What is also important to note is that one change occurs within the now-isolating, newly-Masculine GS-EC as the other change is occurring within the PEC. First, let's look at what happens within the now-isolating, newly-Masculine GS-EC.

AutoGenesism: A Theory of Everything

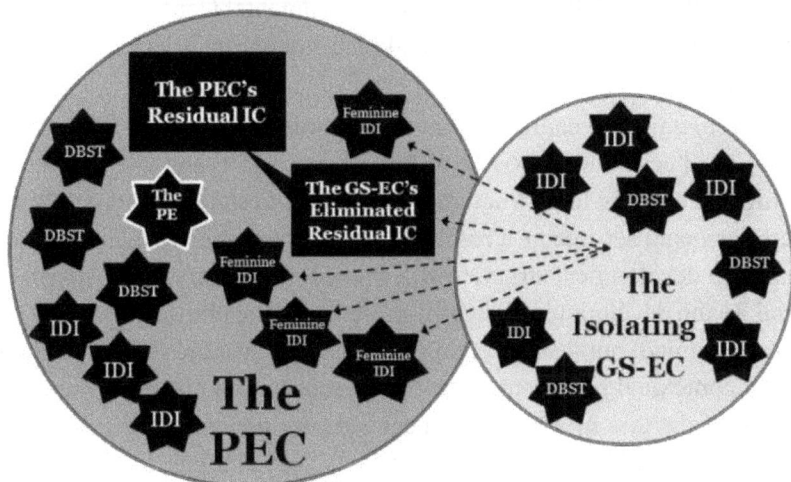

Figure 2:2-C
The Move-To-Isolate Event
sweeps away all IC linkage between itself and the PEC
with a blunt gender-based 50/50 accept-reject protocol
that effectively clears away all relatively *Feminine* holons
[note the now-solidified border between the two]

In order for the GS-EC to ever achieve full maturity [become a completely isolated Environment], that entire linking Residual IC mass has to be eliminated from the GS-EC. When this elimination [the Move-to-Isolate Event] happens, it is a Change/Event. And since it is a Change/Event, it results in the emergence [within the now-isolated, newly Masculine GS-EC itself] of a residual Fact Set representing the factual nature of that elimination Change/Event. At this instant of complete isolation, the GS-EC's Identity is defined only by the relationship between DBST and IBST informational masses, with this residual Fact Set the only residual information set that exists within it. This emergence of this lone residual Fact Set (having emerged to factually represent the occurrence of the Move-to-Isolate Event) changes the overall nature of the GS-EC with its presence, and is therefore a Change/Event in its own right. This follow-on C/E Unit, just like the first-ever residual Fact Set did within the very first URC-DEC, starts the ball rolling again, launching a brand new Residual IC within this newly-isolated [newly *mature*] URC-DEC.

From there, this Residual IC will grow in direct response to all activity within the Environment just like the former Residual IC did. With its Residual

289

IC launched, the new URC-Determined Environmental Confine is forever independent and isolated, and the gestational placenta phase of its eternal existence is completed.

The remaining dynamic information wholes — both DBST and IBST masses — will continue to exist. Not so with every C/E and C/S Trajectory, as each will immediately lose structure, with all still-gestating Dynamic Burst Set Trajectories being set free as a result. What had been the GS-EC's progressive C/E and C/S development structure will immediately lose its cohesion, with all Material Realm development instantly obliterated. The phrase *"The end of time"* does come to mind, but this isn't really the case. It's just the result of a complete loss of all contextual precedent, system preferences, and historical ramification, as a result of the loss of all residual Fact Set continuums and the relationships that established these environmental constants. The elimination of the Residual IC basically resets the entire progressive development chain back to zero to start over.

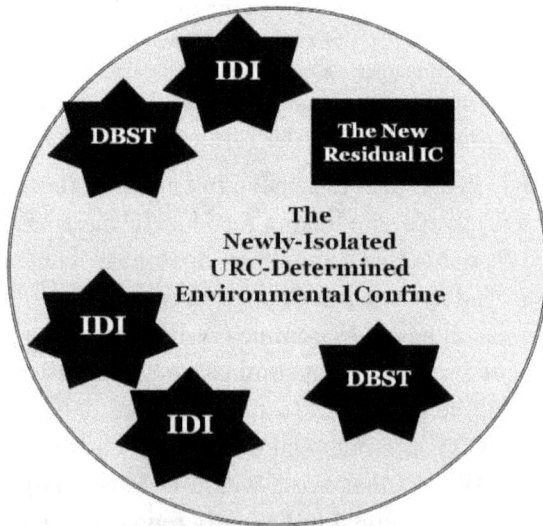

Figure 2:2-D.
The Former GS-EC is initially defined by its remaining DBSTs
as the Move-To-Isolate event launches a new Residual IC
as well as a new C/E progressive development process

The fact that each remaining DBST and IBST were created by C/E and C/S Trajectories [material brains] as material survival responses contextually isolated them from any fundamental Identity relationship with the GS-EC's original Residual IC and its own relationship with the PEC. Once that Residual IC has been eliminated from their own relationship matrix, any tangential link that the former GS-EC's now-defining DBST/IBST relationship matrix might have ever had with the PEC [through that branch of its own Residual IC] is no match for the now-Masculine GS-EC's Identity Survival expression requiring a complete and permanent Isolation response. Basically, The Hierarchy of Kind establishes this as a default ramification.

The new Residual IC will evolve and grow with the ongoing activity within the Environment. In essence, nothing will change for the bulk of what's permanent within this newly isolated, mature Environment. In fact, the loss of the original IC won't be *remembered* by the new Residual IC. The newly isolated URC-Determined Environment will simply have the acknowledgement of its having become a mature Environment, since that Change/Event triggered the launch of its new and isolated Residual IC. Only within the isolated confines of some of the IDIs that remain will there be any reference to what this newly mature Environment had been at one time. And only within those few who ever actually knew what this process was all about to begin with.

Now, let's look at the other immediate result of the Move-to-Isolate Event.

So, what happened to the original Residual IC that was eliminated? Well, since a Residual IC is information, it can't be destroyed or cease to exist. But, since it represents activity that happened at a Unit Rate of Change that is only compatible with the Environment that it was just swept from, it might seem as if there's no real place for it to go. But then, how is that possible? The logical structure of physical Reality could allow it to simply exist as an Environment unto itself if it had no contextual conflicts preventing it, but, as we've already established, it is still contextually linked to the PEC's Residual IC. But that environment's URC is not compatible. How is this dilemma rectified? By default, of course. The same way that all existential dilemmas are rectified.

Where to Go? The Hierarchy of Kind in Action

Yes, you must keep in mind that this rejected Residual IC is forever historically connected to the PEC's Residual IC, even if its URC is incompatible with the whole of that environment. A permanent historical connection will allow any information holon [under a very specific set of Association protocols] to exist within the confines of the Environment that hosted its initiation Change/Event.

The truth is that indivisible DBST and IDIs exist within their home Environments while inside their component Burst Sets are completely isolated from that Environment. It's fairly common. In the case of this mass of residual Fact Set continuums [with its incompatible URC] what would immediately occur is that the entire mass, of what had been freely accessible RFS continuums relative to the entire GS-EC, will become a similarly indivisible, impenetrable unit whole, relative to the rest of its new environmental home with the PEC.

A massing event of this kind will occur at the PEC's Unit Rate of Change, transforming the entire out-of-sync Residual IC into a single, physically impenetrable holon that is now fully contextually compatible with the rest of the PEC and its URC-Determined contents. Very much like a DBST/IDI with its isolated internal component Burst Sets, presenting as compatible to the rest of the environment. Of course, when the Move-to-Isolate Event sweeps through a Gestational Sub-Environmental Confine, its Residual IC isn't the only tenant to become homeless. Let's see if I can explain why, without getting lost in extensive digression.

> ***Note*** — What is really important to keep in mind is that the gender expression trigger that causes the GS-EC to Move-to-Isolate, is [as previously noted] based on a 50/50 Masculine-Feminine accept/reject, environment-wide, default ID Survival response. It's not selective in any other manner whatsoever, so the net implications can be enormous.

Yes, the Move-to-Isolate Event resolves nicely for the GS-EC, and even results in a pretty neat solution for its now-homeless Residual IC. But when you realize that by the time this event occurs, that the development of DBSTs within the GS-EC has very likely progressed in survival sophistication to the stage where human mind/brain survival systems and resulting Intellect Burst Set Trajectories have emerged, then this gender ID Survival Move-to-Isolate Event resolution can affect more than just the Identity threatening Residual IC. It can also result in the permanent displacement of IDIs, as well as those GDIs whose gestation processes have just been *completed* as a result of the sudden structural dissolution of their corporeal brains. Let me explain.

As already stated, the protocol that triggers the Move-to-Isolate Event is very blunt, very broad, and solely based on relative gender expression. It's not intelligent or discriminating in any sense whatsoever. It gets rid of the Identity Survival threat that the original Residual IC's permanent information sets [with

AutoGenesism: A Theory of Everything

their permanent contextual linkage to the PEC's Residual IC] present, and that's what it does. All other ramifications are not even secondary in importance. Since the DBST is relatively Masculine (hell, it's the presence of the DBST that tips the Environment's gender expression to Masculine) it stays put, preserving the GS-EC as a true Environment. However, the emergence of the IBST (the human IDI) adds a fascinating complexity concerning the net ramification of the GS-EC's successful isolation event.

> ***Note*** — It's important to note that the emergence of Intellect brought with it the emergence of relatively Feminine Dynamic Burst Sets. Remember in Track#1, when we took a look at the difference between the human and non-human brain's survival process and examined that PDT Identity crafting process that the GDI uses to develop itself as the brain continues generating new Burst Sets of Intellect? Well, that self-awareness, and high level of sophistication allows for the possibility of Intellect Burst Sets that are surprisingly Feminine in gender expression. Not passive, but very Feminine nonetheless.
>
> Keep in mind that the ID Survival imperative also features Feminine expressions, and there are those brain/mind survival processes that are definitely Feminine in gender expression. Behavior that includes compassion, selflessness, nurturing, symbiosis, inclusion, and the many ways that one can take what is presented within the course of a corporeal life and resist the natural urge to view it as competition. If, over the entire gestation, the GDI maintains this way of dealing with corporeal life, its Primary Expression will remain relatively Feminine.
>
> When one of these human beings is fully gestated, they will present as having a gender expression that is relatively Feminine when compared to the 50/50 Masculine-Feminine gender balance accept-reject trigger that initiates the Move-to-Isolate Event. This being the case, these IDIs [yes, these are human beings] will be seen by this blunt, environment-wide, gender-triggered protocol (based on the gender of their Primary Expression alone) as no different, and therefore no less of an immediate ID Survival threat, than the Residual IC mass.

With the accept/reject protocol as bluntly administered as it is [environment-wide], and as simply as it is [a 50/50 Masculine-Feminine gender expression qualifier] it is impossible to prevent the elimination of all relatively Feminine IDIs when the Residual IC is eliminated. And while this may sound a bit harsh at first glance, in truth, this inevitable ramification is exactly what the GS-EC's authoring PE anticipates. In fact, this is the whole idea behind initiating the GS-EC.

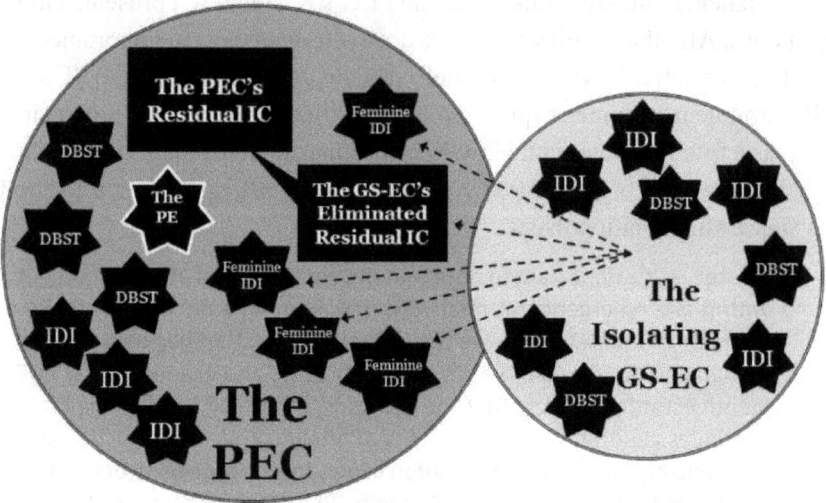

Figure 2:2-C.
Another look at that Move-to-Isolate event
[note the Feminine IDIs that have also been swept from
the GS-EC]

Again, what the Procreating Entity tries to accomplish when it initiates the GS-EC is an enormous scale replication of its own gestational development process. If you look again at the table I put up earlier, the direct alignment is pretty obvious.

The Human Brain Generation	The GS-EC Discharge
Each Dynamic Unit = IBS	Each Dynamic Unit = One IDI
Learns through its PFS Memory Cloud	*Contributes* its full RFS Info mass
Capable of *generating* only one GDI	Capable of *isolating* only once

I've changed the headings to represent the human brain generation as compared to the GS-EC's discharge as it moves to contextually isolate itself, and kicks out both the Residual IC and each IDI with a Primary Expression that is determined to be relatively Feminine. As you can see, what emerges from the Move-to-Isolate Event looks like an enormously scaled IDI.

AutoGenesism: A Theory of Everything

Well, the SDI is not just an enormously scaled IDI. It's also much better equipped for eternal self-aware existence, since it retains a permanently entangled memory cloud — unlike the IDI. And the SDI's memory cloud is the entire GS-EC's Residual IC mass, and not just Perception Fact Sets (as is the case with the human brain's own memory cloud). Okay, this will take a little explanation as well.

When the Move-to-Isolate Event occurs, and the Residual IC and the relatively Feminine IDIs [these are nice folks who aren't competitive or self-focused; actually to an usual degree, making them relatively unique] are physically swept from the GS-EC, the shared authoring Environment and common URC that exists between these IDIs and the eliminated Residual IC is obvious, making the massing of the Residual IC and these IDIs logically and contextually required. We referred to this massing as an **Environmentally-Imposed Contextual Entanglement (E-ICE)** due to the profound and permanent level of contextual entanglement that's imposed as a result of a shared degree of *foreignness* relative to the environment that the constituents have suddenly found themselves within. This brings the Residual IC and this community of Feminine IDIs together as one indivisible holon relative to the rest of the PEC, even as all of these IDIs maintain their relative Identities within the confines of this otherwise massed unity that they've achieved. Again, this is what The Hierarchy of Kind allows.

What's also important to note is that this E-ICE massing is a Change/Event that happens at the PEC's Unit Rate of Change [it occurs within the PEC]. This causes this permanent entanglement of residual and dynamic information to exist within the PEC as just another physical solid that shares a common URC with the rest of the PEC's relationship matrix. The SDI [this E-ICE massed holon] is now a full and contextually associable member of the PEC community.

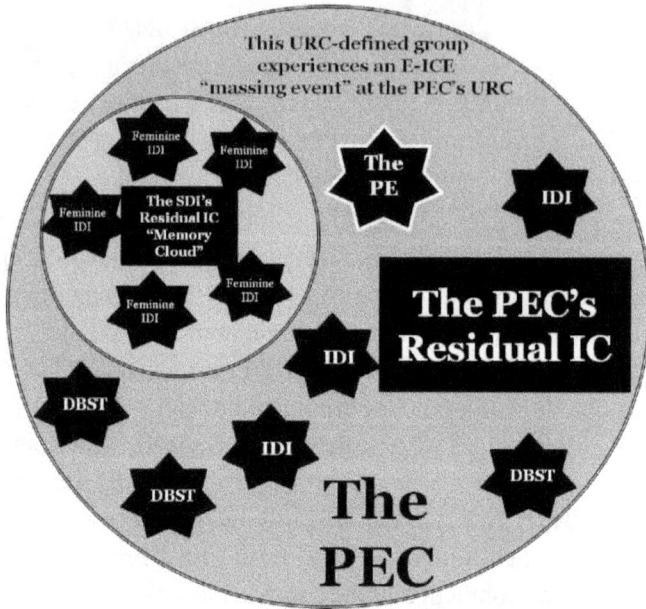

Figure 2:2-E
The incompatible URC of the former GS-EC's
Residual IC and Feminine IDIs imposes an E-ICE
massing event at the PEC's Unit Rate of Change

Of course, within the confines of the SDI, this gathering of dynamic and residual informational holons retains its original shared URC, and the fact that it has fully massed as an identified whole (relative to the rest of the PEC) creates a much more substantial contextual entanglement between these IDIs and their Residual IC. This has the effect of each IDI feeling a level of individual union with the Residual IC that was impossible while they shared that IC with the rest of what made up the confines of the GS-EC. Remember how that Hamburg bar caused you, your coworker and the lunch lady (in that charming Section I analogy) to suddenly become much more intimately bonded? To suggest that this Environmentally-Imposed Contextual Entanglement is more intensely experienced by each IDI than what you'd get from running into coworkers in a German bar would be a true understatement.

Keep in mind that Association and Increase are the original Identity Survival pursuit strategies that the C/E and C/S Trajectories engaged in, and with ID Survival the itch that it is for all IDIs [as the C/E Trajectory hybrids that they are], this sudden and profound sense of union with the massive Residual IC [and the obvious Increase in holon structural size and complexity being granted to each IDI as a result of that new level of direct entanglement] is experienced as absolute bliss. Remember, the pursuit of Identity Survival has always been what drives the now-fully gestated human being; from the instant that its placenta brain went on line with its very first Intellect Burst Set generation. *Increase* of this magnitude (regardless of whether this is how each IDI pursued its own ID Survival while in corporeal gestation or not) comes with a level of satiety that is profound. You might even call it Heaven.

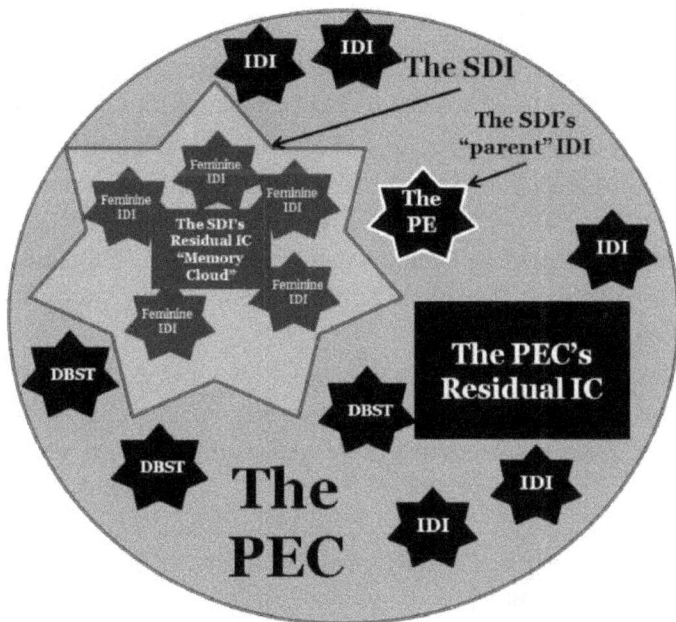

Figure 2:2-F.
The SDI finds a true home within the PEC as a result of
its familial connection to the Procreating Entity, and
its historical entanglement with the PEC's Residual IC

Note — It is due to the fact that its dynamic components are much more deliberately communal than the Intellect Burst Set collective that makes up the average IDI, that I decided to name this intelligent, contemplative, and fully dynamic version of humanity the Symbiotic Dynamic Intellect being, or SDI. I also chose this name to point out that it can only succeed as a fully functional whole if all the IDIs involved are capable of acting in concert with one another — embracing Symbiosis as their ID Survival expression.

As an interesting aside, the gender accept/reject protocol that brings the SDI into existence also ensures its successful functionality as an intelligent, dynamic entity within its new Environment. If not for the relatively Feminine expression of every IDI that makes up its collective nature, it would not take long before the SDI suffered its first internal power struggle. Then again, it's not as if the very human Procreating Entity hasn't probably tried to bring that gender balance as close to the brink of incompatibility as possible.

Butching Up the SDI

Now, concerning THE PROCESS and how the GS-EC's gestational role can be manipulated, as the Procreating Entity *performs* the initiating C/E Unit, there are protocols that will affect how the process — as a whole — progresses that can be embedded within that event [as historical/internal context] as a result of the intent of the PE, but only if those protocols are broad enough and if the desired impact on the process is blunt enough. One way to profoundly affect the nature of the emerging SDI is through the Move-to-Isolate Event; specifically, delaying that event's occurrence.

The Move-to-Isolate Event is the one-off event that, while naturally isolated from the evolving ramification structure that will ultimately define the GS-EC, is a defining part of its resolution as a gestating placenta. This makes the Move-to-Isolate Event a natural target for any PE with a desire to have an active hand in determining the broad nature of the SDI that will emerge in the end. It's not much, but by intending that the Move-to-Isolate Event be delayed, the PE can affect the gender expression of the IDIs that are washed out with the Residual IC; producing an SDI that is more Masculine. This is accomplished by carefully shifting the gender trigger itself, from 50/50 to some other balance [as long as the Identity threatening Residual IC is eliminated, of course]. Shifting the accept/reject protocol in this manner allows some relatively Masculine IDIs to become eligible for inclusion within the SDI's community. But why might this be desirable?

Delaying the Move-to-Isolate Event might allow the GS-EC's IDI community (in general) to have an extended period of evolutionary development before the gender trigger isolates the GS-EC and kicks out all relatively Feminine IDIs. The result could be an SDI that is more highly prepared, with a Residual IC that possesses more sophisticated RFS continuums as a result of more highly developed GDIs [the result of intellectually superior brains and that specific impact on the quality of their PFS memory clouds], positively affecting its immediate grasp of larger concerns.

But, the most obvious impact of delaying this transition [these PEs are human after all] is the increase in relative Masculine gender expression of the SDI that emerges. And while there are many benefits to this more aggressive, more inherently masculine SDI, if not successfully anticipated, the level of increase in Masculine expression could have a devastating effect on the SDI's ability to exist as anything more than an isolated battlefield of competitive IDIs fighting each other for dominance.

This notion of an SDI that's been allowed to become way too Masculine sure brings to mind the kind of monster that religionists have used for centuries to scare each other into coloring inside the lines. The thought of such a tortured beast [complete with all that enormous potential] makes one's blood run cold, and creates a great premise for a horror trilogy.

This crafting mechanism would be accomplished by the PE's initiating intent when the GS-EC is launched as THE PROCESS. Of course, attempts to *intend* any developmental protocols that are more precise than a delayed Move-to-Isolate Event would likely fail to be successful. The GS-EC, once it has been initiated, is nothing more or less than any other naturally developing URC-Determined Environmental Confine, and only an absolutely primordial, environment-wide, protocol would be able to remain intact, given the kind of ramification-driven development process that such an environment endures. The kind of divine micro-management that most theologies suggest is clearly impossible within this process, and it is this freedom of developmental expression what defines the GS-EC as a true procreation placenta.

The authoring Procreating Entity dynamically contributes to its initiation, but then the natural progressive development process itself takes over from there as gestation — with that required amount of the authoring PE's own contextual Identity [in the form of the *swept away* Residual IC's historical context] remaining integral to the inimitable Primary Expression of the SDI when it has emerged as whole and viable. If any term properly describes this amazing deliberately initiated creative process, then procreation is that term.

The ultra-hybrid SDI possesses the dynamic nature of the IDI, as well as the Residual IC's natural capacity for eternal mass increase; replicating the GDI's ever growing memory cloud, and allowing for unique and novel knowledge progress for the SDI's community of IDIs. To the entire parent Environment, the SDI is a single dynamic and determinative entity, even though within the SDI each IDI experiences its own existence as a part of a community of IDIs that are bathed in the visceral satisfaction provided by each one's immediate and intimate contextual entanglement with the Residual IC as it continues to mass new information in response to each instance of intra-community activity.

The SDI is also the authoring IDI's (the PE) solution to its gnawing urge for Identity Survival. Its *parent* relationship with the SDI gives it historical inclusion within what emerges as a new C/E Trajectory holon structure of existent SDIs [a new *subspecies* of humanity], with each SDI a component holon within the next larger holon structure [the ongoing C/E Trajectory that consists of SDIs that have emerged as a result of deliberately initiated GS-ECs]. This more than satisfies that *breeder* IDI's Identity Survival itch since it is the same Increase strategy pursued by each and every C/E Unit within each C/E Trajectory that ensured its own Identity Survival the instant that it joined in the effort to bring that IDI into eventual existence. All for one and one for all. As it's always been for the C/E Trajectory and its DBST/IBST hybrid expression. But there's a lot more that's accomplished (existentially speaking) as a result of the emergence of the SDI. In fact, the SDI is quite an achievement in its own right.

Each SDI is the ultimate expression of physical existence. In fact, it literally represents all possible forms of physical existence in one overwhelming Identity expression. It furthers the Identity Survival of the C/E Unit (in general) as the ultimate Survival achievement of the breeder IDI. It fully expresses the collective Identity of an entire URC-Determined Environmental Confine [its GS-EC's original Residual IC]. It also connects, through the Identity of the GS-EC's authoring PE, to everything that brought that IDI into existence, and in that way, it links to everything within the PEC, as well as everything that is contextually linked to that Environment. In this way, the SDI really is the Alpha and the Omega, connecting the first to the last and expressing the whole Identity of physical existence through its direct link to the original Residual IC.

I generally think of this Residual IC linkage in terms of the DNA that is passed on from parents to their offspring; causing them all to be physically related as a family, even though it allows the offspring to be unique and singular in Identity. I suppose that viewing the GS-EC's authoring PE as family to the emerging SDI is as accurate a way of interpreting it all as any other. It's a contextual entanglement that is clearly significant, and one that's inspired a lot of

AutoGenesism: A Theory of Everything

religiousness in this world of ours over the thousands of years that we've practiced civilization. Which brings me to one last item.

Behold . . .

As I was laying out the agendas of both Track#1 and Track#2 in the beginning of this Section II, I stated that I was going to present a possible explanation for why our own Homo Sapiens version of humanity has so thoroughly embraced the extremely unlikely concept of a creator god that will provide the faithful with some version or other of a paradise reward as a result of being *"good"*. I stated that it would be in this Track#2 overview that I would present this explanation. Well, it's now time for me to do that.

We just got done taking a really detailed look at a procreative reapplication of the fundamental progressive development process, and while it's pretty innovative, what's it got to do with the fact that 5/6 of the modern human population on Planet Earth intellectually default to the belief in *something* that they can't perceive and over 50% submit their will to whatever they're told that it is that this *something* requires of them? Am I now going to offer the authoring PE as our creator god, and sew this entire thing up with a quick wave of my hand?

No, that'd be stupid.

Granted, if it's true that our Universe is a GS-EC, then its authoring Procreating Entity is the IDI responsible for its initiation. But, that's not the same thing as declaring that breeder IDI to be GOD. It's a lot more complicated than that, and I'm going to honestly attempt to explain how certain residual Fact Set continuums that are central to the historical basis of the GS-EC's own Residual IC could easily affect how IDIs view the nature of their own role within Reality [as a result of these continuums being noticed and analyzed] with the net impact being the otherwise impossible conceptualization of a creator god, heavenly rewards, hellish punishments, and the cross-cultural staple that is the divinely predicted and required end of days apocalyptic division of the *good* from the *evil*. Yes, this is what Track#2 has been all about, and at long last here's where I'll be bringing it all together for you. But first, let's review how it could be that even the most brilliant IDI [a human being] could misinterpret even the most obvious and factual indication.

The human mind/brain Dynamic Burst Set generation system can only ever translate its perception of fact. It can't ever generate residual Fact Sets. Hell, it doesn't even have factual Fact Sets available in its memory cloud to refer to.

301

I've been calling those memory cloud data sets *Perception Fact Sets clusters* be-cause they are the factual representations of each perception interpretation that the mind/brain system has achieved; whether those interpretations are accurate or not. This means that the GDI, and the IDI that each GDI eventually becomes, can never contain any Burst Sets that are factual.

Yes, the SDI is different in that it possesses a Residual IC, packed with Fact Sets, but even then, its dynamic nature [its *human* conscious awareness] is a result of the IDI [human] community contained within it. This means that the SDI is also perception addled. Not to the same degree as an average IDI, but still, the SDI is not free of the positive/negative aspects of subjective perspective examination and interpretation as it engages with the Environment and all that exists within that Environment.

So what does this mean? It means that no matter how brilliant or bathed in wisdom any version of a human being becomes, what it knows about Reality is what it has determined through its own interpretation and translation of what it is capable of perceiving. Beyond that . . . well, for the human being, there's nothing at all beyond that, and there never will be.

So what are the ramifications of this absolute barrier between Reality and what the human being experiences as reality? They're extensive, but I want to only focus on one of the ramifications of being human within a URC-Deter-mined Environmental Confine that was purposely initiated and that is still serv-ing as an SDI's GS-EC gestational placenta; the one overwhelming ramification that has literally defined what it means to be a human being that gestated on Planet Earth.

A God is Born

When you think about it, there isn't much difference between the SDI and how most traditional religions view the central focus of their devotion. This is especially true with the Abrahamic religions [Judaism, Christianity, and Islam] where the god in question specifically created humanity *in its own image*. In fact, both [the SDI and any one of the traditional supreme beings] could be de-scribed as generally *human* [in a broad sense of what that suggests] while clearly and exceedingly superior in presence and capacity. Since this comparison [be-tween the SDI and our human race's most popular version of God] is essential to the whole point of this Track#2 overview, let's take a really good look at the SDI with this in mind.

AutoGenesism: A Theory of Everything

The physical structure of the SDI, while it is similar to the IDI in many ways, is unique in the most essential aspects. Of course, it's completely dynamic and self-determining, and like the human IDI, it possesses a *whole-self,* conscious awareness, but the net impact of all that's come together to coalesce as the SDI cannot be overstated.

The most overwhelming difference is the most obvious, but let's examine it anyway. Each IDI is the net result of the lifespan of one human brain. This gathering of every thought, every reaction, every experience, every win, loss, love and unrequited desire that defines the full corporeal human life is certainly not insignificant, but the SDI is the net result of the entire duration of an intentionally initiated URC-DEC's role as a gestational placenta. During this phase of progressive development, the sheer number of GDIs and IDIs alone is impossible to quantify, as is the full impact of all these lives on the depth and sophistication of the Residual IC that ultimately becomes the SDI's compare/contrast information resource.

As a whole, this Residual IC contains an impossible to determine number of RFS continuums that represent what is factually real and what is a factual ramification of the relationships between these RFS continuums, but it also contains the complete PFS continuums from too many corporeal lives and afterlives to count. With such an immense wealth of raw factual information as well as every single human perception and unique perspective that's ever occurred within the GS-EC, from the instant of its origin right up to the Move-to-Isolate Event, as if each were its own truly experienced memory, the SDI's capacity for true wisdom is staggering. Compared to even the most extraordinary IDI, there is no limit to the SDI's potential as it moves throughout eternity with consciousness, and a complete awareness of itself as a unique existential whole.

What is also important to note [relative to this conceptual comparison between the SDI and a traditionally depicted godly entity] is that the GS-EC's Move-to-Isolate Event can only occur once, since its occurrence transforms the GS-EC into a fully isolated Environment, with no access in or out ever again. This means that it takes a whole GS-EC [an entire Universe and everything within it] to produce one SDI being. What this suggests is that when the Procreating Entity produces that out-of-sync Change/Event Unit [launching the GS-EC with its unique URC] that PE knows full well that the resulting SDI will be incalculably *more* than any IDI, and in every possible sense of what that suggests.

As to how all of the PE's foreknowledge [of the overwhelming capacity of the SDI that will inevitably emerge from the GS-EC] could have affected our human race and its unlikely view of Reality, you need to remember that each GS-EC is specifically initiated with the PE's intention of it serving as the gestational placenta of an SDI. This expectation is [it must be] present and available within the Residual IC of each GS-EC that exists. After all, the intent of the authoring PE [including all that the PE knows to reasonably anticipate concerning the full nature of the SDI that will emerge in the end] is an integral aspect of that out-of-sync C/E Unit; historically represented by the out-of-sync residual Fact Set that launches the GS-EC's own Residual IC. As the GS-EC's most primordial identifier, this permanently preserved ideal will always retain a significant level of prominence within this original Residual IC as long as it continues to define the GS-EC's Identity.

> ***Note*** — As I stated before starting this Track#2, this is all speculation, and no matter how precise I get with all of this, I will continue to acknowledge that there's no possible way for me or any other Material Realm inhabitant to chase this mystery down to any degree of specificity.

I realize that there's no way to prove it, but it does stand to reason that if an intellectually sophisticated inhabitant of a GS-EC were to stumble across that very first residual Fact Set continuum, it would contain the factual specifics of the authoring PE's original intention for this GS-EC. The description of this GS-EC's *destiny* [the inevitable emergence of an SDI] and the SDI's significance to this entire Reality confine's existence, could easily be enough to inspire the notion of a creator god that is omnipotent, omniscient, and omnipresent. In fact, the idea itself seems almost too obvious, even if it's just speculation that I freely admit to having engaged in as a result of what I've figured out about AutoGenesism.

The only contradiction is the notion that such a powerful and overwhelming being *created* our Universe, as opposed to the notion that our Universe is *creating* it. But, it's such a direct contradiction that the connection between the two notions is clear and compelling. And, like I pointed out, the human being can only translate what it can perceive.

Oh, and the *"good go to heaven, the bad to hell"* notion [not to mention the apocalyptic *Judgment Day* scenario that the anticipated Move-to-Isolate Event seems way-too obviously capable of suggesting if the factual specifics have been incorrectly perceived]? I would imagine that inclusion within the SDI could easily be seen as a version of heavenly reward, even if being left behind

AutoGenesism: A Theory of Everything

within the hyper-Masculine environs of the now-isolated former-GS-EC might not qualify as a burning lake of fiery torment for most folks. Still, the *"do unto others"* Golden Rule method of dealing with the often angry stuff of life sure qualifies as a thoroughly Feminine Identity Survival expression if ever there was one. And an overtly Feminine gender expression is what gets an IDI swept from the GS-EC [and into the heavenly confines of the SDI] during its Move-to-Isolate Event.

Yes, this is all speculation, even if the dots that seem too obvious to ignore suggest a complete and precise inverse of what's become traditional wisdom concerning the creation and eventual destiny of our world. There's a kid's game called *The Telephone Game* that shows how quickly perception translation can affect a simple single sentence whispered from player to player. It's not difficult to see how such a contradiction could have developed and taken hold as sacred knowledge . . . well, on this planet full of humans anyway.

And So . . .

Again, I'm going to make the statement that this entire Track#2 has been speculative in nature. You don't have to embrace anything in this book, but I especially don't expect anyone to run out and start a religion based on a breeder IDI's procreation process. That said, this track really does give your understanding of the basics of AutoGenesism a proper workout, and as far as I'm concerned, that's all that matters to me. I just want you to better understand what I've been trying to teach you.

Now, from here we will focus on a variety of specifics that require detailing that would've been a bit too extensive if included within either Track#1 or Track#2. I also want to take a moment to suggest a few other cultural predilections that Auto-G might be able to help explain. I'm calling this next section *"Digressions and Speculations"* because I feel some of it to be fairly accurate, while some of it is admittedly a lot more adventurous, and yet each topic is a digression in its own right and connected with something we've already covered.

Kevin Brian Carroll

Section III

Digressions
and
Speculations

Presenting AutoGenesism involves the establishment of some very coun-terintuitive notions, and while I was able to articulate most of them fairly effec-tively within the previous sections, there have been some very resistant notions that require a heck of a lot more room to work through. I originally envisioned this section to be a lot larger than it ended up being, but as I got more involved in the mechanics of presenting This notion as a whole, the explanations became more and more efficient, leaving only a few specifics that simply refused to be streamlined enough for inclusion within the previous narrative structures. That said, the Speculations segment of this section did expand a bit, so I guess it all balanced out in the end.

This section will allow me a chance to stretch out a bit and present some aspects of this logic structure that might end up seeming obvious, but that none-theless require presenting, since they are foundational to how AutoGenesism ends up working out as it does. Like I said, and will keep saying, I didn't invent any of this. I don't have the capacity to invent this stuff. This is based solely on the sort of established protocols and logical infrastructure that most freshman college students already know. The application of it all is pretty wonderful, but again, if one simply scales down their focus and looks to the most primitive expression possible, this begins to be obvious without a lot of intellect being expended on the effort.

I decided that the best way to manage this section is to simply present each digression and/or speculation as a stand-alone essay; to whatever degree is possible, of course. Each digression (being a digression) naturally expounds on a specific aspect of a topic that's been covered, so there's a certain sense of continuity between each of these and the topic's section of introduction. There may even be a bit of reiteration to help with that continuity. The speculations are much more independent in nature, since, while they also maintain a definite degree of continuity with all that's been presented to this point, they don't serve to expand on any aspect that's already been introduced within an earlier section.

It'll all make sense, I promise. So, let's first deal with the digressions.

AutoGenesism: A Theory of Everything

Digression

Concerning My Specific Methodology

As I worked to more fully understand and refine my AutoGenesism theory, there were times when I would grab my assessments and assumptions and present them to a partner for intense review and critique, with the expressed intent that all failures and/or alternative hypotheses be exposed and addressed. As AutoGenesism became more and more clearly revealed as directly connected with widely accepted theoretical staples (i.e. Holon Theory, Quantum Theory, the Expanding Universe Theory) while directly challenging such widely accepted scientific paradigms as the Big Bang, the Standard Model, and Relativity's relationship between Time and Movement, my own efforts to severely challenge it as a useful theoretical basis became more and more a fundamental part of my definition and refinement process.

I knew that the more radical Auto-G became [relative only to all other prevailing theories] the more precise my own understanding of it would have to become. I also knew that as Auto-G became more defined and more precise, my own objectivity concerning its veracity could become increasingly threatened. Embracing Philosopher Helen Longino's view as expressed within her 1990 *"Science as Social Knowledge"*, I accepted this evidential reasoning and deductive effort as a *"human practice and therefore inherently context-dependent"* (that phrase lifted directly from the pages of Massimo Pigliucci's *"Nonsense on Stilts: How to Tell Science From Bunk"*), and decided to thoroughly validate my logic train on an ongoing and repeating basis as a means of constantly checking my own degree of objectivity and dispassion.

AutoGenesism isn't a philosophy or an ideology. It's a theory about why reality is what it is, and why the things that exist, exist. My aim is not to argue for how reality should be, but to determine what forms the basis of reality as it actually is. Sort of like a forensic examination, I suppose; using only deductive logic basics, whatever available dots there are that can be connected to anything of a primordial nature, and some of the most counterintuitive indications that have come out of the last 100 years or so of scientific (and not so scientific) research into what's real. The goal has been no guesswork or irresponsible assumptions at all, with all major questions addressed and all loose ends eliminated.

What I want to offer here is the latest description of that specific examination, with the hope that it helps you fully appreciate the level of intellectual discipline I applied to this effort. Each of the following items are either what I consider to be fundamental aspects of Reality or they are what I consider to be fundamental aspects concerning how to approach any determination of what it is that can be or cannot be real.

Item #1: Reality: The Ultimate Frame of Reference

I cannot believe how much pushback I get whenever I insist that regardless of Einstein and his theories of Relativity, when it comes to the determination of what is and what isn't a fact within an environmental confine, it is the environmental confine itself [the apical holon that hosts whatever occurs or exists within it] that provides the factual frame of reference. Yes, it may be useful to consider other frames of reference if what you're trying to determine is how to procedurally manage an event from a specific frame of reference [applied physics], but if what's being pursued is factual accuracy, then the environmental frame of reference is the frame of reference.

To help illustrate this, I've even drawn my own quick version of the famous Special Relativity non-simultaneity thought experiment diagram that features a stationary observer on an embankment (A), an observer riding a train at 60 mph past the observer on that embankment (A'), and a pair of lightning strikes hitting the front and rear cars of the train, with the question being whether simultaneity is a determination that is at all possible.

AutoGenesism: A Theory of Everything

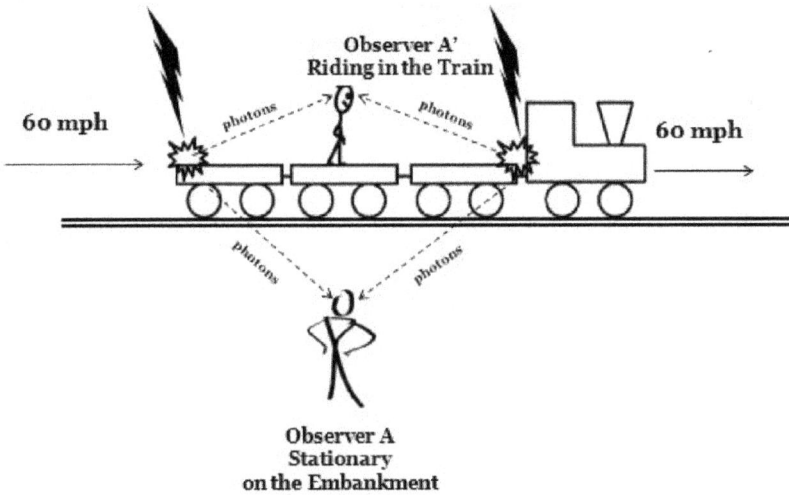

Figure 3-A
Special Relativity Non-simultaneity Diagram

The observers [A and A'] each occupy very different positions [on the embankment and on the train carriage, respectively] that affect their perceptions of the lightning strike events occurring within the very specific environment that they share. This difference in perception is the key to Einstein's *Special Theory of Relativity*, and in this cursory examination, I am going to challenge the notion of allowing either observer to reconfigure Reality as a direct result of the relationship between their cornea lenses and whatever specific subset of photons there might be that may travel from wherever to wherever within that clearly defined theater of activity. I do realize that on a blackboard, and within carefully prepared laboratory experimental systems, that Einstein's time dilation predictions do work out, but perhaps that's the most important observation that exists within this theory and its impact on the way that science in general confirms theoretical veracity, as one works to completely factor out the full ramification suite of these Relativity theories.

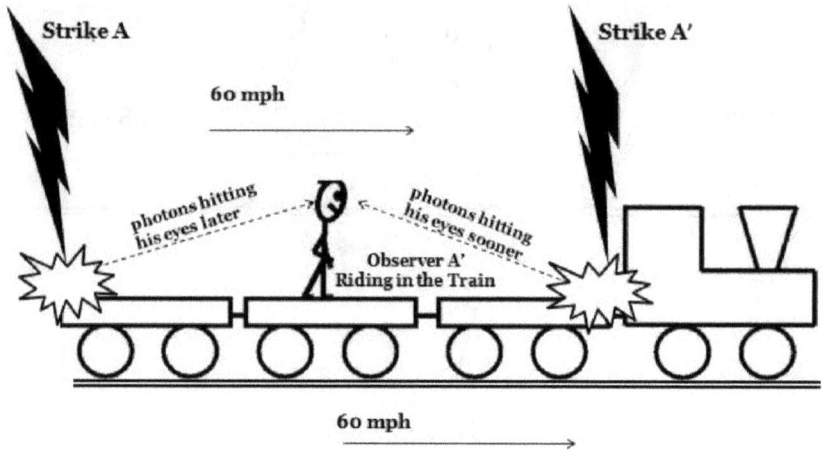

Figure 3-B
Observer A' in Isolation

As we focus on Observer A' here [placed in the exact center of the train at equal distance from both of the lightning strike locations], keep in mind that this thought experiment has Observer A [on the embankment, also equally distanced from both the front and the end of the train, but not in motion toward or away from either strike], seeing both lightning strikes [Strikes A and A'] as having occurred at exactly the same instant, or simultaneously. That said, Einstein's *Special Theory of Relativity* states that due to the existence of Observer A' [the one riding the train] there is no way to factually determine whether the two lightning strikes did or did not happen simultaneously. Basically, the idea is that because of the unique point of perspective that Observer A' possesses, the simultaneity of those strikes is factually nullified. Well, relative to the *universe* [note the italics] that Observer A' occupies, it is.

The theory insists that Observer A' sees the lightning strike [Strike A'] first, since he is racing to that position [at 60 mph] and away from the lightning strike [Strike A] at that same velocity. This seems reasonable enough, but the theory goes on to say that the speed of light [in this case, the speed of the photons traveling from the strikes to the observer's eyes] cannot and does not change relative to the observer, regardless of that observer's position or relative velocity [relative to the lightning strikes, in this case].

Since this is stated as an absolute certainty, and since Observer A' [due to his own velocity of 60 mph toward Strike A' and away from Strike A] sees the strikes as happening non-simultaneously [the photons racing from Strike A' hit

AutoGenesism: A Theory of Everything

his eyes before the photons from Strike A can hit his eyes] then according to Einstein's *Special Theory of Relativity* [working with the equation: **speed equals distance divided by time**, and all inversions of the same] Observer A's additional speed toward the photons from Strike A' as a result of his moving toward that position at a steady 60 mph, must be compensated for within that equation, since the speed of light [photons in travel] is absolute and cannot possibly change relative to any observer's frame of reference, regardless of that observer's position or relative velocity.

In other words, that 60 mph cannot be tacked onto the 186,000 miles per second that light is already traveling to the observer's eyes [theoretically this would make those photons move faster than the speed of light], so something has to give in that equation [speed equals distance divided by time] for this thought experiment to make any sense. And in this case, Einstein throws Time under the train (so to speak) — forcing it to dilate [actually slow down] for Observer A' — and this is due to another assertion that he makes; that each Observer's frame of reference is technically a stationary frame of reference. Therefore, forget about messing with speed or distance in that equation, since relative to Observer A' [or any observer's frame of reference] there is no speed or distance involved. Obviously, time is the only factor available for adjustment. Or is it?

Well, it is if you insist that the only possible frames of reference that exist are those that belong to Observer A and Observer A'. However, if you do, you're artificially manipulating the actual theater of activity in this specific case, and doing so without justification.

Here's another look at Observer A' and his relationship with the lightning strikes, only this time we're going to include the full ramification set that actually exists as the photons from Strike A' and Strike A reach his cornea lenses at differing instances.

313

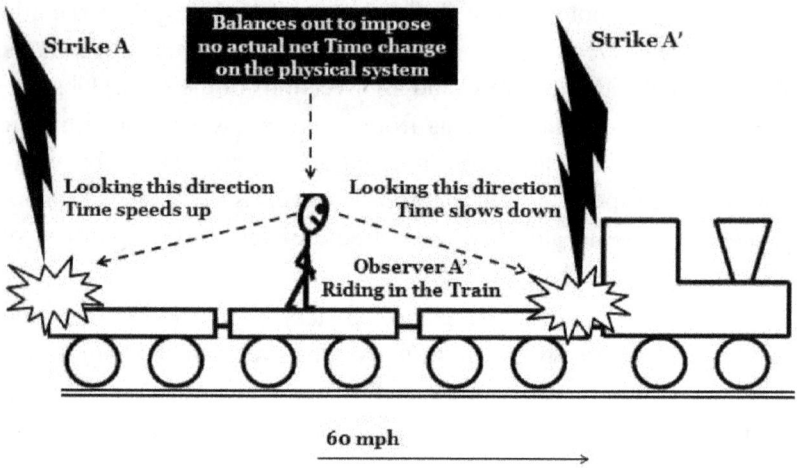

Figure 3-C
Non-simultaneity Debunked?

As you can see, there is something happening here that actually throws the entire thought experiment into a spin that it cannot recover from. Yes, if Observer A' only looks at Strike A', then Einstein's Special Relativity demands that Time slow down to compensate for the rapidity of the photons reaching his eyes as compared to the length of the train cars between himself and the strike. That said, if he only looks at Strike A, then the opposite must occur [Time speeds up] to compensate for the delay of its photons reaching his eyes as compared to the length of the train cars between himself and that strike.

Of course, suggesting that Observer A' can physically alter Time itself by simply turning his head around is (I would like to assume) a suggestion that even Einstein would have trouble making. In fact, since both observers [A and A'], both lightning strikes [A and A'], the train and the embankment are all components within a larger environment that is common to all (as well as to a lot more components than have been listed) it is reasonable to suggest that there is a frame of reference that would supersede either observer's unique perspective; the common environmental frame of reference. Here's the diagram.

AutoGenesism: A Theory of Everything

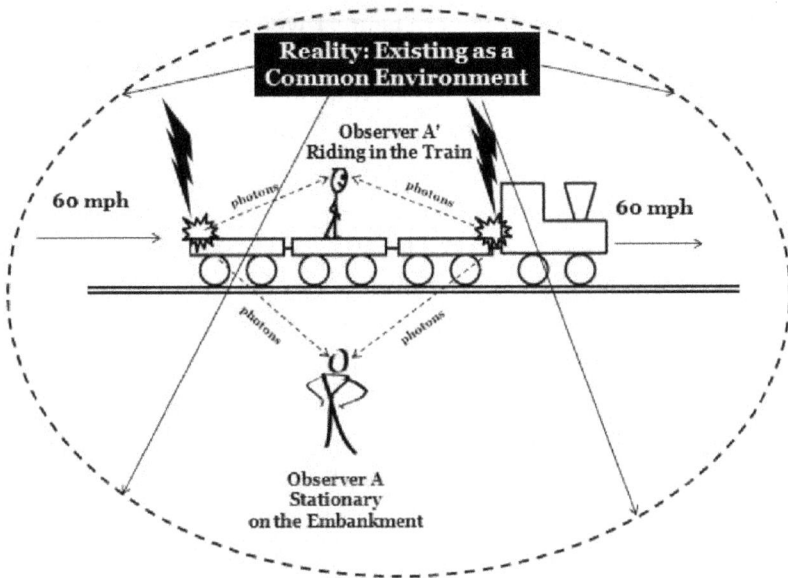

Figure 3-D
Reality: The Ultimate Frame of Reference

In essence, what I'm trying to illustrate is that regardless of the math or the thought experiments, there is a fundamental real that supersedes the perspective or perception of any observer that physically occupies the same environment as that which is being observed by that observer. If those two lightning strikes occurred simultaneously, then they occurred simultaneously regardless of who observed what and from what perspective that observation was made.

In fact, as shown above, in this specific [and famous] thought experiment, a quick turn of the head by Observer A' is all it takes for him to completely alter the flow of Time itself. And I would imagine that the math actually works out in that case as well, which should be a big red flag concerning the use of math equations to establish and/or verify claims concerning the true nature of Reality.

I've read dozens and dozens of lengthy explanations for and against the wisdom of allowing individual perception the power to completely reconfigure the very structure of ongoing Reality, and while I appreciate the brilliant mathematical convolutions that have been routinely employed to prove Einstein's brilliant little prank as somehow being a serious description of nuts and bolts Reality, the truth is that this reign of the observer has likely been academic satire for quite long enough.

315

In fact, as one becomes ever more familiar with the man, the times, and the unusual nature of his theory descriptions, it becomes increasingly plausible that Einstein must've known how brilliant an absurdist satirical commentary [on the requirement that experimentation be the sole arbiter of theoretical verification within the very community he had been, to that point in his life, refused professional entry] his *Special Theory of Relativity* actually was. How could this have not been the case? As soon as one reads how carefully he crafted each sentence [relentlessly shadowing the bizarre ramifications of each casual assertion by relating them to field experimentation protocols] the sly prankster is slowly revealed, yet only to those who are not culturally predisposed to blindly accepting what's been presented with repeatable test study results and/or with math equations that factor out properly on a blackboard.

If so, then it's an absolutely brilliant satirical condemnation of the absurdities of relying solely on the blunt mechanics of The Scientific Method. Perhaps the most astonishing part of this wondrous caper is that when Special Relativity survived peer review [as a presentation specifically designed to successfully navigate the experimentation/math blackboard peer review process, it would] the man doubled down on the whole charade and crafted his *General Theory of Relativity*; earning himself a permanent place of honor as one who achieved true genius in a manner that still transcends the pedestrian muddling of those C students who run this world.

Of course, I can't prove that Einstein intentionally pranked the entire 20th century with his Relativity theories, but, as I quickly illustrated above, I can prove beyond any shadow of any doubt that there is a fundamental real, and that there is nothing at all relative concerning the quantum unit progression of Now that is Time, or the evolving spatial environmental whole that consists of every existing position, proximity, and volume displacement, if one is pursuing the factual nature of Reality as the *everything* that it is. Reality is an ever emerging relationship matrix comprised of everything that is happening and that has ever happened [persisting in factual representation] as a result of one quantum instant of *Now* giving way to the next at a common unit rate of change.

One relationship matrix — one frame of reference. And it's just that clear, concise and easy to understand in spite of what's otherwise suggested by ones experimental results or mathematical calculation. My embrace of the existence of a fundamental real is why AutoGenesism is the Theory of Everything that it is.

Autogenesism: A Theory of Everything

Item #2: System Coherence — "As Above, So Below"

After declaring Reality to be real, this ageless axiom was the very first requirement that I placed on any Theory of Everything that might emerge as a result of this effort to deduce exactly what could be determined to be real about Reality. The reason is as simple as it is inescapable; the physical structure of Reality must be consistent and coherent at all levels. What brings that structure together must not only exist at all levels, it must be fundamental and necessary at all levels. It must be the literal core of every version of physical existence, and set every requirement manifestation; from Quantum Entanglement to the psychological impetus that drives a theoretical physicist to one day solve the mystery of Quantum Entanglement. Perhaps it'd be best if I refer to a couple of primordial staples and detail how they serve as examples of what system coherence is and how it works.

I explain in Section I that I embrace the existence of an actual meta-law [*"first, survive"*] that sets the basis for all subsequent laws and requirements, and that it is the survival of inimitable Identity that is the ultimate definition of what it means to *"first, survive"*. While it can be argued whether or not it's Identity Survival that's being pursued at the primordial level of physical existence (although it does explain C/E Units seeking that version of survival within the internal/historical contextual composition of subsequent C/E Units within the holon structure of a C/E Trajectory, creating the arrow of Time as it does) it can't ever be suggested that within AutoGenesism the pursuit of Identity Survival is theoretically isolated to any specific level of progressive development or physical system.

In fact, I make a strong case for the notion that while it provides the impetus for progressive development at the most substructural levels, it's at the human level of material manifestation, where Identity Survival is most clearly established as the true definition of existential survival. Unlike the Change/Event Units that mindlessly pursue ongoing existence as contributing context within the Identity of an existing trajectory, human beings fully understand that they exist. Each one of us knows that as corporeal beings our days are numbered. And yet, what is our most common response to this inescapable realization? We pursue the permanence of our unique identity; seeking to leave our mark upon the Material Realm. We blatantly pursue Identity Survival, and in a myriad of ways; each as unique and inimitable as ourselves. We don't pursue material survival, and that's really important to understand and acknowledge.

317

What's most fascinating about this seemingly schismatic approach to survival of self is that it involves both fundamental C/E Trajectory Identity Survival [procreation] and a literal modification of the unique strategy that the Environment itself employs as it, too, pursues its own ID Survival [Identity definition and isolation via contextual complexity]. In fact, the often destructive behavior that many people pursue [smoking, drinking, drug abuse, unnecessary risk, self-destructive choices, and even suicide] can be directly connected to the human mind's own pursuit of definition and isolation [defense] of inimitable Identity at the expense of its authoring brain's survival, and in Section II's Track#1, I detail the specifics of this connection.

This deliberate and sometimes tragic contradiction between the pursuits of an otherwise rational human being and what that human fully realizes is fundamental to ensuring its own material survival is powerful evidence that deep within our own subconscious and unconscious assessment of what is true and intractable, survival is not defined by the persistence of the material manifestation. Somewhere beneath our cultural predilections, we understand that true survival of self is achieved as a result of something that is much less amenable to traditional scientific methodology.

And it's this universal impact of Identity Survival that I see as indicative of its place among those staples that lay the foundation of Reality's physical structure. I am swayed by the fact that there is no delineation that exists relative to the nature of this primordial requirement regardless of the specific level of progressive development. Serving that requirement might look like a different process to an observer when comparing ID Survival pursuit as it manifests within widely disparate systems, but that's to be expected. Still, the requirement itself drives all activity, and that fact remains unaffected by change in system complexity and sophistication. This is how it must also be (and is) with each existential staple, and it was this requirement of system coherence (since Reality itself is a physical system) that was the primary determinant as I examined each existential staple's fitness to serve in that capacity.

Another example is the scalable presence of information [yet another existential staple] as a system determinant. Information, in the form of residual Fact Sets (RFS) and RFS Continuums, is equally evident at all levels of progressive development. Its physical presence is clearly the primary concern of each research scientist, [that concern, itself, is a great example of the human brain's own Dynamic Burst Set (DBS) information in full Reality-altering trajectory

AutoGenesism: A Theory of Everything

(DBST) manifestation] as he or she devises and designs those extremely rigorous and carefully isolated systems [this is deliberate RFS management, meant to mitigate the impact of Internal and Relative contextual *"contamination"*] that are featured in all scientific experiments, in what is a common preparatory effort to ensure the replication of the precise study results that are desired and fully anticipated.

It may be hyperbole to declare that these elaborate context/precedent-mitigating system preparations are no different than the precision riggings that ensure the success (and/or survival) of a premier illusionist, but it's not unfair to note the similarity as it pertains to the intellectual diligence that is devoted to system isolation and control in both cases. If system precedent and environmental context doesn't exist, then why the elaborate preparations to filter them out? The truth is that (and this is especially true in connection with the delicate process of entanglement involving extremely primitive elementary systems) precedent and context are like ghosts in the machine, and it's this influence, in the physical presence of residual Fact Sets, that gives headaches to those folks who struggle to achieve some semblance of control over systems that range from stage shows to quantum mechanics.

Residual Fact Sets define the most sophisticated material structures [DNA] and it may just be that 3 dimensional residual *placeholder* Fact Sets also define the open space of the entire universe [Dark Matter, and the impact it has on material existence; Dark Energy]. And so it is that from the bottom to the top, from the first to the last, and within and between every system that exists, the whole of Reality itself is either happening at this instant or persisting as a system-defining contextual impact within any one of an uncountable arrangement of RFS informational continuums and RFS continuum matrices. That the human being cannot appreciate just how consistent and coherent that whole is, is merely a ramification of its own positional restrictions as an integral component within that whole.

That said, it's the refusal to inflict a line of system demarcation (and in any way isolating the quantum from the classic from the cosmological) that separates this ToE from all others. It's this requirement that all systems make immediate and holistic sense with all other systems that literally forces AutoGenesism to be the theory that it is.

319

Item #3: The Meta-Law

In Lee Smolin's *"Time Reborn: From the Crisis in Physics to the Future of the Universe"*, Prof. Smolin suggests the existence of what he terms a *meta-law*, which (to paraphrase Prof. Smolin) would be a primordial law that bases the existence of all other laws, such as the laws of physics, cosmology and biology. While, I must admit that I learned of this *meta-law* idea long after applying the actual concept of such a law within the structure of Auto-G, I immediately embraced this specific label as ideally representative of how I'd approached the concept of existential requirements in general. I've always believed in the existence of a sole existential imperative that bases all other expressed requirements of physical existence and ultimately determines the nature of progressive development.

Considering the extremely primitive and universal nature that such a meta-law must possess, if put into words, that primordial imperative is best expressed as *"first, survive"*. Basically, that there is an intrinsic requirement that if something exists, then that something is naturally compelled to pursue continued existence until it can no longer prevent the loss of its existence. I suppose it can be debated as to whether such an intrinsic imperative does exist, but it'd be really hard to argue that *"first, survive"* is not the simplest and most primordial of all possible requirements that could be imposed upon the existent something, regardless of what it is.

This law has all the characteristics of what could qualify as a meta-law, as you will see, but only after a few clarifications are made concerning what it means to survive; specifically, what survival refers to in the most universal sense. After all, if *"first, survive"* is to be the meta-law, then it must be the law relative to all levels of existential survival. This means that the failure to survive must be precisely defined, and defined relative to what it means to exist and maintain that existence. This requires that the definitional clarification of existence itself be achieved, and this is where we'll start.

The definition of existence, in relation to the meta-law *"first, survive"*, must be as rigidly universal in application as the meta-law itself, if it is to be relevant in any manner whatsoever. The most important criterion must be that the existent something (**IT**) must be capable of losing the existence that **IT** possesses relative to that which is not **IT**. So, what must be embraced is that existence involves placement within the Relative Being State, since this being state is the existential basis of relative existence [this relative to that].

AutoGenesism: A Theory of Everything

I've decided that the qualifying term physical existence is best used as shorthand to symbolize the larger requirement that all that exists within the Relative Being State be objectively real and share the same existential basis; that survival can be lost if the law *"first, survive"* is indeed the meta-law that sets the requirement for all subsequent laws. Of course, this immediately eliminates the philosophical notion *singularity* as having any actual validity relative to that which exists, since the concept itself requires a singularity to exist as the whole of everything unto itself, with no delineations or fragmentations (creating any form of relative state to exist) allowed. Certainly, such an infinitely present manifestation could never cease to exist if it is the sole existent thing, and that's only one of the logical and empirical failures that exist for the singularity; even as it alone is certainly enough to sink the whole damn thing on its own.

Now, concerning the nature of physical existence, for something to exist, **IT** must stand out from within the whole of that which is but clearly isn't **IT**. If **IT** cannot stand out and be defined as being wholly delineated relative to that which contains it, then **IT** cannot be existent. I use the phrase *"stand out"* due to the entomology of the word existence — derived from the Latin *"existere"* which translates as *"to stand out"*, but also because it just provides the best illustration for what it means to exist. The existent **IT** is not conceptual in nature. **IT** exists as physical and actual, and this is critical to establish before we move on. That said, we have to now translate this existent **IT** relative to the most primitive and primordial examples of **IT** that we know of. One of them being the basis of Quantum Theory; the Quantum of Action.

The Quantum of Action is just one kind of physical quantum that is known to exist. It's unique, however, due to the fact that while it is definite and quantifiable it isn't material or measurable, and that it is gone as soon as it has appeared in full within the Material Realm. In fact, it is immediately replaced by an identical quantum of the same nature that is a unique unit of action in its own right, and not simply a repeat of the action quantum that vanished prior to this quantum unit's appearance. The second quantum of action also lasts only until it is fully emerged within the physical realm, to then be immediately replaced by the next identical, yet physically unique, action quantum, with this repeated as a direct chain of action until resolved in one way or another.

A number of questions emerge concerning the physical existence of the quantum of action:

- What gives an action quantum a physical presence?

- What delineates one action quantum from the next?
- What delineates any action quantum from the environment that hosts it?

For these questions to be suitably addressed, the answer or answers must be at least as primitive and primordial as the action quantum itself, and passing it all off as only requiring a statement using the term ipso facto in a grammatically accurate manner is worse than never bothering with the issue at all. The good news is that we do have one answer for all three questions, and that answer is Identity. Let's see if this one answer fully addresses all three questions in a responsible manner.

What gives an action quantum a physical presence?

Each quantum possesses inimitable Identity as a result of the distinction it has achieved even before it has fully developed. This distinction is established by a contextual blend — internal (historical) and relative (comparative) — that each possesses by default as a ramification of existing within the Relative Being State.

What delineates one action quantum from the next?

Each quantum's Identity is singular and inimitable due to the specific contextual blend that defines it. One's Identity, by default ramification, establishes its physical perimeter.

What delineates any action quantum from the environment that hosts it?

The hosting environment is the contextual relationship (relative context) between all physically existent wholes. The quantum's Identity has established its contextual, and therefore physical, presence within that relationship matrix. The logical ramifications are obvious.

So, it does seem as if Identity is the key to physical existence, and it can definitely be argued that unless something possesses its own inimitable Identity, relative to all else that exists, it certainly cannot *"stand out"* as physically existent. It's therefore not unreasonable or intellectually irresponsible to make the statement that physical existence is fully dependent on the possession of inimitable Identity.

AutoGenesism: A Theory of Everything

Now, the definitional effort moves from what it means to exist, to what it means to survive as an existent something. This gets a bit more complicated, but it does help further define what existence is as existential survival itself becomes more and more defined. Let's look at what can be lost by the existent something, and see if that tells us anything about the nature of existence.

When the quantum of action ceases to exist as a manifestation, it is replaced by the next quantum of action. That's easy enough, but if the meta-law is *"first, survive"*, then didn't that quantum of action give up pretty readily as it made way for the very next quantum of action's emergence? One might go so far as to suggest that *"first, survive"* was never even part of that simple action quantum manifestation/replacement process, let alone the meta-law that literally drives all that exists to do what it does and be what it is.

But, there's something that's ongoing within even the most primitive physical manifestations, and it's right there when the quantum of action is replaced by the next quantum of action as well; the pursuit of true existential survival, even if it takes a little clarification to recognize it in its most primordial expression. That survival is being pursued as each quantum emerges contextually defined by the historical precedent that is the prior manifestation of all previous quanta within the specific progression of action that features all associated action quanta as contributing units.

What the meta-law *"first, survive"* insists is that the Identity of the physically existent **IT** be preserved unless and until that Identity can no longer be preserved. At the most primitive levels of physical existence, this is accomplished by contextually entangled quanta (be they action, energy, or what-have-you) establishing defined holons [see Holon Theory for details] of any quantity of such quanta. Each additional quantum unit extends the Identity Survival of the initial quantum another 100% of the duration of its initial manifestation, since the Identity of each quantum within the unit collective [next higher level holon structure] contains the Identity of each previous quantum unit as Identity defining historical [internal] context.

It may, a first blush, come across like a semantics argument, but the truth is that physical Identity is a blend of internal and relative context, and if Identity is existence, then the persistence of Identity, regardless of the nature of that persistence, is the persistence of physical existence. If **ITs** Identity persists within the internal contextual composition of something that is maintaining its own physical existence (or is also persisting within the contextual composition of any number of similars within the holon structure that is itself persisting as physically present) then **IT** exists, and **IT** has (to that instant, at least) achieved Identity Survival and is serving the meta-law *"first, survive"*.

This is not to suggest that contextual Identity Survival is the only kind of survival that is ever pursued. Structural survival and material presence survival are also pursued, as is the preservation of unique and inimitable Identity for those existential wholes that are physically indestructible [information wholes and contextual environments]. Still, when there is a clash between any two or more versions of *"first, survive"*, Identity Survival will always trump all others, and this can be noted at all levels of physical existence and progressive development.

It's the acknowledgement of the existence of a meta-law, and the identification of that meta-law as being the pursuit of Identity Survival that forces AutoGenesism to be the ToE that it is.

Item #4: Time: In Proper Perspective

I hadn't realized that Time, as we intuitively experience it, makes no sense to anyone else who's ever tried to put one of these Theories of Everything together until I started digging into the two primary fields of science that deal with ToE issues; those being Physics and Cosmology. To be honest about it, I was pretty startled to discover that the basic views to emerge, as a result of what's been revealed over the last 100 years or so in both disciplines, have Time as either wildly subjective in nature and relative in structure to any of a wide variety of causal actors, or completely illusory and projected by the mind of each observer that is engaged in any defined system under observation. In other words, Time is not widely considered to be a primordial component of this or any other Environmental sub-structure; material or otherwise.

I see Time very differently, and the way that I view Time's role within the physical structure of Reality is not only a critical aspect of AutoGenesism as a ToE, but it's also very instructive concerning the logic train that gathered together as I developed Auto-G. It's therefore useful to quickly sketch out what I believe Time's true place within the existential structure is, why I perceive Time as I do, and how it is that I came to view Time as I view it.

As I laid out in Item #2, when all is said and done, Identity Survival is the driver that sets all subsequent requirements. This bottom line expression of the meta-law *"first, survive"* will always be the reason why something does what it

AutoGenesism: A Theory of Everything

does and why it ultimately is what it is. What's instructive here, concerning Time, is that even the physical establishment of Time itself (as the fundamental unifier that it obviously is) must be due directly to the *"first, survive"* meta-law dictate.

There's literally no other option, regardless of how elegant one's theory of Time might be. If that specific theory does not have Time's physical emergence occurring as the default result of primordial adherence to that specific meta-law, then that specific theory cannot be an accurate theory concerning the nature or physical structure of Time. As a result of my own devotion to preserving the universality of this meta-law, and to resisting any introduction of a new requirement that cannot be directly tied, by way of default ramification, to that meta-law's natural evolution as a requirement expression or emerging suite of expressions, I simply allowed Time to emerge on its own within the progressive development structure, and kept an eye out for it as it did so.

Of course, as I've established in Section II's Track#1 narrative, physical existence and the Relative Being State itself emerged as the originating series of Change/Event Units found their footing, and the resulting Contextual Environment [Reality] saw its own survival increasingly assured as each emerging Fact Set added nuance and complexity to Reality's inimitable Identity as the rapidly developing contextual relationship matrix that it is. It was *"That works, so do it again"*, permanently established as the meta-law's first-ever response-to-precedent expression, that set the existential table for the ongoing (and it's still ongoing) Change/Event Trajectory, as well as all subsequent versions of the C/ET's own successful survival strategies (the Change/Spatial Trajectory and its own suite of survival strategies, as well as the Dynamic Burst Set Trajectory and its own unique Identity Survival procreation process).

And, there's no point in denying the fact that the relentless basis of all this progressive development is and has always been the simple Change/Event Unit's drive to *"first, survive"* at all costs. That being true, it's also clear and hard to deny that the Change/Event Unit's quantized and indivisible Unit Rate of Change (since the C/E Unit is the primordial quantum of physical existence) is the perfect basis for Time as an inescapable progressing infrastructure upon which the whole of physical reality can then build and develop in complexity and Identity resilience.

I see no other theory of Time as being pure and devoid of indefensible logic schisms. In fact, it's almost as if this most inescapable and clearly present fact

325

of physical existence is specifically designed to clash directly with the way that science and modern reason has developed as tools to verify physical existence. This issue, for instance, the *Rate of Flow* dilemma, seems to suggest that unless all aspects of Time can be properly measured, it can't actually exist.

> "The concept of *"time passing"* can be considered to be internally inconsistent, by asking *"how much time goes by in an hour?"* The question, *"how fast does time pass"* seems to have no satisfactory answer, in which answers such as *"a second per second"* would be, as some would argue, circular and thus false. In addition, even if we do accept the above answer, then the statement *"a second per second"* can be expressed as a fraction which is always equal to 'one'. But this 'one' has no meaning beyond being a number and is thus also the wrong kind of answer. Therefore, the argument goes, the rate of the passage of time is nonsensical."
>
> **http://en.wikipedia.org/wiki/Block_universe#Rate_of_flow**

But, then, our inability to present Time as a stand-alone quantity might just be a clue concerning what Time actually is, or better stated, what it is not. Clearly, if the universe [Contextual Environment] is all there is, then the Rate of Flow dilemma certainly does present a serious problem with the notion that Time is actually anything at all, as opposed to simply the default impact on literally everything that comes into physical existence as a result of the pursuit of Reality's most primordial requirement.

My determination process has always embraced the simplest and least unlikely (as opposed to the most likely, an important distinction in many cases) explanation possible. And, as the inevitable ramification of one C/E Unit's replacing the last, across the whole of a quantized Contextual Environment, with one more synchronized quantum step forward (as each and every *Now* replaces the last) the actual role of Time is no more or less than the role of any other emergent property that is the default ramification of any one existent thing or another's *"first, survive"* effort. In this sense (relative to the thoughts and perceptions of any observer) while Time loses its *meaning*, it gains a more primordial significance as the one stable and reliable indication that Reality actually is the default result of the primordial existential quantum [the Change/Event Unit] and its dogged devotion to the meta-law that bases the existence of all laws and imperatives.

This explanation of Time is indicative of how I see the whole of Reality, and how I've worked to allow AutoGenesism to organically unfold as a common-sense Theory of Everything. Nothing simply is, and nothing exists as a result of anything other than a default reaction to the existence of a prior something, with that reaction serving to enable the Identity Survival of that prior something or a third prior something.

The C/ET and its immutable URC creates the Environment-unifying emerge/replace, change/event chain that we all experience as the *"Arrow of Time"* regardless of whether a philosophical or logical case can be presented to the contrary, and this resulting structure of before and after meets all my own established criteria as a natural and required physical manifestation. When realized in this manner, Time is simple, intuitively natural, and completely lacking in logical or empirical contradiction. And best of all, as an explanation, it presents Time as being related to the rest of Reality in exactly the manner that we've always known it to be, and without any extraneous philosophical or intellectual machinations to clear a space for its obvious existence.

Item #5: Information: Its Physical Nature and Role

There's no Theory of Everything that is as sweeping and as specific as AutoGenesism, and the reason why this is true comes down to how I view the nature of Information and its role in the emergence and progressive development of every system that comes together to create and define the whole of Reality as a physical system in its own right. In fact, of all that comes together to form the theoretical foundation of Auto-G, this seemingly unique view of Information as physical and primordial is what delineates this from every other effort to clarify what is real and reliable about Reality.

I've listed the physical existence of Information as #4 in this digression, not because it is any less integral to the emergence and progressive development of Reality than Items #1, #2 or #3. In fact, while the meta-law *"first survive"* presents all that's achieved physical existence with the requirement to pursue ongoing existence, it is the physical nature and role of Information that presents the means by which that universal survival imperative can be pursued. I've listed Information 4th because the physical emergence of Information is (like Time) a default ramification of cause and effect.

Like Time, Information simply is what it is, even if the existence of Information does manage the ongoing activity that creates and further defines what is real and permanently existent (again, as no more than a default ramification of the fact of its physical presence). And this is a real process that can be fully detailed and directly linked to traditional observations through deductive inference; not a claim that nudges this ToE toward the wilds of metaphysics.

The system-management influence of residual Fact Sets and the RFS continuums that they create isn't exactly an unknown quantity, even if modern science is loath to label it as such. That system precedent exists, and is progressively determinant, isn't all that controversial, although it does depend a lot on the specific scientific discipline, and the kinds of systems under examination. Genetics, for example, embraces the existence of system-determinant Information sets, even if the work focuses on the initial material impact of that Information as opposed to the physical nature of the Information itself.

Still, deductive inference can teach us a lot about the nature of Information, even if present research is confined to the examination of those material holons that react to the precise dictates that (to date) have only been tracked back to seemingly conscious (and inordinately brilliant) protein initiators. Of course, assigning consciousness, or even rote deliberation to proteins does smack of metaphysics, regardless of how you phrase your assertion, and no amount of observation interpretation can resolve the mystery of organic processes unless the physical existence of residual Fact Sets is allowed to rescue you from a materialistically imposed infinite regression.

The truth is that genetics makes the best case for both system precedent and the physical existence of a residual Fact Set informational structure. The inference is inescapable. If DNA information (or any source of information, for that matter) is capable of directly affecting the structural development and fundamental survival dictates of a material manifestation (which is what any organism is) then it must share a physical basis with that material manifestation. This is how Reality works, and even if we can't observe the nature of that physical commonality or measure it with our senses and our technology, the fact of system precedent and historical context is proof enough of the presence of some form of organizational influence. Unless, of course, one embraces the unlikely notion of intelligent, self-interested proteins.

We do know that genetically inherited residual Fact Sets, regardless of how they physically relate to the double helix strands of material DNA we've learned to isolate and manipulate, lay the developmental foundation for all living organisms during gestation. We also know that once fully gestated, this same suite of very specific residual Fact Sets continues to exist as the literal center of survival management for each viable organism until that organism has lived out its entire lifespan. This isn't a matter of controversy, and yet the existence of information as a physical manifestation is still widely dismissed as metaphysics.

Each cell in the body has proven to carry on an absolutely astonishing level of focused, deliberate, and efficient activity without any perceivable means of dynamic coordination or even central control. A skin cells knows to perform the function of a skin cell. A brain cell knows to perform the function of a brain cell. This isn't controversial stuff, and yet the suggestion that information exists as a reactive, responsive physical initiator to what can be observed and measured to be precise and meaningful activity is ultimately a step that science is incapable of taking.

Of course, there are those fringes that do exist within any community, and the scientific community is no different. But, even so, the absolute fringes of physics (as close as it comes to acknowledging the role of information as a physical participant in the progressive development of so much ultra-sophisticated material structure and dynamic capacity) seems incapable of allowing for the existence of residual Fact Sets and RFS Continuums. It does come pretty close though.

After a lot of searching, I did run across a theoretical perspective that sort of agrees with my own view of the role and impact of information on environments and the systems that exist within them. Actually, it's a combination of two theories, but it is a combination that is often made when this question of system response and/or development is raised. What I'm most surprised about is that this suite of theoretical perspectives hasn't become a lot more axiomatic. After all, the evidence is overwhelming, even if the technical specifics (as presented by each approach, relative to the mechanics of how information does what it does) are a bit tortured. Here's how these two approaches to resolving the issue of uncertainty and Quantum Mechanics align with my own view of Information.

In Section I, I go to great lengths to describe the Internal [historical] Context that provides unique intrinsic Identity to the 1st C# note played by a violinist in an analogy that features a concert performance. This very specific view of the impact of Information on the definitional relationship between a system [that C# note] and the environment that contains it [the rest of Reality] is somewhat acknowledged within a theoretical approach known as *"historical consistency"*. Pioneered by Robert Griffiths [Carnegie Mellon University, Pittsburgh] to specifically address the mysterious nature of Quantum Mechanics, historical consistency presents the chronology of a system as being determinant; limiting the possible arrangements that the system can then take to only those that make any logical sense with what's already occurred to and within that system.

Following that lengthy C# note analogy in Section I, I present a second analogy involving two company coworkers and a surprise encounter in Germany whilst on vacation. This analogy describes the impact and ongoing development of Relative Context, and the dynamic nature of relationships between systems existing within a shared environment that emerge as a result of that context. This view is somewhat acknowledged within a theory known as *"quantum decoherence"*. This approach suggests that an environment is physically affected by the existence of a system that exists within it, and that each interaction between that system and that environment results in the exchange of information bits concerning the relative location of that system within that environment.

Quantum decoherence is a notion that's always been loitering around the topic of Quantum Mechanics, but it took a 1985 paper by Erich Joos and H. Dieter Zeh (describing how an object achieves a distinct location naturally as a direct result of interaction with the environment that contains it) for the approach to resurface as a modern consideration. Subsequent efforts by others (most notably by physicist Wojciech Zurek) have further developed quantum decoherence as featuring photon and other particle interactions, freezing larger systems in place (eliminating all superpositional possibilities) in spite of the absence of observers.

It's notable that these two basic approaches are often associated as a system impacting tag-team in the same manner that I present Internal and Relative Context as informational determinants. Where the differences exist are in the mechanics of how a system and/or environment is affected, the physical role of Information as a party to that process, and the impetus behind any system's specific response of any sort whatsoever. I see Information as a physically existent quantity that emerges as a result of change, activity, or material manifestation, but that statement is going to require further elaboration.

In fact, the way that I define Information restricts my use of the term itself. Unlike many who work with Information as integral to their own theories, I cannot use the term to describe a property set of a material manifestation, a contextual confluence, the impact of one system upon another, or the recorded data that preserves or shares the specifics of such identifying delineators. As I view the physical nature of Information, it does not present as a wave or a particle. It

AutoGenesism: A Theory of Everything

doesn't fall into entropic ruin when the system that it defines has finally run its course. It's not stored within the material structure as a form of energy, and it doesn't have anything to do with heat transfer. In short, I do not believe Information to exist as physically compatible with material manifestations. I know material existence to be based on change [activity], and I know Information (in the form of residual Fact Sets) to be the primordial response to each unit of change [activity], and a default emergence with its own unique property set that defies direct observation as it serves the ID Survival pursuit of Reality itself.

If the assertion that Information exists as a nonmaterial, yet otherwise mundane and fully physical, constituent that is integral (along with all that is material and therefore scientifically observable) to the full and functional structure of Reality means that the modern scientific community is forced to then consider this definition of Information as metaphysics, and therefore dismiss this entire AutoGenesism notion out of hand, then so be it. The real of Reality is what it is. At some point it has to be acknowledged that human science is led forward by the evidence if that evidence can be shown to be pervasive; even if it means that the definition of physically existent must be broadened to allow for what's become evident.

In Tom Siegfried's *"The Bit and the Pendulum: From Quantum Computing to M Theory — The New Physics of Information"*, he chats with a variety of individuals who were (in the late 1990s) at the leading edge of trying to determine information's place in Reality. The realization is a little slow in emerging, but after a while, it becomes clear that while you can talk around the omnipresence of a progressively emergent precedent *"scorecard"* of some sort [defining system character and behavior at all levels from Quantum Mechanics to the Universe as a defined macro-system in its own right] if you insist on restricting the nature of Information to bits of data that act and react like particle collectives that add to and subtract from a computational definition of an object until they cease to exist as definable summations, then you eventually arrive at a point where your system development and behavioral assumptions (while firmly based on reliable and repeatable data) are no more than "Just So" stories. Not that your assumptions are wrong, but that you've leaped over the part where you work out exactly why your assumptions are right as you move forward to focus on how to effectively control the system under scrutiny.

"There are huge regions of spacetime and many probability tracks where there aren't any observers," (Murray) Gell-Mann noted. "For example early in the universe there certainly weren't any. But gradually as quasi-classical variables emerge from the quantum fog, at least along certain probability tracks, you begin to get enough regularity so that something could evolve that exploits this regularity in its environment."

Tom Siegfried ~ The Bit and the Pendulum: From Quantum Computing to M Theory — The New Physics of Information

Probability tracks? Quasiclassical variables emerging from the quantum fog? I understand the cultural reluctance to acknowledging nonmaterial existence, but science has imposed a false equivalence between the legitimacy of nonmaterial physical information and the kinds of baseless assertions that present Reality in terms of myths, legends, and modern reconfigurations that seek to blur what edges still exist between that sort of stuff and what can be proven to be real.

Information, like Time, is nothing more than a default ramification that becomes part of the existential landscape of Reality as yet another C/E Unit replaces the last C/E Unit within any one of countless C/E Trajectories, and it doesn't get any simpler than that. The difference is that while the ubiquitous synchronicity of Time exposes the sub-structural contextual commonality that Reality itself is based on (the Environmental URC), the contextual relationship matrix that is Reality itself is informational; a web of residual Fact Sets (RFS) and RFS continuums, with the inimitable Identity of Reality (as the full Contextual Environment that it is) defined by the nature of those informational wholes (individually and collectively) and the historical and evolving relationship that exists between those RFS and RFS continuums.

Again, the role itself is just as simple and primitive as it can get, and yet, as you'll see, the impact of information (in the form of RFS and RFS continuums) on the whole of Reality relative to the meta-law *"first, survive"* extends from the most primordial to the most ultra-sophisticated expressions of progressive development, and within any and all inclusive reality confines. And, this is what I want to clarify here, since what we're discussing is how and why I came to the conclusions I came to concerning the true nature of Reality.

The Identity of the existent **IT** is defined by the precise blend of Relative Context [**ITs** present and emerging physical relationship with the entire rest of Reality itself] and Internal Context [the history of **ITs** physical relationship with the rest of Reality] that **IT** possesses, and it is this blend of contextual specifics that (when its material structure has failed) persists as the environmental presence of the existent **IT**. This is what constitutes **ITs** Identity Survival, and while the concept might be counterintuitive to the materially persisting Homo Sapiens brain as it generates its emerging nonmaterial mind, that material brain's lone survival strategy is based on exactly that counterintuitive Identity Survival concept; even as its mind [that survival strategy itself] rejects the notion out-of-hand.

Context is *earned* as the existent **IT** does (or is) whatever **IT** does (or is) during its own material manifestation phase of existence, and that context persists as residual Fact Set representations of the actual occurrences and/or relationships that defined that material **ITs** span of existence. What this means is that although an occurrence and/or relationship no longer materially exists, the contextual ramification of that occurrence and/or relationship will always exist to represent the net impact of the existent **ITs** material presence within the entire Contextual Environment due to the permanent physical nature of each residual Fact Set that emerged when each occurrence related to **ITs** presence happened or each resulting relationship became actual.

During **ITs** entire span of material manifestation, residual Fact Sets continue to emerge at the Environmental Unit Rate of Change, since the materially existent **IT** physically consists of C/E Units (regardless of the specific structural configuration it features) that replaced one another at that same URC. Yes, these are extremely dense levels of physical emergence, but it's all an extremely simple, repetitive rote response that could not be more primitive. Again, the simplest and most primordial of processes, just as you'd expect from a quality Theory of Everything.

The obvious result is the material **ITs** development of a unique and inimitable Identity, as each contextual specific blends with all previous contextual specifics to create a literal slurry of Identity defining contextual constituents. This blend physically isolates the existent **IT** as individual, establishing it as an identifiable holon within whatever larger inclusive holon (or holons) its physical existence contributes to. And this fact (its holon relationship within whatever hierarchical structure it is that contains it) is also represented by residual Fact Sets within the Contextual Environment, further defining the Identity of the existent **IT** by increasing the density of ongoing Relative Context that is literally 1/2 of **ITs** blend of identifying specifics, as well as further ensuring the Identity Survival of the Contextual Environment by increasing that Environment's contextual density.

Less obvious is the fact that as Identity Survival is pursued by the existent **IT**, each RFS and RFS continuum that emerges further cements the precise nature of the laws and property specifics that will govern all subsequent changes and activities to occur within the Contextual Environment. In fact, this is the means by which the meta-law *"first, survive"* sets the basis for all subsequent laws. As each existing **IT** wins and loses its battles within the material realm, each success/failure precedent is factually preserved within the RFS matrix. This ever-increasing web of evidence combines with the universal survival requirement itself to affect ongoing activities and progressive development processes. This matrix IS the physical Contextual Environment, and as factual precedents are established and further defined, all subsequent laws and requirements emerge to assure that change and activity contribute to the survivability of the Contextual Environment's inimitable Identity. Yes, this is where the *"fine tuning"* of our Universe occurs. Another intractable mystery resolved.

The very specific physical nature and role of Information — while completely passive and no more than a default ramification of the truth that if something happens or changes, then the fact that it happened or changed emerges and persists — is yet another factor that forces AutoGenesism to be the very specific Theory of Everything that it is.

Item #6 - The Inapplicability of Math to Any ToE

This critical requirement of a plausible ToE should be much less controversial than it is, but for whatever reason, mathematical formulas have defined this topic since the day it found its way out of the theology department and into the relative wilds of the secular scientific wing. Maybe, as Professor Lee Smolin suggests, our knee-jerk deference to math in this specific case has to do with something that is based more on culture than on anything else.

> "Our desire for transcendence is at root a religious aspiration. The yearning to be liberated from death and from the pains and limitations of our lives is the fuel of religions and mysticism. Does the seeking of mathematical knowledge make one a priest, with special access to an extraordinary form of knowledge? Should we simply recognize mathematics for the religious activity that it is?"
>
> **Lee Smolin: Time Reborn: From the Crisis in Physics to the Future of the Universe.**

Of course, Prof. Smolin properly predicates that statement with a detailed examination of the pristine and esthetically pure (perhaps resembling a divine) nature of mathematics. And this is pretty much how I've always seen the practice of math, and its relevance to how it actually goes when dealing with reality; with mathematics as an adventure one can have within a perfect and predictable world; the kind of imaginary world where the messiness inherent when dealing with the presence of incalculable layers of historical context and precedent is not available to gunk up the elegance of how things maybe should work. And that, as opposed to the sort of world we all live in, where what's true has been true long enough to impose itself on whatever it is that you wish could just be different, maybe more immediately logical, every now and then.

That any Theory of Everything, which is a theory concerning how everything actually works, could ever make sense with mathematics (which is logically based on a perfect world that doesn't have much at all in common with reality itself) is itself a logical schism that should have been obvious to anyone who's ever taken more than a few minutes to consider the point of such a theory. It almost seems as if it should be unnecessary to make such an observation, but for whatever reason there is for such an extreme intellectual dichotomy to exist and clearly persist, the fact is that it does.

It's also a fact that Auto-G will be criticized for its absence of formulas and mathematical equations. That being the case, maybe it'd be best to use such an equation to illustrate my point concerning the inappropriateness of formula balancing as the proof basis of any ToE. Here's a very simple logical equation statement.

A+B=C
therefore
C-B=A

Clean, simple, and easy to see that, on the face of it, it is true. Now, let's apply a little reality to this statement, by having the letters factually represent actual physical items, and see if it holds up as being true.

Chocolate + Coffee = Mocha
therefore
Mocha — Coffee = Chocolate

I suppose that you could insist that in the abstract, this statement is true, but in reality (at least in the reality that we all share and contribute to) this statement is ludicrous. This is because we all know that if you mix Coffee and Chocolate together to create the liquid solution that is Mocha, there's no means of un-mixing such miscible solutions to, in this case, extract the Chocolate from the Coffee or vice versa. In the real world that actually exists, the statement "A + B = C therefore C — B = A" (depending on what you have each letter represent as actual physical items), may end up being not only false, but ridiculously so.

Of course, you could probably find immiscible physical items to assign those letters to in an effort to allow the statement to remain true, but the blended "C" item would not actually be a true blend in that case (and besides, the true mathematical purity of the statement has already been destroyed since it can be set up to fail, regardless of what you do to try and salvage it) and this is the problem with trying to explain physical reality with nonphysical mathematical formulas and equations. To make the predictions of such statements come true, you end up having to invent artificial realities and severely isolate them from the rest of what's real. That completely renders irrelevant the entire point of any ToE that is based on such proofing efforts if such a ToE is meant to explain the true nature of what's real.

My effort to understand the basis of physical reality has never considered the impact of formula math on what I might determine, since such pristine and context-free math has no actual alignment with the nature of Reality itself. Reality is buried in incalculable densities of historical and interconnecting contextual contamination, and the best we can do is allow reality to show us how it has developed as a result of all that contamination, and to then figure out why it developed as it did.

This is why I based Auto-G on the most primitive staples and avoided Inductivism at all costs. It's always been about working with the fundamental defaults and the primordial meta-law that bases those defaults. And if anyone can create an $E=MC^2$-style formula that will work in all possible situations, then give that person a Nobel Prize for figuring out how to encapsulate what will have to be the hardest working formula to ever exist. Not a Nobel in Physics, but a Nobel in Literature for excellence in descriptive communication.

As for me, I'm going to never worry about the language I use to describe the basics of physical reality. Words work just fine, and when they stumble, I'll draw a picture to help them out. I'm not restricted by any specific method of communication. Hell, if it takes hand signals or interpretive dance, then I'll be there to make sure that what's real is communicated to the full extent of my own capabilities, and to hell with anyone else's arcane elocutionary requirements. Physics Math just won't cut it for explaining or proofing a true and fully functional Theory of Everything, and for the simple reason that *Everything* includes a lot more than physics. AutoGenesism isn't a theory of 1s and 0s, and what it

AutoGenesism: A Theory of Everything

states concerning the nature and structure of physical Reality can't be represented by numbers, symbols, or cleverly balanced equations. Auto-G is a description of Reality, and its acknowledgement of just how relentlessly dirty Reality is, forces it to be the ToE that it is.

And, So . . .

So, there you have it. You can agree with it or you can dismiss it, but you can't suggest that I simply or recklessly grabbed at the concepts and notions that base Auto-G or cherry-picked a few established ToE staples and reapplied them with new labels and new marketing literature. AutoGenesism didn't start out as a Theory of Everything. It started out as my own effort to better understand the actual nature of the human being, and why it clashes so profoundly with the rest of what has been declared to be the nature of Reality as a whole. Obviously, it didn't remain limited to the nature of the human being, and the reason it didn't was because it quickly became obvious that there was literally no way to logically explain the physical existence of the human being within the established paradigm that hosts the most widely embraced theories concerning the nature of Reality itself.

It took tracing the forensic evidence that's piled up everywhere backward toward the physical initiation of all existence, yet without accepting any established axioms or dismissing any of them out-of-hand either, as I headed back toward the point of existential genesis. It also took extreme discipline when connecting the empirical and inferential dots, and not allowing any flashes of intuition to supersede the grinding work that is deductive reasoning and logical verification.

And throughout all of this effort, I remained dedicated to keeping the basis ridiculously simple and primitive, and to always follow the design axiom that requires the reuse of available parts whenever possible. They call it designing for part reduction, and if I've learned one thing, it's that Reality is as efficient as one could ever imagine anything being. Three unique *parts* and the devotion to scalable reapplication, and look at what you've got. Even now, I am floored when I stretch it all out before me and look at how brilliantly it falls together without a single conscious intent existing to muck things up as it does.

Kevin Brian Carroll

Digression

Contextual Precedent
and the Mechanics
of Progressive Development

If ever there was a moment to step out and isolate an extended explanation, this would qualify as that moment. Not that the concept of "stuff happens, so the fact that *'stuff happens'* happens" is all that hard to get your head around. In fact, that's pretty easy to manage just as long as you're not in rigid denial of the existence of information. But then, if you are, then this entire AutoGenesism premise is a complete waste of your time, and you wouldn't be reading this digression, so I'll be assuming that as far as you're concerned the existence of residual Fact Sets is not in question.

If you've got any level of acceptance concerning science in general, then I'll also assume that you're comfortable with the concept of Nature allowing repetition of those processes and systems that have succeeded, while not allowing those that have failed to become established as ongoing efforts (as thoroughly noted in evolutionary biology). Again, if this is not how you see Reality working at a fundamental level, then this is not a digression that will serve you, since there are basics that I'm assuming to be firmly in place as I begin this specific examination. The reason for this is that this is an examination of how progressive development occurs as a result of Contextual Precedent and the residual Fact Sets that establish it and enforce its influence within the URC-Determined Environmental Confine.

Now, fitting these two basics together to come up with what we've got sitting all around us (not to mention the obvious existence of us as well) without inventing a mind capable of establishing and controlling the whole progressive development process is where the difficulty lies. In fact, it's really hard to detail how it all can happen if you refuse to pop a god of some kind into the system. The speed bump? Time.

Actually, it's the technical aspects of how such an empirically established concept [system management via contextual precedent] fits into the much more empirically established concept of *"Time's Arrow"*, without crashing it by suggesting that Time runs in both directions when it come to the net impact that each *fact that 'stuff happens'* actually has on stuff that hasn't even happened yet. Believe me, as simple and obvious as it might appear at first blush, this Time's Arrow versus precedent/ramification issue is anything but simple regardless of how obvious it might be that both concepts work in complete harmony within all naturally evolving systems.

In Rupert Sheldrake's latest book, *"Science Set Free: 10 Paths to New Discovery"*, he expounds on his hypothesis *Morphic Resonance*; concerning the formulation of system *"habits"* that evolve as a result of patterns of activity within any defined system. It was here where I learned just how tortured the physics of Time versus progressive development can actually become, and where I learned that one cannot simply assume that what might seem obvious can be just as simply declared to be self-evident.

I don't embrace Sheldrake's notion that each evolving system possesses a capacity for its own *"memory resonance"* (regardless of the mathematics concerning how such resonance might theoretically be achieved) that can then *"reach back in time"* to affect that system's ongoing development, but I do embrace the notion that all progressive development is based on a default imposition of *success* as defined by Contextual Precedent, and that the specifics should be explained concerning how such an imposition is achieved. I had hoped to introduce a conceptual framework for my own explanation of how progressive development is managed by Contextual Precedent within a brief digression at a point during Section I's introduction of the relationship between residual Fact Sets and the Contextual Environment, with the plan being to further develop the minutiae within that explanation as Section I's overall presentation progressed. However, as you'll see, a brief digression on this topic wasn't possible, so I ended up placing the entire digression here in Section III.

AutoGenesism: A Theory of Everything

Time as a Dimensional Isolate

I suppose that the first thing to establish is that, as previously stated, I agree that Time is a full physical dimension in its own right; the 4th such physical dimension, with the other three being spatial. This is the standard view of the world that is shared by most scientific disciplines; Theoretical Physics being unique in its rejection of the traditional 3-D world on the basis of issues that String Theory and M Theory (whatever that actually is) have with such restrictions. What I want to suggest is that Time, as a full dimension, is even more physically isolated when compared to either, or all, of the other three dimensions than some might assume to be the case, and that this profound property distinction directly contributes to the capacity for organizational development that defines the 3-D Material Realm.

> *Note* — In *"Our Emergent Universe: How the Change/Event Became Spatial"*, I detail exactly how Time brought kinetic energy, movement, and ultimately space and proximity, into physical existence. If you have not read that digression yet, you might want to do so if the notion of Time's existential primacy is going to be a problem for you. The most difficult aspect of this entire AutoGenesism notion is that it is so comprehensive, while completely upending so much that's become axiomatic, that it requires the establishment of large, fundamental Reality redefinitions before other equally large and fundamental Reality redefinitions can be addressed and thereby established. That said, there's no possible way to avoid that intellectual dilemma, and one must simply compartmentalize as one makes one's way through the whole of it all without misplacing anything that's become settled as one does.

Length, width, and height — the three spatial dimensions (yes, I realize that it's all much more complicated than this) — are the dynamic, malleable products of ongoing activity, and activity occurs within the progression of Time. The length, width, and height of a three dimensional system can increase and/or decrease over time within a given environment, but as it does, each quantum of Now (the unitary basis of Time) brings residual Fact Sets into physical existence (they actually emerge as a default ramification — something happens, the fact that something happened *'happens'*).

These residual Fact Sets never cease to exist [they ensure the ID Survival of the macro-system, but the bottom line is if it happened, it cannot un-happen, leaving the fact that it happened permanently existent], so they *collect* and a relationship matrix emerges between all of these permanent residual Fact Sets as they each represent changes and occurrences that happened within the macro-system over Time. Yes, it gets pretty densely packed after a while, and that's the point.

The Identity Survival of the macro-system that we'll refer to as Reality (you can think of it as our Universe if you wish) is and must be served by all that exists as part of it. Identity Survival is the only true imperative that exists, with all other requirements based on its fundamental demand that what exists must persist until it cannot. Successful progressive development, and the increase in system complexity that such development guarantees, is how Reality's own Identity Survival is ensured. This requires that sub-system success be repeated and that failure be noted within the residual Fact Set relationship matrix and avoided. We know this strategy as The Laws of Nature, Natural Selection, and The Laws of Physics.

As each residual Fact Set, and each relationship between permanent residual Fact Sets, emerges and further cements the definition of system success, the range of available change options becomes increasingly defined and restricted within that system. We observe this as material systems possessing specific properties and behavioral predilections. At the subatomic level we observe that each class of particles has a defined size, mass, and charge, with some possessing a defined spin or other characteristic. At the cosmological level, we observe diameters, spatial proximities, mass/gravity relationships, and velocities that adhere strictly to established rules and protocols. The existence of system structure is only questioned by the most radical theorists, and in the face of overwhelming evidence.

To help in my own intellectual grasp of how each sub-system's ongoing change trajectory moves through Reality's own developmental progression I envision all change within the macro-system that is Reality as a thin line aggressively attacking from the left of a precisely defined battlefield as Reality's own definitional specificity (the result of more and more success-versus-failure precedent emerging as representational residual Fact Sets and residual Fact Set relationships) steadily fills in the possible open space within that battlefield, further restricting how that thin line can progress as each change occurs.

As the diagram (Figure 3-E) illustrates, this growing mass of residual Fact Sets has the net impact of moving that quantized line of change trajectories in the opposite direction [here, I visualize an ever-growing mass meeting that thin line's attack from the right of the same battlefield, and pushing that point of interaction steadily to the left as that mass grows larger with each quantum of

Now], increasing the truth that the range of ongoing change options that can occur within that macro-system will become more and more restricted over time.

The Battle Line of System Evolution

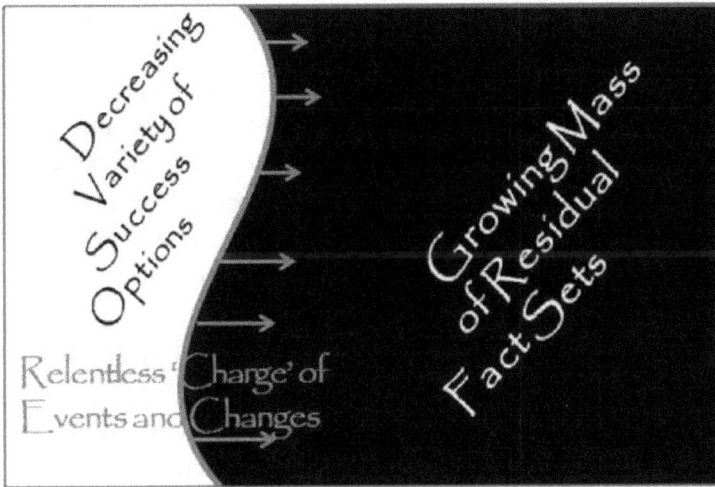

Figure 3-E

Now this is not to suggest that Contextual Precedent [that enormous dark mass of residual Fact Sets that's pushing back against the thin gray line of change that's moving from left to right across that otherwise white battlefield in Figure 3-E above] is reaching back from the future into the past to affect ongoing change, and it's important that I make it clear that I am NOT suggesting such a thing. Time only moves in one direction, and change moves through Time in only one direction, in spite of the opinions of some that Quantum Mechanics suggests that change is theoretically free to move in any causal direction it sees fit.

All system development forces [all dynamic Change/Event Trajectories as well as the passive, default ramification of the increasingly restricted freedom of available options for change — as ongoing change defines that system via Contextual Precedent] move through Time in the same direction. How they engage one another within the course of each system's own lifespan [a Change/Event Trajectory in its own right] can cause an observer to view that engagement as evidence of a dynamic time reversal, but that's just an erroneous observation interpretation since a bi-directional arrow of time would necessarily present many other indications; most would be very obvious, and some pretty spectacular.

Getting Specific Through System Definition

A system's specificity is produced and developed by gathering residual Fact Sets, with each emerging to represent the contextual impact of each Change/Event Unit within that system as one quantum unit of Now replaces the last quantum unit of Now. Each residual Fact Set permanently preserves the Contextual Precedent that a unit of change presented to the contextual balance as a whole, and as each new Change/Event Unit occurs (keep in mind that each Change/Event Unit, while existing within its own ongoing trajectory, concurrently affects the system in quantized lockstep with an uncountable quantity of other Change/Event Units that also exist within their own ongoing trajectories) it's sort of like the way that the physical activity of painting a wall decreases the area of wall that's left to be painted with each brush stroke.

The act of applying the paint lasts only as long as it takes to apply the paint, but the coat of paint itself persists. In this sense, the factual impact of Contextual Precedent persists long after the occurrence and/or change that caused an adjustment in the system's overall contextual Identity to become a fact.

As to how this relates to the development of the kinds of systems that define the Material Realm, since the Change/Spatial Trajectory serves as an Identity Survival strategy of the more primordial Change/Event Trajectory (ultimately producing Reality's three dimensional material structure) the three spatial dimensions are no more than fleetingly temporary physical manifestations of environmental/contextual change within a given universal system. They happen from Now until Now is completed, and then they happen again, but only for the next quantized duration of Now. The only persistent real is the full, factual ramification of each *Now*, preserved by a residual Fact Set that will never cease to exist.

This means that the progressive change momentum of our three spatial dimensions is physically (if passively) challenged by the increasing specificity of system-defining residual Fact Set continuums, but the advancement of both are directionally locked into a shared arrow of Time that neither can break free of. The future doesn't reach back and manage the development of the emerging present; field resonance or no field resonance. It is the physical existence and system impact of residual Fact Sets, Fact Set continuums, and the constantly developing relationships between residual Fact Sets and Fact Set continuums (serving the primordial Identity Survival requirement of the macro-system) that provides a default defiance against potentially destructive cancerous growth activity, as Time's wide variety of Change/Event Trajectories trudge on in mindless deference to the same Identity Survival imperative that drives everything forward.

And So . . .

A lot has been made of a few highly prepared artificial systems that, when treated in a very specific manner, have yielded result indications that suggest that Time is inherently malleable, or even that Time is an illusion that the human mind has imposed on Reality as a whole. Yes, these indications can be very intriguing, but when one looks at such indications, the totality of the rest of Reality must be included within that examination, along with the impact of such a possibility (that Time is bidirectional or perhaps even nonexistent) on what's obvious and essential about Reality and all that exists within Reality's relationship matrix.

After all, if Time isn't sequential or unidirectional, then it's never been sequential or unidirectional. And if that's true, then why is everything else (other than those experimental results indications) progressing in lockstep along a sequential and unidirectional progression of Time?

If you insist that this is a result of the difference between Quantum Mechanics and the rest of how Reality operates, then you need to provide the line of system demarcation that prevents larger sub-systems from breaking free of Time's resilient lockstep, and where that line of demarcation exists between these two extremely incompatible forms of system structure. Obviously, larger systems can't defy Time's imposition of definite and disciplined *now and then*. If quantum systems can, then the demarcation between those systems and all other systems must exist and be determinable.

So, what can explain such counterintuitive indications? Well, a look at the true nature of observation is a good place to start whenever paradigm-altering indications are observed.

Observation has its value, but only if it is applied in deference to established facts concerning what is and what can possibly be real. When dealing with Time's Arrow, the overwhelming nature of Time and its unidirectional impact on Reality as a macro-system flirts with omnipresence, and that must be seriously considered when an experimental indication suddenly pops up to challenge Time's unidirectional impact on the rest of what clearly exists (including the fact that the experiment in question also existed as ensconced within that unidirectional progression of Time).

It's probably best to understand that while observation can be perceived (and therefore experienced) as Reality, Reality (and Time as its most primordial fundamental) cannot be projected by the observer. Nor can Reality be fundamentally redefined as incompatible with what's already become overwhelmingly obvious if that redefinition is due solely to any number of extremely isolated and finite experimental indications. Even as the observer observes what exists within Reality, the observer also exists within Reality, and must always include Reality's impact upon the act of observation. This includes the potential for larger system dynamics that the observer has had no prior experience with or previous knowledge of.

The bottom line here is that there is no observation that is capable of determining what's truly and fully real, since the observer cannot be separated from the macro-system under examination. Only through intellectual abstraction and a rigid adherence to disciplined inference concerning what can be proven as universally reliable can the nature of Reality ever be known.

Our Emergent Universe:
How the Change/Event Became Spatial

Regardless of the approach you take, if what you're trying to establish is a plausible hypothesis that details the uninterrupted progressive development chain that started with the genesis of physical existence and worked its way naturally to where the whole of Reality features all that sits right there before us, there are specific transition points that you're going to have to spend time and effort on. That means diving into detail, and getting really specific about your theories associated with these critical transitions.

Since AutoGenesism is primarily focused on the earliest stages of progressive development, and how those primordial drivers and qualifiers set the existential table for higher level rinse-repeat developmental progress, the real key is to fully flesh out how Reality makes its way from the simple Change/Event Trajectory to the kind of trajectory that material existence is based on; the Change/Spatial Trajectory. And to do it without any sleight of hand or reinvention of what constitutes physical Reality — like adding dimensions and other stuff like that.

What is so special about the Change/Spatial Trajectory, and what's all that about material existence [particles and energy fields] being based on spatial change? In the off-chance that you've stumbled upon this digression without the benefit of having read and understood Sections I and II, I'll briefly overview the true structural nature of matter's building block; the particle. In the interest to keeping this digression from falling prey to further digression, I'll be specific and keep my focus as elementary as possible as I do this.

Of all true particles, the Quark is widely considered to be the most elemental. Let's bullet point a description of any one from a family of Quarks

347

[doesn't matter which family we choose] and describe it as it is, and not as it's perceived and/or measured by an observer with a super-collider.

This Quark:

- Exists within the arc of a Change/Event Trajectory
- Consists of a relative density of entangled Change/Spatial Trajectories (each of which exists within an arc of an individual Change/Event Trajectory)
- Features a trajectory entanglement that is based on each spatial [Change/Event] trajectory serving as holons that are contextually associated (as a result of how they were formed) in a manner that provides the apical holon structure [the Quark itself] its full contextual identity, and thereby its own physical existence.

And there you have the physical structure of a Quark; any Quark.

> ***Note*** — In Section I, I fully explain the reason why these Change/Spatial Trajectories have become entangled [massing with a specific density] but for the sake of this quick overview, I'll simply state that each trajectory holon extends its own Identity Survival by becoming integral to the internal [historical] context that defines and provides Identity to the Quark as the apical holon that it is. Simple Identity Survival; the impetus for all that occurs and develops.

So, with entangled Change/Spatial Trajectories comprising the material structure of the Quark, it's important that we deal with the emergence of the Change/Spatial Trajectory, since everything that is comprised of Quarks is ultimately constructed of entangled Change/Spatial Trajectories. And if we want to connect the true quantum of material existence [the Change/Event Unit] to the Change/Spatial Trajectory, we'll need to go through the kinetic energy field (arguably the most primordial of all potential energy fields) to get there. And this is exactly what we're going to do.

Fields, Energies, and Mass

The build-up of force in any system is called potential energy, but what does this actually mean? What's true about any force potential is that to create it, there must be a requirement that is introduced into whatever system it is that will ultimately contain this force potential. As to what the nature of this requirement must be, it's fairly wide open. It can be as primitive as an object that's been lifted off the ground to create the gravitational requirement that it travel back to the ground again. It can be more highly developed. Perhaps an isolated electrical current that is naturally required (once inductively established) to complete its flow to ground. Whatever it is, it is the requirement that has been introduced that creates that energy potential, and it's just that simple.

Physicists refer to this existing requirement as a vector field of force or a force field, and it can get pretty confusing if you think of these fields as being anything that's material in nature; an elemental slurry perhaps. This can be especially troublesome when you're dealing with extremely primitive, or even primordial, development systems. In fact, if you run a process back far enough you will necessarily leave all forms of matter (as well as matter in general) in your wake. You'll be examining forms of physical existence that set the stage for fermions, bosons, quarks, particles, and all that stuff to then collect on the plates of theoretical physicists. As we start in this segment, this is what we'll be working with to establish the first field (an existing requirement) that produced a recognizable form of energy.

The primordial form of energy is kinetic energy. Well, there is potential energy, but once set into action, it becomes kinetic energy. Kinetic energy is simple movement. All other forms of energy are based on kinetic energy, with the specifics concerning what it is that is moving or why it's in movement that determines the form of energy [e.g., electrical energy is the movement of free electrons, and gravitational energy is released when you drop a rock]. The release of that potential energy causes acceleration (force) and the resistance against that acceleration is called mass. Mass achieves increasing density [moving toward a resting state — matter] as it triumphs over energy within a specific system. And that's pretty much what is known about both kinetic energy and mass.

To be fair, there's a lot that's been determined about how to predict and determine and even control the gathering potential and rate of kinetic energy release within a closed system, as well as how to calculate the amount of mass that exists within an object that is under assault by the force of an energy release. But, the actual physical nature of energy and mass, as well as the physical substructure of matter [the literal offspring of this relationship between kinetic energy and mass] is still pretty mysterious within the professional confines of physics and related fields of science.

So what can be suggested about the true quantum of physical existence [the Change/Event Unit] and this specific ongoing relationship mystery that sits directly beneath everything that we know to exist as material, and therefore physically tangible, within our own universe? Actually, it's pretty compelling, but as I did when discussing the possibility that 3-D spatial place-holding residual Fact Sets are what scientists have termed *dark matter*, I was originally going to present this examination as a Speculation Alert so that I wouldn't be declaring something that — frankly — no one is going to be able to validate or falsify at this stage of our actual capacity for either. Then I realized that not only is my logic rock solid and every inference responsibly leveraged, there aren't any actual competing theories that exist if falsifiability via experimentation is the minimum requirement for theories. The truth is that there's no such thing as valid experimental falsifiability concerning this pre-material level of progressive development. Still, that shouldn't mean that examination of pre-material developmental processes are to be considered off limits, so I decided to present it without any apologies.

The bitch was that this extremely critical overview eventually became much too expanded to be presented within a quick digression, so I had to open up room for it within Section III. Still, I want to reiterate that this is a process description that cannot be verified or falsified. I have no illusions concerning my ability, or anyone's ability, to validate any of it beyond what can be determined concerning the contributing facts as they exist.

> *Note* — This general hypothesis concerns the transition from simple chain-of-event existence to what can be truly considered material existence. I intend to make the case that this involves the progressive development of the URC-Determined Environmental Confine as a whole (universe, if you like) to include the emergence of the Change/Spatial Unit trajectory (or simply *spatial trajectory*) as a critical contributing factor to the survival of its [our universe's] inimitable contextual Identity, and to detail the spatial trajectory's part in the creation of physical space, physical distance and relative proximity. I also intend to show that physical existence does make this transition the only way that anything develops; as a result of Identity Survival [the lone existential requirement] specifically pulling that transition forward.

Now, I've made the case that Identity Survival is the sole existential imperative, and provided plenty of evidence to that effect. That means that if I'm to remain consistent here, I need to show that the emergence of the spatial trajectory can only occur (or have ever occurred) if it serves that specific requirement

AutoGenesism: A Theory of Everything

[Identity Survival] for something that already exists. In this case, I'll be declaring that the existence of the spatial trajectory serves the Identity Survival requirement of both, the Change/Event Unit trajectory (or simply *event trajectory*) and the relationship matrix involving all that physically existed at that instant [both change/event and information] that we refer to physical Reality.

This is due to the fact that the Change/Event Trajectory, at this stage of progressive development, is the only dynamic physical thing pursuing Identity Survival, and the URC-Determined Environmental Confine itself [Reality] has always and will always be dependent on increasing complexity to prevent duplication by any rival environmental confines. Okay, so duplication isn't an imminent threat to a URC-determined Reality confine, but the pursuit of Identity Survival isn't specific about what is or isn't an immediate threat. There's no sophistication involved in what's essentially a blanket imperative.

So, what I'm going to be laying out for you here is how the Change/Spatial Trajectory serves as a successful Identity Survival strategy for the Change/Event Unit trajectory and for Reality as a physical macro-system, and how that transition from change/event to change/spatial is not only logically possible, but completely plausible and efficiently successful.

Now, the first thing I want to remind you of is The Emergent System; particularly, the part concerning how emergent systems emerge. As I stated, they are the result of a specific confluence of contributing factors or systems, and I used a tornado as my example. I also made clear that some emergent systems are created by a combination of material/force factors and non-material factors, and that these noumenal factors — if present — are generally of particular significance; using the difference between a crowd and a mob as an example of such a generated emergent system. I then finished that overview off by stating that strong emergence features an emergent system that cannot be reduced to its contributing components without being destroyed as the unique system that it is; that it is literally irreducible, even though it is clearly comprised of contributing components.

With that refresher behind us, I want to suggest that the transition from Change/Event Trajectory to actual matter begins with an emergent system that is commonly referred to as the vector field of force, or force field, which, as we just noted, are terms for existent kinetic energy potential.

Yes, it seems as if potentials [energy and otherwise, but mostly energy] populate every other Theory of Everything, and there's actually a good reason for that; the bottom line concerning mass (and that next critical and directly re-lated stage toward everything we know as present and accounted for: matter) is mass's hand-in-glove relationship with energy. So, it's a no-brainer that seething potentials of primordial energy are central to whatever has been tossed together to explain the secular genesis of all that is tangible. That said, how can a field of energy potential exist as an emergent system and satisfy the requirement that it serve the Identity Survival needs of the most primordial staples [the Change/Event Unit, and the developing relationship matrix between information sets] as a follow-on survival strategy?

I know that I need to first present my case for why I believe that the Change/Spatial Trajectory [that kinetic energy itself] came into existence ini-tially as a classic emergent system. After all, we're not going to assume anything at all within the confines of this examination. The good news is that we won't have to. There actually is compelling evidence to suggest that everything asso-ciated with the Change/Spatial Trajectory [movement, proximity, space and dis-tance] can be explained quickly and relatively easily by simply approaching the whole of it in the same general manner that science has often approached similar irreducible forms of physical manifestation; by allowing for the existence of The Emergent System, and examining if the manifestation in question qualifies, and if the contributive confluence necessary for its spontaneous emergence could reasonably exist without unnatural influence. So let's take a moment to look at what constitutes a kinetic energy field of potential.

When kinetic energy potential is reached, depending on the form of energy being examined, this can mean something as simple and nondescript as a ball positioned on an incline or a foot off the ground. The energy potential is nothing more than the capacity for force (of some sort) to manifest immediately (or whenever it's allowed to manifest) as a result of a suite of factors associated with that specific circumstance that has created an unresolved requirement. In the case of the ball, its position relative to its resting position creates an unre-solved gravitational requirement that insists that it return to its resting position, or a position of similar rest relative to the force of gravity. And this requirement can be imposed in as many different ways as there are ways that energy can become manifest; possibly including ways that we have yet to discover. In sum-mary, it is the unresolved requirement that we're seeking to create if what we want is an energy potential.

What is true about any emergence initiating confluence that could exist as a connecting state between the Change/Event Trajectory and an energy potential

AutoGenesism: A Theory of Everything

state resulting in the Change/Spatial Trajectory as a kinetic energy manifestation is that it is (by the very definition of what it is) a primordial transformation confluence that cannot be immediately likened to other, more commonplace, emergence confluences.

> ***Note*** — A tornado's emergence confluence involves low pressure, warm and cool air masses colliding in a precise manner, moisture, and geographic factors, whereas a mob's emergence confluence involve people, circumstance, cultural predilections, and psychological-emotional triggering specifics, with these factors ultimately balancing out in ways that bring the specific manifestation into existence for as long as all of those factors remain within a supportive confluence.

Naturally, it must be assumed that a pre-material, primordial emergence confluence involves contributing factors that are not material. But is this sort of thing even possible? Of course it is. A mob emerges from the confines of a simple gathering of people as a direct result of non-material contributing factors. The correlation is clear and unambiguous.

Besides, the fact is that matter came into existence as a result of factors that were not material. That much is obvious. All that is physical and relatively existent before the appearance of matter is the Change/Event Trajectory and the residual Fact Sets that emerge (and persist) as a direct result of the Change/Event Trajectory, so physically, this is all we have to work with. But maybe this is enough.

What we know is that Identity Survival — at this point — is only being dynamically pursued by the Change/Event Unit via the Change/Event Trajectory. We know that by this stage of progressive development, Contextual Association, Relative Context, and Contextual Precedent have all become Reality-shaping influences as a direct result of the permanent nature of emerging residual Fact Sets and how the Informational Continuum operates as a whole. We also know that these existential staples are being leveraged where possible (by the macro-system's relationship matrix as the apical holon that it'll always be) even as every Change/Event Trajectory that exists strives to persist by any means available, and to employ these staples to develop those means of dynamic trajectory survival yet to become available. After all, the macro-system can only improve its own Identity survivability through the dynamic activity of each existent Change/Event Trajectory and the residual Fact Set continuums that this activity brings into existence.

As we factor out how the Change/Event Trajectory achieves its own profound increase in Identity survivability by way of the properties inherent within the kinetic energy release of the Change/Spatial Trajectory, this is what we have to work with in total; both physical and noumenal. And as you'll see, this will be enough.

Kinetic Energy: The Basis of Matter

The reason that scientists have been chasing down the Higgs Boson (and its suggested indication of the existence of the Higgs Field) is because they know that material existence is ultimately the result of energy release; specifically kinetic energy. What they need the Higgs Field for is to *"slow down"* the kinetic energy's velocity enough for some things to coalesce into bits and pieces and particles and whatnot. Not that they suggest what these things might be, other than bits of energy [fermions, bosons, whatever], but that's not actually important at our point of examination, since bits and such have yet to become bits and such. All we have are Change/Event Trajectories, residual Fact Sets, and the developing relationship matrix between them all (that we call Reality).

So, what we need to do is focus on what they do know, and that is that everything that exists as material is the impact of a constant battle between kinetic motion and whatever it is that's getting in the way of that motion. The entire material realm exists as either Change/Spatial Trajectories or an entangled confluence of Change/Spatial Trajectories. The only difference between what becomes matter and what doesn't is the amount of mass [resistance to velocity that is fighting for inertia], with matter arising from those things that have enough mass to become at rest.

In their Standard Model theory, the Higgs Field is the 21st century's version of the 19th century aether, externally imposing mass on that which would otherwise zip right on by and never find cause to coalesce with anything else, with matter originating as a result of the inherent resistance of this aether. Of course, the Standard Model doesn't address the issue of how this aether or these zipping whatever-they-are have come into existence, but we will.

Still, what we want to take away here is the fact that no one is arguing the basic notion that the Change/Spatial Trajectory is the literal building block of matter. Nor is anyone debating the idea that the degree of resistance facing the Change/Spatial Trajectory [amount of mass in a specific system] affects the kind of material existence that ultimately manifests as a result of that Change/Spatial

AutoGenesism: A Theory of Everything

Trajectory's contribution to whatever system develops. With that settled, let's examine how a kinetic energy potential can emerge as a direct result of the factors [Change/Event Trajectory, Identity Survival Imperative, and Informational Continuum] that were available before the advent of matter.

Emergent System Confluence Suite

I want to make it clear that the confluence suite that initiated the very first Change/Spatial Trajectory was unique. Although the Change/Event Trajectory had become established, there was no precedent for the Change/Spatial Trajectory (for actual spatial movement) and this is important to take note of. You can assert that the initiation of such a revolutionary system as proximity change was necessarily tenuous and that there was no system in place to force any confluence to create what this confluence obviously created, and you'd be correct in that assertion. But, you would still have to concede to the fact that the Change/Spatial Trajectory, and the material realm it launched, does exist, and that unless you want to insist that matter (and the universe that hosts it all) simply is, was and always will be, you've got to account for how it initially came into existence. And I'm sorry, but copping out to some magical Big Bang that came from nowhere with everything it takes to be an entire universe hidden inside of itself is immeasurably more unlikely than what I'm going to suggest here.

So, what I want to do is bullet-point some of this stuff to give us both a break. First, let's examine the initial confluence, and let's keep in mind that all it needed to do was launch that very first change from here to there. After all, the first change/event was a single Change/Event Unit, and we saw how that took off as soon as it was launched. With the Informational Continuum containing the specifics of that survival success, the follow-on quantum of action — in this case — was no more than rote response. Just rinse and repeat.

The Initial Confluence Suite

- Identity Survival Imperative — Identity Survival = true = ongoing existence
- A Change/Event Trajectory seeking Identity Survival
- Informational Continuum
  - Contextual Precedent

- Change/Event Unit Identity Survival = holon structural collaboration [Increase]
- Change/Event Trajectory Identity Survival = Contextual Association

All it takes is for one instance of this powerful requirement/ precedent configuration to hit a win as a result of the emergence of a field potential; which is what an emergent system is, even as it plays out from moment to moment until all the potential is exhausted into released energy of one sort or another. It is the focused requirement itself [*"first, survive"*] that creates the energy potential, in the same way that lifting a rock off the Earth creates the focused requirement that gives that rock a kinetic energy potential that it will expend immediately as soon as it's allowed to expend that potential energy by being dropped.

In the case of the Change/Event Trajectory's constant requirement, it must create ongoing Change/Event Units, and in the only form that residual information has ever noted Change/Event Units to occur (in follow-on Change/Event Trajectories) in order to survive as an identified whole. This sets up the building potential until it's expended as energy; obviously kinetic energy in our own Universe. The result being the Change/Spatial Trajectory.

As we saw with the Change/Event Trajectory, once it started, there were plenty of ramifications that kept it going. Of course, the fact that the Residual IC had already established the follow-on quantum as the primary means of unit survival (launching the trajectory) back when the Change/Event Unit came into existence, set a pretty stable foundation for the basic structure of the Change/Spatial Trajectory when it emerged. Still, there's a lot that was suddenly revealed to be survival improvements over how the Change/Event Unit was getting by beforehand, and this was why the Change/Spatial Trajectory was so immediately embraced and promoted (by the event trajectory and by the entire relationship matrix that constituted the macro-system Reality) as a primary means of building forward toward eliminating the constant threat of existential oblivion for all that (by that point) had come into existence.

So, let's look at what that first Change/Spatial Trajectory brought with it as far as Contextual Precedent is concerned.

> ***Note*** — Now remember, Contextual Precedent (the basis of all laws of nature and physics) is what the macro-system itself adds to this emergence confluence. It remains on permanent standby (along with the universal primordial imperative: Identity Survival) awaiting the next Change/Event Trajectory to launch as the necessary 3rd factor, rounding

out the necessary factor confluence for the emergence of an energy field potential, and the next Change/Spatial Trajectory's kinetic energy release. Like I said, rinse-repeat. Kind of amazing how simple the whole thing actually is. Of course, not all Change/Event Trajectories spawn Change/Spatial Trajectories, but then not all thunderstorms spawn tornadoes either.

Change/Spatial Emergence: An ID Survival Pursuit

- Kinetic Energy Potential becomes Kinetic Energy unless restricted
  - Kinetic Energy release results in the occurrence of at least one Change/Spatial Unit
- A change from one proximity position (relative to all else that exists) to a new proximity position (relative to all else that exists)
  - A Change/Spatial Unit's occurrence launches a residual Fact Set that fully and permanently represents the contextual ramifications of that occurrence
  - The emergence of that residual Fact Set is a Change/Event Unit, with each quantum of spatial-centric change and its associated residual Fact Set occurring as a follow-on (and therefore contextually entangled) Change/Event Unit.
  - This default result creates a Change/Event Trajectory that is contextually entangled with the Change/Event Trajectory that was 1/3 of the Change/Spatial Trajectory's originating vector field of force emergent system confluence suite.
  - This newest Change/Event Trajectory is now available (as are all Change/Event Trajectories with the same primordial requirement to independently pursue Identity Survival by any and all means possible) to be part of another field-creating Emergent System Confluence Suite (along with Contextual Precedent and The Identity Survival Imperative that are perpetually available) that can produce yet another kinetic energy potential field and subsequent Change/Spatial Trajectory.
  - This specific confluence is perpetually replenished as soon as it produces this specific emergent system, with each Change/Spatial Trajectory succeeding in extending the Identity Survival of the

original, as well as all subsequent (and therefore contextually entangled) Change/Event Trajectories, requiring it to be repeated by existential default, in service of the macro-system's own Identity Survival strategy [Increase and system diversification].

As you can see by the bullets, the Contextual Precedent has become a lot more robust following that first flurry of ramifications that were brought on by that very first Change/Spatial Trajectory's release. The success literally establishes the inevitable nature of the next success and so on. This is system survival via natural selection at its most primitive,

I specifically like how when each quantum of action occurs (satisfying the originating Change/Event Trajectory's ongoing need for contextually associated occurrence) a new residual Fact Set comes into existence and alters the physical nature of the Informational Continuum, and, by direct ramification, increases the relative sophistication of the contextual *slurry* that is Einstein's *Global Geometry*. This change is also a Change/Event Unit, and with each Change/Event Trajectory quantum adding yet another IC-extending residual Fact Set to the Environment, this new Change/Event Trajectory presents its own need to address its Identity Survival.

Of course, with the confluence of Identity Survival imperative and Informational Continuum (with its Contextual Precedent concerning how that survival was just achieved as a result of the emergent system that is the kinetic energy potential) already in place, the road forward has now been paved for what will happen with this Change/Event Trajectory and its own survival effort.

What is most remarkable is that the resulting Change/Spatial Trajectory will be intimately entangled (possessing a direct contextual in-kind association) with the Change/Spatial Trajectory that (in a sense) caused its own existence to emerge. Later, when the recurrent orbital trajectory is established (with its own revolutionary survival success imprinted within the Informational Continuum to ensure that it will become a common survival strategy for future Change/Spatial Trajectories) this contextual entanglement will ultimately result in the isolated densities of Change/Spatial Trajectory activity that we note as the fundamental basis of matter [this is what a particle is] when we perceive them.

It's important to note here that open space is a byproduct of this trajectory survival process, and it serves to allow an apical holon trajectory structure (like a particle) the dielectric that it needs to establish and maintain its own contextual Identity relative to all other such trajectory matrices. As to how such open space

Autogenesism: A Theory of Everything

is created, well, it's not as open as it seems, even if it doesn't host material existence. I do cover this extensively in a speculation; *"Dark Matter: How the Change/Spatial Trajectory Serves the URC-Determined Macro-System"*, but basically, it's just the macro-system's Identity Survival being aggressively assured by residual Fact Sets that have been brought into physical existence by Change/Spatial Trajectories that have occurred on a massive scale.

And So . . .

So, this should help bring AutoGenesism into a clearer view for those who've spent time within more traditional scientific pursuits. Yes, it does careen dangerously close to speculation, and I did preface this presentation with an admission that there's no way to falsify any of it. Still, it does bear noting that this explanation of how we got from the primordial Change/Event Unit and its default trajectory to the initiation of what we call the universe has a pretty palpable ring of truth to it, and comes across as especially credible when placed alongside those theories that have wasted billions of dollars and decades of the finest minds our world has to offer without moving the ball forward in general over the last 40 years or so.

But, in the totality of what AutoGenesism presents, this is a minor point of interest. So much more of obvious significance is revealed as one moves forward within this labyrinth.

Kevin Brian Carroll

Digression

Human Consciousness

and the

Personality Development Trajectory

If you read Track#1 of Section II you'll notice that several subsections are devoted to the examination of a very deliberate and clearly defined Identity Survival pursuit effort involving the gestating human mind and its authoring material brain; the Personality Development Trajectory (PDT). We looked at how the PDT effort is structured, and why it succeeds as it does. What we didn't do was examine some of the evidence that suggests that the PDT is more than an adventurous speculation. In this digression, I want to address that requirement with the kind of patience and focus that it deserves.

The existence of the PDT is central to the entire premise that there is a brain/mind relationship (and a very defined survival process that has emerged as a result of that relationship) that is fundamental to how a material brain that produces a human being does what it does. It is this unique process that makes the human brain very different from all other material brain survival systems.

While it may be easy enough to assert that such a trajectory exists, what is more difficult is proving that the PDT exists. In fact, it may ultimately be impossible (given our present technological capacity to observe and/or measure such a thing) to prove the physical existence of the PDT by way of the Scientific Method; specifically identifying the PDT and separating it out from the overall system that includes it and the process that it enables as a result of its inclusion.

Still, the impact of the process can be examined, and there may be ways of inferring its existence if we examine the PDT from a perspective that allows for its existence (if only for the duration of the examination) as a plausible explanation concerning the emergence of the human mind. Of course, inference should never be offered as definitive proof, but if it's strong enough, inference can go a long way toward inspiring professional research into the existence of this dynamic process. Perhaps even developing a verification profile that could be used to prove that the kind of process this is can, in fact, exist.

The Emergent Mind

In the first segment of this examination we'll focus on the emergence of consciousness, with a quick look at one theory that suggests how conscious thought arises from material activity. I've chosen this theory due to the fact that it does a good job of making its case that the brain itself manufactures the consciousness stream through globally coordinated synaptic Change/Events. Of course, my affinity with the basic approach of this theory has most to do with its obvious alignment with what I embrace concerning the Change/Event Unit as the quantum basis of all developmental structures, but I also appreciate its capacity to effectively describe a reasonably plausible **Dynamic Burst Set (DBS)** generation event in a concrete manner. That said, I do not embrace what this specific theory offers as the process that triggers and guides the brain's configuration and launch of consciousness, and it's important that I make sure that this is emphasized before we move forward with what I do feel it provides as compelling evidence that the brain does generate the mind.

I've chosen Dr. Sam Parnia's description of this theory due to its effective clarity and brevity.

> Professor Susan Greenfield (Oxford University) has proposed that the mind may arise from the activity of brain cells at the level where the cells are connected together (the synapses). Rather than arising from a single isolated region of the brain, she suggests that consciousness arises diffusely from the brain-cell connections.
>
> The reasoning, Greenfield argues, is that there is no single complete function that takes place in one region of the brain. As mentioned above, it is known, for example, that vision is divided up into many separate components that are connected together to give rise to the conscious experience of seeing, such as color, motion, and form processing, and the function of vision can preoccupy over 30 brain regions. So brain regions are smaller parts of a wider brain stage and not units that work alone. Thus we know that conscious experience arises from the actions of many different parts of the brain.

AutoGenesism: A Theory of Everything

However, when we break each area of the brain down into its smaller constituents, we see that each area is a complex circuit that is ultimately reduced down to the connections between the cells, or synapses, or in other words, to the individual wires of the circuits themselves across which electrical signals are passed. This signaling is dependent on a series of different biological products, or proteins, which are themselves products of genes. Therefore, Professor Greenfield has proposed that the neuronal correlate, and in effect, the physical substrate of the "mind" is a process that occurs at the level of the brain connections, or synapses, which are not only highly dynamic, but which also reflect experience through their strength and extension of connections.

According to this theory, consciousness, or our sense of self-awareness, is thought to arise from the interaction of assemblies of neurons involving up to tens of millions of neurons all connected together. It is proposed that at any one time, there may be many neuronal assemblies present; however, the largest assembly will dominate and determine that moment of consciousness.

The degree to which cells are recruited, and hence the degree of consciousness, will be determined by a variety of factors, such as the strength of the input coming into the brain — for example, from the eyes and the fingers, as well as preexisting connections and the degree of competition, as shown by the smaller assemblies starting to form.

Sam Parnia MD, PhD: WHAT HAPPENS WHEN WE DIE

So, it's the word *competition* that catches my eye here. Is Dr. Parnia suggesting that Greenfield's theory rests upon the idea that these sub-assemblies actually compete for primary influence within the corporeal brain's function as the generator of human consciousness? Maybe, if I read on, his interpretation of Greenfield's theory will reveal that choice of "competition" as an operative description to be a quick slip, and not integral to this specific theory concerning the brain's actual configuration and generation of each conscious awareness burst set per specific instant.

So, let's imagine that we're standing on the street holding something in one hand. An assembly of brain cells related to "touch" is active, so we're aware of what we're holding. Then, suddenly, we see something that interests us — for example, an accident. We then stop feeling what we're holding and just experience what we're seeing. At that time, the activity of the assembly of brain cells related to touch would be overtaken by the new assembly of cells, which would have become active in relation to what we have seen.

The activity of these cells is in turn determined by the activity of various proteins, which may change in response to other signals, including Change/Events taking place in our body, such as hormone changes, immune changes, or changes in the levels of neurotransmitters. So in the same scenario, if we had the flu and were feeling very ill, certain chemicals and hormones would be released by our body and immune cells that would also interact with the brain cell networks, so we would feel "unwell" while seeing an interesting Change/Event.

It has thus been suggested that the subtlest influences either from outside or inside the body modulate consciousness at the level of cell synapse in the brain, and hence, lead to differences in consciousness, and that there's always a competitive process going on between different assemblies of cells.

Okay, so it does seem to be Dr. Parnia's interpretation of Prof. Greenfield's theory that this process is the result of cell assemblies winning within a competitive environment, with stimuli launching a literal scramble for assembly dominion within a theater of many such assemblies poised at the ready for their chance to take the helm. As this excerpt is taken from a traditionally published work of non-fiction, I'm going to assume that Prof. Greenfield's theory has been accurately described by Dr. Parnia, including his own use of that theory as the basis of the specific vignette he offers as further clarification of how Greenfield's theory translates to real world moments.

I generally find that rephrased presentations (if allowed by the theory's original author, of course) give me a slightly better view of the theory itself, and this is why I'm using Dr. Parnia's interpretation of Prof. Greenfield's consciousness theory in this examination. Especially since it's probably not absolutely critical that I deal with the minutia of that theory here. In fact, my issue with it focuses not as much on what's been stated here, but more on what has been neglected. In that sense, the minute specifics of Prof. Greenfield's theory are not even germane to this examination at all, and Dr. Parnia's broad overview will serve nicely to set up the examination.

Managing the Initiation of Perception

What we have here is an extremely complex response process that has evolved to allow an ultra-sophisticated biological holon structure to successfully manage its ongoing pursuit of survival within a relentlessly dynamic, yet exceedingly nuanced, theater of competition. Now, while I have to agree that Prof.

AutoGenesism: A Theory of Everything

Greenfield's connection (synapse) network response (as a definite, globally diffused, event involving concurrent exchanges of information signals) is very likely the generation *"burst"* response that we're seeking when looking to define the instant of consciousness emergence, what I have a problem with (concerning Professor Greenfield's determination, as detailed by Dr. Parnia) is the means by which a response requirement is presented to the brain's entire assembly community, and the management process involved in the brain's choice of which assembly will be activated to the level of dominating the sentient experience and for how long that dominance will last.

What is clear is that consciousness — intellectual self-awareness — did not evolve casually as an inevitable capacity within the material brain. Descriptions of the depth of precision and the breadth of complexity involved in the simplest of structural responses to mundane Change/Events suggest that the sentient brain evolved as a result of specific requirement. After all, nothing just emerges within the Material Realm.

Opportunity can explain how something developed, but it can't explain why it developed. Requirement provides the impetus for what comes into material existence, and when examining requirement, if you dig down deep enough, what you're left with is survival, and that's all your left with. Whatever else you find is directly associated with survival and with filling the role of defining specific expressions of survival [the most effective and efficient means of achieving survival].

When addressing the development of something as epitomical as the human brain (for instance), the fact is that the corporeal structure's pursuit of survival is what's driving that development. While this obviously presents a requirement that certain feature sets be embraced as integral to that development, it is also required that some be avoided, since whole system survival is the lone achievement being sought.

Abraham Lincoln once wrote that *"a house divided against itself cannot stand"*, and he was correct in that observation as it pertained to the corrosive impact that slavery was having on 19th century America's capacity to remain a functioning union of states. What Lincoln wrote is true for all unions; regardless of how they're structured. Disease is what we call the progressive destruction that such a schism creates within the union of assemblies and sub-assemblies that make up the corporeal body. Even the most localized structural failure can have an immediate impact on the entire body. And, the changes emerging as a result of the direct and indirect influence of that failure can be impossible to unwind as ramification, with a growing schism continuing to build in complexity and influence, as more and more of what results, reacts to what has been initiated.

If the human brain's response to external and/or internal stimuli was actually based on a free competition between cell assemblies that (as any brain/mind researcher will admit) are completely incapable of independent sentience (let alone human sapience), then the pursuit of apical system survival could not have been the driver that led to its development. To even suggest that simple chemical triggers and hormones make the decisions concerning what the conscious mind will perceive as not only significant, but even apparent, is to grant these chemicals and hormones a level of intellectual capacity that no one is willing to acknowledge.

True competition for the helm — between cell assemblies; the champion having to immediately organize and reorganize its instant-to-instant response protocols in aggressive defense of what's been achieved — does not seem like a system that would serve the entire organism by default. Nor does this system offer any global management structure. We can imagine a structural complexity that is so vast that it has achieved self-management as a holistic, materially configured system capacity, but when such a material structure is conceptually dissembled, the life within that system evaporates like a ghost and you're left picking over molecules for clues as to where it went.

So, what is the management activity involved in the triggering of conscious awareness as a survival response to the complexities of corporeal existence within a competitive environment? For that, we need to take a look at the nature of information as a physical reality, and the possibility that there are more versions of information than raw data that simply represent the occurrence of activity and being.

The Executive Brain

What we do know is that DNA provides survival directives within each cell of virtually all living things. I say virtually because of what's known about specific pseudo-organisms called prions, which appear to accomplish dynamic existence without DNA. However, that's another issue entirely. DNA provides default protocols that have been established as a result of a process of progressive development that is specific to an organism and its species' history. Successes

AutoGenesism: A Theory of Everything

and failures have established the unique system preferences, with the DNA itself as the informational account concerning what succeeded and [by its absence] what failed to succeed. In the brain-equipped organism, this information is what the brain translates into specific and detailed action-items — to be pieced out and delivered to the assemblies and sub-assemblies that make up the independent, materially apical whole that is the organism itself.

A DNA-driven central management system's processes are relatively simple and somewhat apparent, with species behavior mostly consistent even among the more sophisticated organisms that employ this basic management system. We have labeled this DNA-driven survival system *natural instinct*, and even the most sophisticated of brain-equipped mammals are largely driven by natural instinct. The truth is that even with training, in the end, a dog will always resort to breed, and this is why people bred dogs to fill specific requirements. Natural instinct is what generally governs the generation of ongoing dynamic information *action-items* within the corporeal brain. The sophistication and nuance capacity (regarding this translation of the DNA's broad directives) provides the only real differentiation between one species' intelligence and another.

If you take a close look at the human brain, the process immediately presents itself as being fundamentally different. The most obvious difference is the heavily documented fact that the corporeal human being is not only capable of, but is generally prone to, directly challenging — often, even aggressively rejecting — what constitute primordial dictates of the basic survival imperative itself. This odd predilection is especially glaring when the human being in question is otherwise completely normal and functional in every sense as a corporeal organism. Philosophical and theological notions acknowledged, if the human brain's sole function is to translate DNA survival dictates into dynamic action items — as is clearly the case with nonhuman brains — then there's no adequate explanation for the fact that so many functionally healthy people deliberately pursue their own physical and psychological destruction.

The truth is that a drive for self-destruction is only widely exhibited within the Homo Sapiens species [our own version of corporeal humanity], and this drive is expressed in an impressive variety of ways. I see no sense in presenting statistics to prove that this is true, since the evidence of this human predilection for self-destruction is overwhelming, with examples littering virtually every society, community and household in ways that have defined, and in new and novel ways that continue to define, Earth's human race. Clearly, this drive is not an aberration that's taken command of the brains of only a small subset of Homo

Sapiens, but rather, a profound departure from the DNA driven survival management system that governs all other high functioning corporeal wholes that populate the Earth.

So, what could possibly explain this stark difference between how the Homo Sapiens [human] brain approaches the primordial issue of raw survival and how all other normal brains approach it? Obviously, if DNA information is what provides the basic survival directive suite for all other brains, there must be a competing information source involved in crafting the survival directive suite for the Homo Sapiens [human] brain.

What it Means to be Human

This is where it might be good to examine the actual nature of the dynamic information that is generated by the two major types of corporeal brains; the human brain and every other brain that exists on this planet. Yes, we can draw the specific line here at this divide due to the fact that full human consciousness is clearly that unique when compared to the sentient response/reaction nature of what the animal brain produces as action-item information.

No one really denies that the human brain's end product is completely unique and that this is not about intelligence or capacity for intelligence. Intelligence isn't even the issue when comparing human and animal brains, and that's been long settled. The fact persists that human intellect is in a class all its own, and that its capacity for full and textured self-awareness is (so far as we know) unique to the brain of the Homo Sapiens hominid; at least on this planet.

What we need to do is take a good look at the ramifications of a brain that produces dynamic action-item information that can engage in conceptual abstraction concerning the fact of its [the information itself] own physical existence. And what are the ramifications of dynamic information that, when brought into existence, is immediately aware that it possesses an Identity that is singular and unique?

Let's look at the basics of a simple **Dynamic Burst Set (DBS)** for a moment. A DBS is information; a dynamic interpretation of DNA dictates, configured to actively address a requirement that DNA dictates cannot address. It has emerged as a result of the activity of the material brain (a synaptic Change/Event, if you agree with Prof. Greenfield's theory) and is therefore not a material part of the brain itself once it has emerged whole and operational. This suggests that each synaptic Change/Event [happening at whatever

AutoGenesism: A Theory of Everything

Change/Event rate can be determined] results in a quantum [not materially divisible] burst of dynamic information that occurs on the heels of the last quantum burst of dynamic information [also the emergent result of a synaptic Change/Event within the brain].

The Identity Survival expression *Association* [in-kind entanglements that ensure extended holon Identity Survival via inclusion within the structure of a more complex, more durable holon] requires every DBS that originates as a result of the activity of the same authoring brain to seek this in-kind Association if such Association can be achieved, which, in this case, it can. This suggests that if these Dynamic Burst Sets of information do persist, then they must gather as a fully entangled holon collective. But do these brain-generated Dynamic Burst Sets actually persist?

What is known is that when information [a residual Fact Set] emerges as the default result of a Change/Event Unit [the occurrence of Change A is a fact] then it [the residual Fact Set] persists with no possible half-life rate of decay [if Change A happened, then it can never NOT have happened]. This means that information [Fact Set or continuum], once brought into existence by a Change/Event [unit and/or trajectory of units], can never cease to exist. It might seem a bit simplistic, but the basis of physical Reality is, by definition, as simple as it gets.

The truth is that Reality is a contextual environment that is literally defined by the permanent physical existence of information — residual Fact Sets (RFS), RFS clusters, RFS continuums — and the complicated contextual relationships that emerge and evolve between all such information holons. And as we learned in Section I, what connects all this information and isolates it as one defined environment is the uniform and immutable Unit Rate of Change (I suppose you could refer to the URC as the quantum duration of *Now*), since each RFS that exists within a Reality confine was necessarily brought into existence to represent a quantized Change/Event Unit that occurred at that URC. All this noted, what the brain creates is a very different form of information.

Yes, although the action-item burst set (DBS) that is produced by the brain's synaptic event is information, it is very different than the simple residual Fact Set that comes into existence as a result of the quantized Change/Event Unit. This is because these are dynamic process directives that must then initiate specific activities or system changes that are not actually defined within the DNA information itself. These synaptic Change/Events (as described in Prof.

Greenfield's theory) are producing actual information directives that did not previously exist; original, coordinated to an amazing degree, and capable of physically initiating Change/Event activity within entire areas of the corporeal body that have been targeted for response and/or initiation.

In the simplest version of this dynamic information generation process, each DBS contains information concerning the required DNA dictate interpretation; the precise action-items specifics; the subsection of the body to be targeted; the coordination between that subsection and all other assemblies and sub-assemblies; and how that single DBS of direction will coordinate with the single DBS that preceded it and the single DBS that will follow it. Obviously, this level of sophistication can't be accomplished by way of simple cellular DNA coordination, so these synaptic Change/Events are definitely producing a true form of information that is then actively addressing the processes targeted by those Change/Events in a real and physical manner.

The fact that these burst sets of information do not establish a passive, default preference management presence based on precedent (creating avenues of progressive development potential, as is the case with RFS information), but actively initiate immediate responses to instances as they present themselves, means that this is dynamic information; an actual hybrid form of physical existence that features a permanently existent information mass that possesses the dynamic physical capacity of the Change/Event Trajectory

And as we noted in Section II, the human version of this hybrid manifestation is fully self-aware; meaning that it knows that it exists, and it understands this at an extremely sophisticated level. And since it knows that it exists [and as a persisting and growing mass of fully entangled Dynamic Burst Sets no less], what is there to prevent it from developing a vested interest in its own progressive development? Nothing. Certainly not the intellectual rejection of such a notion that's based on a traditional belief of what can and cannot be possible. In fact, if survival is the primordial imperative that it proves itself to be in all other matters of existential development, the existence of this vested interest is more than plausible; it's required by the same law *"first, survive"* that governs all other forms of physical existence.

But, if information survives by default anyway, then where is the danger of failing to maintain existence? What is the survival expression that drives this self-aware form of information? The quick answer is to point to the URC-Determined Environmental Confine and its own translation of the *"first, survive"* meta-law to the universal natural selection dictate *"do this again"* as each

AutoGenesism: A Theory of Everything

win establishes a success precedent and, in some cases, the development of a full system preference within its own ongoing progressive development structure.

The emerging DBST is a true contextual sub-environment that presents to the rest of physical Reality as an indivisible holon; a literal solid. This is due to the fact that each DBS that comprises the DBST was configured and launched by an apical material system [the brain] and it did not come into physical existence as a default representation response to a Change/Event Unit that occurred within the macro-system that is Reality. This contextually [therefore, physically] isolates each DBS within the trajectory whole; collectively creating the sub-environment that is the DBST. This being the case, one can simply point to the fact that the macro-system pursues inimitable Identity Survival (through its promotion of successful structures via contextual precedent and established system preferences; i.e.; natural laws), creating a powerful precedent for all such contextual environments to also pursue inimitable Identity Survival. But, in this case, there's reason to suggest that the DBST, as a true environmental confine in its own right, is vulnerable to an even more aggressive pursuit of inimitable Identity Survival. This being especially true if the specific DBST under examination is fully aware of itself as existent and unique.

As with most emergent systems, the whole is generally more than a simple sum of the parts, even if some of those parts are identifiable within that whole. In the case of this emergent hybrid, the Identity Survival drive [innate within the dynamic factor of the emergence confluence — the Change/Event Trajectory that is the lifespan duration of the holon structure of the brain itself] must persist as integral to this emergence due to its primordial nature as Reality's lone existential imperative. [see Sections I and II for an extensive overview of how C/E Unit survival is pursued and accomplished] For our purposes here, we'll simply acknowledge this fundamental aspect of the Change/Event Trajectory and how it impacts this hybridization of action and information; since it is only this confluence factor that possesses any survival expression whatsoever.

What the Change/Event Trajectory does is provide the only actual survival imperative drive that exists within this dynamic information hybrid, due to the fact that information has no survival imperative drive whatsoever. True, the DBST doesn't face existential oblivion, but neither does the URC-Determined Environmental Confine (both are information relationship matrices after all). What each faces (if only in the most unlikely scenario) is a threat to its inimitable uniqueness; a successful challenge to its Identity by a perfect pretender. Yes,

371

this is so unlikely as to be beyond improbable, but the meta-law *"first, survive"* is not a sophisticated directive; possessing nuanced application. It's the only primordial, universal requirement that exists, with all other requirements emerging in reference to it.

The establishment and defense of inimitable Identity is job #1 for that which possesses progressive development capacity. This is true for the entire Material Realm, for the constantly emerging information [both residual and dynamic] relationship matrix [Reality], and for every DBS relationship matrix that emerges and/or has emerged from a living brain's ongoing effort to manage the material survival processes on behalf of a corporeal organism of some sort. Of course, the impact of this as an actual impetus is subject to quite a variety of evolving influences, so its presence expression within each DBS can vary widely, as we'll discover within this digression.

> ***Note*** — What's extremely important, regardless of what level of survival you're examining, is to remember that Identity is the lone requirement when trying to determine existence. We covered this in Section I, and really get specific about it within Section II, but just to quickly emphasize how it works here . . . for it to exist, **IT** must possess unique and singular Identity. If **IT** doesn't, then **IT** cannot be said to actually exist. This means that the primary definition of existential survival is the establishment and promotion/defense of inimitable identity; Identity Survival. This is pursued and accomplished in a variety of ways, with Identity Survival manifesting in some ways that may seem counterintuitive, depending on how one views the nature of Reality.

When examining what the human brain produces, this pursuit of Identity Survival is what you need to focus on. The human brain's self-aware DBST has an environmental confine's view of what constitutes Identity Survival, and there's no possible way to overemphasize this one critical difference between what drives the human brain/mind survival system and what drives the non-human brain survival system. In the interest of making sure that this difference is emphasized, we'll be referring to human brain generations as **Intellect Burst Sets (IBS)**, as we do in Section II.

As I stated above, these burst sets mass together after they've accomplished whatever it was that they were configured and launched by the brain to address. The laws of contextual precedent that rule the nature of progressive development (detailed in Section I and emphasized in Section II) require them to become permanently entangled and physically indivisible, with the resulting mass growing with each burst set that's generated by the one authoring brain responsible for that mass.

Each precise instant of conscious awareness that occurred at some point within the ongoing Change/Event Trajectory that is the material existence of that specific brain, persists as originally generated; meaning that each IBS maintains its relative contextual relationship with all others that comprise that **Intellect Burst Set Trajectory (IBST)**. This is a hyper-sophisticated dynamic burst set relationship matrix that is wholly conscious and self-aware; when fully gestated, an indivisible human being with a true personal history and an abstract sense of itself relative to the whole of Reality. This being the case, as soon as enough Intellect Burst Sets have collected, this emerging human mind begins to realize that it has its own unique and inimitable Identity that it must now promote, defend, and (while still being presented with new burst sets by the brain) further define and develop.

> ***Note*** — It's important to keep in mind that each IBS is further defined as occupying its own place within the gestating Intellect mass itself (which is actually a permanently existing trajectory of sequentially generated Intellect Burst Sets and specifically entangled IBS Trajectory segments) as just one of an uncountable number of unique manifestations of self-aware existence that occurred within a timeline. Each IBS is, therefore, incapable of conscious self-awareness independent from the IBST mass itself as a whole, since none can possess any sense of independent historical context [its own place within the relationship matrix that is Reality] if isolated from the IBST it occurred within. Again, the IBST is a true sub-environmental confine that exists whole and indivisible within the larger macro-system that is Reality. No burst set that comprises its holon structure has any contextual relationship with the larger URC-Determined Environmental Confine, since it was the material brain's activity that specifically created it, and not the general environmental activity that causes residual Fact Sets to emerge by default.

Once the entangled mass of Intellect Burst Sets begins to experience its own emerging sense of self, an Identity Survival agenda naturally begins to formulate. In Section II, Track#1, human Identity Survival gets really worked over, with its own digressions here and there concerning the ways that Planet Earth's own human race [the Homo Sapiens hominid species] chooses and pursues inimitable Identity. What I will reiterate is that the emerging human being's own pursuit of inimitable Identity will often overwhelm the Homo Sapiens' DNA material survival considerations, and this can affect the brain's response to even the most immediate concerns. It's this uniquely *human* focus on the ID Survival of the brain's generated output (as opposed to the more common corporeal focus on the survival of the brain/body material system itself) that results in the mind's establishment of the **Personality Development Trajectory (PDT)**; radically altering the nature and function of the human brain/mind survival system in comparison to how all other brain/mind survival systems function and serve their own apical material structures.

The Personality Development Trajectory

As I made clear in Section I, the PDT is not a spatial trajectory, and it's not like the *gathering forward* DBST either. It's a constant and seamless activity that the human mind is engaged in; a Change/Event Trajectory. It consists of a definite process that each human mind learns from other human minds [initially, family members] through interaction and simple proximity. The PDT is why communities and cultures emerge, and why some differences between people can have such a powerful impact on their ability to overcome those differences. It's also the reason why some people can become so determined to physically destroy themselves, while others, who are afflicted by the same circumstantial and environmental motivators, are never similarly driven.

Keep in mind that the IBS Trajectory is active and it's fully capable of physically affecting both the Material Realm and the Informational Realm. After all, that is what it was configured and launched into existence to do [one IBS segment after another]. When this massing IBS collective eventually achieves its own sense of self [some suggest that this transition takes place when the authoring brain has been generating IBS Trajectory segments for around 4 or 5 years], it actively takes on the task of crafting its own emerging identity [through imitation of others, as is how all human behavior develops and solidifies].

Once this holistic sense of self emerges, the mind realizes that it has a stake in its own emerging Identity development. As the mind does this, the PDT is its response to that specific realization as an active effort to affect that development; a Change/Event Trajectory. The Personality Development Trajectory is exactly what it professes to be; the effort that the human mind puts toward defining and developing its personality while it's still physically associated with its authoring brain. As I detail in Section II, the PDT is the emerging mind *reaching back* and doing what it can to manage its own ongoing development.

AutoGenesism: A Theory of Everything

What is surprising is the efficiency with which this developmental management is accomplished, and how little actual interaction there is between the mind and the brain's response configuration processes. In fact, generally speaking, the PDT leaves no real *fingerprints* on what it does, since the impact it has on the cognitive generation process is never made by actually *touching* that process in any direct physical sense. As with all other information management processes, this PDT effort employs precedent, precedence, and default ramification, even if (in this case) the specific precedents and precedence defaults are actively crafted by the mind itself.

Here's a quick and broad overview of how the PDT process works. As with any sort of overview of this kind, minute specifics are not indulged, since each brain/PDT relationship will have its own peculiarities and exception doesn't prove the rule in this or any other case.

- The brain has been operational long enough for a substantial mass of Intellect Burst Sets to gather in-kind [an IBS Trajectory] as a result of that brain's activity.
- That IBST has achieved a full and abstract awareness of self as a result of the organizational complexity of the brain — due, of course, to the DNA structural specifics of the corporeal whole itself; this capacity is inherited. We refer to this IBST-governing sense of whole self that emerges and evolves while the living, functional brain continues to feed the IBST with new burst sets as the human mind.
- Once this *human* level of sentience has been achieved, the self-aware mind is naturally compelled to initiate its own survival strategy — this involves the establishment and development of inimitable Identity; the primordial means by which any existential whole is defined as existent.
- The evolving human mind learns from other human minds that Identity development is achieved by managing its own brain's ongoing generation of all subsequent burst sets of Intellect. It witnesses how this strategy affects the overall Identity [character and predilection suite] of each IBS, and how, as they gather, the crafting of the IBST Identity as a whole gradually progresses through this management of its own evolving contextual composition [the IBST being a relationship matrix of Intellect Burst Sets].

- The actual management process involves carefully selecting the residual Fact Sets that are allowed into its own brain's *memory cloud* and manipulating the attribute specifics of each Fact Set that is selected. These will be the data sets against which its brain will compare and contrast all incoming internal and external stimuli. How this information library evolves will be critical to how its brain will respond to the demanding task of moment to moment survival.

- As each IBS generation occurs [it is an actual change/event] a residual Fact Set (RFS) comes into existence to factually reflect that generation and application of that burst set, as is the case with all change/events that happen. Each RFS that represents an IBS is no more or less than any other fact set brought into existence by an occurrence, and simply contributes to the increasing complexity and nuance of Reality's overall Identity. That said, when it comes to the complex, ultra-sophisticated human brain's clearing of its in-box, there are IBS generation events that are more important to the survival of the whole than others. These are the IBS generation events that will need to be remembered.

- In short, each IBS event that addresses a requirement involving the human brain/mind system's unique capacity for cognition, abstraction, circumstance awareness and evaluation, or even simple awareness of self in contextual juxtaposition with Reality as a whole, is a densely packed generation, causing the emergence of a residual Fact Set (RFS) cluster that factually represents that burst event by the brain/mind survival system. Since this kind of generation involves the self-aware experience and translation of external and/or internal stimuli, what this RFS cluster actually represents is the factual nature of the brain/mind system's experience and translation of *perception* as an IBS generation event [generally involving multiple IBS generations]. This IBS generation event is the human mind/brain system's subjective interpretation of whatever the stimuli event was that created the requirement for its generation as opposed to the true factual nature of that stimuli event. While subjective, these events are extremely sophisticated and generally valuable survival response generations, and are the foundation of what it means to be human. These RFS clusters are, therefore, rote selected and processed by the PDT for use within the brain's memory cloud. We'll be referring to these unique RFS clusters as **Perception Fact Sets (PFS)** More — below — on the relationship between Perception Fact Sets and the residual Fact Sets that otherwise represent the lifespan of the material human brain within a common RFS continuum.

- When an IBS event is *launched* by the brain, it's not immediately experienced as conscious awareness [conscious awareness occurs when the selected PFS clusters are attributed to become contextually entangled with the brain's memory circuits, and become experienced as *immediate memory*]. In fact, research has established that a delay of anywhere from .5 seconds to a full 7 seconds between an IBS generation and the conscious experience of that generation is common (see the segment *Free Will?* coming up next for specifics). Of course, this delay is synced up within the PDT process before the conscious experience of that IBS event is allowed, to avoid the perception of obvious hitches in flow or sequencing.

- This delay is actually a survival strategy that ensures a rigid consistency of ongoing reality perception, as one instant follows the last and sets up the experienced instant of *Now* for the arrival of the next in a lifelong series of perceived moments that will need to make sense to the human brain as one seamless flow of experience. This is accomplished by the emerging mind's PDT activity, which provides the ultra-sophisticated dynamic information capacity needed for such a trajectory analysis and experience crafting process. Of course, part of this process includes the PDT's IBST Identity crafting effort; a seamless selection and attribution process that prepares a steady stream of Perception Fact Sets to serve both efforts before allowing any of them into the brain's memory cloud.

- Over time, the PDT process develops and solidifies response trends and predilections; cognitive yeses and nos; weighting standards for all categories of experience and perception translation; human archetype identity protocols and divergences involving interpretations of those protocols; specific competitive survival strategies [corporeal and postcorporeal]; and all manners of definitions concerning reality and the proper translation of reality to ensure a consistency of progressive experience.

- This is all accomplished before any PFS is ever allowed to exist enter the brain's memory cloud [become available for the brain to apply to the business of IBS generation and application] and be experienced [remembered] by the emerging corporeal mind as conscious awareness.

- Keep in mind that this memory cloud exists as a contextually isolated residual information mass, and is not actually part of the IBS mass that manages the ultimate nature of its composition. The PDT is merely how each PFS is assigned an arrangement of attribute identifiers to make some of them more significant (and therefore, more readily available to the brain) than others; with corporeal survival being served on the one hand, and the mind's own emerging Identity development being served on the other. When the brain has ceased to function, its memory cloud ceases to be contextually unique among the other residual Fact Sets that comprise that brain's RFS continuum. This is because the PFS clusters that comprised the memory cloud were only attribute entangled with the material structure of the brain, and never contextually associated with the IBST [the human being] that remains.

Note* — Concerning The Perception Fact Set. It's important here to remember that perception is an activity; a Change/Event Trajectory. As is the case with each and every unit that makes up any C/E Trajectory, when a perception activity C/E Unit occurs, an entangled residual Fact Set emerges to accurately and permanently represent that occurrence. Seems obvious enough, but it's here where the PDT gets its Identity sculpting material.

And yet, keep in mind that nothing is ever actually removed from a RFS continuum and physically placed within a data vault at any time. The RFS clusters are simply affected with a relative contextual modification that makes them immediately accessible to [entangled with] specific referencing circuits within the material brain whose activities brought them into existence. Relative contextual relationships between residual Fact Sets (RFS) and between RFS continuums are constantly evolving, and dynamic informational wholes are every bit as capable of altering relative contextual relationships as any C/E Trajectory [the primary adjusters of relative context within the URC-DEC]. Once you finally allow for the physical existence of information, none of this is a stretch. A little complicated, but not a stretch by any means.

Because the human mind is self-aware, what each human brain's memory cloud consists of are those Perception Fact Sets that have emerged as a default ramification of each mind's unique experience of every cognition IBS configuration/launch event performed by its authoring brain. This is because what the PDT sees as critical is the

AutoGenesism: A Theory of Everything

Change/Event Trajectory that is the perception activity itself. Reality is one thing, and the self-aware interpretation of Reality is another. The human mind launches the PDT as its own ID Survival strategy, so why would it be focused on anything other than its own interpretation of Reality? Especially since all it knows is its own interpretation of what is real. The truth is that its focus is, and should be, on its own development; the net result of its own perceptions.

So, how do we know that this process even exists? Let's face it, while it sounds perfectly reasonable, how can anything like this be verified as being more than one version of an engineering solution that could exist given the requirements as they are? Well, we can take a look at the absence of the process and see if its elimination teaches us anything about its active and ongoing presence.

We can also look at whether this PDT activity persists in the manner that self-aware information would if denied its constant source of ongoing information feed in the same way that energy ceases to manifest as a dynamic force within the Material Realm if cut off from its source of potential (thereby examining the viability of the claim that human consciousness is, in fact, a form of energy and not a form of information). In the digression *"From Here to There: The Crossing Over Event"* we'll be doing that.

But first, let's examine the claim (above) that each bit of memory is processed and that this processing activity actually requires a period of definable time to complete. This lag in conscious experience would certainly be one indication (albeit, only one of many required) that the mind's PDT activity does exist and is an ongoing process that specifically impacts the human brain's generation of conscious awareness.

Free Will?

In 2008, the following paper appeared concerning a consciousness study conducted by a team of researchers.

Published online: 13 April 2008 | doi:10.1038/nn.2112

Unconscious determinants of free decisions in the human brain

Chun Siong Soon, Marcel Brass, Hans-Jochen Heinze, John-Dylan Haynes

There has been a long controversy as to whether subjectively 'free' decisions are determined by brain activity ahead of time. We found that
the outcome of a decision can be encoded in brain activity of prefrontal
and parietal cortex up to 10 s before it enters awareness. This delay presumably reflects the operation of a network of high-level control areas
that begin to prepare an upcoming decision long before it enters awareness.

The paper that this abstract refers to — offered as a download PDF that's
obtainable by logging onto . . .

http://www.nature.com/neuro/journal/v11/n5/abs/nn.2112.html

. . . and paying a fee — details follow-on research inspired by Benjamin
Libet's mid-80s controversial determination that the human brain has already
finished deciding (at least 500 milliseconds) before the human being has experienced having made an A/B choice. These folks went Libet one better, and employing an fMRI machine, discovered an actual two-stage process that signals
the intent to decide in one sector of the brain, followed by the actual decision in
another sector, before sending the memo on to the conscious mind that selection
A or selection B will be taken as the preferred choice between the two.

Now, some who've investigated this (and the actual lengthening of lead
time that the brain achieved against the mind once modern technology was applied and some of the messier bits of Libet's own methodology were cleaned
up; as much as a full 7 seconds in some instances), have insisted that this is proof
that the human being has no free will whatsoever, and that its conscious mind is
nothing but a slave to the gray glop that sits behind its eyes. Others have pointed
to this irresponsibly broad assertion concerning free will as just another indication that the secular humanist will go to great lengths to dismiss the true separation that exists between the mind and the brain; a notion that the non-secular
mind has so feverishly promoted for centuries.

Me? Well, I immediately saw it as evidence of my notion concerning the
presence of the Personality Development Trajectory. After all, that's a lot of
information to approve, weight, and tag with the right attribute values. And the
fact that this study indicates that the actual time it takes to experience consciousness varies from moment to moment suggests that this is a dynamic result of
something else that is equally dynamic; such as an ongoing and relentless process occurring between the brain's activity and the individual's experience of
that activity.

AutoGenesism: A Theory of Everything

I can imagine that there are other suggestions that have been offered to explain this unusual indication, but to be honest, none that I've read actually addresses the primordial impetus for all material processes that occur naturally; raw structural and Identity survival. To examine whether the PDT experience-vetting process does address the human being's extremely complicated material survival requirement, let's look at what happens when the immediate memory of a person is completely obliterated as a result of disease or brain injury.

I Can't Remember What It Is That I Forgot

There was a movie several years ago [Memento] that actually did a pretty reasonable job of illustrating what a complete absence of short term memory might be like for one so afflicted. The protagonist struggles with anterograde amnesia, which isn't even a full loss of short term memory and certainly not a loss of immediate memory, which is what the elimination of the PDT vetting process (and the resulting contextually isolated, logically structured memory cloud) would present as a crippling survival challenge.

In the movie, the viewer is treated to a scrambled and disjointed experience that somewhat mimics the impact of chronic short term memory loss, but if the entire PDT vetting process did not exist for the human brain, the confusion and information chaos would be literally crushing; resulting in a complete collapse of the entire brain's capacity to manage even the simplest processes. To be more precise concerning the importance of only this very specific PDT process, extremely severe autism is probably a better example of the kind of impact that an absence of the PDT would have on a human brain; with no means of filtering the incoming data stream for relevance, consistency of experience, synchronicity of progressive experience, survival significance, or for any of the kinds of ways that information is attributed for use by the brain on behalf of the business of simple survival.

So, it seems obvious that some sort of information management process exists, and that (more importantly) the process is a requirement. And since information (like DNA) serves as the default management function for all other organic processes, it stands to reason that the presence of an intimately related information source as an active and immediately responsive management process (given the speed and complexity of functionality necessary) would be more than plausible, and actually more of a requirement in itself.

As I pointed out above, when the data flows in from the body's external sensory systems (which constantly arrives as a literal wash of stimuli) it must be processed before a response can be initiated. If not, then all stimuli will be equal in significance, urgency, relevance and historical/relative context, which means that none of it will possess any significance, urgency, relevance or historical/relative context whatsoever. The entire wash will remain a wash, and the brain will be incapable of responding to any of it.

It takes the PDT to process the incoming data wash, before it can be allowed — as prepared information sets — to be experienced as conscious thought and the moment-to-moment awareness of existence.

When I was a kid, I remember being told that in every interaction between two people, there are three different events happening; what I'm experiencing, what the other person is experiencing, and what's actually happening. Yes, there is only the one interaction happening, but the experience of that interaction is also a true event, and this is the point that I want to make here.

If a ball falls off a table, and no one saw it or heard it, then all that occurred was that a ball fell off the table. Only one string of residual Fact Sets will reflect that lone trajectory of Change/Event Units involved.

If there was one person present, then two Change/Event Trajectories occurred as a result of that ball falling off the table; the ball fell off the table and someone experienced the ball falling off the table. Increase the number of witnesses and you increase the number of unique Change/Event Trajectories. Of course, each event unit brings a residual Fact Set into existence, and each RFS will be factual and accurate concerning each event unit it emerged to represent as having factually occurred.

The self-aware experience of witnessing the ball falling off the table causes a unique cluster of residual Fact Sets to come into existence. This cluster will always be integral to the RFS continuum that reflects the IBS generation trajectory of one human brain, but as the factual representation of a sensory perception event, this RFS cluster (a Perception Fact Set cluster) will be targeted by the mind's PDT for potential selection, and if selected, will be processed for inclusion within the authoring brain's memory cloud using a very sophisticated contextual attribution protocol that, as noted above, can take from .5 seconds to a full 7 seconds to happen, before that PFS cluster can be consciously experienced by the corporeal-focused mind as immediate memory.

AutoGenesism: A Theory of Everything

Perception Fact Sets are factual, but only concerning the perception of the brain/mind survival system that then brought them into existence. Their representation of Reality is tenuous at best, and can be wildly inaccurate, depending on a variety of factors that we've already discussed. Still, they are critical to the survival of the brain-body system (establishing and developing quick-response protocols) and extremely handy to the Identity development efforts of the PDT (in the many way we've already noted).

The bottom line here is that the PDT aligns each PFS with a *memory cell* activity trajectory, after weighting that PFS properly, with the intent of providing the brain what it needs to successfully manage the survival of itself and the body. It does this much like a parts bin manager along a production assembly line or a bar back in a really busy nightclub; feeding the configuration effort while controlling how that configuration is comprised by affecting the nature of the components that are readily available from moment to moment.

So yes, the Personality Development Trajectory is the mind rigging its own progressive development process, since it sits right there with complete and overwhelming access to exactly what it takes to game that process without all that much additional effort. That said, the mind's PDT activity is still largely focused necessarily on providing the brain with what it needs for a lot more than basic corporeal system survival, since the range of possible ways that human response to external stimuli can, and often must, be nuanced is far beyond the capacity of any brain that is only translating DNA instinct to manage successfully. The DNA dictates are present, and they will pitch in when instinctive response is called for, but the PDT often finds ingenious ways of prepping the Identity development effort through its management of the raw structural survival effort, even if it can be the case where the two are at odds as larger ongoing efforts.

From my own point of view, it's a pretty nifty arrangement, and it sure answers a lot of questions if I start factoring in the mind's realization of self, counterproductive personality archetypes, and that whole self-destruction dichotomy that seems to only belong to the human being to any degree whatsoever. In fact, if the PDT doesn't exist, then I'm afraid that you're left with no reasonable notions concerning the confounding nature of humanity.

Kevin Brian Carroll

Summary

So, what have we proven? Strictly speaking, we've proven nothing. Still, we've taken the Personality Development Trajectory as an Identity crafting effort of the generated Intellect whole to a point of being an entirely plausible notion and maybe even a process that is required by the nature of the primordial imperative Identity Survival. It's not proof, but it's not insignificant either. But, maybe what's important isn't that the PDT be yanked out and placed between glass slides and under a microscope.

Perhaps it's more important to consider how the realization that such a process does exist would actually affect the average person and their own effort to get through a day without breaking a nail? If it did become widely understood to exist, just the awareness of the PDT's constant impact on the average person's life would inevitably shift every paradigm in existence; societal, philosophical, scientific, cultural, and ultimately crippling theology altogether after a few generations of strident resistance. Let's look at how your own life might be affected by as much a certainty in the PDT's existence as the average person's certainty in the occurrence of the Big Bang.

Of course, if the PDT's existence were to be accepted then it would be widely accepted as evidence that you'll persist indefinitely; carrying on after the death of your brain and your span as part of the Material Realm. That'd be pretty great in itself, but then, even if you don't know about the PDT, if it does exist, you'll still persist whether you expect to or not. If we persist, then as soon as corporeal death has its way, that's revealed whether we understand the how or why of any of it. Knowing about the PDT would help with that transition, but it wouldn't be a true game-changer relative to the life-after-death question. Knowing about the PDT delivers its biggest impact while you're still alive and while your brain is still working to deal with the stuff that confronts you from moment to moment.

Having a full knowledge of the PDT, and what it does for you and (more important) to you can be the difference between succeeding and failing as a gestating human being, or (more likely) ending up somewhere lost within the anonymous herd of fellow drones; drifting between good and bad and whatever else there is that's neither here nor there, as larger presences steer your forever as they see fit. Sounds ominous, but let me see if I can explain exactly what I mean by this.

AutoGenesism: A Theory of Everything

When you were born, you didn't get to choose your parents. You didn't get to choose your gender, or your appearance, or your genetic structure, or the circumstances surrounding your birth. If your family was wealthy, then good for you, but you never had a say in what those circumstances were going to be relative to the life you had awaiting you. In fact, you never had any input on any of it, regardless of what the New Age self-help books try to claim about *Soul Contracts* and whatnot.

You came out of that placenta as the completed product of a gestation process that initiated long before you ever knew what was happening. And as your life has littered out behind you, it's always been clear that your level of success and failure, contentment and disappointment, and all the shades that have manifested between each of these polar extremes within your own daily life have been greatly affected by what occurred within that placenta.

Well, if what I believe about the PDT is true (and there is a lot of inferential evidence that this PDT does exist), then the final version of who and what you can be is entirely up to you. This is a very important thing to realize. The PDT's existence literally suggests that our own version of the human being — while manifesting as the material Homo Sapiens hominid of Planet Earth — is actually making its way through a 2nd stage of physical gestation, as are all human beings while their material brains are managing their survival systems.

If the corporeal human lifespan can be revealed to actually be a 2nd stage of physical gestation, then as long as your brain is still feeding your mind with Intellect Burst Sets, you still get to consciously shape and form the human being that you'll be when this stage is completed. You get to decide what is important, what is trivial, what is beautiful and what is divine. You get to be as strong and as noble and as wonderful and as transcendent as you want to be, but only if you actively focus on accomplishing what it takes to become exactly the way you wish to be. And the best part is that you really can become that wonderful version of yourself just by visualizing that wonderful you and being that you as you meet each trauma and opportunity that comes your way.

Your strength is built as you weather each storm with dignity and self-reliance. Your wisdom is built as you allow each failure to teach you what it has for you. Your power is built as you respond to each petty aggression with kindness and magnanimity of character. In fact, every decency you express is more power and brilliance added to the ultimate expression of the eternal human being that you're crafting.

Yes, this is your ultimate opportunity and you are fully in charge of how well you leverage this opportunity. As you can see, the Personality Development Trajectory and its crafting process isn't just some esoteric notion. It's an entirely plausible explanation for most of what we know to be the nature of a human being's corporeal existence.

And all it takes to fully benefit from knowing of its existence is to be conscious of how you allow it to craft your ultimate self. If you respect strength of character, then be resilient in the face of hardship and magnanimous in the face of both victory and defeat. As the years pile up behind you, those predilections will become more and more cemented into your permanent character.

Sounds like no more than behavioral modification? Sure it does, but that's why behavioral modification works (if the prospect engaging in behavioral modification is still young enough, of course). Did you think that leveraging knowledge of the PDT would be revealed to be anything other than what's passed for common sense? It's never been more than the simple effort of human survival, but knowing why things are as they are goes a long way toward taking the mystery out of how to get some good out of what's already ongoing. And when all that's ongoing is completed, if you've been smart about how you've consciously leveraged what you've learned, you'll be presented with the final reward; an eternal Identity that you can be happy with.

Digression

From Here to There
The Crossing-Over Event

It was a bit of a struggle to finally decide whether this essay would be a digression or a speculation, but in the end, I decided that the purpose of its inclusion is to round out parts of Section II that (as far as I'm concerned) are not speculative at all. I do acknowledge that there are plenty of people who absolutely reject the notion of human life after death, and I also acknowledge that they honestly embrace that view, having arrived at it as a result of what they firmly believe to be definitive empirical evidence (or lack of same).

That said, I have to also acknowledge that there are even more people who fully embrace the notion of life after death, and have their own reasons to honestly believe that they know exactly who and what awaits them as soon as they close their eyes for the last time. These folks are just as stridently confident of their view concerning the eternal nature of the human being as the hardcore materialists are that the whole topic is patently ludicrous. And me, I'm just as happy to let them both have their beliefs remain unmolested by anything that I might add to the debate.

Still, in the interest of fully fleshing out a significant aspect of AutoGenesism, I'm going to include this piece about what actually happens when a person passes away, and I'm not going to slip it into the Speculations area of this section. I've already laid out the logic and physics involved in my own determination that the human being emerges from the sentient/sapient brain as an entangled holon of dynamic, proactive information burst sets.

As far as I'm concerned, the question of whether there is conscious, self-aware life after death has been thoroughly addressed, even if the public debate itself continues to rage on forever. In fact, it'd probably be a good idea for me to flatly state a few things before we even get into the central theme of this piece, since some readers might view this as a standalone presentation. It's also likely that this specific topic will draw the highest percentage of skip-through readers, and without a quick dash of context (at the very least), what awaits these readers will be certainly misinterpreted.

In Section II (at the end of Track#1 and all throughout Track#2) we looked at the physical emergence of the human being, and we made the point that, as far as we know, it is only the Homo Sapiens brain that produces the human being on our planet. Of course, this implies that the human being is not a flesh and blood, material thing, and I'm going to state it straight out and for the record that the human being is NOT made of bones and flesh and blood and chemicals that are affected by tiny electrical charges and other bits of energy. The human being is an informational hybrid that (on our planet) the Homo Sapiens brain generates — one Intellect Burst Set (IBS) at a time — over its entire life span. I really hope that this settles any questions concerning exactly how the human being is structurally defined within AutoGenesism.

I also want to make sure that we're straight on a couple other commonly debated aspects of the human being; mainly its overall role within the whole of Reality (as the epitome of naturally evolving progressive development) and the relationship it has (on our own planet) with the Homo Sapiens brain.

Concerning the larger role of the human being, the truth is that the human being has no role; larger or otherwise. No role has ever been assigned to the human being by any larger, higher authority, and if any human being has ever embraced a larger, greater calling, it's one that it dreamed up on its own and imposed upon itself. The only requirement that actually exists is the meta-law *"first, survive"*, and beyond that, there's no other imperative, and no need for any other imperative. The human being simply exists, and the unique nature of its existence serves no larger function.

The emergence of the human being is pretty remarkable, and as a contributing factor within the contextual composition of physical Reality, it's a really tough act to follow. But, the emergence of the human being is a net result of how the sentient, time-aware brain serves its corporeal whole. It's not, and has never been, a pursued outcome by anything that is not human that exists with the drive to achieve Identity Survival.

The second issue concerns the human being's relationship with the material system that brings it into existence (on this planet, that's the Homo Sapiens

AutoGenesism: A Theory of Everything

hominid). Unlike other progressed forms of physical existence, each human being merely *"happens"* as an unintended ramification of how its authoring brain serves its function as a corporeal survival system. Yes, its informational mass does provide permanent contextual Identity representation to every Change/Event Trajectory that's ever existed as a contributing holon within the entire lifespan of its authoring body/brain system, but what it is that makes the human being *human* is pursued and achieved in spite of its authoring Homo Sapiens' own pursuit of Identity Survival.

Basically, it's a case of the human being having its own agenda, and regardless of what the Homo Sapiens brain is actively pursuing as it generates that human being; burst set by burst set. One indication of this is the fact that the functional cognitive processes of the corporeal Homo Sapiens hominid are clearly designed to serve the immediate survival needs of the corporeal Homo Sapiens creature, and not functionally designed to serve the developmental needs of the gestating human being. Still, as we see in *"Human Consciousness and the Personality Development Trajectory"*, each human being's PDT surreptitiously works its own agenda into how these processes serve the Homo Sapiens creature's ongoing survival concerns as it manages the raw wash of sensory input and transforms it all into useable reference data sets.

The fact that the human being's physical development and ultimate emergence isn't even of interest to the brain that creates it is really important to remember. This is especially true when examining the complicated relationship that each human being has with the Homo Sapiens hominid that brings it into existence.

As we sketched out in Section I, what's necessary for the successful development of the human being is not always good for the Homo Sapiens that's providing that development's heavy lifting. Often it's downright destructive and when this is the case, more often than not, the brain knows it. Many times it's the brain survival system that literally drives the corporeal whole that it exists to serve and protect to its own clearly inevitable failure in a relentless pursuit that it (with its own ultra-sophisticated sense of self-awareness serving as nothing more than a helpless witness) has no understanding of, nor appreciation for.

So, how is this possible? I mean, it's obvious that this is true, and the relative health of the self-help industry, the mental health industry, and the alcohol and drug industries are proof enough that there's a lot more to being human than simple survival pursuit. And the fact that anyone actually cares enough to devote their lives to unraveling the brutal mystery of how it is that any person can so purposefully destroy their own ability to survive is evidence that the mortal human is more than the impact of nature/nurture, the spiritual shackles of original sin, the grinding predilections of selfish genes, or an aggregate of them all in any possible balance.

There is an explanation for this vexing dichotomy, and we're going to look at it. When we do, we'll be discovering something equally revealing; what actually happens when the human mind transitions from providing the PDT perception processing effort to finally becoming the conscious perspective of the fully developed and fully emerged human being.

But, First . . .

There's a lot more to why any one person does what they do, sees what they see, believes what they believe, and ends up becoming who and what they become, than can ever be fully detailed in any book — let alone an essay overview like this one — but, I'm not going to be detailing any of this to that level of specificity. Hell, I know that it's going to be really tough to even clearly articulate the difference between full human conscious awareness and the version of conscious awareness that you and I are working with right now. I'm not delusional concerning the sheer complexity of the human mind/brain survival system.

Still, there is that one striking distinction concerning the way that the human mind and its authoring brain work together that we've just touched on, and it does go a long way toward explaining a lot about those aspects of mortal human behavior that so stubbornly violate Reality's most basic law. In this digression, I want to focus on the actual experience of being a gestating human being, and existing with that unique survival schism as it becomes more and more the case that serving one master involves taking from, or perhaps even destroying, the other.

This could get extremely complicated for anyone that's dropped into this presentation with no real point of reference. So, in the interest of eliminating the need for any further digression within this digression, I'm going to re-introduce a few terms that we used in Section II's Track#2. In fact, I'm going to simply copy them from that section and paste them into the following space here . . .

AutoGenesism: A Theory of Everything

Intellect Burst Set (IBS) — Introduced in Section II's Track#1, this is a Dynamic Burst Set that is configured and set into existence by a human brain. It is a hybrid that is Information in structure while possessing the dynamic characteristics of a Change/Event Unit. The primary feature that sets it apart from other forms of brain-generated information sets is that it contains a unique manifestation of full self-awareness that is contextually tied to the instant and circumstances of its original generation.

Intellect Burst Set Trajectory (IBST) — A Dynamic Burst Set Trajectory that is launched and fed by a human brain. This is the term we'll be using to refer to the physical structure of the human mind.

Personality Development Trajectory (PDT) — As detailed in Track#1, the PDT is the activity that the IBST, in its role as the developing human mind, is engaged in as it carefully selects what **Perception Fact Sets (PFS)** are allowed into the brain's memory cloud, and assigns contextual attributes to each PFS relative to significance, accuracy, and immediate survival relevance. Once the brain has died, the PDT ends as an ongoing activity and the mind's collective self turns to managing the awareness and perception interpretation of itself as a free-form IBST. The PDT effort is the mind's primary survival focus (intelligent perception, proactive and re-active sentience, and moments of sapience) during its gestational stage of physical development.

Gestating Dynamic Intellect (GDI) being — The human mind (IBST) that exists and is in ongoing gestation as the human brain is alive and feed-ing it with Intellect Burst Sets. I will refer to this emerging information mass as the GDI in reference to it as an intelligent and proactive entity in its own right, as opposed to when I'm solely referring to its physical struc-ture. The primary description of the GDI as a distinct phase of the human being is that its mind is deeply focused on the PDT process.

Isolated Dynamic Intellect (IDI) being — The fully developed and phys-ically independent human being that has become freed of the material au-thoring brain upon the death of that brain. I note its contextual isolation in this label, but the IDI is fully capable of perceiving and interacting with the rest of the Contextual Environment. This is the active and self-aware hu-man being whose mind is no longer engaged in short-listing corporeal sur-vival references or personality development.

391

If you've been reading along to this point, then these terms will be familiar, but I have to accept the fact that some readers approach books like this in a much less disciplined manner. Hopefully, this quick glossary will help those readers stay with the rest of us as we move forward. However, AutoGenesism is deeply nuanced in some parts, and without a full understanding of how it all fits together and how the whole of it integrates factually with what's already become established as true and reliably existent, it's not hard to lose sight of how precisely it does represent Reality and fill in the gaps in our knowledge concerning what is real and why. This digression is focused on one of those deeply nuanced aspects of AutoGenesism that profoundly delineates it from all other Theories of Everything; the physical birth of the human being.

Corporeal Conscious Awareness

The most impressive aspect of AutoGenesism, as a Theory of Everything, is how it literally expands as an explanation as soon as you look to it in connection with those mysteries that have nothing at all to do with the questions that it had originally addressed so succinctly. This is a property that David Deutsch describes, in his book *"The Beginning of Infinity: Explanations That Transform the World"*, as being evident in a *"good explanation"*. Well, the fact that Auto-G can equally address the quantum unitary basis of Time and the reason why individual human beings are so widely capable of complete and relentless self-destruction across and in spite of a wide variety of cultural norms, mores, and predilections suggests that it is a *good explanation*. In fact, it's absolutely unique in its capacity to be of equal efficacy regardless of the nature of the system in question.

As I covered in *"Human Consciousness and the Personality Development Trajectory"*, the following research paper made an enormous impact on how I felt that the existence of the mind-brain survival system could be both verified and effectively described as an active and ongoing process. The lag time between the brain's initiation of response and the consciously aware human mind's experience of that response initiation seemed to definitively establish that something was happening to process the mind's experience of ongoing Reality and its own involvement with that Reality.

AutoGenesism: A Theory of Everything

Published online: 13 April 2008 | doi:10.1038/nn.2112

Unconscious determinants of free decisions in the human brain

Chun Siong Soon, Marcel Brass, Hans-Jochen Heinze, & John-Dylan Haynes

There has been a long controversy as to whether subjectively 'free' decisions are determined by brain activity ahead of time. We found that the outcome of a decision can be encoded in brain activity of prefrontal and parietal cortex up to 10 s before it enters awareness. This delay presumably reflects the operation of a network of high-level control areas that begin to prepare an upcoming decision long before it enters awareness.

http://www.nature.com/neuro/journal/v11/n5/abs/nn.2112 .html

In that digression, I dig into the specifics of this research paper, and then detail exactly what is happening — during the .5 second to 7 second lag — between the brain's generation of a dynamic informational response and the mortal individual's experience of actively initiating that response. Here, I feel it necessary to get deeper into the impact on the human experience itself, and how this mind/brain survival system shapes the experience of being mortal for each of us.

Although it has nothing at all to do with the physical survival of the human consciousness, *"Unconscious determinants of free decisions in the human brain"* did open my eyes concerning the very real need for a difference between corporeal conscious awareness and what human conscious awareness consists of once the body and brain have become a thing of the past. I cover this in *"Human Consciousness and the Personality Development Trajectory"*. But, there was something else that this research suggested to me. Something that was never stated or even vaguely reference by the research or the paper.

What I found to be stunning about what these folks had discovered was that it allowed me to fairly accurately place the corporeal brain/mind survival system's unique point of perspective, and even figure out why it's placed there during IBS generation. Until I ran into this research, I hadn't even considered this issue to be an issue at all. Now that I've become aware of the implications of it, I've become even more convinced that I'm really on to something definitive and extremely significant with this AutoGenesism notion.

Now, this bit of research data doesn't really definitively declare all that much on its own, but when approached from the perspective that the Auto-G premise presents, it takes on a whole new level of immediate significance. For one thing, it's become clear to me that regardless of what one might think, none of us have ever actually experienced what it's like to perceive, assess, recall, or initiate a response through the direct use of a human mind. We know what it's like to remember having done so, but that's a very different experience, since memory is even more removed from the immediacy of Reality than perception.

Before I go any further into perception versus Reality versus immediate memory of perception, there are three new terms with which I want you to become familiar.

The first is **Point of Perspective (POP)**. This refers to the precise and relentless focus of attention that the intelligent, sentient, sapient, self-aware human mind has devoted itself to. The mind doesn't really have any say in its POP, although as a self-determining dynamic agent, it can (and does) challenge what has naturally evolved as the most practical and expedient target of the POP. Still, exceptions don't prove the rule, and the vast majority of brain/mind survival systems feature the mind's POP in a consistent position while that system is in operation.

The next two terms represent the impact of the mind's POP on what constitutes the human experience of self. **Corporeal Conscious Awareness (CCA)** refers to the impact on the human experience of self that results from the emerging mind's devotion to the Personality Development Trajectory activity, and **Post-Corporeal Conscious Awareness (P-CCA)** refers to the impact on the human experience of self that results from the redirection of that devotion to the management of sentience, sapience, perception interpretation, and response-reaction for the free-roaming IBST; the IDI (or fully gestated human being).

The Corporeal Perspective

You already know what Corporeal Conscious Awareness feels like. You've been dealing with it for as long as you've existed. It consists of a blend of visual, auditory, olfactory, tactile, and taste sensations that are concurrently being evaluated and reacted to by an ongoing stream of conscious thought, and perhaps even internal dialogue from time to time. You feel, you sense, you consider, you remember, you imagine, you react, you touch, you smell, you taste, you enjoy, you suffer, you reflect and you wonder about the significant of the whole of what constitutes physical existence. And, hopefully, you learn a thing or two as a result.

AutoGenesism: A Theory of Everything

As we've recently discovered, you do all of this between .5 seconds and 7 seconds after your body has already moved on to the next item to be addressed. And yes, that fact about what being consciously aware actually means for you should take a bit to wrap your head around, even if it can be proven to be true and explained as the best possible solution to the larger problem of effective and efficient corporeal survival. It really doesn't seem possible that our entire experience of self is actually a memory, and not an immediate manifestation, and yet the evidence is all around us.

The National Geographic Channel's *"Brain Games"* TV show offers plenty of evidence that the Point of Perspective that creates our CCA is designed to keep us alive, as opposed to putting us at the spear tip of ongoing change within the Material Realm. Any street magician can prove to you that your capacity to detect skilled initiation is more than just limited by your individual capacity to be aware of what's going on around you. That external-internal stimuli data wash has to be properly vetted and attributed before it can be useable, and the fact is that until that's done, you're deaf, blind, and otherwise experientially isolated from the rest of Reality; for your own good, I might add.

During the human being's corporeal gestation the mind's POP is resolutely fixed on the PDT Perception Fact Set vetting and loading process (into the brain's memory cloud) to ensure that the brain's needs for logical consistency are met as effectively and efficiently as possible. From there, it's the brain's part to fit itself in with what's being presented as Reality. When the brain is operating properly, it all works out rather nicely.

In cases where the brain's short term memory region is damaged or destroyed, the mind itself has no capacity to develop beyond flashes of momentary sensations. When mental illness creates data routing havoc, there's no possible way for the emerging human mind to avoid the impact on its ongoing development. When trauma causes the emerging mind to reach into the PDT process and dramatically affect the consistency of what's become an established attributing protocol, the net effect can range from simple cognitive dissonance to post-traumatic stress disorder. Extreme disturbances can inflict any of a wide variety of negative results on the developing whole that is the gestating human being.

The experiential effect of having the CCA's POP located where the brain's memory cloud receives initial PFS loading (as opposed to placing it anywhere else) is that the GDI experience of physical existence is completely immersed within and is defined relative to the Material Realm, even though it doesn't actually exist as part of the Material Realm. And this is obviously the best way for the GDI's PDT effort to be most effective at providing the brain with the best and most suitable data sets for its use in configuring new burst sets in response to the ongoing business of material survival; even if this means that there's a half-second delay that's included as part of the package.

Of course, the delay is never perceived since the mind's CCA is synced properly with all other sensory stimuli that is being streamed, and to be honest, the few seconds of lag time only affect the brain/mind survival system in moments of extreme and immediate physical threat. Moments that the body generally doesn't survive anyway. That said, intense reaction training can mitigate the downside of that natural lag, but it can only mitigate it. It can't eliminate it. In the overall balance, the processing of experience benefits the brain a lot more than it would be benefited by a CCA that was instantaneously experienced.

So, now that we have examined the corporeal version of consciousness, let's move on to the post-corporeal version of consciousness. In one sense it's pretty similar, but in many other ways, it could not be more different. After all, a significant shift in point of perspective can literally change one's view of Reality.

The Eternal Mind

It's become a cliché that people see their life flash before their eyes when they have a close call with the bus to the hereafter, and the reason it's become a cliché is the same reason that all clichés become clichés; because when people have a close call with the bus to the hereafter, they often get a really fast view of their entire lives. Seems simple enough, but oh, that anything would ever be that simple.

Of course, not everyone experiences this overview, but the ones that do (or that get a flash that seems like such an overview) are experiencing something that is a lot more significant than you might think, even if only for a second or two. What they're experiencing is a complete shift in their POP from the PFS loading-into-the-memory-cloud process to the actual POP that they'll have as a fully viable human being, when the brain's been shut down for good and they're done with this 2nd stage of physical gestation.

AutoGenesism: A Theory of Everything

When this happens (generally when the GDI is convinced that the destruction of the corporeal matrix is at hand) some people look outward, and experience what many consider to be an OBE (Out-of-Body Experience) while others look within, and experience an assortment of Intellect Burst Sets that comprise their physical structure; actual moments of extremely vivid and full spectrum cognition that were actually configured and launched into existence by their material brain at some point during its existence.

Of course, there's the fact that these are near-misses (and with that, the brain/mind survival system's placing the errant POP back to the PFS loading process once again) putting that experience under the processing hand of the PDT (as it has become established to that point in the development effort) and the net result is that the corporeal experience of this event isn't pure by any means. Still, such an event can be instructive concerning the nature of Post-Corporeal Conscious Awareness (P-CCA), even if it's been modified for usability by the PDT in accordance with what the individual has experienced as acceptable Reality up to that particular moment.

What I mean to suggest is that a Near-Death Experience (NDE) can serve to inform the materially-focused GDI that there really is an afterlife, even if the specifics of that information have been altered (as all CCA experience is) to serve the agenda of the PDT's overall effort, generally strengthening preexisting biases and expectations. This would be why some people meet deceased relatives during NDEs, and even travel to their firmly-embraced version of Heaven, where Jesus and angels and even a version of God exist to reaffirm their faith before sending them back to be of greater service on Earth, whereas the more secular mind often experiences a much less structured P-CCA experience.

It is important — again — to keep in mind that the POP (whether CCA or P-CCA) is not free of bias. It is based on only a translation of perception, and even when that POP is freed of the linear confines of the memory cloud input stream it remains profoundly attached to that same fundamental perception translation. The human mind will always exist to manage the experience of existence in service of the Intellect mass' inimitable Identity, so it should not be assumed or suggested that the individual is blessed with all knowledge and realization once the body has hit the coroner's table. The truth is that once the brain has stopped taking in new and unique external information (like from books and such) the human mind (having graduated from its gestational GDI state to its fully developed IDI state) has only what it already possesses at that point in IBS information to work with.

So, what does it feel like to be free of the corporeal data stream? I don't know. I've never been dead or even near-dead. The logical requirements suggest that the P-CCA has an awareness of before, now and after, but that this experience is significantly altered due mainly to the fact that the physical nature of each realm is so incompatible with the other.

Is there Time in the informational realm? Yes, there is. Within the entire contextual environment, which contains both the Material and the Informational Realms, the Unit Rate of Change *"sets a common clock"* for everything. The only question is one of harmonic frequency rates, one realm compared to the other. Most say the informational realm *"vibrates"* at a higher frequency, but I have yet to hear or read a technical explanation of what this actually means. I'm going to admit that I have no idea what the harmonic rate of change is for the informational realm, or if there are multiple rates (as suggested by a lot of those who claim to know) that correspond to levels of enlightenment, whatever that actually is.

What I want to do now is wind this up with a quick look at the crossing-over event, what that actually is, and why it is what it is. Eventually, you will experience this, and when you do, I'm hoping that this entire overview will help you avoid the sort of confusion and distress that many encounter. It's just a quick shift in your mind's POP and if you remember that you'll be all set.

The Actual Crossing-Over Event

What I want to define now is exactly how the human being transitions from its 2nd stage of physical gestation (which is the stage that you and I are both deeply involved in at this very moment) and emerges as a fully functional, fully viable, and fully developed inhabitant of the Contextual Environment that we call Reality.

This is the big one. The great equalizer for the entire human race. No matter how rich, powerful, famous or infamous you became during your corporeal run, this one event wipes that slate clean and hands you over to the rest of your physical existence as no more and no less than any other human being that has ever existed, or that will ever exist. Forget the stuff about saints and sinners. When the crossing-over event occurs, we all emerge from it as brand new babies within the Informational Realm.

Of course, as with the babies that we all are so familiar with in this world of ours, we'll each be the direct result — the culmination — of what did and did

AutoGenesism: A Theory of Everything

not occur during our gestation, and certainly not clean slates that the Informational Realm can do with as it pleases. No, for better or worse, we'll each be who and what we crafted of ourselves while we had the chance during this, our 2nd stage of wholesale development. Some of us, big fat bouncing babies, eager to learn the ways of our new world, and some of us, not so much.

The slate is clean as it pertains to the relative status, success, or notability we each achieved for ourselves during our corporeal run. All that sort of thing remains behind (think of it as wrapped up within the discarded placenta, I suppose) and what we're all left to begin again with is what does accompany us into the final phase of human existence; our character, our strength, and our capacity to flexibly respond to our new world as it actually is. In short, we've got only ourselves (the person that each of us has become) to rely on. That said, we also have each other, and for many, the afterlife is all about community and the mutual support it promises. After all, the human being is a communal being. Always has been, and it always will be. But enough about this, let's look at what actually occurs during the crossing-over event. Knowing the truth about this might just make all the difference in how you take your first baby-steps into eternity.

The Traditional Narrative

We've all heard or read about the crossing-over event. Books, movies, documentaries; there is so much that has been presented to the modern public concerning the specifics that it almost seems unnecessary to go over it yet again, but I do need you to know that I've done my own homework in this area. In fact, I've come to the conclusion that these narratives are based on actual experiences that the *nearly passed* have had, and there's a reason why I need to address this issue of the traditional narrative. That reason involves the nature of perception, and what expectation can bring to the experience of perception.

In a court of law, the most compelling form of evidence is the testimony of an eyewitness. It is also widely acknowledged to be the least dependable form of evidence. Even the most credible eyewitness suffers from a powerful vulnerability when it comes to reliable accuracy. The eyewitness can make a very compelling case for a presentation in the minds of a jury, but for a real slam-dunk, it takes forensics to nail it all down tight. Perception isn't fact, even if it does make the most impact on the perceptions of others, and really, this is the problem with perception. It only knows what it knows, and in many cases, that consists of

399

what it has allowed itself to consider to any degree whatsoever. In court, that aspect of perception has sent innocent people to the death chamber, and more than just a couple of people here and there.

In the instance of crossing from this Material Realm to the Informational Realm, perception (and the expectations that definitely affect perception) will become enormously influential, even if only during the initial stages of orientation. If you expect a tunnel, there will be a tunnel. If you expect a light that radiates love and acceptance, there will be light that radiates love and acceptance. If you know that your grandfather and grandmother, your first dog, Sammy, and an angel with silver-tipped wings will be waiting for you to lead you through the tunnel to the loving light that accepts you without reservation, then guess what? Your grandfather, grandmother, Sammy and an angel with silver-tipped wings will be waiting for you to . . . Okay, you get my point.

However, I have another point that's related to that point, and it's that initial greetings are pretty easy to configure when we're dealing with expectations and the perception adjustments that bring them to life. Full and ongoing Reality isn't so easy to configure, and at some point you'll be forced to deal with Reality as it actually exists. My own view is that the sooner one confronts the real that persists in spite of the embraced perception, the better, and that this is true regardless of the situation. Tunnels, angels, grandparents and feel-good balls of light aside, your best bet as you enter the hereafter is to walk in with your eyes wide open and your vision unobstructed.

"You? You Ain't Goin' Anywhere, Pal"

Yes, in spite of tunnels, ferryboats being poled across dark, murky rivers, lights that beckon, pearly gates, and whatever else has been imagined to the contrary; when you die, you're not really leaving to go anywhere. In fact, if you were to watch someone cross over (from a post-corporeal point of view) you wouldn't see much of anything happen at all. Then again, you'd see the affected GDI much more clearly than the corporeal body/brain that's failing, as it materially reconfigures and reconfigures at the URC. The actual *crossing-over event* wouldn't seem like much of an event at all.

I remember when I watched my grandson's eyes turn on as he made his way through his third week of corporeal viability. Before that moment, his eyes had been like impenetrable barriers between me and whatever was going on within his little head, but suddenly it was as if someone had opened the blinds and his bright blue eyes were tracking mine. That sudden shift instantly granted me a deep, visceral connection to him (one human to another) that hadn't existed until that moment.

This is probably what it's like to witness the crossing-over of a GDI (its transition from a CCA-addled gestating potential to a full-fledged human being) from the perspective of an IDI. The visceral emergence of a fellow member of the human race from within the confines of what's perfectly resembled a person, even as (until that transition) it's offered no perceptible connection whatsoever. That shift of POP from the corporeal brain's survival effort (CCA) to the dynamic awareness of being a fully developed human being (P-CCA) probably feels (for the concerned IDI that is present for this event) like it did for me when Patrick's eyes suddenly focused on my own. *"Welcome to the world, little man"* is what I said to him. It must feel that same way for the IDI that greets one who's newly crossed at that moment.

So what does it feel like from the perspective of the one who is crossing over? Again, what do you expect it to feel like? The mountains of evidence suggest that it's deeply affected by your own beliefs concerning what can happen, what can't happen, and what's likely to happen. There's a lot of research (to the extent that anything can be scientifically determined about something so resistant to traditional scientific methodology), and from what I've been able to eliminate as preposterous nonsense (still leaving plenty of room for a broader range of experience potential than I actually expected), the plausible scenarios that await the crossing-over individual are still too numerous and too widely varied for anyone to honestly suggest a typical experience. But that doesn't mean that you're completely vulnerable to the whims of circumstance.

Expectation will definitely affect your experience, and while that's to be expected, if you do keep focused on the true nature of what's actually occurring (or in this case, what's NOT occurring) then you won't get lost, get hoodwinked by someone, or subject yourself to trials and tribulations that really don't await you regardless of who or what you made of yourself during your gestational development phase. What's happening is your mind is ceasing its focus on managing your brain's survival effort, and it's finally allowing you to stand up from that effort and take your first-ever look around at what's been right there all along. In that instant, it becomes clear to you that you've been right there the whole time, only now you're free to do as you wish.

Kevin Brian Carroll

In the end, perception is not Reality, and even if it does a great impression of it, perception doesn't have the juice to become Reality to any great extent or for any length of time. Knowing what actually happens when you shuffle off this mortal coil will clearly ease the transition, and put you on the right foot a lot sooner than if you take such a profound step toward your eternity while laboring under a traditional delusion or even while completely (and ignorantly) open to the first indication that presents itself to you (and whatever it is that might just be tucked in right behind it). God knows what that might be, and why would you want to chance it?

Entanglement:

The Laws and Dynamics of
Contextual Association

Physical Reality is not just the totality of all that exists, it is also the very specific and complex relationship matrix that has emerged as a result of every-thing that has every occurred, everything that exists or has ever existed as a re-sult of everything that has ever occurred, and everything that has ever occurred between everything that exists at this very instant. That relationship matrix is the result of both the impact of precedent on everything's dynamic adherence to the universal meta-law *"first, survive"* and the ultimate definition of survival within the relative being state; *Identity Survival*.

As we discovered in Sections I and II, Identity Survival is pursued in a variety of manners, depending on what's become established through successful holon structuring and/or preservation of contextual Identity. We established a gender-based system of descriptively defining a relative handful of primary Identity Survival pursuit expressions, with one group [Competition and Isola-tion] described as *Masculine*, and the other group [Increase, Association, and Symbiosis] described as *Feminine*. We even explored some less-than-obvious examples of these expressions, with Strong Nuclear Interaction [Isolation] and Time [Increase] as two that are particularly notable.

What I want to work through in this digression is the manner in which the pursuit of Identity Survival is affected by holon structuring as a result of the relationship matrix that is Physical Reality. Since we're taking a quick look at a relationship structure that features a depth and breadth that no one can ever claim to know in full, what I'll be focusing on is a very broad hierarchy of contextual weights that have proven themselves to exist, and to be logically amenable to a reasonable amount of inductive application.

Kevin Brian Carroll

A Rising Tide Lifts All Boats

For instance, the Masculine expression Isolation is commonly encountered as working in congress with the Feminine expression Association in complex material holon matrix structures [the cells that make up the human body are a great example of this]. The existence of a hierarchical influence structure seems fairly obvious, since Association (as an ID Survival expression) should otherwise directly challenge (or perhaps cancel out completely) the Isolation expression that prevents one cell from losing its own composition as a result of combining with other cells in structural collaboration. And yet, this obviously is not the case, with each cell maintaining its own compositional integrity [Isolation] even as it solidly contributes [Association] to the rigid holon composition of the system that is the corporeal body.

What is important to understand is that the reason that this hierarchy rules the holon structuring of the Material Realm is that it is the primary structure that defines the Informational Realm and provides a predictable, reliable order for change within Reality's relentlessly evolving relationship matrix. And yes, this hierarchy is critical to the Identity Survival of Reality itself as a macro-system that's in constant contextual development.

As for Physical Reality's initiating realm, that which exists as dynamic is a direct expression of the Change/Event, regardless of what form it takes. We need to keep in mind that at its existential core, even the most complex and sophisticated matrix of Change/Event holon structure is forever in a war against impending oblivion. It fights this ongoing war through activity organization, constantly seeking increased complexity and sophistication to ensure as prolonged a definable structured Change/Event as possible. Basically, in its own effort to survive it seeks entanglement with relative similars.

What this accomplishes is Identity Survival by way of the survival of that which shares and/or represents that Identity in a relative or historic manner; that which is its own Kind. It's not a perfect solution, but as Change/Event holon matrices join to create multi-tiered assemblages of structured circumstance, they can logically survive as a contextually entangled form of physical existence for longer than the instant (at the very least). In the end, this presents the Identity of each of those contextually entangled units as having existed over the entire duration of the identified Change/Event whole that they gathered in union to create.

AutoGenesism: A Theory of Everything

When you translate this concept into something tangible and relatable (the existential duration of the Earth, as an identifiable Change/Event Trajectory, for instance) the survival win per Change/Event Unit involved becomes obvious.

Now, this developmental focus doesn't simply happen, and this is important to note as well. It is imposed upon that which is in dynamic struggle against oblivion by Reality's own requirement that it pursues its own version of Identity Survival, and the fact that a survival win for progressive development (in general) is a survival win for Reality's own drive for contextual density, which protects its Identity (as the relationship matrix that it is) from being duplicated (or otherwise threatened in any other manner) as a unique and inimitable existential whole. The meta-law *"first, survive"* is translated into *"do that again"* when a success is noted within Reality's relationship matrix, and *"don't do that again"* when a failure is noted. What is important to point out here is that it is residual Fact Sets and their precise relationships between one another that establish and enforce Reality's translation of the meta-law for the entire Material Realm.

The Hierarchy of Kind

The residual Fact Set does not pursue Identity Survival, but physically persists as a natural result of what it is; information that factually represents the raw occurrence of change and all factual ramifications of change within a URC-Determined environment. However, the URC-Determined Environmental Confine (Reality, the macro-system) does actively seek a physical increase in contextual complexity and adding new and ever increasingly dense continuums of residual Fact Sets is the only way that this is possible. Reality is the physical relationship structure of permanently existent physical holons, and information sets are the only permanently existent physical holons, with continuums presenting these holons in historical and relative context.

We established the Identity Survival benefits that Change/Event Trajectories provide the Material Realm's unitary basis; the Change/Event Units that collect in an in-Kind contextual survival strategy. The informational continuum provides a similar role, only the beneficiary is not the arrangement of residual Fact Sets that similarly collect within a continuum. The beneficiary of this entanglement is the URC-Determined Environmental Confine, with each RFS continuum locking all in-Kind units within its holon structure to create an actual layer of inimitable identity as additional contextual specificity (preserved in Isolation, even as it joins in Association with other similarly Isolated holons) on behalf of the URC-Determined environment's own battle for Identity Survival.

Each continuum can also become contextually entangled with other continuums in ways that further delineate the URC-Determined Environmental Confine from any and all pretenders, with the layers emerging at a rate that's limited only by the kinds of contextual in-Kind relationships that emerge as a result of the Material Realm's ongoing battle for holon survival. And if that sounds like it could get really out of hand, really fast, then it's because it could, if there was no structure imposed upon this contextual growth by the URC-Determined Environment's own deference to the meta-law *"first, survive"*. Fortunately, there is such a structure, and I've labeled it **The Hierarchy of Kind**.

In the case of the Material Realm's dynamic Increase and the establishment of organized trajectory matrices, the laws that govern such development involve established basics of success versus failure that are passively presented (like walls and/or speed bumps) with plenty of flexibility depending on immediate circumstance and even incidental contextual influences. However, contextual relationships between informational holons involve much more primitive and intractable laws, especially concerning the act of full association between information sets and continuums. These entanglements are not incidental or insignificant (given the permanent physical nature of information and the critical role that each RFS continuum plays in the Identity Survival of the apical holon Reality) and as such, requirements are universal, and can't be variable per environment.

> ***Note*** — For ease of presentation, we'll be giving the physical Increase of any form of in-Kind information holons the term massing. This will also serve to give this form of Increase a visual representation of the unique manner that information sets can remain contextually fluid (relative to one another) depending on the overall Identity of the relationship matrix itself as it further develops and becomes more precisely defined.

Since it is a relationship matrix, the URC-Determined Environmental Confine's Identity is threatened by any level of inconsistency within the countless contextual relationships that combine to ultimately define it as the apical holon that it is. It is therefore a matter of survival that the Hierarchy of Kind exists as the base logic structure that governs all such permanent and tangential massings. As a logic structure, it's pretty straightforward. In fact, most of its impact on

AutoGenesism: A Theory of Everything

how residual Fact Sets and RFS Continuums *affect* each other is fairly obvious and intuitive in structure.

For instance, the most substantial contextual commonality (or entanglement potential) that can exist between information holons is a shared origin of emergence. Origin of emergence refers to whatever Change/Event Unit or Change/Event Trajectory it was that was responsible for bringing the information holon [either RFS or RFS Continuum] into physical existence. An example of this might be two Change/Event Units, occurring within the same trajectory will bring two residual Fact Sets into existence that will permanently exist within the same RFS continuum. These two residual Fact Sets will occupy the same relative sequential position within that continuum as the two Change/Event Units (that caused their emergence) occupied within that trajectory. As a result of that shared origin of emergence, they'll always enjoy a profound level of entanglement potential. Pretty simple, but also extremely consequential; as those laboring over the commercial viability of quantum computing technology are discovering. Naturally, the requirements get more demanding as the complexity of the systems increase.

The capacity for two highly progressed Change/Event holon structures to even respond in shared Identity Survival pursuit will be nonexistent if the RFS continuums that they're defined by do not share an in-Kind contextual relationship at any level. Microbiologists have been trying to create life in the laboratory for a long time, and the problem hasn't been a lack of knowledge concerning the ingredients required to make the resulting recipe gel into something that's alive. It's known that there is an unknown initiator that has eluded them, and there's been a lot of attempts to jump-start life from the collection of contributing bits that have covered a pretty fascinating range of ideas. Probably, the most successful work-around was described in May of 2010 by Richard Alleyne, Science Correspondent for The Telegraph™ in a story titled: *"Scientist Craig Venter Creates Life for First Time in Laboratory Sparking Debate About 'playing god'"*.

> Dr. Venter, a pioneer of genetic code sequencing and his team at the J Craig Venter Institute in Rockville, Maryland, have been chasing the goal for more than 15 years at a cost of £30m.
>
> First they sequenced the genetic code of Mycoplasma genitalium, the world's smallest bacteria that lives in cattle and goats, and stored the information on a computer.

Then they used the computer code to artificially reproduce the DNA in the laboratory, slightly modifying it with a "watermark" so it was distinguishable from the original natural one.

Finally they developed a technique of stripping bacteria cells of all original DNA and substituting it with the new artificial code.

The resulting "synthetic cell" was then "rebooted" and it started to replicate. The ability to reproduce or replicate is considered the basic definition of life.

Dr. Venter compared his work with the building of a computer. Making the artificial DNA was the equivalent of creating the software for the operating system. Transferring it to a cell was like loading it into the hardware and running the program.

It's notable that Dr. Venter and his team took an already existent group of bacteria cells and simply stripped all original DNA from them before implanting the artificially engineered DNA into the cells and manipulating the resulting hybrid to initiate replication. Basically, they performed a successful DNA transplant, not that unlike gene therapy treatment. The main point is that they didn't actually cause life to emerge whole from a fresh confluence of contributing factors, which no one has ever been able to accomplish.

So, what's preventing research teams from finally getting a stew of appropriate chemicals from springing to life? I'm going to suggest that it could be the impact of the Hierarchy of Kind on the very specific residual information sets that either allow or deny developmental entanglement between the C/E Trajectory matrices of which any such stew of appropriate chemicals is comprised. It would take all such trajectory holons to get the *go ahead* before a progressive entanglement [Increase] could occur, with any one holon's denial preventing the emergence of life, regardless of what initiator trigger is inflicted upon that collective.

Another powerful example of the Hierarchy of Kind's impact on the holon structure of the Material Realm is the mysterious nature of Strong Interaction, Weak Interaction, Electromagnetism, and Gravity. Obviously, each of these forces serves to hold together what has become an entangled system, and preserves that system's Identity, with the only true difference being the intensity and range of the force required to accomplish that Identity preservation per system being served. Each basic force — having been established and then enforced in the same manner that all such laws of physics and nature are established and enforced [success precedent as represented by the URC-Determined environment's Residual IC] — possesses distinct properties that serve the degree of

AutoGenesism: A Theory of Everything

contextual entanglement that's required between two or more material systems (relative to all other historical and/or relative contextual entanglements that also exist between these systems and the rest of what constitutes physical Reality), while allowing for multiple levels of relative contextual entanglement to coexist within those systems that are more complex and intricately structured.

Material holons are held together via Strong Interaction and Electromagnetism, even as they are held fast to Earth within its gravitational field, while Earth is held in the Sun's orbit, and our solar system adheres to its own position relative to the rest of the Milky Way galaxy. So, how many unique forces are interacting here? Three, if you embrace current scientific wisdom concerning gravity, but the truth is that there may be as many as five unique expressions on display within this very small example of the Informational Realm's imposition of system entanglement on the Material Realm's contribution to the Identity Survival of Reality's relationship matrix.

The Hierarchy of Kind lays out the relative importance of each level of contextual entanglement, with some much more critical than others. This rigid hierarchy of how physical attributes impact Isolation and Association between Identified holons serves to enforce the efficacy of the various Identity Survival pursuit expressions, and stabilize the ID Survival process of the URC-Determined Environmental Confine as a whole.

There are those developmental entanglements [multi-cell organic structures are a good example] that would not exist if not for the fact that the Hierarchy of Kind imposes a rigid Isolation at more primordial levels of contextual juxtaposition, only to suddenly promote an in-Kind Association between the very same holon structures once a specific level of progressive development has been achieved. Without this logically driven default system of allowed/deferred system entanglements, the achievement of sophisticated material development, in the form of higher-level, multi-system holon structures, would've been impossible. In these cases the pursuit of Identity Survival is definitely served by the delay that's been imposed.

The Environmentally Imposed Entanglement

In Section I we covered this impact of the Hierarchy of Kind in our examination of Relative Context.

Let's imagine that you work in a large customer service center, and you

are one of fifty employees who have been isolated into five product support groups of ten employees for as long as you've worked for this company. This is due to both the established organizational data routing structure, and to the actual physical cubicle layout, with the result being that it is rare that any of you engages with anyone that works outside of your assignment group. Even the group work schedules are staggered over five 1/2 hour periods, to ensure a constant and somewhat extended coverage of customer service activity throughout the day. In essence, your associations — professional, and as a result, personal as well — within that specific society are constant and have been rigidly determined by the structure established for that society.

Now, let's imagine that you take a vacation, and you travel to Europe. While you're in Europe, you happen upon another employee of your firm, and although that person works in the same customer care center as you do, they do not belong to your specific product group. You recognize them, having seen them before, but within the strict environmental context of your job, this person does not share contextual association with you as a member of your ten person team.

But the two of you have just discovered each other in a bar in Hamburg, Germany, and regardless of what you do about it, this fact has immediately caused a major change in your relationship. The company's structure that prevented contextual association between you as employees, has now — by default ramification — established a new level of direct contextual association between you as employees of that same company in the US. In fact, this environmental shift has established a definitive in-kind contextual relationship that you did not share before this change. What you now share is relative context as two people with a similar contextual history, relative to the local environment. After all, this is a bar in Germany. Not your work center in America.

This contextual bond will now survive while you continue to associate in this or any subsequent environment that pits you both as a relatively similar pair against this overarching attribute [the fact that where you are is an equally foreign environment for both of you] that will be a dominant factor within each of these environments, relative to your established identities.

If any other contextual similar becomes part of the equation, (let's say, the cashier from your company cafeteria bumps into you both as you're walking together to another Hamburg bar) you will both adopt that similar, (whether conceptually or in fact) and this new association will exist for the duration that each of you shares the same level of relative contextual isolation within the environment you're presented with.

AutoGenesism: A Theory of Everything

Of course, if that level of relative context changes (say, the cafeteria cashier hooks up with a local and becomes less of a *relative foreigner* as a result) then the relative association between the three of you will adjust accordingly. In fact, it's likely that the initial two of you will establish an even closer relative contextual bond, since now you both are also without local romance in Germany, unlike the lunch lady.

It's a commonly experienced phenomenon, especially among professional people whose careers can bring them into repeated periods of tangential, yet significant, association with those whose professions support their own or vice versa. Professional sports is definitely an arena where an Environmentally Imposed Contextual Entanglement (**EICE**) is de rigueur to the degree that one comedian once quipped that as sports fans, we're basically rooting for laundry:

> Loyalty to any one sports team is pretty hard to justify. Because the players are always changing, the team can move to another city, you're actually rooting for the clothes when you get right down to it. You know what I mean, you are standing and cheering and yelling for your clothes to beat the clothes from another city. Fans will be so in love with a player but if he goes to another team, they boo him. This is the same human being in a different shirt, they hate him now. Boo! different shirt!! Boo.
>
> ~ **Jerry Seinfeld**

And that's probably the best example of EICE that I can think of, since who hasn't dealt with a favorite pitcher or running back's sudden *betrayal* as he shows back up in town to inflict misery where he once granted a measure of hope and optimism.

In the physical comings and goings of Reality, an EICE is the result of any number of contextually isolated informational masses [a mix of residual and Dynamic, or a number of Dynamic masses] that share a common origin suddenly experiencing a profound level of contextual entanglement as a result of being physically placed in a foreign URC-Determined Environmental Confine. Like the coworkers who suddenly found themselves in the same bar in Germany, the shared origin entangles these permanent holons at an extremely primordial level.

In Section II's Track#2, we examine a scenario that's even more complicated, since the residual Fact Set continuum involved is (properly) drawn back into the URC-Determined Environmental Confine of its own origin, yet as a whole it immediately entangles with the Dynamic IDIs (as an entangled cluster in its own right) that were ejected from the URC-Determined environment of

411

their own origin, due to the fact that for them (as materially generated informational hybrids) the Unit Rate of Change that they share with the RFS continuum (which is now back in its own environment of historical origin) is the most primordial level of in-Kind entanglement that's available. What's also true is that due to the URC that all of these informational masses share, and due to the fact that this URC is not in sync with this new environmental confine's URC, while these information holons can exist within this *foreign* environment, they will remain profoundly entangled to the degree that the entire collective will present as one indivisible informational holon to that environment, even as within the confines of that apical holon, each previously independent mass will remain independent relative to all other masses that comprise that entangled collective.

Yes, it's complicated, but it works, and because of the Hierarchy of Kind, it always works. And that's the point.

What can and cannot happen within any environment is determined by the precedent that has been established and enforced by residual Fact Sets, Fact Set continuums, and the intricate relationships between them all. I call this web of influence *Reality*, and the simple logic that stabilizes the whole thing *The Hierarchy of Kind*. The Identity of each existent something is what matters to the whole of Reality, since Reality is defined by the collective Identity of everything that shares, or is a result of a shared, Unit Rate of Change. The Hierarchy of Kind simply defines the relative impact of one existent thing on the Identity of another existent thing, and vice versa. From there, that definition determines how the meta-law *"first, survive"* will regard that potential relationship. The rest is either *yes* or *no*, and the whole of Reality moves on from there.

Speculation

Time Dilation and Gravity

An Indication of
Identity Survival Enforcement
Within the Macro-System

Those that have been exposed to the specifics of Albert Einstein's General Theory of Relativity come away from that exposure with a very counterintuitive notion; a change in either acceleration or gravity field strength will alter Time itself for that which has that change inflicted upon it. This theory's treatment of Time as a malleable variable that is vulnerable to the relative strength of a gravity field is the result of Einstein's Special Theory of Relativity and Einstein's belief in a physical equivalence between acceleration and gravity stemming from the fact that increases in acceleration and Gravity are experienced by an observer as feeling the same.

In the digression *"Concerning My Specific Methodology"*, I address Einstein's Special Theory of Relativity as it pertains to non-simultaneity, and the famous train-observers-lightning-strikes thought experiment as an example of why I embrace the notion of a common frame of reference for all activities and observers that exist within a defined macro-system, as opposed to the multiple frames of reference notion promoted by Special Relativity and the full ramification suite that emerges as a result of that notion. Here, I would like to challenge Einstein yet again, only this time, it's the impact of acceleration — in the specific form of gravitational field strength — that I wish to focus on.

This bizarre relationship between Time and Gravity (or acceleration) has been termed Time Dilation by the scientific community, and the truth is that experimentation has produced proof that such dilation of time can be measured.

That said, in this examination, I won't be allowing either Time or Gravity a break as far as the basic property set that it possesses relative to all other constants within the relationship matrix that is Reality. In other words, in spite of all indications, I'm going to insist that Time and Gravity remain consistent and constant as Reality fundamentals, regardless of what even the most precise clocks have to report concerning their unique relationship.

I'm not going to allow that interaction to fundamentally alter the basic property set of either constant. What I will do, instead, is offer a plausible interpretation of the experimentation results (arising from that interaction between Time and Gravity) that will allow for those results without allowing for any alteration of the basic property set of either Time or Gravity to exist as the explanation for the nature of those experimentation results. In fact, I will explore any and all other constants to see if any one of them, or any combination of them, can shed new light on the Time Dilation phenomenon.

The effort here is to eliminate what's been presented as a fundamental contradiction between the stability and consistency of Time as a structural platform within the material realm of physical Reality, and what Time must actually be if Time Dilation can be imposed by simple proximity changes within a gravitational field. After all, if Time is inherently malleable (and as a direct result of something as easily adjustable as relative position within a specific gravity well), then there must exist a ramification suite (emerging as a default response to that obvious lack of macro-system stability) that would necessarily be both exceedingly profound and universal in its impact on all systems that exist as constituents within Reality as a whole.

If Time Dilation (as presented by the studies and papers that support the notion) does exist, it cannot simply exist as a mere curiosity. It cannot be something that is fundamental to the basic relationship between the quantum of Now and material reality while existing as nothing more than a localized factor to be corrected for within manmade systems that transverse gravitational field strengths or operate under a wide range of relative velocities. The very existence of a quantum structure of material reality would be severely challenged by Gravity's ability to affect the stability of the common clock within that macro-system; Time being the progressive quantum unit exchange of Now within that system.

Since the issue is fairly complex, I'm going to bullet-point a sentence as discrete phrases concerning the fundamental problem with intra-system Time Dilation before we start really getting into examining those indications that have

AutoGenesism: A Theory of Everything

suggested its existence. I think it might be a good way to make the specifics of that intractable dilemma more immediately graspable for the average reader.

- Random internal shifts in the structural consistency
- of the ongoing progression of change/event quanta
- within a physical macro-system (a holon that arcs within its own ongoing trajectory of change/event quanta, as is true of all physical systems),
- inflicted on that macro-system by a variety of component systems that each contribute to its holon composition as a result of their very existence,
- especially as a result of something as dynamic and potentially random as a change in relative placement within any one of a countless number of sub-system *"gravity wells"*,
- create a holon structural schism that can never be resolved,
- namely, that a macro-system can never possess or enforce a fundamental holon structural commonality due to its structural deference to the subtle and not-so-subtle movements of bits and pieces within the gravity wells of relatively insignificant sub-systems that are scattered within that macro-system.

In essence, if the scientific community is correct, and physical/material existence is quantized (which seems to be an assumption that's been repeatedly borne out over the last 100 years or so) then the progression of change/event quanta (we refer to each of them as *Now*) can't shift within a relatively insignificant sub-system like Earth without severely compromising the basic physics of the entire macro-system that we call the Universe, as a direct and progressing ramification of just that one shift.

Imagine if a shift in the progression of change/event quanta could be inflicted upon the component composition of each and every sub-system within the Universe as a result of differing gravitational field strengths? The exponential nature of the ramification confluence, as the universal quantization of progressive action alone disintegrates with some bands of gravitational field strength forcing system action quanta to leap far ahead of sequence, while other gravitational field strength bands force system action quanta to stall, and still other systems that move between gravitational field strength are subjected to constant stutters and lurches in quantum progression, would necessarily oblite-rate the entire nature of quantization, since quantization requires uniformity of unitary presence or structure.

Of course, Einstein's rather cavalier equivalence — declaring acceleration and Gravity to be literally one and the same — has its own severe challenges; the capacity of Gravity to actually alter Time only being one of those challenges. It's this equivalence notion that forces General Relativity to be based on the same speed equals distance divided by time equation that had Einstein originally throwing Time under the train in his Special Relativity thought experiment that we examined in that earlier digression *"Concerning My Specific Methodology"*. In fact, it's this equivalence with acceleration that forces Einstein to declare that Gravity is akin to a marble circling an enormous drain in search of a straight line to follow.

So, the truth is that it's pretty easy to describe just how universally prob-lematic the notion of Gravity-inflicted Time Dilation actually is. But then, as I noted, there have been experiments that have shown indications of changes in gravity well placement affecting the synchronization between carefully prepared precision clocks. So, what's that all about? Maybe it'd be good to take a look at these clocks.

The Atomic Clock

Let's take a look at the measuring devices that have been used to determine exactly what impact Gravity is having on the relative stability of Time quanti-zation. After all, it goes without saying that our best and most precise observa-tions are only as good and precise as the instruments we're using, as well as how accurate they can be within a given application.

The following is a very quick description of the history and mechanical basis of precise time measuring systems. To save time and trouble, I lifted it from Wikipedia.com, since this isn't a dissertation. I've also taken the liberty of highlighting [with bold font] the several passages that I feel suggest a critical, yet overlooked, role that atomic clocks have likely played in the scientific com-munity's progressive embrace of Time Dilation through experiment indications.

AutoGenesism: A Theory of Everything

History

The idea of using atomic transitions to measure time was first suggested by Lord Kelvin in 1879. Magnetic resonance, developed in the 1930s by Isidor Rabi, became the practical method for doing this. In 1945, Rabi first publicly suggested that atomic beam magnetic resonance might be used as the basis of a clock. The first atomic clock was an ammonia maser device built in 1949 at the U.S. National Bureau of Standards (NBS, now NIST). It was less accurate than existing quartz clocks, but served to demonstrate the concept.

The first accurate atomic clock, a caesium standard based on a certain transition of the caesium-133 atom, was built by Louis Essen in 1955 at the National Physical Laboratory in the UK. Calibration of the caesium standard atomic clock was carried out by the use of the astronomical time scale ephemeris time (ET). This led to the internationally agreed definition of the latest SI second being based on atomic time. Equality of the ET second with the (atomic clock) SI second has been verified to within 1 part in 1010. The SI second thus inherits the effect of decisions by the original designers of the ephemeris time scale, determining the length of the ET second.

Since the beginning of development in the 1950s, **atomic clocks have been based on the hyperfine transitions in hydrogen-1, caesium-133, and rubidium-87.** The first commercial atomic clock was the Atomichron, manufactured by the National Company. More than 50 were sold between 1956 and 1960. This bulky and expensive instrument was subsequently replaced by much smaller rack-mountable devices, such as the Hewlett-Packard model 5060 caesium frequency standard, released in 1964.

In the late 1990s four factors contributed to major advances in clocks:

- Laser cooling and trapping of atoms
- So-called high-finesse Fabry–Pérot cavities for narrow laser line widths
- Precision laser spectroscopy
- Convenient counting of optical frequencies using optical combs.

In August 2004, NIST scientists demonstrated a chip-scale atomic clock. According to the researchers, the clock was believed to be one-hundredth the size of any other. It requires no more than 125 mW, making it suitable for battery-driven applications. This technology became available commercially in 2011.

Kevin Brian Carroll

Mechanism

Since 1967, the International System of Units (SI) has defined the second as the duration of 9192631770 cycles of radiation corresponding to the transition between two energy levels of the caesium-133 atom.

This definition makes the caesium oscillator the primary standard for time and frequency measurements, called the caesium standard. Other physical quantities, e.g., the volt and the metre, rely on the definition of the second in their own definitions.

The actual time-reference of an atomic clock consists of an electronic oscillator operating at microwave frequency. The oscillator is arranged so that its frequency-determining components include an element that can be controlled by a feedback signal. The feedback signal keeps the oscillator tuned in resonance with the frequency of the electronic transition of caesium or rubidium.

The core of the atomic clock is a tunable microwave cavity containing the gas. In a hydrogen maser clock the gas emits microwaves (the gas mases) on a hyperfine transition, the field in the cavity oscillates, and the cavity is tuned for maximum microwave amplitude. Alternatively, in a caesium or rubidium clock, the beam or gas absorbs microwaves and the cavity contains an electronic amplifier to make it oscillate. **For both types the atoms in the gas are prepared in one electronic state prior to filling them into the cavity. For the second type the number of atoms which change electronic state is detected and the cavity is tuned for a maximum of detected state changes.**

Most of the complexity of the clock lies in this adjustment process. **The adjustment tries to correct for unwanted side-effects, such as frequencies from other electron transitions, temperature changes, and the spreading in frequencies caused by ensemble effects.** One way of doing this is to sweep the microwave oscillator's frequency across a narrow range to generate a modulated signal at the detector. The detector's signal can then be demodulated to apply feedback to control long-term drift in the radio frequency. In this way, the quantum-mechanical properties of the atomic transition frequency of the caesium can be used to tune the microwave oscillator to the same frequency, except for a small amount of experimental error. **When a clock is first turned on, it takes a while for the oscillator to stabilize.** In practice, the feedback and monitoring mechanism is much more complex than described above.

http://en.wikipedia.org/wiki/Atomic_clock

As stated above, our capacity to measure the progression and stability of the change/event quantization of Time is *"based on the hyperfine transitions in*

AutoGenesism: A Theory of Everything

hydrogen-1, caesium-133, and rubidium-87" with the International Second universally defined as *"the duration of 9192631770 cycles of radiation corresponding to the transition between two energy levels of the caesium-133 atom"*. Of course, there's a ± as there is with pretty much everything, but as you can tell (below) they're pretty strict with the International Second since it's the basis of all units of time in use.

> Under the International System of Units (via the International Committee for Weights and Measures, or CIPM), since 1967 the second has been defined as the duration of 9192631770 periods of the radiation corresponding to the transition between the two hyperfine levels of the ground state of the caesium 133 atom. In 1997 CIPM added that the periods would be defined for a caesium atom at rest, and approaching the theoretical temperature of absolute zero (0 K), and in 1999, it included corrections from ambient radiation. Absolute zero implies no movement, and therefore zero external radiation effects [i.e., zero local electric and magnetic fields].
>
> The second thus defined is consistent with the ephemeris second, which was based on astronomical measurements. The realization of the standard second is described briefly in a special publication from the National Institute of Standards and Technology, and in detail by the National Research Council of Canada.
>
> **http://en.wikipedia.org/wiki/Second#International_second**

Now, I'm going to simply state the obvious here, and suggest that while these time measuring devices are designed to mitigate changes and fluctuations of the frequency of the caesium oscillator system (caused by external radiation effects, frequencies from other electron transitions, temperature changes, and the spreading in frequencies caused by ensemble effects — as listed in the description above) there are no adjustment processes in place to compensate for changes in the oscillator system's relative placement within the gravity well as a system-disturbance factor. Not that such an adjustment process could be designed to fit within a clock, if a gravitational field stabilization mechanism were to exist; it doesn't. This is true, even though it is a fact that changes in relative placement within Earth's gravity well are often a significant disturbance factor in all other dynamic systems.

The truth is that when a precision clock is brought into service, regardless of the method of leveraging the caesium 133's unique properties, *"the atoms in the gas are prepared in one electronic state prior to filling them into the cavity"*. Yes, that does sound as if the entire mechanism depends upon the stability of what can easily become a highly sensitive dynamic system, and one that's extremely vulnerable to external forces.

Gravitational Field Strength is an Environmental Factor

Let's play with the notion that when any one of the variety of caesium 133 based atomic clocks is precisely prepared and finely tuned, and its elaborate system of adjustments is properly set into place, that this is done at a specific and unchanging position within Earth's gravity well. Maybe the entire process is carried out between a few rooms at that position, or perhaps initiated at one level and finished at another, but I think it's safe to suggest that before any measuring is done, the atomic clock in question has been properly acclimated to its resting position relative to the gravity well that keeps everything on Earth, on Earth. This list of the world's atomic clocks suggests that they aren't generally moved around much if they're being used as precise reference clocks:

http://en.wikipedia.org/wiki/List_of_atomic_clocks

Even when a caesium clock has been prepared for operation at a high altitude, the impact of the decreased gravitational field strength at that altitude on that caesium oscillator system (perhaps naturally speeding up the resonant frequency compared to an exact same system located deeper with Earth's gravity well) is going to necessarily be tuned out of the system, if that oscillator system is going to be useable as a precision time-keeping device. Thereby effectively compensating for the slightly different (yet consistent) gravitational field strength by slowing down the oscillating frequency of the system to make it accurate relative to other, similar time pieces located around the world. In essence, no atomic clock is designed for ultra-precision time measurements while being subjected to radical changes (or even subtle changes) in gravitational field strength.

Then again, there have been those incidents when an atomic clock hasn't been allowed to properly stabilize after a change in gravitational field strength has been inflicted upon it, before being applied to the precise measurement of Time. Such as when one has been used to experimentally prove the concept of gravitational Time Dilation. In fact, the most commonly referenced experiment, said to prove that Time Dilation does exist, involved atomic clocks taken onboard Boeing 747 airliners in 1971, and flown around the world in opposite directions.

AutoGenesism: A Theory of Everything

I don't believe that I'm going out on a limb here by suggesting that the accuracy of these clocks could easily have been affected by not only the G-forces of take-off, the electronic field environment within the planes, and the physical disturbances inherent in any version of such an endeavor, but just the fact that each of these hyper-sensitive systems (the caesium oscillators, themselves) had been brought into existence within a larger environmental system that featured a very specific and consistent gravitational field, begs the question: *Why wasn't something as significant and universally determinant as gravitational field strength understood to be a system factor in the same manner that temperature, radiation fields, and random frequencies were?*

The basic fact is that all systems — regardless of relative stability (even the newest optical clocks, poised to take over for the aging caesium clock designs) — have one common system factor that cannot be dynamically compensated for with an automatic response adjustment mechanism; relative placement within Earth's gravity well. And changes in gravitational field strength is a very real and very influential factor within any dynamic physical system, and (of course) within any mechanism that's based on the natural operation of a dynamic physical system.

And This Has 'What?' To do With Identity Survival?

Entropy is a well-researched phenomenon, and has been inextricably associated with Time's arrow of progression. This is most likely due to the fact that all material systems experience entropy over a period of time, but some have made the claim that entropy causes Time to progress in the manner that it does. Others assert that Time is entropy. Entropy is the progressive destruction of a defined material system, and while some systems can take billions of years to break down, no material system is immune to entropy.

Many factors contribute to or mitigate the rate of entropy within most systems, and while it's not as easy to observe as heat or friction, changes to gravitational field strength have been observed and noted as being a factor that contributes to the rate of entropy in dynamic, material systems. While this may not be as easily observed on living material systems that are moving between relatively similar positions within Earth's gravity well, it becomes very noticeable when one of these systems is placed well outside of its normal position within that gravity well over an extended period of time.

Certainly it's been proven that human beings, when subjected to a prolonged period of placement far removed from their normal base level within the gravity well of our planet, suffer serious physical deterioration. It would seem that any system that has evolved within a constant and specific gravitational field strength is compositionally dependent on the ongoing presence of that gravitational field strength (within a reasonable range, of course, depending on the system in question) for its continued survival. And, the evidence (when examined from this perspective) does suggest a distinct correlation between placement within the *gravity well* of a macro-system (like Earth) and system stability (and normal survivability) relative to that placement.

But, how can we know that removing the delicate and ultra-precise caesium 133 oscillator system to a position that is further away from its *home* gravity well placement is having a deleterious impact on its own survival as an existent system? At the moment, all we have are the indications that suggest that the caesium system is being affected; its oscillations are speeding up. When lowered into Earth's gravity well, the system's oscillations are slowing down. The placement within the gravity well is affecting the oscillation rate. That much we can know for certain.

So again, what's this got to do with Identity Survival? This is where we slip out into the part of this speculation that is speculative, and play with a very interesting idea concerning the survival of a larger system, and how that survival could be enforced by that larger system right before our eyes without our even realizing what it is that we're observing.

Earth possesses a gravitational field. No one actually knows why it possesses a gravitational field, or what a gravitational field's physical properties consist of. This isn't a speculative statement. This is as established a fact as you're going to find out there in the confusing world of theories and hypotheses. Regardless of whether we understand Gravity or not, Gravity is what keeps everything that is of Earth . . . on Earth.

Earlier in this book, we examined the influence of the sole existential imperative Identity Survival on systems that range from simple Change/Event Trajectories to the most complex and sophisticated system to ever exist; the human being. I stated flatly that Identity Survival is what drives everything that exists to do and be what it is. Well, I'm going to hold firm to that statement, and suggest that gravity is the means by which a large system (like our planet Earth) pursues Identity Survival; more specifically, how it enforces that Identity Survival through the Masculine imperative expression Isolation.

AutoGenesism: A Theory of Everything

Isolation is the ID Survival strategy expression that isolates the contributing holons of a holon structure from competing holon structures, and prevents the loss of any contributing holon by that holon structure. A good example of this is the atom. The atom's nucleus remains intact as a result of Strong Force interaction between the quarks that make up the protons and neutrons that then bond together in a constant configuration to form that very specific nucleus, and Electromagnetism keeps the electrons (in a consistent number and formation) orbiting that nucleus in their proper positions, thereby maintaining the very specific structure of that atom (and its ongoing identifiable property set) for as long as possible. This is the most well-known version of the ID Survival expression Isolation, and it literally prevents each atom from falling apart, and ceasing to exist as the holon structure that it is.

Obviously, as the system gets larger, the way that it inflicts Isolation upon the holons within its identified structure is going to be noticeably different, with many emerging considerations (such as allowing for the ongoing survival of all contributing holon systems) affecting that strategy. That said, an ID Survival Isolation strategy must exist if that macro-system holon is to remain physically existent.

What starts out on Earth, for the most part, stays on Earth. Even the moisture that evaporates collects within Earth's atmosphere and rains back down upon her. Earth's gravity is weak, relative to other forces, but its universality succeeds in keeping much of what comprises Earth in place (as the widely diverse collective that it is and is constantly becoming from moment to moment). What's truly remarkable about this Isolation strategy is that it does so without negatively affecting the survivability of each system that exists as integral to the extensive macro-system [Earth], and that therefore must be encouraged by Earth itself to flourish if it [Earth] is to survive as a healthy and progressing macro-system.

In fact, what holds the Moon in devoted orbit around the Earth is the same force that allows a breeze to lift the seeds of a flower and scatter them across a field. What's even more amazing is that it is the flower that is deeply ensconced within that gravity well, which means that the actual force itself (if gravity is but a dumb attracting or pressuring force) must be greater on the flower than on the Moon. Curved space-time, acceleration, or waves of gravitons (or whatever the theory concerning the nature of gravity that one embraces), the sheer brute force that locks the Moon in place, and 25,000 miles away, is the same brute force that allows bubbles to float around a laughing baby's face on a warm, sunny summer afternoon. I suspect that this gravity is a much more complex and nuanced system survival mechanism than has been — to date — suggested by the range of theories that have emerged to explain it.

What I do know is that each system that exists within any macro-system (such as Earth) is integral to the Identity definition of that macro-system (as the defined holon that it is). This means that the macro-system itself must enforce the requirement that every system that exists as integral to its Identity remain integral to that defined Identity. In terms that are relative to this examination, what exists as part of the whole of Earth must remain on Earth if Earth is to maintain its own unique and inimitable Identity. This means that there must be a means by which Earth (as well as all such macro-systems like Earth) can enforce the requirement that all integral sub-systems remain as part of the collective that defines Earth relative to the rest of Reality. I think it's pretty clear that gravity (whatever it actually is as a highly nuanced Isolation mechanism) is how this requirement is enforced.

"You Can't Hold Us Here Forever"

Now, we all know that the human race has slipped the surly bonds of Earth and . . . well, we've left the Earth for short periods of time. We've calculated the possibilities and imagined ourselves littering the cosmos far into the future, as Earth stays behind like a mom sitting by the phone, hoping for a call now and then. We've sent out radio waves and we've sent out a variety of drones to explore what exists beyond the thin band of gases that separates us from the rest of the universe. We've balanced Earth's gravitational pull against the influence of centrifugal force, to place stable technology platforms just beyond those gases. In short, we've learned how to work with Gravity, and even leverage it accurately and consistently.

Still, we haven't overcome it, nor have we overcome the relentless and holistic impact it has on our own bodies. And this is what I want to take a closer look at; this less obvious aspect of Gravity as Earth's clearly successful Identity Survival strategy — the entropy-accelerating impact that profound reductions in gravitational field strength have on all auto-animated dynamic material systems.

What is true is that when a naturally occurring physical system comes together, the basic environment that it comes together within [air pressure, range of temperature, range of gaseous blend, and yes, gravitational field strength] is a critical part of the overall confluence that made the emergence of that system

AutoGenesism: A Theory of Everything

possible. Once that system has become established (and replicated, perhaps) the confluence itself is capable of slight modifications, but as the tenuous nature of mutation survival indicates, there are limits to how radical the changes can be to that system's component confluence before the system itself becomes threatened.

Some changes to the system's environment can immediately threaten that system's survival. Probably the most aggressive threat would be a radical change in the gaseous blend within the environment that contains a living system (like a dog, for instance). Throw the air mixture out of balance and the dog is immediately threatened. Easy enough to verify, that's for sure.

Other changes to the system's environment (like temperature) can be initially endured, even if the long range impact on the system will accelerate entropy, and ultimately system death. Still, an extreme change in temperature (if extreme enough) would have the same immediate impact on both living and nonliving systems as the radically adjusted gaseous mixture had on the dog; immediate system death.

Placement with the Earth's gravity well is just another environmental factor that exists along with many other such factors (like gaseous mixture and temperature) that are integral to the successful survival of some physical systems. Especially those systems capable of leaving Earth's gravity well under their own initiative. The only significant difference between Gravity and other environmental factors is the universal nature of Gravity's presence regardless of where you're located across the surface of the earth (albeit; there are small field strength differences between relative latitude positions, but none that overtly affect the survivability of auto-animated dynamic material systems).

Nonliving systems are not affected by the specific mixture of gases that make up the air available to breathe. Mineral systems are not affected as readily by radical changes in temperature as organic systems. The truth is that the more static the system, the less affected it is by environmental changes. Obviously, extremely sensitive systems — specifically sensitive dynamic systems — are the most readily affected by changes in environment, which brings us back to the extremely sensitive caesium 133 based time measuring system.

This system can be very precisely tuned, carefully shielded, and environmentally encased to protect it from changes in the environment that hosts it, but nothing can be done about the change in gravitational field strength that results

425

when its gravity well proximity position is changed. Yes, the reduction of gravitational field strength that we're discussing is really subtle, but this is an extremely sensitive system that depends on a remarkably precise balance of system factors. While it can be protected from many external factors, and automatic adjustments can be designed to correct for other factors that it can't be protected from, changes in gravitational field strength is a universal factor that can't be protected against or automatically adjusted out of the system.

And, while the caesium 133 oscillator system that bases the atomic clocks that appeared to verify Time Dilation is an extremely precise and stable oscillator, we've already seen how sensitive it is and how easily it is affected by external factors when it's being applied to the task of measuring Time to within 1 part in 1010 . Earth's Identity Survival enforcement strategy of consistent gravitational field strength as an essential system survival factor may not endanger the caesium 133 oscillator system, but when you're using such a system in the manner that they're being used to measure such precise increments of Time, the entropy-accelerating impact of removing such an system from Earth's gravity well doesn't have to be significant to be noticeable. Especially if you're specifically looking for evidence of that impact.

It may be premature to declare that a macro-system's gravitational force inflicts a survival threat upon any lesser system that threatens its own Identity Survival by extracting itself from the collective (of lesser systems) that defines that macro-system as the identified holon that it is. However, the indications do suggest that the physical processes within a variety of systems that we employ as time measuring devices are affected relative to how deeply ensconced they are within Earth's gravity well. Of course, this change in gravitational field strength affects the system's rate of oscillation, with Time Dilation the observed impact.

When utilizing an ultra-precise, ultra-sensitive process to accomplish a specific end (as is the case with the most accurate and sophisticated time measuring/keeping systems) why should it be assumed that the precise integration of gravitational field strength would not be a factor in how that system decays (or otherwise operates)? Wouldn't this make more sense than the blanket assertion that Time itself is altered by shifts in gravitational field strength? Especially if such alterations can also be readily imposed by changes in relative acceleration between objects sharing the same position within Earth's gravity well.

AutoGenesism: A Theory of Everything

Perhaps if Gravity were viewed as being based on the same requirement as the other three forces as a coercive system Identity Survival strategy, with system size (and therefore strategy specifics) being the only real difference, the eventual unification of these forces wouldn't be the intractable problem it is for the brilliant minds that are focused on solving it.

Kevin Brian Carroll

Speculation

Determining the Unit Rate of Change

In a quantized Reality, the span of Now is specific, concrete, and uniform in duration. It is also possible to determine the duration of Now relative to whatever it is that has been established as the official base unit of time measurement; in our own case, the Universal Second. Stating that the quantized nature of Time progression (making each unit of Now permanently and eternally uniform in duration) makes the determination of that duration possible is not the same as declaring that determination measurable. Still, getting close to determining that Unit Rate of Change (URC) and measuring that URC are two very different efforts, and two very different ways of looking at the value of scientific discovery.

One way of looking at the value of scientific discovery is through the lens of application and usefulness. This is generally how most funding sources view the value of science and scientific examination; how it can be turned into a benefit for mankind, perhaps even a profitable benefit? There's nothing inherently wrong with that way of viewing scientific value, but there is too much that exists yet to be determined that can never be leveraged as a benefit for that to be the only reason to keep reaching for answers.

The other way of looking at the value of scientific inquiry is through a much more holistic approach of what is beneficial to the larger needs of the human race, as opposed to its immediate or easily imagined requirements for material survival. This approach is much more aligned with how the effort to establish AutoGenesism relates to the overall journey of scientific inquiry. Not as an effort to ultimately master the nature of physical Reality, but to eventually understand it, and to better fit within it as Reality's most stunning accomplishment.

Kevin Brian Carroll

As for determining the actual duration of the quantum of *Now*, there's obviously no tangible benefit to be had or advantage to be gained as a direct result of achieving that determination. Still, the value in having a concrete appreciation for exactly what it is that rests at the base of this incredible holon structure of matrices within matrices within matrices might help the human mind find a moment of ease and comfort within the blistering cacophony of it all. Not all human minds, and not all the time, but some and for a moment or two. And maybe that alone is worth the effort?

The Duration of Now

How many billions of Change/Event Units actually occur within the confines of one caesium clock-determined second of measured time? That's a good question, but while it might be a question we cannot answer, it's not a question that we can't consider. The Physics department has its own strategy for determining the URC, and in honor of Max Planck, they've termed the results Planck Time. Here's a quick look at how they suggest the duration of the Quantum of Now be determined.

In physics, the Planck time (tP) is the unit of time in the system of natural units known as Planck units. It is the time required for light to travel, in a vacuum, a distance of 1 Planck length. The unit is named after Max Planck, who was the first to propose it.

The Planck time is defined as:

$$t_P \equiv \sqrt{\frac{\hbar G}{c^5}} \approx 5.39106(32) \times 10^{-44} \text{ s}$$

where:

$$\hbar = h/2\pi$$

is the reduced Planck constant (sometimes h is used instead of $\hbar$ in the definition)

G = gravitational constant
c = speed of light in a vacuum
s is the SI unit of time, the second.

The two digits between parentheses denote the standard error of the estimated value.

AutoGenesism: A Theory of Everything

As you can see, the strategy is based on several assumptions that we have no real means of verifying through measurement, or even through mathematical calculation, since the structural constant itself — the Planck Length — can't actually be determined without a standard error of estimated value.

The Planck length ℓ_P is defined as

$$\ell_P = \sqrt{\frac{\hbar G}{c^3}} \approx 1.616\ 199(97) \times 10^{-35}\ \text{m}$$

where c is the speed of light in a vacuum, G is the gravitational constant, and $\hbar$ is the reduced Planck constant. The two digits enclosed by parentheses are the estimated standard error associated with the reported numerical values.

http://en.wikipedia.org/wiki/Planck_time

Of course, actually timing the photon's journey from one end of a Planck Length to the other is a thought experiment, since there are no technologies capable of measuring such a thing. The Wiki page itself offers a pretty clever visualization for those who'd like to try and imagine just how small this unit of measure actually is:

> The size of the Planck length can be visualized as follows: if a particle or dot about 0.1mm in size (which is at or near the smallest the unaided human eye can see) were magnified in size to be as large as the observable universe, then inside that universe-sized "dot", the Planck length would be roughly the size of an actual 0.1mm dot, that is, about the size of smallest object the naked human eye can see. In other words, the diameter of the observable universe is to within less than an order of magnitude, larger than a 0.1 millimeter object, roughly at or near the limits of the unaided human eye, by about the same factor (10^31) as that 0.1mm object or dot is larger than the Planck length. More simply - on a logarithmic scale, a dot is halfway between the Planck length and the size of the universe.

http://en.wikipedia.org/wiki/Planck_length

I'm going to suggest that a 0.1mm dot is *roughly* halfway between the Planck length and the size of the Universe. Especially since we have no idea how large either the Planck length or the Universe actually is.

431

Clearly, there's no actual headway being made in determining just how minute the quantum instant of Now actually is, but is there a way of getting closer to that Unit Rate of Change without becoming unhitched from objectivity altogether? Maybe one of the central mysteries of Special Relativity — Time Dilation — can help us in a way that pure theoretical math can't? The following statements concerning experimental results obtained as a result of efforts to prove the theory of Time Dilation are widely considered to have been verified and proven to be accurate:

In the theory of relativity, time dilation is an actual difference of elapsed time between two events as measured by observers either moving relative to each other or differently situated from gravitational masses.

Velocity time dilation tests

Ives and Stilwell (1938, 1941). The stated purpose of these experiments was to verify the time dilation effect, predicted by Larmor–Lorentz ether theory, due to motion through the ether using Einstein's suggestion that Doppler effect in canal rays would provide a suitable experiment. These experiments measured the Doppler shift of the radiation emitted from cathode rays, when viewed from directly in front and from directly behind. The high and low frequencies detected were not the classically predicted values.

$$\frac{f_0}{1 - v/c} \quad \text{and} \quad \frac{f_0}{1 + v/c}.$$

The high and low frequencies of the radiation from the moving sources were measured as:

$$\sqrt{\frac{1 + v/c}{1 - v/c}} f_0 = \gamma(1 + v/c) f_0 \quad \text{and} \quad \sqrt{\frac{1 - v/c}{1 + v/c}} f_0 = \gamma(1 - v/c) f_0,$$

as deduced by Einstein (1905) from the Lorentz transformation, when the source is running slow by the Lorentz factor.

Rossi and Hall (1941) compared the population of cosmic-ray-produced muons at the top of a mountain to that observed at sea level. Although the travel time for the muons from the top of the mountain to the base is several muon half-lives, the muon sample at the base was only moderately reduced. This is explained by the time dilation attributed to their high speed relative to the experimenters. That is to say, the muons were decaying about 10 times slower than if they were at rest with respect to the experimenters.

AutoGenesism: A Theory of Everything

Hasselkamp, Mondry, and Scharmann (1979) measured the Doppler shift from a source moving at right angles to the line of sight (the transverse Doppler shift). The most general relationship between frequencies of the radiation from the moving sources is given by:

$$f_{\text{detected}} = f_{\text{rest}}\left(1 - \frac{v}{c}\cos\phi\right) / \sqrt{1 - v^2/c^2}$$

as deduced by Einstein (1905).[15] For ϕ = 90° (cos ϕ = 0) this reduces to f detected = f rest γ. Thus there is no transverse Doppler shift, and the lower frequency of the moving source can be attributed to the time dilation effect alone.

In 2010 time dilation was observed at speeds of less than 10 meters per second using optical atomic clocks connected by 75 meters of optical fiber.[16]

Gravitational time dilation tests

In 1959 Robert Pound and Glen A. Rebka measured the very slight gravitational red shift in the frequency of light emitted at a lower height, where Earth's gravitational field is relatively more intense. The results were within 10% of the predictions of general relativity. Later Pound and Snider (in 1964) derived an even closer result of 1%. This effect is as predicted by gravitational time dilation. (See Pound–Rebka experiment)

In 2010 gravitational time dilation was measured at the earth's surface with a height difference of only one meter, using optical atomic clocks.

Velocity and gravitational time dilation combined-effect tests

Hafele and Keating, in 1971, flew caesium atomic clocks east and west around the earth in commercial airliners, to compare the elapsed time against that of a clock that remained at the US Naval Observatory. Two opposite effects came into play. The clocks were expected to age more quickly (show a larger elapsed time) than the reference clock, since they were in a higher (weaker) gravitational potential for most of the trip (c.f. Pound, Rebka). But also, contrastingly, the moving clocks were expected to age more slowly because of the speed of their travel. From the actual flight paths of each trip, the theory predicted that the flying clocks, compared with reference clocks at the U.S. Naval Observatory, should have lost 40±23 nanoseconds during the eastward trip and should have gained 275±21 nanoseconds during the westward trip. Relative to the atomic time scale of the U.S. Naval Observatory, the flying clocks lost 59±10 nanoseconds during the eastward trip and gained 273±7 nanoseconds during the westward trip (where the error bars represent standard deviation). In 2005, the National Physical Laboratory in the United Kingdom reported their limited replication of this experiment. The NPL experiment differed from the original in that the caesium clocks were sent on a shorter trip (London–Washington D.C. return), but the clocks were more accurate. The reported results are within 4% of the predictions of relativity.

The Global Positioning System can be considered a continuously operating experiment in both special and general relativity. The in-orbit clocks are corrected for both special and general relativistic time dilation effects as described above, so that (as observed from the earth's surface) they run at the same rate as clocks on the surface of the Earth.

Muon lifetime

A comparison of muon lifetimes at different speeds is possible. In the laboratory, slow muons are produced, and in the atmosphere very fast moving muons are introduced by cosmic rays. Taking the muon lifetime at rest as the laboratory value of 2.22 μs, the lifetime of a cosmic ray produced muon traveling at 98% of the speed of light is about five times longer, in agreement with observations. In this experiment the "clock" is the time taken by processes leading to muon decay, and these processes take place in the moving muon at its own "clock rate", which is much slower than the laboratory clock.

http://en.wikipedia.org/wiki/Time_dilation#Velocity_time_dilation_tests

If we accept the validity of each of these experiment results statements, then we can take the exact amounts of dilation, as measured by each procedure, and begin calculating a common denominator that unifies all of the measured dilation amounts within a common synchronization rate. This would be required since the ± percentages between mathematically calculated dilation amounts and amounts actually measured (regardless of whether statistically significant or insignificant) would definitely not be instructive when seeking progress toward establishing the actual Unit Rate of Change that our entire Universe is based on. The exact dilation amounts, and to the most precise decimal position possible, would be required.

Working With the Data

What we'd be trying to establish would be the *"common clock"* rate of exchange from one quantum *Now* to the next quantum Now. Any dilation indication would be locked within that rate of exchange, regardless of how accurate or inaccurate the indication itself. If the dilation were a loss of 59±10 nanoseconds during an eastward trip around the world or a gain of 273±7 nanoseconds during a westward trip around the world (using Hafele and Keating's 1971 caesium clock flight results as an example), then both measurement changes would necessarily be in sync with the URC that bases this Universe since the dilations (as well as the measurement ± deviations) occurred within the confines of this Universe.

> ***Note*** — This [the fact that all dilations and ± deviations are in sync with the universal Unit Rate of Change] would be true regardless of the reason for the measurement differences. For an examination of what else could account for time dilation, see *"Time Dilation and Gravity: An Indication of Identity Survival Enforcement Within the Macro-System"*.

The fact is that all that occurs within our Universe does so in sync with the fundamental Unit Rate of Change that defines our Universe as the Contextual Environment that it is by quantizing all activity and information emergence. This forces all dilations and deviations that we measure with our precision clocks to remain in sync with that fundamental URC, regardless of what it is that is causing dilations in Time measurement (as well as all measurement ± deviations) to occur when clocks and other standardized rate measuring devices or items are subjected to experimental and/or environmental manipulations.

Establishing the common rate of change would require gathering all base results that have been established through the use of the highest frequency oscillating systems that can be engineered; repeating the exact same system manipulations within the exact same structured procedural environment and gathering all repeated measurements of these exact same experimental processes (noting precise deviations and not merely ± percentages); repeatedly employing a measuring platform that's capable of noting precise deviations to their extended decimal positions; and embracing the expectation that these extremely precise deviations would be of great importance as unit delineation measures since all such deviations would also be required to exist in sync with the Universal URC.

Of course, there's no guarantee that the calculated common denominator between each and every indication of dilation and all deviations thereof would ultimately reveal the actual URC. That said, we'd have a much better appreciation for the incredible intricacy that sits at the base of all that unfolds before us, around us and within us, as well as a much more realistic view of what it will take for us to really get a firm handle on the true nature of physical reality. It would certainly give us a better feel for how incredibly brief the quantum of Now is (and therefore how astoundingly precise the quantization of Reality actually is) than a vague thought exercise (above) involving a 0.1 mm dot and the visible diameter of our Universe.

Dark Matter:

How the Change/Spatial Trajectory
Serves the URC-Defined Macro-System

So, let's try out another bit of speculation here. Mainly, just to see how it all pans out relative to the more serious examinations that are occurring all around it, but also to give the more intellectually adventurous among us the chance the sit back and play with a rogue thought that's based on what we've established thus far without anyone getting pitched off-track as a result. What I want to look at for a moment (within the safe, secure confines of this Speculation section) is the notion of using the physical nature of the residual Fact Set, and its symbiotic relationship with the Change/Event Unit to challenge the Big Bang theory.

Now, this speculation is based on a very new way of looking at open space and what could be the physical basis of open space. Of course, our entire universe is a sea of open space with islands of material existence here and there. Galaxies of stars, to be more precise, with vast expanses of what appears to be nothing whatsoever between these islands of dense activity. Furthermore, all evidence points to the possibility that these vast expanses are growing ever more vast, and at an increasing rate of speed. Obviously, something is going on within these vast expanses of nothing whatsoever, and not in the sense of goings on that are happening within these open spaces, but in the sense that these open spaces are involved in what's ongoing, and evidently so.

Probably, it's best if we start at the beginning, and see what we've got as a basis for deeper evaluation.

Kevin Brian Carroll

The Big Bang: A Traditional Speculation

We speculate that the universe itself launched into material existence as a result of a massive, primordial explosion, and that this is evident due to the fact that everything that can be perceived as material within the universe is racing away from everything else in the universe. Yes, there is the cosmological radiation constant that leads some to suggest that this primordial explosion did happen, but the basic indication that caused the original hypothesis was that galaxies are in a race for the exits (so to speak) and at an ever increasing velocity. On a radio interview, one scientist irreverently tagged this theory a *"big bang"* and the name stuck. Since then, it's become the primary notion concerning how our entire universe, and Time itself, came into existence. But how plausible is the Big Bang when all the evidence is critically examined?

As the following, very well-known, illustration suggests, regardless of where in this universe you are, the rest of the whole of it seems to be racing away from you.

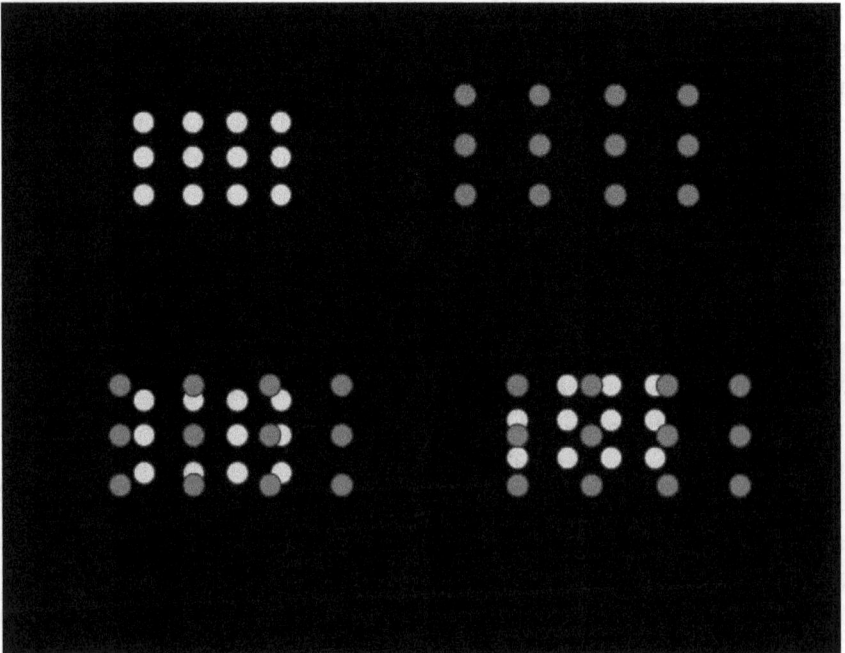

Figure 3-F
Note that in C and D the pattern expands
from completely different centers

AutoGenesism: A Theory of Everything

This is what cosmologists have noted about the relative expansion of the universe as a result of measuring that expansion relative to our own position within the whole. Of course, it suggests that the entire universe of galaxies is moving specifically away from us. Scientists suggest that regardless of where the point of observation is placed, the universe of galaxies will be perceived as racing away from that point of reference. Naturally, there's no means to prove this hypothesis, but if true, what does this suggest about the actual nature of the primordial Big Bang?

What it suggests (in fact, it insists) is that there is no Big Bang proximity position of origin or even general direction that can be determined, since all measurements will reposition the point from physical expansion to be wherever the measurement is taken. If we accept that there is no predetermined point of demarcation between the physical properties of basic Reality that exist within one system as compared with another system that is comprised of the same fundamental units of material existence, then this inexplicable malleability (relative to the proximity point from which all expansion is progressing outward) is a serious problem that must be addressed.

Surprisingly, no one seems to see this one glaring inconsistency as a problem with this specific theory. Well, we're going to notice this *'problem'*, and see if we can apply what we've learned about the representative nature of Residual Information Fact Sets to provide a plausible alternative explanation for how and why this expanding universe we inhabit is expanding in the manner that's been observed.

Displacement Fact Sets and Macro-System Identity

One constant that we've noted is the primordial imperative that we've termed Identity Survival. We've determined that it is the sole imperative, and that whatever it is that exists, it serves this lone imperative for as long as it continues to exist; even if doing so means that it does so in any of a myriad of ways. In other words, how one existent whole pursues Identity Survival may not be how another existent whole pursues it. That may seem obvious, but it's worth stating as a fact anyway; as is the basic fact that Identity Survival is Job #1 regardless of what's being done by what from one end of Reality to the other.

When a Change/Event Trajectory initiates, arcs, and completes, it does so relative to everything else that has also initiated, arced, and completed. And as it does (until it is finally completed, and then forever afterward) the full and accurate contextual relationship that was established as a result of that trajectory persists as a default ramification of the emergence and existence of the Fact Set that will always exist to fully represent that specific Change/Event Trajectory and the historical context that it provides to the contextual environment's own Identity as the existential whole that it is, and that it will continue to become.

All material manifestations [this is what layers of spatially expressed Change/Event Trajectories, in contextual Identity Survival entanglement actually are] contribute one common contextual aspect to the Identity of the macro-system they occupy, and therefore define; relative spatial proximity. This is the actual physical distance and position each material manifestation occupies or occupied in relation with other material and/or representative informational wholes that are occupying their own relative spatial proximity positions. In fact, spatial proximity is a primary identifier when qualifying the contextual impact of anything that is material, and therefore change/event-centric, on the universal environment.

What's true about even the most massive material system manifestation is that it displaces a defined 3 dimensional volume at a relative proximity position during a specific instant of time progression (commonly described with the use of a space-time coordinate system based on where and when that manifestation occurred as a discrete event). This proximity position — relative to all other existing 3 dimensional volumes that concurrently occupy the same instant of time progression within the same macro-system — changes as that time progression advances. These ongoing proximity position changes (even those position changes involving entire galaxies) are Change/Event Trajectories, as is true with all Change/Spatial Trajectories. This being the case, these Change/Spatial Trajectories (involving change/spatial and change/event material manifestations featuring 3-D volume displacements within spacetime) produce residual information Fact Sets that permanently represent both relative proximity position per specific quantum instant of *Now*, and the precise amount of three dimensional volume displaced within the macro-system and relative to all that exists within it.

AutoGenesism: A Theory of Everything

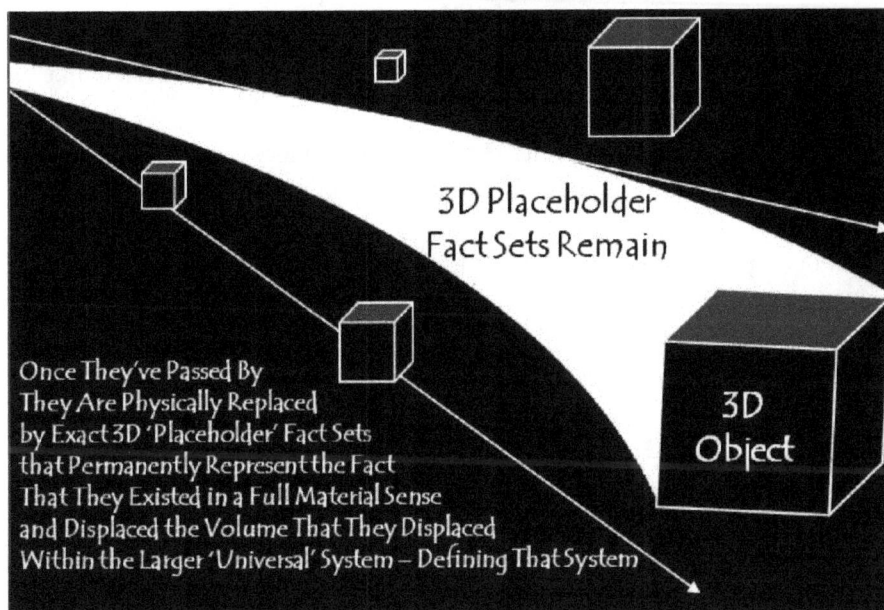

Figure 3-G

These volume displacement Fact Sets serve as literal placeholders within the dynamic theater, even if only relative to all other existing **Placeholder Fact Sets** that are representing their own specific Change/Event Trajectories in the same manner.

While displacing a defined volume, each three dimensional material manifestation cannot share a proximity position (relative to all else within that macrosystem) with any other physical manifestation (material or otherwise) without clashing with what has become a fundamental premise within any structural matrix; contextually or materially based. We call this a collision when this occurs between two material manifestations, but it's just as destructive when it occurs between a material whole and an informational whole. Two or more permanently existent informational wholes certainly cannot occupy the same relative proximity position, and when considering the existence of open space, this fact suggests a very plausible (even if presently counterintuitive) explanation concerning the existence of what (to us) seems to be an empty vacuum.

The primary issue here is that open space obviously exists, and yet, for anything that is physically existent to exist (even a relative material void) a cause must exist or have existed to bring it into physical existence. For something that is as ubiquitous as the void of open space, the cause must be primordial and universal in nature. After all, the space between material objects is as defining as the material objects when establishing the Identity of a macro-system like our universe.

That Identity definition (if its survival is the primary concern of the macro-system, as has been declared) is more established by relative expanses of open space than by relative proximity positioning between material manifestation within that open space. This suggests that Placeholder Fact Sets are of primary importance to the Identity of our universe, and that when they've been brought into existence (as a default ramification of activity and/or change — as all Fact Sets emerge) their position, volume displacement, and relative proximity are constantly emerging aspects of the inimitable Identity of our Universe as the system it is.

Many Huge 3D Objects
Take Up Volume Space
as They Orbit
and They Spin
and They Do What They Do

Figure 3-H

Obviously, as our own Earth spins and rotates and revolves around our own Sun, the contextually available *space* (at some point) needs to make room for more Placeholder Fact Sets [relatively large, as well as relatively small] to anchor their unique contribution to the contextual Identity of the universe as the existential whole that it is. This isn't an issue, since our Sun is just a tiny part of the entire Milky Way galaxy, and as such, it slides along with our galaxy into new, *virgin* proximity positions relative to other galaxies and to the Placeholder Fact Sets that have emerged as a result of the movements of those galaxies.

AutoGenesism: A Theory of Everything

Meanwhile, within each galaxy, Identity Survival (in whatever way it's being enforced at that level) is holding each star system to its unique galactic position unless or until a more powerful force challenges that system enforcement. Not unlike the application of rocket engine thrust to the task of breaking our own planet's relentless hold to allow us travel into space. Again, the pursuit of system Identity Survival, yet on an enormous and easily observable scale. No line of demarcation between what drives one system and another, regardless of the size of each system.

And as for our expanding universe, it should be obvious that with the requirement that all Placeholder Fact Sets permanently occupy each relative proximity, position and volume displacement that's been previously established, all ongoing Change/Event Trajectories [the solar systems, galaxies and whatnot] are passively deflected ever outward. And, while we can't perceive their orbital trajectories being altered, we can perceive the fact that they are becoming increasingly distant from one another, and in no unified linear direction.

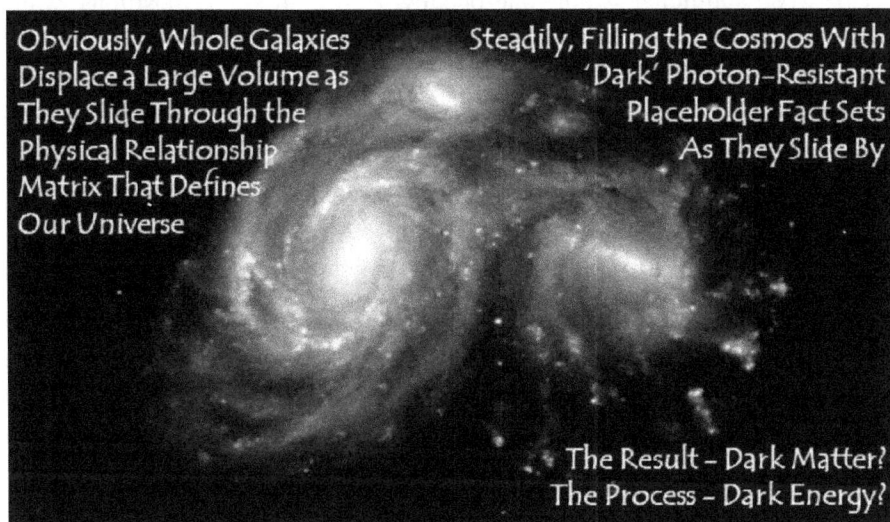

Obviously, Whole Galaxies Displace a Large Volume as They Slide Through the Physical Relationship Matrix That Defines Our Universe

Steadily, Filling the Cosmos With 'Dark' Photon-Resistant Placeholder Fact Sets As They Slide By

The Result - Dark Matter? The Process - Dark Energy?

Figure 3-I

The fact that these galaxies are not actually racing from any one point of initiation, or heading toward any one point of ultimate destination is a clue that should be earning more attention than it is. Then again, while it's that fact that really challenges the Big Bang as a workable theory, it doesn't challenge the idea that existing residual Placeholder Fact Sets are forcing large material systems ever outward to establish new relative proximities, positions and volume

443

displacements that will then be permanently represented by new Placeholder Fact Sets.

When one considers that information (while it does exist as a physical determinant within every system) doesn't absorb or deflect photons (or any other form of material, for that matter), an entirely different mystery begins to falter, as is often the case when (as David Deutsch stated in *"The Beginning of Infinity: Explanations That Transformed the World"*) a *good explanation* is discovered. That mystery is the physical nature of Dark Matter and Dark Energy.

The Displacement PFS Continuum Matrix

If you take another look at **Figure 3-G**, you can see that as each large material system moves, it leaves a representative swath of Placeholder Fact Sets in its wake. These swaths, while certainly not dovetailing together as a residual field of impenetrable information, would definitely establish a relationship matrix between additional swaths that occupy nearby proximity positions, while permanently adhering to the relative position (between each swath and the actual trajectory path, relative to all system trajectory paths that persist in residual representation) that a galaxy (for instance) occupied as it slid by at some point during its existence. Like a screen or web, the open spaces exist, even as the structural whole remains firm and concretely defined.

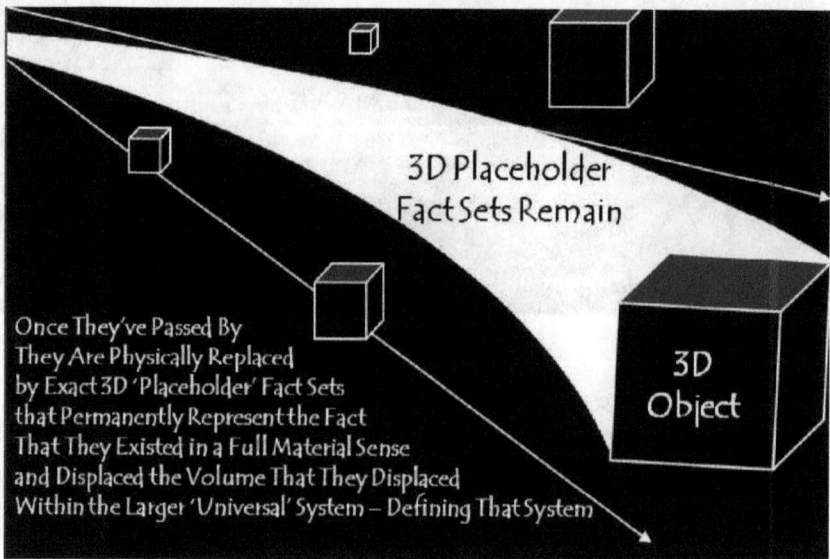

3D Placeholder Fact Sets Remain

Once They've Passed By They Are Physically Replaced by Exact 3D 'Placeholder' Fact Sets that Permanently Represent the Fact That They Existed in a Full Material Sense and Displaced the Volume That They Displaced Within the Larger 'Universal' System – Defining That System

3D Object

Figure 3-G

AutoGenesism: A Theory of Everything

In fact, considering the holon structural requirements of full galaxies, the unoccupied proximity between actual Placeholder Fact Set *orbital tracks* that physically define the relative here-to-there of *open space* is potentially enormous in some places. They'd be literally imperceptible, depending on our technological capacity to thoroughly measure these open regions versus the placeholder orbital tracks occupied by residual Fact Sets.

To our own observations, this entire relationship matrix would be nothing but open space, and yet, our devices are picking up something. Dark Matter might just be that relationship matrix of Placeholder Fact Sets, and Dark Energy might just be the requirement that ongoing activity, by enormous material systems (like galaxies), keep moving outward as they slide along the outer edges of that established matrix creating relative spatial proximities that aren't already occupied by Placeholder Fact Sets.

As for the universe itself, if it really is the entire relationship matrix that exists between material and informational wholes that share a common Unit Rate of Change, then there's no limit to how large it can become. No contraction, no entropy death. Nothing but an ever expanding proximity relationship between residual Placeholder Fact Sets and the Material manifestations that brought each PFS into physical existence. In that sense, if this is true, then the whole of our universe is a lot less complicated than we will ever allow it to be.

Yes, this notion is probably impossible to falsify, and that's why it's relegated to the confines of this Speculation section Then again, if the expanding universe and the cosmological constant are all that supports the Big Bang as one of Cosmology's most successful modern era theories, then maybe it needs to be reexamined. At least challenged now and then. At any rate, this bit of speculation does succeed in further defining the extremely specific nature of residual information Fact Sets and how they define the Identity of a macro-system like our own universe. That's valuable in itself.

Kevin Brian Carroll

So, What Have We Learned?

In the Preface, I quoted either Dale Carnegie's or Paul White's *"Tell them what you are going to tell them, tell them, then tell them what you told them."*, and said that this was how I was going to present my Theory of Everything — AutoGenesism — to you. And from there, I proceeded to do exactly that. I told you what I was going to tell you, and then I spent the Introduction, Section I, Section II (Track#1 and Track#2) and Section III (Digressions and Speculations) telling you what Auto-G is all about and how it makes sense of so much that has been overlooked or even further mystified as a result of other ToEs and their unique narratives concerning the physical nature of physical existence.

Well, now it's time for me to wrap this whole thing up by telling you what it was that I told you. I'm thinking that a quick review of each major section will be the best way of handling a proper review of this presentation as a whole, with a full acknowledgement that if you did missed anything important, you can certainly return to the section where it's covered and see where and how it was that it slipped past you during your first glance through.

The Introduction

The Introduction establishes what a Theory of Everything must address if it's to qualify as a full and comprehensive ToE. Each requirement is listed, with a detailed explanation concerning why it must be addressed by a full Theory of Everything. That list is comprised of the following issues that must be fully addressed:

- The Genesis of Physical Reality
- Coherence Within and Between Systems
- The Existential Foundation of Order
- A Sufficient Explanation For That Which Exists

- The Arrow of Time
- The Emergence of Spatial Environment
- The Existence of Natural Laws
- Quale: The Experience of Experience
- The Why of Esotericism
- The Fundamental Requirement: What Is It?
- The Legitimacy of the Basic Approach

This is no small requirement, since a failure to fully address each and every issue with the one ToE should doom that theory as being not even a step forward toward a more comprehensive ToE still under construction. In other words, if the raw conceptual core of the theory is intractably incompatible with any of the above listed requirements, then that theory should be DOA, and not worth pursuing. If we've learned anything from the impending collapse of the Standard Model, it's that you can work for decades to patch the leaks in an unworkable theory, with the most ingenious fillers and workarounds, but no matter how brilliantly you work to preserve it, eventually it's all going to fall down around you if at its core it was logically flawed.

The Introduction also makes the point that the established theories are getting ready to fall; not that anyone with even a passing interest in the subject could be honestly surprised at such a statement. String Theory, M Theory (whatever that actually is), the Big Bang Theory, General Relativity, and the Standard Model are all feeling the pressures of technologically amplified clarity and access of information and the inevitable ramifications of that clarity and access. This flood of new information has resulted in increasing numbers of reputable and responsible voices calling for a wholesale reconsideration of scientific assumptions that have been viewed as foundational for decades on the one side, and on the other, an army of wild-eyed hucksters pasting together ad hoc theophilosophical contraptions loosely based on the contradictory indications arising from sketchy attempts to preserve those assumptions in the face of overwhelming evidence that somewhere along the line, someone got it all wrong but refused to admit it. In short, we started this presentation off in the traditional manner.

The Introduction section promises a new and unprecedented Theory of Everything, describes what a full ToE must contain, and lays out why it is now time for such a full and comprehensive theory to be seriously considered and thoroughly examined. Let's take a look at each of the subsequent sections to see how the information they contained contributed to the satisfaction of the listed ToE requirements.

AutoGenesism: A Theory of Everything

Section I

In Section I, the basics of physical existence are established, with much of what's been verified as factual interwoven with what's emerged as rock-solid inference and logical ramification due to the inescapable impact of what's been factually verified as real and dependable. The existential staples are introduced: quantum unitary existence, uniform quantization, physical system emergence, the relationship between change and information, context and contextual precedent, Identity and physical existence, the lone primordial imperative [*"first, survive"*] and what that actually means relative to the progressive development of physical Reality [Identity Survival], the physical nature of Reality as a relationship matrix of permanent and transitional holons that is based on quantized synchronization of physical emergence [Unit Rate of Change], and the difference between passive, residual influence and the dynamic impact of real-time directives inflicted upon material systems by information sets and informational masses. And each staple is briefly overviewed.

Section I then introduces some very broad and critically important fundamentals that will serve as the basis of everything else that this examination will reveal. From the physical structure of the actual quantum of material existence to the unlikely hybridization of change and the fact of change, and how that hybridization transformed the basic nature of Reality itself, Section I serves to set the stage for the revolutionary information contained within Section II's Track#1 and Track#2.

Theory of Everything requirements met within Section I:

- The Existential Foundation of Order
- A Sufficient Explanation For That Which Exists
- The Existence of Natural Laws
- The Fundamental Requirement: What Is It?
- The Legitimacy of the Basic Approach

Section II

After a brief introduction of AutoGenesism and a bit about how really unprecedented Auto-G is as a Theory of Everything (especially considering the issue of existential genesis, and how all other ToEs — including those based on theology — have aggressively avoided the issue), Section II breaks into two tracks with the launch of Track#1 *"From Nothing to Everything"*.

449

Section II — Track#1

Track#1 wastes no time in taking on the traditionally intractable dilemma of true existential genesis, devoting over 4,000 words to detailing exactly how physical Reality came into existence from a true physical absence of anything whatsoever. No semantics bait and switch, no redefinition of the term *nothing*, no infinite multiverses, no beginning-less/endless expansion-contraction cycles, no mathematical positive/negative integer-morphing trick shots, or any of that nonsense; this explanation absolutely reeks of what we all know to be true about what's there right in front of us, and the terminology is succinct and consistent. Using the basics of quantum mechanics and extremely disciplined deductive logic, the emergence of physical Reality is quickly and easily revealed, with the only question remaining: *why did it take so long for someone to figure this out, when all the fundamental knowledge required to solve this mystery had already been so firmly in place for such a long time?*.

From there, Track#1 leads the way through the essential and common developmental cycles of a naturally progressing URC-Determined Environmental Confine [Reality, or as we refer to ours — The Universe]. The emergence of spatial proximity, movement, kinetic potential and realization, contextual precedent and natural law, the primordial precedence of Identity Survival and how Reality is defined as a universal macro-system with an ID Survival expression all its own, and how all of the staples that were introduced in Section I come into play as physical Reality climbs out of a literal nothing to become what we know it to be; a vibrantly teeming matrix of multi-layered relationships and evolving relationship dynamics.

Track#1 introduces the impetus and brute logic behind the emergence of life, of brain-equipped life, and finally, of the sentient, occasionally sapient, human mind, and then lays out the basic premise behind what will be covered in Section II's speculative Track#2; the human mind's need to breed.

Theory of Everything requirements met within Section II's Track#1:

- The Genesis of Physical Reality
- Coherence Within and Between Systems
- The Existential Foundation of Order
- A Sufficient Explanation For That Which Exists
- The Arrow of Time

AutoGenesism: A Theory of Everything

- The Emergence of Spatial Environment
- The Existence of Natural Laws
- Quale: The Experience of Experience
- The Fundamental Requirement: What Is It?
- The Legitimacy of the Basic Approach

Section II — Track#2

Yes, Section II's Track#2 is unique in that it's resolutely speculative, and makes no bones about it. It never professes to be any more than an intuitively educated guess concerning why the human mind that originates on Planet Earth is so devoted to the concept of a creator god, and why some forms of creator myths have become so profoundly successful as ToE explanations; even in the face of devastating evidence to the contrary.

What's really unique about Track#2's take on myths and theologies is how absolutely secular and commonsensical that take actually is. A procreative workaround that requires next to no effort on behalf of the procreating entity, making it the epitome of return on expenditure. I'm personally labeling this track *genius*, and especially if it's not true, since if it's not true, then how long will it be before it is true. In the end, you have more than a plausible explanation for every theological premise that's ever existed, and that's only the obvious win here. The latent victory is Track#2 as a masters class in exactly how every imperative, qualifier, default, and ramification works as one amazing structure of cause, effect, and progressive ramification. Track#2 is worth the effort even if just for the deep dive into some inky depths of pure theoretical logic. It's here that you really see just how expansive AutoGenesism really is.

Theory of Everything requirements met within Section II's Track#2:

- Coherence Within and Between Systems
- The Existential Foundation of Order
- A Sufficient Explanation For That Which Exists
- Quale: The Experience of Experience
- The Why of Esotericism
- The Fundamental Requirement: What Is It?
- The Legitimacy of the Basic Approach

451

Kevin Brian Carroll

Section III

In this section we get a chance to really dig into some of the more intricate aspects of how physical Reality is structured, as well as stretch out a little on some speculative notions concerning just how expansive this Theory of Everything might ultimately become as the years ahead allow us a better (perhaps, more accurate) perspective on some really mysterious present day indications. In order to properly deal with these two very divergent efforts, Section III is divided into two distinct segment: *Digressions* and *Speculations*.

In the Digressions segment I start off with a detailed presentation of my specific approach to this entire effort. Better to place this here in Section III, than to waste anyone's time with it before they've actually decided to invest their time and effort in Section's I and II, even if this overview seems legitimately necessary, given the nature of this presentation. From there, the titles of the following digressions should be instructive concerning the scope and focus each contains:

- Contextual Precedent: The Mechanics of Progressive Development
- Our Emergent Universe: How the Change/Event Became Spatial
- Human Consciousness and the Personality Development Trajectory
- From Here to There: The Crossing-Over Event
- Entanglement: The Laws and Dynamics of Contextual Association

Each topic was introduced and covered to a degree within a prior section, but as you'll discover, the depth and/or breadth of the topic itself proved to be too much of a digression for it to be properly addressed within the section of its introduction. There are bits of reiteration here and there, but the need for each of these topics to be expanded upon within this section becomes apparent quickly, as does the value in taking the effort to flesh each topic out within the confines of a section specifically devoted to that process.

The Speculations segment showcases the ways that Auto-G, as a theoretical basis, might help make some significant headway in efforts to determine the true nature of some very mysterious indications that continue to puzzle the best minds on our planet. As with the Digressions segment, I'll let the titles reveal the mysteries that are under investigation as being vulnerable to Auto-G's revelatory impact as a fully expansive Theory of Everything.

- Time Dilation and Gravity: An Indication of Identity Survival Enforcement Within the Macro-System

AutoGenesism: A Theory of Everything

- Determining the Unit Rate of Change
- Dark Matter: How the Change/Spatial Trajectory Serves the URC-Determined Macro-System

Speculation, yes. But, only due to the fact that there's no way (at present) to verify the suggestions contained here. Certainly not due to the existence of better, less counterintuitive explanations. In fact, each speculation is thoroughly based on peer reviewed science and widely accepted interpretations of that science, even if the dots between that science and these specific conundrums have yet to be discovered by the mainstream scientific community. But then, without the fundamental theoretical infrastructure that AutoGenesism provides, how were those dots ever to be connected? I guess we'll just have to see.

Theory of Everything requirements met within Section III's Digressions and Speculations segments:

- Coherence Within and Between Systems
- The Existential Foundation of Order
- A Sufficient Explanation For That Which Exists
- The Arrow of Time
- The Emergence of Spatial Environment
- The Existence of Natural Laws
- Quale: The Experience of Experience
- The Why of Esotericism
- The Fundamental Requirement: What Is It?
- The Legitimacy of the Basic Approach

And, in the End . . .

AutoGenesism is a Theory of Everything that actually offers a functional and logically consistent explanation of the whole of physical Reality and a very reasonable explanation of how it could have come into existence. It's the only ToE that does, and in that sense it's a very unique and singular accomplishment. In every other sense it's no different than waking up to what's always been sitting right there in front of you, and simply allowing it all to be what it is as you do what it takes to make the necessary adjustments to your own perspective. It's not about being creative or ingenious. In fact, it's about being able to be exactly the opposite of creative or ingenious.

The need for the human mind to have a reasonable working theory of what's real and what's not real is as fundamental as it gets. You can call that need human weakness or original sin or a failure to achieve enlightenment, but all it takes is a look back over human history to see just how physically difficult it's always been to impose a logically unreasonable working theory of what's real and unreal upon a people to get a good idea of just how damaging such a schism is to the mind/brain survival system of a human being.

While it's true that for millennia the human race on this planet has embraced many unreasonable working theories concerning Reality, it's also true that these theories were autocratically imposed and ground into the culture of these people, with basic survival depending on individual acceptance and embrace of the community view of what's real. All the while, profound ignorance of the true nature of physical structure definitely played its own part in providing a level of plausibility to whatever Reality theory had emerged to unite a community in survival of self and kind.

What's changed that status quo (of random Reality theories coexisting effectively with the factual nature of physical Reality, for the variety of communities based on those theories) is the emergence of scientifically obtained and verified evidence that directly and successfully challenges the validity of these long-established Reality theories. And the impact on the modern, science-served world has been predictably devastating.

What couldn't have been predicted, was the overwhelming impact that such powerful evidence would have if presented devoid of accurate context to a world of humanity that had just been stripped of its existential narrative by the proven existence of that evidence. An afternoon in a book store is all that's needed to acquire a deep appreciation of just how intellectually destabilized the modern world has become over the last 100 years or so, and how intense that instability has become within the last decade.

The most respected popular science magazines have begun to resemble the gossip tabloids in their breathless reporting of groundless speculation as if each irresponsible anecdote coming out of a gathering of two or more theorists were an announcement of the beginning of the end of humankind's search for ultimate truth. Worse yet, no one from within the air-locked depth of academia is challenging any of it, as Reality gets *"weirder and weirder"* for anyone and everyone who cares enough to pay attention.

So, why bother with any of this? Why not let people believe what they want to believe? Well, the main issue is that people don't begin by believing what they want to believe. They begin by believing what someone else wants them to believe. Moms, dads, priests, ministers, media, governments, friends, peers; the list of those who shape the beliefs of each and every one of us is long, and it's impossible to accurately determine who it was that started the chain of influence that's culminated in the fact that each one of us embraces and defends a viscerally defined Reality theory that we've employed from day to day as the lens through which we perceive ourselves and the life that we pursue. That Reality theory defines every instant of our existence, and yet, most of us instinctively know that the Reality theory that defines us is wrong, and intractably, irreparably wrong.

So, why bother with any of this? Why not let people believe what they want to believe? To be completely honest, as far as I'm concerned, if what a person believes truly serves them, then I've got no interest in challenging that belief. What I know about human perception and the afterlife of the human mind tells me that those folks will be just fine as they continue to believe what they believe and create the naturally evolving experience that their beliefs provide them as they enjoy their ongoing existence in the manner they've been prepared to experience. If they can be happy and fulfilled, then I'm certainly not going to get in the way of that happiness and fulfillment.

The only reason to bother with any of this is on behalf of the millions of modern world folks who simply cannot force themselves to embrace a Reality theory that doesn't seem real to them. And there are many millions of these folks, with many millions more moving from the ranks of believers every year. I don't seek to dissuade anyone from their beliefs. I only seek to serve those who've already realized that the traditional wisdoms can't be true, and who've seen the recent popular science spectacle for what it is; the disjointed theoretical flailings of yet another fundamental Reality structure that's in the initial stages of its own death throes. It's for them that I've bothered with any of this.

Go ahead and challenge AutoGenesism with whatever you've got. I'll welcome it. As far as I can tell, it's as airtight as any Theory of Everything has ever been, and much more airtight than most theories of anything whatsoever, so don't expect me to waffle on any specific that's necessary to the survival of the whole of it. It's not my own belligerent nature at play here. It's that this ToE is constructed like any *good explanation,* as described in David Deutsch's *"The Beginning of Infinity: Explanations That Transformed the World"* . . .

"The better an explanation is, the more rigidly its reach is determined — because the harder it is to vary an explanation, the harder it is in particular to construct a variant with a different reach, whether larger or smaller, that is still an explanation."

I've also constructed a website designed to supplement the information in this book, with a very specific focus on the experience of human existence. Located at http://TheAutoGenesist.com it's full of quick, clever bits concerning life's ultimate questions, and some surprisingly succinct presentations that might just help some folks with a few questions of their own concerning who they are, what they are, and what awaits them after all is said and done. Basically, this site will address the uniquely human issues that I felt might clash with the focus of this presentation, even as it offers information that's based on the default ramification structure that is AutoGenesism.

One thing I'm very sure of is that we're living in a time that literally pulsates with the need for a paradigm shift in what collectively constitutes the human view of Reality. I firmly believe that AutoGenesism can be that paradigm shift, but I'm also aware of just how intractable the current view is and will remain in spite of how poorly it serves those who embrace it and defend it. I've got no illusions concerning any of this, and while I will certainly work to make this revolutionary perspective available to all who might benefit from its clarity and sense of reasonable cohesion, I'm just grateful for the fact that I've finished this presentation and I've done so without failing Auto-G in the process.

Reality is what it is, and no one can invent it. AutoGenesism is only an explanation of Reality, and if it can be verified or added to in a manner that expands it without compromising its logical integrity then by all means grab on and do what you will with it. Yes, Auto-G is my Theory of Everything, but Reality itself belongs to no one. Perhaps this ToE will someday contribute to our species of human beings finally finding its own true place within Reality. If so, then that's all that anyone could ever ask of anything.

About the Author

Kevin Brian Carroll is not a physicist, a cosmologist, or a theologian. He doesn't have a PhD in Philosophy, Neurobiology, Astrophysics, or Cognitive Sciences. He's never been abducted by an alien life form, spent time under the tutelage of a transcendent master, left the confines of his corporeal body, or experienced the death of his ego; either intentional or accidental. Whatever he knows or believes he knows about the true nature of Reality is the result of no more than an open mind, careful critical thinking, and a general ignorance concerning decades of established and emerging scientific and philosophical thought.

If genius is a freedom from the constraints of widely embraced convention in pursuit of what so many others have dismissed as unattainable, while remaining thoroughly ensconced within the unforgiving confines of the most precise of ramification structures, then perhaps Kevin Brian Carroll is a genius. Beyond that, he just another guy trying to honestly figure out what's going on above, below, before, behind, inside, outside, because of, and in spite of all that he's become and all that's become of him.